# An Idea Which Went Wrong
*Commercial Microfinance in India*

By
Ramesh S Arunachalam

Copyright © 2014 Ramesh S Arunachalam
All rights reserved.

ISBN: 1494792486
ISBN 13: 9781494792480
Library of Congress Control Number: 2013923762
CreateSpace Independent Publishing Platform
North Charleston, South Carolina

# Acknowledgements

I would like to express my deepest and profound gratitude to my family, friends, professional colleagues and all other stakeholders who helped immensely in completing this book. They are far too numerous to name and hence, this simple acknowledgement. Thank you folks very much for the wonderful support!

# Table of Contents

**PART I** .................................................................................................................. 1
Chapter 1     The 2010 Andhra Pradesh Microfinance Crisis ................................................ 3
Chapter 2     Setting the Context for the 2010 Andhra Pradesh Microfinance Crisis: The Tale of Zaheera Bhee ................................................................................................ 9

**PART II** ................................................................................................................. 15
Chapter 3     The Precursors to the Present Indian Microfinance Crisis—The NABARD High-Level Policy Conference and the Krishna Crisis .................................... 17
Chapter 4     The MFI Resurgence, Thanks to Equity Investors ......................................... 24
Chapter 5     The Return of the Banker(s) ........................................................................... 34
Chapter 6     The General Growth Story of MFIs ................................................................ 40
Chapter 7     Intervening Events from March 2009 to March 2010 .................................... 46
Chapter 8     The Run-up to the First Indian Microfinance IPO .......................................... 49
Chapter 9     The Runaway Success of the SKS IPO ........................................................... 70
Chapter 10    Andhra Pradesh Crisis and Microfinance as India's Subprime ...................... 77
Chapter 11    Responses by the State Government, RBI, and Microfinance Associations to the Andhra Pradesh Crisis ........................................................................ 81

**PART III** ............................................................................................................... 87
Chapter 12    Does a Five-Star Board Always Guarantee Good Corporate Governance? ...... 89
Chapter 13    Can Independent Directors Promote Good Governance? ............................ 98
Chapter 14    What Can MFI Boards Do to Implement Corporate Governance in Practice? ..... 110
Chapter 15    The Governance of Compensation at NBFC MFIs: Is There a Need for Serious Regulatory Reform? ..................................................................................... 115
Chapter 16    Can the Credit Bureau Stop Multiple Lending? ........................................... 126
Chapter 17    Establishing Minimum Standards for Effective Management Information Systems (MISs) in MFIs ................................................................................ 136
Chapter 18    Can the Governance of Risk Management Be Managed in Microfinance? ..... 141
Chapter 19    Do Independent Internal Audits Have Real Value? ...................................... 152
Chapter 20    How Reliable and Valid are Code of Conduct Assessments? ....................... 156
Chapter 21    MFIs and SROs: Critical Issues and Lessons ................................................. 179

| | | |
|---|---|---|
| Chapter 22 | Zero PAR, Legal Notices, and Insolvency Petitions: Delinquency Management from the Field | 192 |
| Chapter 23 | What is the Real Secret Behind the Burgeoning Growth of Indian Microfinance? | 200 |
| Chapter 24 | Is Lending to the Poor Costly? | 204 |
| Chapter 25 | How Safe is the Securitized Microfinance Portfolio? | 210 |
| Chapter 26 | Developing a Robust Regulatory Architecture for Microfinance: What Past Experience Tells Us? | 218 |
| Chapter 27 | Safeguards against Notorious Broker Agents: A Consumer Protection and Regulatory Imperative | 231 |
| Chapter 28 | Does the RBI have the Capacity to Regulate and Supervise Microfinance in India? | 243 |
| Chapter 29 | Should Not Microfinance Investment Vehicles Be Judged by the Same Standards Set for Retail MFIs? | 262 |
| Chapter 30 | Understanding the Role of MIVs in Microfinance: An Urgent Task for Central Banks and Regulators in Recipient (Host) Countries | 273 |
| Chapter 31 | Regulation and Supervision of Microfinance Investment Vehicles: A Suggested Practical Framework | 276 |
| Chapter 32 | Effective Control Systems at MIVs: The Key to Accountable Investing and Responsible Microfinance Globally | 282 |
| Chapter 33 | Redeeming the Indian Microfinance Industry: What Needs to Be Done? | 287 |
| Chapter 34 | The 2010 AP Microfinance Crisis: Lessons for International Agencies like CGAP! | 298 |

| | | |
|---|---|---|
| **PART IV** | | **307** |
| Chapter 35 | Epilogue - Eliminating Conflicts of Interests in Financial Sector Regulation | 309 |

| | | |
|---|---|---|
| **PART V** | | **327** |
| Appendix 1 | Growth of Number of Active Borrowers and GLP From 2000 to 2005 | 329 |
| Appendix 2 | The Financial Marketplace for Low-income People in India | 330 |
| Appendix 3 | Growth of Equity Investments, GLP, and Number of Active Borrowers for the Two Reference Periods | 331 |
| Appendix 4 | Loans Disbursed by Banks and SIDBI and Loans Outstanding to Banks and SIBDI | 332 |
| Appendix 5 | AP versus Other State MFIs, Clients and GLP Added | 333 |
| Appendix 6 | Growth of AP-headquartered MFIs During April 2006-March 2010 and Various Critical Parameters | 334 |
| Appendix 7 | E-mails to RBI Board and SEBI Chairman | 335 |
| Appendix 8 | E-mail to Buy ESPS Shares for Consultant | 341 |
| Appendix 9 | E-mail to Bankers | 343 |
| Appendix 10 | Tampering with Legal Records | 348 |

| | | |
|---|---|---|
| Appendix 11 | Laundry List of Issues Corporate (Mis)governance that was Internally Shared at a Large NBFC MFI in 2009 | 350 |
| Appendix 12 | Who is an Independent Director and Who Should be Treated as an Independent Director? | 352 |
| Appendix 13 | Open Letter to Right Honorable Andrew Mitchell | 354 |
| Appendix 14 | Glossary | 360 |

# PART – I

# Chapter 1:
# The 2010 Andhra Pradesh Microfinance Crisis

*"The micro-loan recovery agents were due to come knocking by the end of that week. She did not wait for them.[1]"*
— Soutik Biswas, BBC News, Andhra Pradesh, 2010

Two lines that matter-of-factly sum up the tale—not just of a life lost but also of an industry gone horribly wrong—an industry plummeted into a crisis by the loss of the very lives that it swore to elevate! The year 2010 saw the Indian microfinance industry suffer a crisis of faith that questioned the very basis of its existence. In October, the government of Andhra Pradesh[2] (AP), a state often described as the microfinance capital of India, reported that around 54 people had committed suicide as a result of harassment related to debt repayment. For a country that had yet not recovered (*emphasis added*) from the agrarian crisis claiming the lives of farmers at a regular rate, this was another body blow! The champions of the downtrodden had turned into agents of oppression and harassment—or so it seemed!

The year 2010 will certainly go down as a watershed in the history of Indian microfinance, when the industry consistently made headlines in the mainstream media. It all began with India's largest microfinance institution (MFI), SKS Microfinance Limited (SKSML), filing its draft red herring prospectus (DRHP) with the Securities and Exchange Board of India (SEBI) in the first quarter. There was all-round optimism,[3] along with the belief that the industry was poised for greater glory. However, the turn of events was tumultuous, to say the least—*from the filing of the DRHP through the controversial SKS initial public offering (IPO) and the sudden and unceremonious removal of the SKS CEO*[4] *after a spectacularly successful IPO, to the devastating suicides in AP (said to be caused by*

---

[1] http://www.bbc.com/news/world-south-asia-11997571
[2] In this book, the State of Andhra Pradesh stands for the undivided State of Andhra Pradesh, as it existed before January 2014!
[3] At the height of this optimism, some of them even likened the "arrival of microfinance" on the national and international stage to the information technology (IT) boom of the 1990s.
[4] Suresh Gurumani.

*multiple lending and over-indebtedness), the promulgation of the Andhra Pradesh Ordinance,*[5] *the related court drama and the subsequent enactment of the act, and finally the appointment of a Reserve Bank of India (RBI) board subcommittee* for microfinance. Reeling from multiple shocks, the captains of industry, as also other stakeholders, were left scrambling for answers.

One stakeholder[6] famously noted, "Microfinance in India has become a macro-mess." As someone who has been involved with what is now described as the microfinance industry for a little over two decades, I must admit that I was indeed saddened to see perceptions about microfinance change, and that too rather quickly, during this period. Microfinance, in the past, had been widely regarded as a tool for poverty alleviation and MFIs were always held in high esteem. However, in the light of the events of 2010, they began to be viewed as *'mere profiteers'* who accumulated *'huge wealth'* at the expense of the poor. Microfinance had clearly become a word to be avoided.

That microfinance in India turned into a macro-mess is a sad truth. In fact, much of this was predicted in May 2005, when Dr Thorat and I presented a paper[7] at the National Bank for Agriculture and Rural Development (NABARD) high-level policy conference[8] in New Delhi. This paper had suggested that the burgeoning growth of microfinance could result in a number of not-so-desirable practices being adopted. As The Hindu Business Line[9] noted in October 2005:

> "A recent paper (May 2005) by Mr. Y.S.P. Thorat (Managing Director, Nabard) and Mr. Ramesh S. Arunachalam, styled 'Regulation and Areas of Potential Failure in Microfinance' has argued for a single regulatory authority for all models and forms of microfinance. 'It will also help overcome the problem of using alternative legal forms to overcome microfinance regulations,' they write. ... And they cite three factors (to back themselves) which are: a) significant proportion of loan funds to the sector are coming from commercial banks - in ways, these are indeed public deposits being on-lent and the sector virtually has unlimited access to 'condition less' collateral free loans at 'soft' interest rates; b) the sector has grown considerably and should continue to grow even more and perhaps at a more scorching pace. The volume of money invested in the sector and institutions (individuals) is therefore by no means small by any standards; and c) there are some striking similarities to the NBFC failure scenario of 1990s and the early warning signals available point to several potential areas where market failure could indeed occur. Their study has found quite a few infirmities in the MFI sector: several entities under a promoter group offering funds; possibility of opaque transactions between group entities not ruled out; no single serious regulator — multiple regulators with different levels of supervision and no serious co-ordination among regulators and supervisors; ghost clients are possible along with ghost branches and ghost fieldworkers; same clients are shown as borrowers for loans

---

5 Andhra Pradesh Microfinance Institutions (Regulation of Money Lending) Ordinance, 2010.

6 Mr Aloysius Fernandez, noted microfinance and livelihoods practitioner and chairman, NABARD Financial Services Limited, [NABFINS] (http://nabfins.org/Chairman), made this comment at several fora, including in papers written by him.

7 The antecedent issues from this paper are dealt with in Chapter 3.

8 Regulation and Areas of Potential Market Failure in Microfinance, by Thorat, Y. S. P. and Ramesh S. Arunachalam (2005). Paper presented at the NABARD high-level policy conference in New Delhi.

9 The Hindu Business Line, October 1, 2005.

from multiple lenders; financial intermediaries in microfinance tend to have weak governance, management information systems and controls and perhaps, very weak risk management functions; by and large collateral free, soft interest, condition less (no personal guarantee) loans — virtually on an unlimited scale today. The money mela of MFIs in the rural areas looks more than a trifle scary."

When the AP microfinance crisis occurred in 2010, almost 5 years since Dr Thorat and I had written the above-mentioned paper, many of the serious issues identified in the 2005 paper seemed prevalent in the Indian microfinance sector. The key ones included the following:

- Corporate governance in Indian MFIs had become even more weak and numerous incidents/examples were available by then, ranging from related-party transactions (such as loans to founder promoters), to the sudden sacking of a highly successful CEO, to the silence of nominee/independent directors (IDs) on such issues, and several other aspects including tampering with board minutes, placing of items not discussed at the board meeting for approval with directors, and the like. M. Rajsekhar and M. Anand (The Economic Times) highlighted these governance concerns in an article, which, in my opinion, changed the course of Indian microfinance in 2010:

  "It just doesn't add up. This May, the board of directors of SKS Microfinance gave CEO Suresh Gurumani a 50%-plus increment, hiking his annual compensation from Rs. 1.5 crore to over Rs. 2.3 crore. It also awarded him a Rs. 80 lakh cash bonus. Three months after that, Mr Gurumani helped complete a spectacularly successful IPO, the first by a microfinance institution (MFI) in India and the second the world over, fulfilling a key mandate the board had given him when he was hired in December 2008. The stock listed at a market cap of Rs. 8,000 crore, exceeding most analyst expectations. And yet, within two months of what was a landmark listing for India's microfinance sector, the board fired Mr Gurumani. No official explanation was offered by the company, though CFO Dilli Raj, in a conference call with analysts, ruled out any financial irregularity. Many directors, all speaking on the condition of anonymity, chorus a one-line explanation for the termination—non-performance. ET interviewed over a dozen sources close to both Mr. Akula and Mr. Gurumani—investors, directors, current and former employees, bankers and regulators. Sources on Mr. Akula's side paint this as a difference in business strategy. Those close to Mr. Gurumani say this was a personality clash, a power struggle. They point to Mr. Akula's changing roles in the company as evidence.... Still, questions on the SKS board's U-turn—giving a 50%-plus hike to the CEO and then firing him five months after that—refuse to go away."[10]

- The artificial burgeoning growth of some MFIs caused, in significant measure, by multiple lending, ghost lending, fraudulent transactions, and the like, was a major issue. This strategy had been adopted to enable these MFIs to show great operating results and declare abnormally high profits so

---
10 *Source*: Quoted from "More to SKS script than meets the eye" by M. Rajshekhar and M. Anand, *The Economic Times*, October 8, 2010.

as to (perhaps) attract equity at higher valuations and build wealth for their stakeholders through various means, including IPOs.

- The creation of a new set of intermediaries called *broker agents* or *micro-agents* (in fast growing and urban areas) who caused (and were causing) havoc in the lives of poor women/men at the grassroots by using coercive methods to collect loans, ranging from kidnapping of daughters[11] of clients to force them to repay to several such harsh measures. In fact, Leo Hornak[12] summed up the arrival of the microfinance agent beautifully:

    "I remember the day three years ago when I decided I no longer wanted to be a part of the microfinance industry. I was standing in a one-room house in a small town in southern India, meeting a family that had taken out a microfinance loan. The mother and father were tired and nervous – both had the gaunt, prematurely aged look that is the hallmark of rural poverty in India. With them was their daughter Laxmi, a tiny eight-year-old girl, hiding in the folds of her mother's sari. 'For the three days that they took her away, I couldn't touch food,' Laxmi's mother told me through a translator, pointing at her daughter. 'We are just glad to have her back.' A few weeks before, Laxmi had been kidnapped and held hostage by a local moneylender called Mrs. Lalitha. Laxmi's parents had failed to keep up with payments on a debt. The debt was not to a loan shark or a mafia boss, however. It was to a registered Indian microfinance company which still claims in its brochures to be dedicated to fighting poverty, with a particular emphasis on women's rights and 'empowering the girl child.' Loan repayments had been informally outsourced to the moneylender.
    ...
    A few months after I left the microfinance consultancy, I again visited the town where Laxmi's family lived. I was told the moneylender was still working with the local microfinance bank, even though a kidnapping court case was pending against her. Weekly loan meetings were even being held in her house. The bank still listed women's rights and "empowering the girl child" as its key priorities. If microfinance ever does build a museum to poverty, Laxmi's one-room home would be a good place to lay the foundations."

- An integrated transparent management information system (MIS) continued to strangely escape the attention of the microfinance sector—data and information were not easily and transparently available at the headquarters level. In fact, there was lack of integration of data/information across branches, products, and geographies. Further, for example, not all charges collected from clients were transparently available in the existing MIS, the business rules of which were also perhaps not clear and transparent.

---

11  I first wrote about the kidnapping on my blog www.micro-finance-in-india.blogspot.com. The aspect of kidnapping and other issues are highlighted in the article "Why the dream of microfinance is turning sour" by Leo Hornak, May 8, 2011.

12  "Why the dream of microfinance is turning sour" by Leo Hornak, The Independent, May 8, 2011. http://www.independent.co.uk/news/world/asia/why-the-dream-of-microfinance-is-turning-sour-2280814.html

- Client protection was at best available as a lip service or, at worst, did not exist at all. The Reserve Bank of India's (RBI) code of conduct was not followed in practice and the RBI simply watched the happenings unfold, assuming greater financial inclusion of the poor all through. The spate of suicides in 2010 in AP clearly suggested the (negative) role played by brokers/micro-agents and others in harassing poor clients and their consequent impact.

- Defaults and delinquencies were burgeoning, especially during the months just before the crisis of September 2010, which perhaps led to multiple lending and greening being used as a strategy to overcome nonpayment of loans. Given the lack of a transparent, integrated MIS and the fact that both MFI corporate governance and MFI operations were like a black box, it had become difficult to believe the numbers and figures provided by Indian MFIs.

- A clear regulatory framework for microfinance backed by a national microfinance policy was lacking, and this had resulted in serious regulatory arbitrage, among other things. It goes without saying that the RBI's indifference to regulating and supervising microfinance and (NBFC) MFIs was responsible for the sorry state of affairs in no small measure!

Thus, the popular perception of microfinance had hit a low, and much of the good work done by many stakeholders, including some MFIs, was beginning to be viewed suspiciously. How did microfinance, once regarded a noble profession, come to be viewed this way? To what extent did the change in the microfinance paradigm (to hardcore commercialization) cause this negative perception? These and other questions started to flit across my mind and I decided to pen my thoughts as a book—*An Idea Which Went Wrong: Commercial Microfinance in India.*

I made a set of ground rules to follow while writing the book. One, it would have to be objective in terms of narration and content, but, at the same time, it would have to try and analyze the various happenings in a candid, analytical manner. Two, while describing problems and events, where there is no conclusive evidence, it would have to offer plausible explanations and leave it to the readers to judge for themselves the various cause–effect relationships. Three, it would need to be forward looking, in terms of suggesting practical lessons and strategies on what exactly would need to be done to reengineer microfinance to serve the needs of the poor and low-income clients.

From the outset, this book is clear in focus—it examines antecedents to the commercialization of Indian microfinance and demonstrates that this commercialization is an idea that went horribly wrong—both in design and implementation—with significant ground-level consequences. Specifically, it shows that improper design and poor implementation of the commercialization strategy led to the 2010 AP crisis in the first place. And using empirical data and hard facts, it seeks to debunk the hypothesis (or myth) that the Andhra Pradesh government, by enacting the ordinance and the subsequent act, effectively killed microfinance in India.

I state things as I saw them unfold over the past few years, backed by relevant data wherever available, taking off from a little before the Krishna district crisis of 2005–2006 in AP. Even before that, I narrate the story of Zaheera Bhee and her daily struggle for survival amidst severe poverty and adversity, to provide the readers with an overall context of (enthusiastic) financial inclusion that preceded the 2010 AP crisis. This is followed by a description of the antecedents to the 2010 AP crisis. I thereafter attempt to seamlessly weave in various happenings during this crisis with my own field-based analyses, before outlining the various lessons gleaned thereon.

The remainder of this book is organized as follows: **Part I**, which includes this chapter and the next, sets the overall context for the book; **Part II**, comprising *Chapters 3–11*, looks at the antecedents to the 2010 crisis and takes the reader through the various happenings during the crisis and brings them up to date with events as of December 2013; **Part III**, which incorporates *Chapters 12–34*, offers critical issues and lessons for global and commercial microfinance, as discerned from the 2010 and previous microfinance crisis situations in India, with regard to a number of specific topics—ranging from corporate governance to risk management, compensation, MIS, internal controls, microfinance agents and staff, client acquisition, effective interest rates, n*onbanking financial company* (NBFC) supervision, priority sector lending (PSL), self-regulation, code of conduct, and the like; and **Part IV**, concludes with a critical chapter—*Chapter 35*, which is the epilogue that focuses on the crucial aspect of making the RBI more accountable to the people of India, especially in the light of the 2010 AP microfinance crisis and recent events that occurred in the financial inclusion space. **Part V** is an appendix containing data, tables, exhibits, and other relevant material including references and glossary.

# Chapter 2:
# Setting the Context for the 2010 Andhra Pradesh Microfinance Crisis: The Tale of Zaheera Bhee

The year was 2010, which witnessed the worst ever microfinance turmoil. The setting was Kurnool, a small town in Western Andhra Pradesh and the month was October.

Locating the Nabee Saheb household in Kurnool[13] was not difficult as it stood near the *kabrasthan*, the Muslim graveyard. On entering the house, a thin-roofed structure built on about 60 sq ft of land, we noticed a wailing little girl in the arms of a middle-aged man who was struggling to console her. We soon found out that the man went by the name Nabee Saheb and the child was called Ayesha, Zaheera Bhee's three-year-old daughter.

The tiny house, built of mud walls and stone, had just two rooms—one where the entire family ate, lived and slept and the other, which was used for cooking and storage. There was a toilet outside. The size of the house became more telling with the piteous cries of the girl asking for her mother—a mother whom she lost about a month previously. Zaheera Bhee is believed to have committed suicide on September 13, 2010, as a result of huge debts. Or at least, that is what her family told us.

Zaheera Bhee's tragic story was narrated to us alternately by her husband Nabee Saheb and their eldest son, Khaza (20), a painter by profession.

Nabee Saheb, the head of this household, was a tailor by profession and he had no stable income. He worked in a tailoring unit near their home, and his salary was dependent on his owner's ability to procure work locally. Talking about his livelihood, Nabee Saheb said,

> "By and large, I make around Rs. 3000 to Rs. 4000 a month (between Rs. 750 and Rs. 1000 per week and Rs. 900 on an average), but that is not assured as most of the young people buy readymade garments these days. During festival seasons, the unit gets orders from older people and in those months (which are not many), I make Rs. 4000 per month. In the lean months, I sometimes make about Rs. 2000 a month."

---

13 The exact place of residence has been withheld at the request of the client family, for security reasons. The case study has been videotaped and the protocols are available.

Khaza added,

> "I came back from Hyderabad because my parents wanted me to help out at home. My mother, Zaheera Bhee, used to pick up odd jobs in the town markets but she too had no regular source of employment. So, my coming back helped as I was able to find work as a painter for six days a week and bring home about Rs. 1200. However, this was not sufficient because there were three more children to clothe and feed—Parveen (18), who is now married and lives with her husband, Muzambil (10), and Ayesha (3)—as well as several loan repayments to be made, day after day for weeks together."

Nabee Saheb affirmed this and added that Khaza's ability to pick up work fairly regularly is what kept them afloat, along with the grace of God (Table 2.1).

| Table 2.1 Family's Source of Income (Weekly, in Rs.) | | |
|---|---|---|
| Nabee Saheb (tailor; head of the family) | 900 | Not stable and could go as low as Rs. 500 or as high as Rs. 1000 |
| Zaheera Bhee (the deceased) | 600 | Was not stable |
| Khaza (eldest son, painter) | 1200 | Regular |
| Total | 2700 | |

According to Khaza, his mother became a member of a five-member women's group [*what we call a joint liability group (JLG) in microfinance parlance*] in the neighborhood. The main (supposed) purpose of this was to access a loan from the MFI to engage in some business and meet the family's cash flow requirements. However, the business was never really set up.

> "To my family's surprise, we found that the group was a willing and easy source of loan money—even the local moneylender would hesitate to give us more money," Khaza added.

Thus, Zaheera Bhee, along with her group members, started taking loans for various reasons with no serious questions asked about the purpose. The family naturally felt happy, taking and using the loans. The details of the various loans taken by Zaheera Bhee[14] are given in Table 2.2.

---

[14] The family claimed that moneylender loans were usually settled quickly as they had a very high rate of interest and also because they were usually small [often borrowed for paying small (MFI) loan installments]. We probed further but could not get complete details on all informal loans taken by Zaheera Bhee and her family and their status, as there were no records whatsoever. Khaza also said that his mother was the one who borrowed and, therefore, they were unable to provide the specific details. It is, however, possible that the family also had some informal loans.

| Table 2.2 Loans and Repayment Schedule of Zaheera Bhee |||||||
|---|---|---|---|---|---|---|
| Name of institution | Loan amount (in Rs.) | No. of installments | Period of installments | Loan repayment (in Rs.) | Weekly Repayment (in Rs), real and amortized | Meeting days |
| SKS [pedda (big) loan] | 20,000 | 50 | Weekly | 450 | 450 | Monday |
| [Chinna (small) loan] | 14,000 | 50 | Weekly | 315 | 315 | Monday |
| SHARE | 40,000 | 50 | Weekly | 900 | 900 | Wednesday |
| SPANDANA | 30,000 | 50 | Weekly | 675 | 675 | Tuesday |
| Local MFI | 18,000 | 50 | Weekly | 450 | 450 | Thursday |
| ASMITHA | 20,000 | 50 | Weekly | 450 | 450 | Saturday |
| BASIX* | 18,000 | Not known | Monthly | 1200 | 300 | Monthly |
| SRIRAM* | Not known | Not known | Monthly | 1750 | 437.5 | Not known |
| Total | 160,000 | | | | 3,977.50 | |

\* Loan repayment for monthly repayment loans has been amortized to a weekly structure to get a proper sense of repayment commitment for the family

While Khaza claimed that the family spent the money (from various loans) for regular consumption purposes, Nabee Saheb added that a significant portion was used for his daughter Parveen's *nikkah* (wedding)! This apart, Khaza clarified that surplus loan money was kept safe and used for unforeseen emergencies and to repay (if required) MFI loan installments that fell on successive days every week.

According to the family, there were quick or notional meetings on almost every day of the week for different MFIs. For example, Monday was the meeting day for SKS (pedda and chinna loans), while Tuesday was for SPANDANA SPHOORTY MFI, Wednesday for SHARE, Thursday for one local MFI, Saturday for ASMITHA, and a day each in a month for BASIX and SRIRAM. The meetings were to ensure that the member remitted the money to the group/center leader/agent every week.

Both Khaza and his father emphasized the fact that it was quite a struggle between day-to-day survival and repayment of loans (which was Rs. 3977.50 per week for all the loans). They said that the strategies used by the family to repay included borrowing from another MFI or such source and borrowing from moneylenders, even for one or two installments. Khaza further said that

> "it was only when my mother, Zaheera Bhee, ran out of options that she committed suicide. Now, My father and I are also in a similar situation and do not know what to do, as we have no source to repay the loan."

With a weekly income in the range of Rs. 2700, the repayment situation has always been a critical one for the family. With each successive loan (see Table 2.2), the family's repayment pressure mounted! After Zaheera Bhee's death, the repayment pressure further increased as the family was now bereft of her weekly income of Rs. 600.

In fact, data from Tables 2.1 and 2.2 clearly suggest that Zaheera Bhee's earnings were hardly enough to service the loans, particularly after the second loan was taken. Even when the entire family's earnings were taken into account (Rs. 2700), servicing the cumulative loan repayments after the fifth loan left the family in a deficit situation. And when one takes into account the reality that the family of six had to meet their living and clothing expenses apart from satisfying the educational and other needs of the children, one can clearly see that it was a no-win situation for the Zaheera Bhee household. *Therefore, I cannot help but question the basis on which these many loans were disbursed in the first place to the Zaheera Bhee household. That is the most critical issue which needs to be understood by all stakeholders who work in microfinance.*

Talking about the loan sanctioning process, an informed bystander remarked:

"There are at least 10 such microfinance institutions operating here. All of them have their field offices and anyone who wants a loan can approach group leaders. They will arrange the loan through the concerned agents (senior center leaders) and MFI staff. There are no serious procedures nor is there any proper questioning on the purpose and source of income before giving loans. God alone knows how they hoped to recover loan upon loan from such people, with poor livelihoods. Also, the loans are mostly used for consumption/consumer finance purposes and/or clearing old loans, and there is a time until which these people can manage repayment. After that, they have to either run away or take their own lives. And almost all the loans are scheduled as weekly repayments. It is compulsory that the borrowers pay the loan installment on the scheduled day of the week, and the field staff/agents will not spare the borrowers until and unless the installment is fully recovered."

Nabee Sahib's eyes moistened as he spoke of the repayment process:

"That is what drove my wife to suicide as she did not have the courage to face the group members, leaders, and loan staff, without making payments, and there was no way we could repay all the money. Also, *MFI staff and group leaders/members obstructed the normal life and work of my wife and family and thereby forced us to repay through several means, including borrowing from moneylenders at very high rates of interest (even 10% sometimes). They also threatened to resort to physical violence if the money was not repaid on time and we have all been scared since. They insulted and abused us until they got the repayment on the specified day—they would follow us from place to place, abuse/pester us, and embarrass us in front of our neighbors, forcing us to somehow repay the money.*"

The Zaheera Bhee case study and news about other similar debt-related suicides have given us enough cause to study the multiple lending phenomena. It is time we research this aspect, introspect with integrity, and usher in appropriate changes to Indian microfinance. That alone can, and will, help Indian microfinance deliver in terms of enabling clients to lead dignified lives and reduce their vulnerabilities, caused by a complex multipronged web of factors.

Having thus set the context of the 2010 AP microfinance crisis, which was all about over-included people like Zaheera Bhee (and her family), let us now rewind in time to 2005. The year was an interesting one, not just for being the UN year of micro-credit but also for the famous initial crisis in AP in Krishna/Guntur districts. As the next chapter suggests, the happenings in Krishna/Guntur in 2005 were among the real antecedents for the 2010 AP microfinance crisis.

# PART - II

# Chapter 3:
# The Precursors to the Present Indian Microfinance Crisis—The NABARD High-Level Policy Conference and the Krishna Crisis

As noted in Chapter 1, much of the problems evident in the 2005–2006 Krishna crisis were articulated by Dr Thorat (then Managing Director, NABARD) and this writer in a paper presented on the second day at the NABARD high-level policy conference in New Delhi in May 2005 (see *Business Line* article[15]). A senior Joint Secretary, Ministry of Finance, Dr Amitava Verma, chaired the panel. The discussions (with people at the plenary) were rather animated, as the paper and its presentation appeared to have ruffled a few feathers. This was evident from the fact that a number of presenters, especially the proponents of the MFI model, focused almost entirely on issues raised in the paper, rather than making their own presentations at the post-lunch session on products and innovations.

Senior microfinance industry stalwarts said (on record) that MFIs had good governance and systems were in place. They also went out of the way to emphasize the fact that MFIs were not engaging in any bad practices. A well-known commercial banker, Dr Nachiket Mor,[16] then Executive Director of ICICI Bank, which had been almost solely responsible for the fast growth of MFIs in the previous three years (and especially in AP), stated publicly that *"All of our partners have excellent MIS and none of them pursue any bad practices. And if such things start to occur, we will use technology for retail delivery and ensure that key mistakes do not happen on the ground."* Mr Mathew Titus, Executive Director, Sa-Dhan, said they, as an association (and unofficial SRO[17]), were taking steps to ensure better governance and systems and also trying to establish a best practices code for MFI operations. Dr Ajit Kanitkar, then a freelance consultant, said the paper was malicious and did not recognize the good work done by Sa-Dhan and others. Ms Achla Savasachhi, Senior Vice-President, Sa-Dhan, ridiculed

---
15 Tread warily on MFI loans; but spare a thought for rural poor (http://www.thehindubusinessline.in/bline/2005/10/01/stories/2005100102220600.htm).
16 Presently, Dr Mor is a member of the central board of RBI. He was nominated in May 2013, as a representative of the Eastern Board of the RBI. He also holds multiple positions in several RBI panels and committees, as at October 2013.
17 Self-regulatory organization.

## Chapter 3: The Precursors to the Present Indian Microfinance Crisis

the paper as being totally off target. Only Ms Moumita Sen Sarma, then Vice-President, ABN AMRO Bank, mentioned at the plenary that the skeletons needed to be emptied from the microfinance cupboard. Many of the donors were conspicuous by their silence, although they did admit in private that the issues raised would have to be dealt with in a firm and expeditious manner. Yet, none of these so-called torch bearers of governance, accountability and transparency were candid enough to admit the 'wrong doings' in the Indian microfinance industry.

Overall, I left the conference with an uneasy feeling. I strongly felt that the issues mentioned in the paper were going to prove critical to the microfinance industry's survival (at a later date), and yet the industry had dismissed these critical issues as either nonexistent or mere aberrations, whereas I knew for a fact that the malaise was spreading fast. So, when the Krishna crisis of 2005–2006 came to the limelight, I was not surprised. While the media in AP went overboard at times, by and large, they highlighted (real) ground-level problems. *The Hindu*[18] even described MFIs as a new breed of moneylenders, something I heard again in October 2010 from no less a person than Dr Y. V. Reddy, the former RBI Governor.[19] I reproduce portions of *The Hindu* article below:

> "A NEW breed of moneylender is seen in the rural areas, quite unlike the stereotype of the village moneylender. Agencies hiring this breed can boast of chief executive officers with management degrees and foreign accents. Collectively, they have acquired a fancy generic name, micro-finance institutions (MFIs). For many borrowers, a deal with an MFI agent is turning out to be as risky as one with the traditional moneylender. At last count, 60 people have committed suicide in Andhra Pradesh unable to bear alleged harassment by MFIs. It is a seeming replay of suicides by debt-ridden farmers during the last decade. This is the official toll: the actual figure is said to be around 200.
> 
> …
> 
> Mr. T. Vijay Kumar, an IAS officer, and the chief executive officer of the government-sponsored Society for the Elimination of Rural Poverty, has…in a report submitted to Chief Minister Y.S. Rajasekhara Reddy, stated how in one instance the members of a borrowers' group were made to stand in the sun till the defaulting member brought the installment due. According to the official, even alleged cases of outraging the modesty of women by MFI staff have been reported. 'They pass very humiliating comments whenever the women are unable to pay the week's installment,' he observed. … Noted Mr Vijay Kumar: 'Their loan officers have no technical appraisal skills. They are rude to the poor borrowers. There is no analysis of the incremental income generated on account of the loan and how much of the income can be set apart for servicing the loan.'
> 
> …

---

18 "The Makings of a Debt Trap in Andhra Pradesh" by S. Nagesh Kumar, *The Hindu*, April 20, 2006.
19 Microfinance Industry in India: Some Thoughts," by Y Venugopal Reddy, October 8, 2011, Vol xlvi no 41 *Economic & Political Weekly* (EPW).

In fiscal 2005-06, banks are estimated to have disbursed loans to the tune of Rs. 1,500 crore to Rs. 1,800 crore to MFIs, the report said."

That the 2005–2006 Krishna crisis was preceded by such large-scale growth[20] is beyond any doubt, as the data[21] suggest. SHARE and SPANDANA led the way, growing several times both in terms of number of clients and gross loan portfolio (GLP, in US$). SPANDANA, in fact, overtook SHARE in terms of GLP (in US$) in financial year (FY) 2005. Likewise, *Asmitha* Microfin Limited (AML) experienced phenomenal growth during FY 2005.

Thus, it is in this context of the huge growth by SHARE, SPANDANA, and AML in FY 2005 (April 2004–March 2005) that the Krishna crisis came into being. It effectively started in March 2005, when the late Dr Rajasekhar Reddy, then the Chief Minister of AP, visited Guntur/Krishna districts in the last week of March (I recall the date as March 29) and asked the then collector, Mr Naveen Mittal, IAS, to enquire into the allegations against some MFIs made by then sitting MLA, Mr Venkat Rao, and others. A consequence of the crisis was that the partnership model[22] of ICICI was done away with and at least 50 branches of some MFIs were closed, to be reopened later after assurances from the MFIs and key stakeholders including ICICI Bank.

*At this point, it seems useful to look at the situation in the Indian microfinance industry.* In 2005–2006, the Indian microfinance industry was a complex financial system[23] with an increasing number of stakeholders involved in it, from NGOs, NGO-MFIs, cooperatives, MFIs, NBFC(s), commercial banks (public and private sector), regional rural banks (RRBs), cooperative banks, development finance institutions (DFIs) and others. Explicit *legitimacy* to the sector was still lacking and microfinance was being delivered through a complex array of institutions governed by multiple laws. Regulation of microfinance was also complex, from very passive (for some types of entities) to very active (for others). In fact, some of these laws and hence regulatory/supervisory mechanisms even had the potential to work at cross-purposes; the scope for conflict of interest also existed. Regulatory arbitrage was indeed huge.

The key loan and outreach data of the microfinance industry, as of March 2005, as per the Mix Market database were: (i) loan outstanding of all MFIs (74 MFIs in total) was Rs. 1144.62 crore and (ii) client outreach of these 74 MFIs was 2.27 million approximately. Of this, the top five AP-headquartered MFIs[24] had a loan outstanding of Rs. 594.57 crore and client outreach of 1.05 million approximately. From this, it is interesting to note that the five large AP-headquartered MFIs accounted for almost 52% of the total

---

20 Large-scale for the context that existed then.
21 See Appendix 1.
22 For a description of the partnership model, see http://www4.gsb.columbia.edu/filemgr?file_id=646440
23 See Appendix 2.
24 SHARE, SPANDANA, AML, BASIX AND SKS.

GLP (of 74 Indian MFIs) as per the Mix Market database. Likewise, these five MFIs accounted for about 46% of the total active clients (of 74 Indian MFIs), according to the same database. Thus, even as of March 2005, the top 5 AP-headquartered MFIs had a huge (almost 50%) market share of the total microfinance sector in India.[25]

If growth was a trigger for the 2005 crisis, policy pronouncements also had an impact. Specifically, it was around this time that the RBI came up with its financial inclusion policy that sought to enhance delivery of financial services from the formal financial sector to large sections of the unbanked. This directive is part of the larger financial inclusion paradigm.[26] The key point here is that it was around 2005 that policy also started to give a strong push to ensure that financial services reached large sections of the excluded and low-income people. And this policy support led to great enthusiasm[27] on the ground with regard to microfinance as well.

That said, the key trends,[28] as they existed in the Indian microfinance industry in 2005, are summarized here: (i) MFIs were growing fast and handling larger portfolios and larger volumes of cash. Cash management therefore became a critical aspect; (ii) the burgeoning growth also meant that the MFIs did not have the administrative and managerial capacity (systems and human resources required) to handle increasingly larger and rapidly growing portfolios. The systems were being severely tested and had to be redesigned. Also, while the general design of systems tended to be good on paper, ground-level (consistent) implementation was poor and needed to be enhanced significantly; and (iii) This had implications for risk management and portfolio quality management, which, in turn, have implications for market and institutional failures.

Therefore, it was no real surprise when the so-called Krishna crisis of 2005–2006 actually occurred. The paper (by Dr Thorat and this author in May 2005) had already anticipated this based on the ground situation in AP and clearly warned the Indian microfinance industry. That the warning went unheard is a different matter. In fact, as part of a team, I (along with others) wrote a report for The MicroNed Network, the Netherlands, and I reproduce a diagram (Figure 3.1[29]) from that report that looks at the 2005–2006 Krishna crisis. You may find this interesting as it has many similarities to the 2010 AP microfinance crisis. Déjà vu indeed!

---

25 Keep this critical aspect in mind and compare it with the growth and market share of the top five large AP-headquartered MFIs during the 2010 AP crisis and you will be understand the enormity of the 2010 AP crisis.

26 The Dr Rangarajan-led Committee on Financial Inclusion and the Dr Raghuram Rajan-led Committee on Financial Sector Reforms are some the important reports with regard to financial inclusion in India.

27 I would like readers to remember this as well as it is relevant when we analyze the 2010 AP microfinance crisis.

28 Source: Regulation and Areas of Potential Market Failure in Microfinance, by Thorat, Y. S. P. and Ramesh S. Arunachalam (2005). Paper presented at the NABARD high-level policy conference in New Delhi.

29 Figure 3.1 tries to broadly map the *causality* (with regard to the crisis) with a tree diagram. Again, most of the causes apply equally well to the 2010 AP microfinance crisis as well.

## Figure 3.1 Andhra Pradesh Krishna Crisis (2005–2006) and Some Inference on Causality

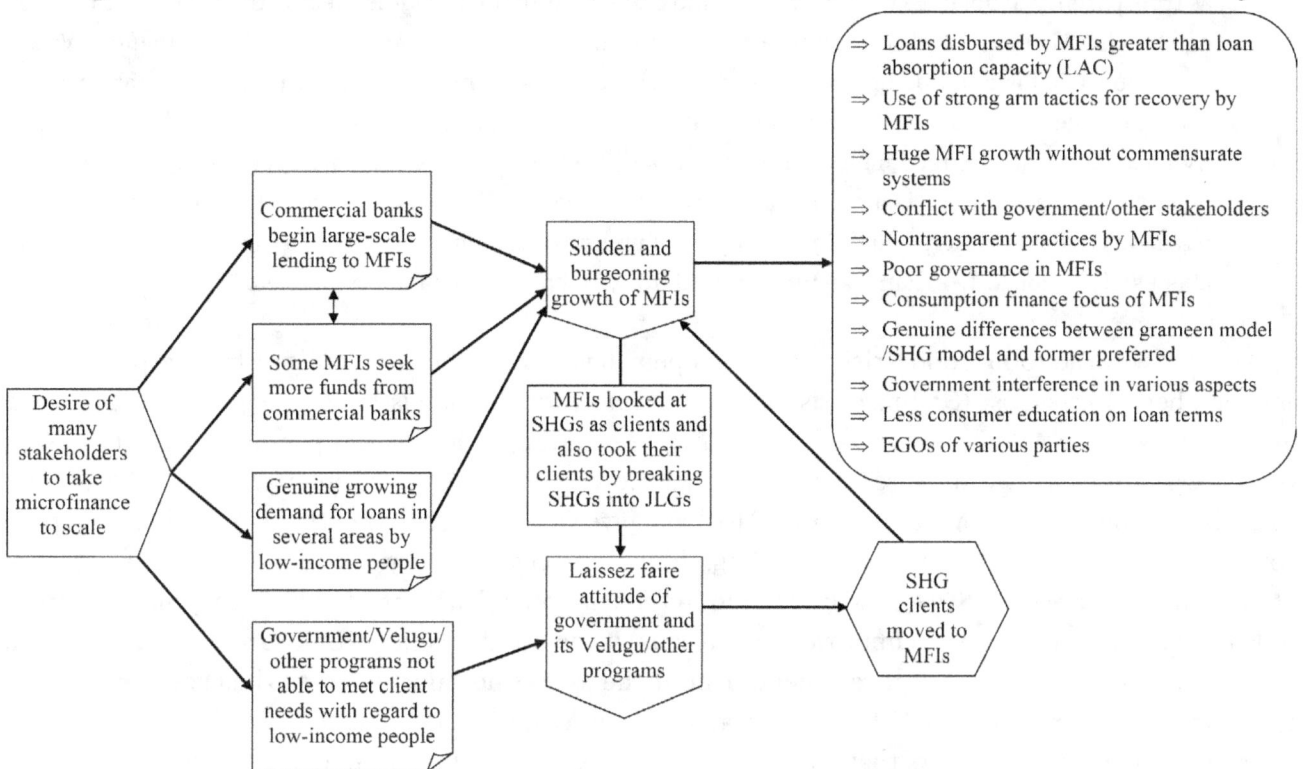

And interestingly, Dr Ghate concurred with the earlier analysis, while outlining the causes of the Krishna finance crisis. Commenting on the causes of the Krishna crisis, Dr Ghate, in the 'State of the Sector Report,' noted:

> "The most important enabling (or contextual) cause was the near-saturation of coastal Andhra Pradesh with microfinance. ...
>
> The second enabling cause was the rapid expansion of bank lending to MFIs that took place after 2003 with the introduction of ICICI's partnership model. With the financial constraint on expansion lifted, the MFIs were free to grow as rapidly as they could recruit and lend to new borrowers, or existing borrowers of Velugu or other MFIs." ...

One of the longer term causes was clearly the 'quest for numbers' relating to outreach and profitability that is the main motivation of many MFIs. While extending the depth and breadth of outreach is clearly central to microfinance's mission of making an impact on poverty through financial inclusion, and while sustainability is essential if MFIs are to attract lenders and investors in order to grow, the crisis serves as a useful reminder that there are other just as important client-centered consumer protection objectives such as transparency in dealings with borrowers and being careful not to saddle them with more debt than they can handle. These are goals that apply equally to minimalist as well as more holistic microfinance. We are all responsible for building up a climate of expectations (including perhaps the preceding chapter!) that celebrates the interrelated achievements of rate of growth of outreach, efficiency, field worker productivity, etc. without always remembering that they can (i) lead to shortcuts in client selection and training, field worker training and sensitization, and loan size determination, (ii) be used as the only criteria for incentive payments to field workers and (iii) put a degree of pressure on them that leaves no time for issues affecting client satisfaction, other than loan turn-around time, and progression in loan size etc."[30]

Much of why the 2005–2006 Krishna crisis happened has already been articulated, but one point needs emphasis here. In the post Krishna crisis situation, *the microfinance industry came together and promised several things to the AP government to cool the heat*. Accordingly, during and just after the 2005–2006 Krishna crisis, the buzzwords were "code of conduct (CoC)," "client-led microfinance," and the like. Many MFIs (backed by the major MFI association Sa-Dhan) gave assurances (some of them in writing) that they would *not*: (i) engage in multiple or over-lending, (ii) use coercive recovery methods, (iii) charge usurious interest rates, (iv) break up SHGs, and (v) offer (only) consumption loans, and the like. They also promised to clean up their governance and improve their various systems and practices, after several systemic issues were highlighted by the then AP government. Overall, the MFIs said valuable lessons had been learnt from the Krishna crisis, and they would hereafter practice *client-led and people-oriented microfinance*.

What happened in the years that followed is well known and is briefly articulated here:

Sa-Dhan framed its CoC (see article[31]), and assured the AP government that it would ensure its strict implementation. The code was said to be pro-client and supposedly contained several features to alleviate client problems, apparently caused by MFIs. The CoC was discussed at a subsequent Sa-Dhan general body meeting and approved by its members, who promised to adhere to it. I was witness to this event and also participated in the group exercises held. The AP government was apprised of the above, and several guarantees (including written assurances) were given by some of the MFIs involved in the Krishna crisis. That a few of the MFIs even gave letters is a fact often mentioned by Dr C. S. Reddy, CEO of Andhra Pradesh Mahila Abhivruddhi Society (APMAS).

After the Krishna crisis, *banks were reluctant to lend to MFIs*. However, slowly, things started to get better for MFIs as the AP government, on the strength of assurances given by the microfinance industry and the RBI, let go of its iron grip on MFIs and let them function again. Part of the understanding was that banks would finance microfinance clients and MFIs would adopt a 15% interest rate on diminishing balance. In fact, some banks like ICICI and the AP government supposedly signed an agreement to this effect, the basis of which I still question because servicing the last mile end-user client in microfinance is indeed costly.

---

30 *Source*: Quoted from 'Microfinance in India: A State of the Sector Report,' by Prabhu Ghate, 2006.
31 AP: MFIs adopt conduct code (http://www.thehindubusinessline.com/todays-paper/tp-economy/ap-mfis-adopt-conduct-code/article1728519.ece).

However, despite these assurances, commercial banks were still not forthcoming to lend to MFIs, as some of the private sector banks (like ICICI Bank) had lost significant amounts during the Krishna crisis. Thus, even after the seeming resolution of the Krishna crisis, the MFIs seemed to be stuck in a situation where they had little resources to finance their increasingly ambitious growth plans, which had not been altogether abandoned and/or altered after the crisis. Again, as Dr Ghate notes, "One short-term impact of the crisis was a heightened perception of political risk among banks, who both increased interest rates, and reduced new lending to MFIs in Andhra Pradesh, especially SHARE and SPANDANA, in the first few months of the current year."[32] So, MFIs had to look at other avenues for capital, and thus came the equity investor bandwagon into Indian microfinance—first social investors and subsequently commercial investors.

As the Economic Times article[33] in 2011 by S. John and M. Rajsekhar notes:

"The current crisis in microfinance in Andhra Pradesh has parallels with another episode in the state in March 2006. Back then, in Krishna district, the state shut 50 branches of two of India's largest microfinance institutions, Share Microfin and Spandana Sphoorty Financial, for charging "usurious interest rates" and "forced loan recovery" practices. According to researcher Ramesh Arunachalam, of the Rs. 2,000 crore Andhra Pradesh loan portfolio, Rs. 1,000 crore was in the Krishna district and another Rs. 600 crore in neighbouring Guntur. The 'Krishna crisis', as it came to be known, threatened the very existence of MFIs as banks stopped giving them loans. The stalemate lasted about eight months. Once they managed to assuage the state government, MFIs needed capital to write off old loans and start giving new loans.

Private equity (PE) investors stepped up. PE, which had invested $6 million in MFIs till 2006, pumped in $679 million in the next four years, says Arunachalam. Between 2007 and 2009, client accounts of the top 14 MFIs grew at a compounded annual rate of 79%. The episode illustrates how a lifeline of cash can save MFIs."

Yes, as noted, most certainly, it was indeed the PE investors who stepped in to support the MFIs, after the 2005–2006 Krishna crisis. They used their social (and later, commercial) investment route—an aspect that was unassumingly taken for granted by the MFIs, who perhaps did not know that these very same PE investors would extract their pound of flesh through faster growth, better operating results, and higher returns at a later date. In effect, the real commercialization of Indian microfinance started with the advent of equity investors, which is certainly one of the major antecedents of the 2010 AP microfinance crisis (as you will understand later when you travel through the book). I draw your attention to this milepost so you can come back to it when analyzing and understanding the burgeoning growth of the Indian microfinance industry that led to the 2010 AP microfinance crisis.

---

32 *Source*: Quoted from 'Microfinance in India: A State of the Sector Report,' by Prabhu Ghate, 2006.
33 *Source*: http://m.economictimes.com/Andhra-crisis-is-now-hurting-MFIs-national-interest/PDAET/articleshow/8380924.cms

# Chapter 4:
# The MFI Resurgence,
# Thanks to Equity Investors

If the 2005–2006 Krishna crisis left the MFIs cash strapped and struggling, they had a savior to answer their SoS—the social equity investors, who came running. These social equity investors (including some donors) provided the much-needed financial relief to MFIs, helping them overcome the temporary liquidity problem. Aided by such pioneers, some MFIs started to grow again, and very rapidly. They were rewarded almost concurrently as they received significant equity from other so-called social and commercial equity investors. These and other aspects related to equity investment in Indian microfinance are discussed in this chapter.

Figure 4.1 provides an overview of equity investments[34] in Indian microfinance, especially during the years preceding the 2010 crisis:

The figure is self-explanatory. It is clear that the equity investments had grown significantly from April 2007 and very much so from April 2008. The total investment—until July 2010—was approximately $680 million ($0.68 billion). Equity investments from April 2007 to July 2010 (a whopping $646.97 million) were almost 20 times the size of the investments before April 2007 (a minuscule $32.51 million). This is one *major* reason as to why MFIs were able to get over the 2005–2006 Krishna crisis and the liquidity constraints (caused by the partial withdrawal of banks from microfinance) thereafter. In many ways, April 2007 appears to be a watershed with regard to equity investments, as that is when the pioneers of social equity investment moved into Indian microfinance. And their success, in turn, led to commercial equity investors following suit.

---

34 After a lot of struggle, I was finally able to create a reasonably valid database (I say this because the data I had was published and quasi-published) on equity investments in Indian microfinance. However, I would therefore like to caution you to view the data and numbers accordingly. That said, it is also my belief that any further data revaluation will not significantly alter the trends-at best, some numbers for the respective years may increase or decrease. Any inconvenience caused is sincerely regretted but this is the best information on equity that I could get my hands on in 2010–2011 and thereafter!

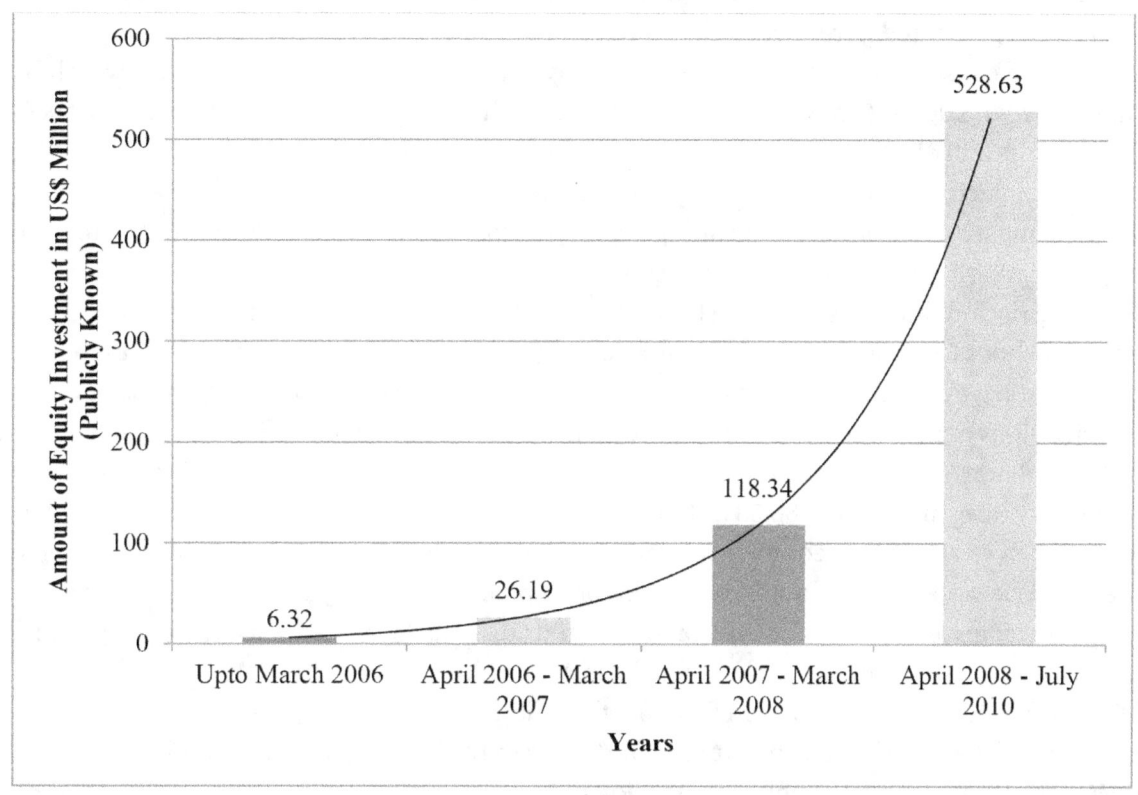

**Figure 4.1 Equity Investments in Indian Microfinance**

In fact, this burgeoning investment had prompted experts such as Mr N. Srinivasan to suggest that perhaps *"microfinance was the preferred sub-sector of choice in the financial sector for investment bankers."*[35] This is especially a curious phenomenon, given the fact that equity investments into other sectors had (sort of) been less than encouraging during the years of the global financial crisis.[36] Incidentally, it was almost during those very same years that Indian microfinance attracted significant equity investment. This curious anomaly was apparently also brought up by a person no less than Ms. Naina Lal Kidwai, Country Head, HSBC, at a national microfinance conference in India in March 2010. I am not sure whether the RBI[37] had taken note of the burgeoning equity investments

---

35 *Source:* 'Microfinance in India State of the Sector Report,' by N. Srinivasan, Sage Publications, 2010.

36 Financial services firm Lehman Brothers filed for Chapter 11 bankruptcy protection on September 15, 2008. The filing was the largest bankruptcy filing in U.S. history (until then), as Lehman was holding over $600 billion in assets at that time. This time period is often viewed as the period of global financial crisis, although, the practices that led to the crisis started much earlier.

37 That there is lack of a reliable national database on equity investments is an aspect that should not go unnoticed at this juncture. Also note what the Mix Market article (http://www.themix.org/publications/microbanking-bulletin/2010/11/how-has-growth-indian-microfinance-been-funded) said with regard to equity investment: "In light of the recent SKS IPO the composition of the equity base of Indian MFIs has received substantial attention, at least at the leading MFIs. While MIX does not (currently) track detailed data on shareholders, we do have details about different classes of equity and their evolution over time. Four main classes of equity are likely to be of interest for practitioners—Donated equity: the accumulated historical donations to the MFI. Retained earnings: accumulated profits retained by the MFI. This represents the historical net balance of revenue from clients and other sources and expenses for operations. Share capital: represents the capital contributed by investors along with any premium over the share price. Reserves: while not required in

in the Indian microfinance industry after 2007. That said, what basic trends can be discerned from the data and analysis presented here?

First, with no causality being implied, all I can say is that the period of very rapid growth in Indian microfinance (April 2008–March 2010[38]) is *associated* with the significant equity investments ($486.58 million) into Indian MFIs.

For example, during April 2008–March 2010, the six large AP-headquartered NBFC MFIs increased their GLP by almost $ 1.912 billion[39]—by doing so, they accounted for almost 73.16% of the total portfolio increase (during April 2008–March 2010) of the top 14 MFIs[40] (which stood at $2.613 billion). Likewise, it is in the same period that the six large AP-headquartered NBFC MFIs added almost 9.76 million active clients—this is about 68.34% of the total clients added (14.27 million) by the top 14 Indian MFIs.

Thus, irrespective of whether the growth of active borrowers or GLP is considered as a measure, April 2008–March 2010 is clearly "the period" of burgeoning growth in Indian microfinance and it was driven primarily by the six large AP-headquartered NBFC MFIs. It is noteworthy that this period is also associated with significant equity investments of $486.58 million. And interestingly, five of these six large AP-headquartered NBFC MFIs received significant equity investment during this period of fantastic growth. Therefore, there is definitely a clear associative (if not causal) relationship between equity investment and very fast-paced growth (both in terms of number of active borrowers and GLP) that occurred during the period April 2008–March 2010 in Indian microfinance, at least for these AP-headquartered NBFC MFIs.

Second, April 2009–July 2010, which is part of the fastest growth period (of April 2008–March 2010), *shows the highest equity investment in a single year* in Indian microfinance–approximately, $387.30 million. What then are some possible explanations[41] for the above trends? Let me attempt to provide a few plausible answers.

- It appears that some MFIs (first movers) perhaps grew rapidly during April 2008–March 2010, probably because the equity investors from previous years (rounds) required them to do so. And while doing so, they perhaps accessed more equity from the investors.

- Other MFIs (followers) perhaps saw the impact of equity investment (in terms of liquidity, growth etc.) for their peer MFIs (first movers) and they also began (trying) to emulate the first mover MFIs, resulting in perhaps more rapid growth in the industry, which may also have resulted in more equity investment. This perhaps began to drive further burgeoning growth and led to more investment with increasingly higher valuations.[42]

---

general, many MFIs choose to retain some equity balances in reserve for times of crisis. This article notes that investors, rather than clients or donors, provide the majority of equity financing to Indian MFIs."

38  See Appendix 3.
39  US $ unless specified otherwise.
40  13 NBFCs and 1 Trust.
41  While these are a few possible explanations, more research would surely be required to understand these relationships in a conclusive manner.
42  According to many industry experts, these valuations were very difficult to justify in the microfinance context.

- In fact, as this plausible cycle continued and gathered momentum during April 2009–March 2010, valuations skyrocketed and this is aptly summarized by the following quote. In a balanced informative article,[43] Xavier Reille of *Consultative Group to Assist the Poor* (CGAP) asks: Are MFIs in India overvalued? He goes on to argue:

  > "Current valuation levels are a cause for concern... **Firstly, the earning prospects of Indian MFIs do not justify such high level of valuations**. Current profitability is moderate. Micro-finance NBFCs in India are only generating a median ROE of 14.4% (although the largest five institutions show substantially higher numbers). Moreover, I see few prospects to increase profitability. Interest rates are more likely to go down as a result of competition. MFIs might not be able to sustain such record high levels of asset quality over a long time, as we have seen in other fast growing markets. Finally, there is not much room for increased equity leverage as NBFCs already have a X7.2 debt-to-equity ratio, more than double the global average for NBFCs.
  >
  > **Secondly, overvaluation might be driven by excess capital flows**. A significant share of equity investment in India comes from investors whose objective is to realize profits by floating or otherwise exiting their investments in a relatively short timeframe. In many cases in the past, this type of capital has produced overvaluation of equity prices in the short term and disappointment in the long term. After all, India is the only micro-finance market that has attracted large private equity funds.
  >
  > But I might be missing the upside. Perhaps investors are expecting MFIs to boost profits through other ways, for example, they might value MFIs as extensive distribution platforms for goods and services beyond finance?"

Thus, from the above-mentioned argument, it can be said that equity investment perhaps induced faster growth[44] in the Indian microfinance sector, leading to more investment and causing further rapid growth[45] and, thereby, attracting more social and commercial equity investments at very high valuations.[46]

Let us try and understand these issues/trends better using data on two sets of MFIs–equity leaders and followers.

As noted earlier, I had, subject to various caveats, pegged the total equity investment in Indian microfinance (until July 2010) at around $679.48 million. This investment went to around 28 MFIs that can be broken into two groups for further analysis: (i) the equity leaders—Group A consisting

---

43 http://microfinance.cgap.org/2010/03/05/are-mfis-in-india-overvalued/.

44 Note that this growth was achieved by leveraging PSL funds from commercial banks (like HDFC Bank, Axis Bank, ICICI Bank) and DFIs like SIDBI. The four named institutions were among the largest lenders to the microfinance sector in years preceding the 2010 AP crisis.

45 This issue is almost similar to the aspect of which came first, the chicken or the egg.

46 Data from international databases (Syminvest and Luminis) clearly indicate several investments by social and commercial PE investors into five of the six large AP-headquartered NBFC MFIs, who eventually led and caused the burgeoning growth of Indian microfinance between April 2008 and March 2010, albeit with disastrous consequences. Also refer to later chapters that deal with issues concerning microfinance investment vehicles (MIVs).

of six MFIs that each received equity of at least ≥25 million dollars; and (ii) the equity followers—Group B comprising 22 MFIs that each received equity <25 million dollars. The following trends are discernible:

- *The favorite MFIs for equity investment:* The six equity leader MFIs[47] received a major share of the equity investment, roughly totaling $549.26 million, which represents about 80.83% of total estimated equity inflows into Indian microfinance. This is indeed a significant percentage.

- *Range of equity investment:* Within this group, the highest investment was over $250 million for one MFI and the lowest was about $25 million for another. The other four MFIs had equity investments in the range of $25–125 million, with an average equity investment of around $60 million. What is interesting is that of the $549.26 million of equity received by these six MFIs, only $32.51 million came in as equity before April 2007. The bulk of it, $516.75 million, came in after April 2007 (and until July 2010).

- For long, people have talked of an association (and not necessarily a causal relationship) between equity investment and growth pattern of MFIs; let us use the principle of reductionism to understand this better. And for a start, let us look at how these six equity leader MFIs grew across the three main reference periods that I have been using to understand the AP crisis: (i) before March 2007; (ii) April 2007–March 2008; and (iii) April 2008–March 2010. Let us look at changes in GLP first and in the number of active borrowers later.

| Table 4.1 Equity Investments in Indian MFIs Across Equity Leaders and Followers ($ million) | | | |
|---|---|---|---|
| Years | Equity leader MFIs (6) | Equity followers (22) | Total |
| Before March 2007 | 32.51 | 0 | 32.51 |
| April 2007–March 2008 | 118.34 | 0 | 118.34 |
| April 2008–July 2010 | 398.40 | 130.23 | 528.63 |
| Total | 549.25 | 130.23 | 679.48 |

- *Changes in GLP across the reference periods:* The six equity leader MFIs grew at a CAGR (over a 4-year period) of 86.18%, adding $ 2.52 billion as GLP during April 2006–March 2010. Of this, a whopping US $2.014 billion (or 79.99% of the total GLP increase from April 2006–March 2010) was added during April 2008–March 2010. That is a very significant percentage and it is equivalent to the six equity leader MFIs adding portfolio worth $ 83.94 million (or Rs. 3861.11 million[48]) every month, during the 24-month period. Indeed, a staggering growth statistic, at least for me. In turn, this is equivalent to

---

[47] Not the same as the six large AP-headquartered NBFC MFIs referred to earlier. For reasons of confidentiality, I have withheld the names of the MFIs, at the request of people supplying the data. I must, however, add that the five large NBFC MFIs from the equity leader group are also present in the set of 'six large AP-headquartered NBFC MFIs.'

[48] I have used a dollar reference rate of Rs. 46 per dollar, which seems appropriate for that period.

each MFI adding a portfolio of $ 13.989 million (or Rs. 643.52 million) every month, and that is certainly a lot of money.

- Contrast this with their growth during April 2006–March 2008, *when they added just over US $0.504 billion*, to be exact. This is about 20.01% of the total portfolio added during April 2006–March 2010. Adding $0.504 billion over 24 months is equivalent to these MFIs adding portfolio worth $21 million (or Rs. 966.15 million) every month for 24 months.

- *The interesting conclusion is there for everyone to see:* For the six equity leader MFIs, the equivalent monthly portfolio addition during April 2008–March 2010 (which is $ 83.94 million or Rs. 3861.11 million) is almost FOUR times as large as their monthly portfolio addition during April 2006–March 2008. This clearly establishes April 2008–March 2010 as a period of very rapid portfolio growth, both in relative and absolute terms. And, surely, it is not a coincidence that April 2008–March 2010 also saw the highest inflows of equity investment into Indian microfinance.

- *Changes in active borrowers across the reference periods:* Likewise, when you look at *growth in terms of number of active borrowers across the reference periods, the following trends are discernible.* During April 2008–March 2010, the six MFIs grew at a CAGR (over a 4-year period) of 61.19%, adding 12.91 million active borrowers during April 2006–March 2010. Of this, nearly 10.46 million active borrowers (or 81.03% of the total additional active borrowers covered from April 2006–March 2010) were added during April 2008–March 2010. This is equivalent to the six MFIs adding 0.44 million active borrowers (or 435,971 active borrowers) every month during the 24-month period. In turn, this translates to each MFI adding 0.072 million clients (or 72,661 active borrowers) every month, which is certainly a lot of active borrowers! The above number equals about 2389 new clients (or about 479 new JLGs or 69 new centers) to be added every day by every MFI, and that is a huge task, under any circumstances. *Ask someone who has worked at the grassroots level and you will surely understand that sourcing clients and developing the JLGs and associated centers do take a lot of time indeed.* And that is why I would rate the above as very, very rapid growth by any standards.

Likewise, during April 2006–March 2008, the following trends are visible—the concerned MFIs added just over 2.45 million active borrowers (or 2,449,769 active clients), which was about 18.97% of the total clients added during April 2006–March 2010. Adding 2.45 million clients over 24 months is equivalent to these MFIs adding 0.102 million clients (102,073 clients) every month for 24 months. This translates to a figure of 20,414 active borrowers every month per MFI and even this appears to be a rather difficult task. And what is interesting is that the number of clients (JLGs, and centers[49]) added

---

[49] The MFIs could be using different terms and a different structure of client aggregation. The idea of using the terms JLGs and centers was to illustrate the real growth of clients, JLGs, and centers (where they are applicable) and notional growth of JLGs/centers where they are not applicable.

during April 2008–March 2010 is *almost 4.27 times the number of clients (and corresponding JLGs and centers) added in the previous period of April 2006–March 2008. This is very significant growth*. As noted earlier, the GLP of these MFIs also grew at very significant rates during April 2008–March 2010-*almost four times* that in the previous period (April 2006–March 2008) GLP. Taken together, this is clearly stupendous growth by any standards. And, of course, as mentioned earlier, these MFIs received significant equity infusion during April 2008–March 2010 and also thereafter. A summary of the key data is given in Table 4.2.

| Table 4.2 Growth of Equity Investments, GLP and Number of Active Borrowers for the Two Reference Periods ||||
| Group A MFIs (equity investor favorites or equity leaders) | Period: April 2006–March 2008 | Period: April 2008–March 2010 | Remarks |
| --- | --- | --- | --- |
| Number of MFIs | 5 | 6 | One extra MFI in April 2008–2010, which started operations in 2008 |
| Equity infusion (in million dollars) | 144.53 | 486.58 | A sum of $646.97 million came in after April 2007 (and until July 2010); of this, $528.63 million came in during April 2008–July 2010 |
| Total portfolio addition for all MFIs in 24 months (in million dollars) | 504.08 | 2014.49 | This represents an increase of 4.00 times across the two periods |
| Total portfolio addition for all MFIs per month (in million dollars) | 21.00 | 83.94 | Note that the equivalent amount added every month during the 24-month period of April 2008–March 2010 is almost equal to one-fourth of what SKS received through its relatively huge IPO. In other words, at the pace of growth during the period, the IPO money could have been exhausted in just four months by the six MFIs. This reflects the burgeoning rate at which these MFIs grew |
| Total portfolio addition per MFI per month (in million dollars) | 4.20 | 13.99 | One extra MFI in April 2008–2010, which started operations in 2008 |
| Total new clients added for all MFIs for 24 months | 2.45 million | 10.46 million | This represents an increase of 4.27 times across the two periods |
| Total new clients added for all MFIs per month | 102,073 | 435,971 | One extra MFI in April 2008–March 2010, which started operations in 2008 |
| Total new clients added per MFI per month | 20,414 | 72,661 | One extra MFI in April 2008–2010, which started operations in 2008 |
| Total new clients added per MFI per day | 671 | 2389 | The value for a day is derived by dividing the (monthly) number by 30.42 |
| Total new JLGs per MFI per day | 134 | 478 | A JLG typically has five members |
| Total new centers per MFI per day | 20 | 69 | A center usually consists of seven JLGs, but could vary according to the adaptation strategies used by the MFI in its model |

*What is the story conveyed by the numbers?* The six equity leader MFIs received significant equity infusion during April 2008–March 2010 and thereafter. Their GLP grew at very significant rates during the same period (April 2008–March 2010)—*almost four times the GLP growth from the previous period* (April 2006–March 2008).

This raises several questions for various stakeholders and it would be useful if these stakeholders try to understand *the rationale behind such phenomenal growth:*

- *What drove this very rapid grow*th during April 2008–March 2010, especially *a*s it came in the backdrop of the 2005–2006 Krishna crisis, and especially given the fact that five of the equity leader MFIs had their headquarters in AP?

- Did equity investors drive this growth? Or did the MFI promoters—*perhaps looking for more investments, better valuations and so on*—turbocharge the growth of the GLP, which eventually led to the 2010 AP crisis?

- Without question, the per-MFI per-month increase in GLP across these two periods is significant and it would be interesting to see whether and how exactly the systems of these MFIs coped with this rapid growth. The happenings during the 2010 AP crisis clearly indicate that the systems of many of these equity leader MFIs were indeed sheared because they lacked the managerial and administrative capacity as well as systems to manage such rapid growth–*that is precisely why there were huge frauds and the like caused by multiple, ghost and over-lending done (especially) through an agent led decentralized microfinance model.*

Honestly speaking, the period from April 2008–March 2010 is a watershed for the investments, as "serious" equity came in then (although it had started flowing from April 2007 onwards). Of course, the taste of success[50]—in whatever terms they are defined, including the stupendous growth of GLP of MFIs, number of active clients, profits, and so on—during this period perhaps prompted more equity investments during the next few months. But, the icing on the cake was the July 2010 IPO,[51] which was a significant achievement. Not to forget the subsequent listing at a huge premium—again, something very remarkable.

So what then are the implications of all of this for the Indian microfinance industry? It would be useful if the Indian microfinance industry, the MFI associations, RBI, and other stakeholders try to understand the relationship between equity investments, growth numbers (both in terms of active clients as well as GLP) and the associated processes and procedures. Some of the key issues (in this regard) are highlighted here:

---

50  No sarcasm is implied or intended. This is a genuine statement!
51  See Chapters 8 and 9.

- *Shortcuts in client acquisition processes:* In many MFIs, the normal and established processes of client acquisition were altered because of the urgency to grow fast—and shortcuts were adopted to facilitate fast growth—this indeed had a huge impact on client preparation and client relationship building, which until then had been considered fundamental for the success of microfinance.

- *Use of agents for client acquisition, loan disbursement, repayment collection, and other processes:* Several MFIs outsourced (through agents) client acquisition and other processes (such as repayment collection). In fact, it became an established strategy during this period and this certainly impacted client education/literacy, borrower sensitization/preparation and their well-being. This strategy also led to excesses in terms of loan disbursement (over-lending, multiple lending, ghost lending etc.), loan repayment collection (coercion, etc.) and the like. In the earlier years, MFIs used to sensitize their clients to neither over-borrow nor spend unnecessarily. All of the 'good' practices were thrown out of the window in the desire for fast growth—some MFIs even coaxed and cajoled borrowers to buy mobile phones.[52]

- *Reasons for rapid growth after the Krishna crisis:* It should be noted that the very rapid growth during April 2008–March 2010 came in the backdrop of the 2005–2006 Krishna crisis. This makes it even more significant, given the fact that five of the MFIs that drove this growth are headquartered in AP, which is also home to the Krishna 2005–2006 microfinance crisis. Subsequent to the Krishna crisis, some of these MFIs supposedly provided letters and commitments to the then AP government—post the Krishna crisis—with regard to not pursuing multiple lending, not using coercive repayment, not chasing fast growth, and other aspects/practices like not breaking up existing SHGs. Despite these assurances, they again grew at phenomenal rates and engaged in various undesirable practices to promote fast growth. This makes one wonder whether equity investment was one of the key drivers for the MFIs to again use undesirable shortcuts to achieve rapid growth.

- *Stakeholders who drove such rapid growth:* It seems necessary also to understand who (in terms of stakeholders) drove this growth and why they did so. Three specific aspects need to be understood here in terms of whether: (i) equity investors looking for quicker returns led the MFIs to grow faster; (ii) MFI promoters/senior management, who were perhaps looking for more investments and better valuations to create greater wealth for themselves and shareholders, also turbocharged the growth; and (iii) commercial banks and DFIs as well as the overall (financial inclusion) policy framework induced MFIs to grow faster. In my humble opinion, each of them had a mutually reinforcing role to play in turbocharging the growth.

---

52 http://www.indianexpress.com/news/andhra-s-smalldebt-trap/701577/4

- *Impact of rapid growth on MFI systems (with special focus on frauds):* Without question, the per-MFI per-month (and per-day) increase in new clients across the two reference periods mentioned earlier is significant and it should be noted that the systems of these MFIs just could not cope with this rapid growth—I have already touched on[53] the issues of nonexistent clients, repayment frauds, and other aspects of staff frauds (based on an analysis of some MFI financial statements) and it is clear that the agent-led outsourced model resulted in increasing frauds in Indian microfinance.[54]

- *Impact of rapid growth on MFI human resource (HR) practices:* Last but not the least, it would also be important to note the negative impact of this burgeoning growth on employees and staff at the field level in terms of working and living conditions, their case load (which I have analyzed elsewhere[55]), their overall morale, their mental stress/health, and the like. Available evidence seems to suggest that the already weak HR practices in MFIs (in 2005) perhaps got much weaker during the period of escalating growth (April 2008–March 2010). Also, outsourcing appears to be another reason for the rapid deterioration of HR practices as all and sundry (even people with criminal records, in some instances) were brought into the MFI fold.

That said, while part of the critical capital for MFIs came from equity investors, with passage of time, the 2005–2006 Krishna crisis was soon forgotten by the banks (such as HDFC Bank, Axis Bank, and ICICI Bank) and DFIs such as SIDBI. With enhanced equity infusion into the MFIs, these banks/DFIs felt that the already overleveraged MFIs were in a better position to leverage even more debt–this led to these banks and DFIs throwing in their weight fully behind the equity-laden MFIs and the next two chapters unravel the story of the burgeoning growth turbocharged by the commercial banks and DFIs, who were also the immediate and short-term gainers in the whole process of (over, multiple and ghost) lending to bottom of pyramid (BoP) clients in Andhra Pradesh and elsewhere in India.

---

53 See chapter on internal control in this book.

54 Increasing frauds, internal lapses at MFIs: Need to strengthen supervisory arrangements to protect the poor (http://www.moneylife.in/article/increasing-frauds-internal-lapses-at-mfis-need-to-strengthen-supervisory-arrangements-to-protect-the-poor/18309.html), by Ramesh S. Arunachalam (July 22, 2011).

55 http://microfinance-in-india.blogspot.in/2011/01/day-in-life-of-mfi-loan-officer-some.html

# Chapter 5:
# The Return of the Banker(s)

Equity investors had done the trick as, post equity investments, the banks started to get back, slowly but surely, to financing MFIs. Thus, progressively MFIs were also able to leverage higher amounts of priority sector bank funds (which, in fact, almost doubled as compared to each preceding year). Together, SIDBI and the commercial banks (HDFC Bank, Axis Bank and others[56]), ensured that soft DFI loans and priority sector funding emerged as one of the biggest financing sources for the MFIs. It is important to remember that the *biggest additionality of equity funding was that it helped restart bank financing to MFIs in a big way, in the aftermath of the Krishna district crisis.*

| Table 5.1 Loans Disbursed to MFIs by SIDBI and Commercial Banks ||||||
|---|---|---|---|---|---|
| Year | Commercial bank loans disbursed to MFIs during the year (in Rs. crores) | SIDBI loans disbursed to MFIs during the year (in Rs. crores) | Total commercial bank and SIDBI loans disbursed with MFIs as on March 31 (in Rs. crores) | Commercial bank loan disbursed (%) | SIDBI loans disbursed (%) | Total of commercial bank + SIDBI loans disbursed (%) |
| 2006–2007 | 1151.56 | — | 1151.56 | 100.00 | 0.00 | 100.00 |
| 2007–2008 | 1970.15 | 695.80 | 2665.95 | 73.90 | 26.10 | 100.00 |
| 2008–2009 | 3732.33 | 1686.75 | 5419.08 | 68.87 | 31.13 | 100.00 |
| 2009–2010 | 8062.74 | 2665.75 | 10728.49 | 75.15 | 24.85 | 100.00 |

*Rs. 1 crore = 10 million*
Source: *Compiled from Status of Micro Finance in India – 2009-2010, by NABARD.*

Surely, as can be seen from the data in Table 5.1, commercial banks and SIDBI leveraged the equity infused into the MFIs. They turbocharged the growth by providing huge amounts of loan funds for deployment as microfinance assets. Without any doubt, if only commercial banks and SIDBI had been more sensitive to the unfolding scenario, the 2010 AP crisis could have been avoided. While MFIs have all along been blamed for the 2010 AP crisis, the role of commercial banks and SIDBI in fostering conditions that led to this crisis should not be discounted. Put crudely, SIDBI and commercial banks enjoyed all the benefits (including receiving huge amounts of interest, processing fees, and the like),

---

56 See Appendix 4 for individual bank data with regard to MFI lending.

while much of the blame went to the MFIs. This is an aspect that should not be ignored under any circumstances.

While SIDBI's role is taken up in detail later, it must be mentioned that among the commercial banks, HDFC Bank was by far the most aggressive followed by Axis Bank.[57] I was indeed shocked to see HDFC Bank shed the conservatism of its parent company, HDFC, which is rather well known for its slow and steady growth approach. Likewise, while AXIS Bank was conservative in the initial years, since 2008 it transformed to becoming an aggressive lender. I seriously hope that the Boards of these banks will look into what caused such changes[58] at their (originally) conservative institutions.

Moving on to SIDBI's role in fostering fast-paced growth in the Indian microfinance sector, it is evident from the data given in Table 5.2 that SIDBI's loan outstanding to MFIs (as a proportion of total SIDBI + Commercial Bank outstanding to MFIs) was at least 25% on a yearly basis across the years preceding the 2010 AP microfinance crisis. This clearly establishes the fact that for each of the four years preceding the 2010 AP microfinance crisis, SIDBI had a minimum 25% market share[59] of the MFI loan market and was by a large margin, the single largest and most consistent financier to the MFIs (at least in the three years preceding the 2010 AP microfinance crisis).

| Table 5.2 Loans Outstanding with MFIs for SIDBI and Commercial Banks | | | | | | |
|---|---|---|---|---|---|---|
| Year | Commercial bank loans outstanding with MFIs as on March 31 (in Rs. crores) | SIDBI MFIs loans outstanding on March 31 (in Rs. crores) | Total commercial bank and SIDBI loans outstanding with MFIs as on March 31 (in Rs. crores) | Commercial bank loan outstanding (%) | SIDBI loans outstanding (%) | Total of commercial bank + SIDBI loans outstanding (%) |
| 2006–2007 | 1584.48 | 550 | 2134.48 | 74.23 | 25.77 | 100.00 |
| 2007–2008 | 2748.84 | 950.38 | 3699.22 | 74.31 | 25.69 | 100.00 |
| 2008–2009 | 5009.09 | 2136.89 | 7145.98 | 70.10 | 29.90 | 100.00 |
| 2009–2010 | 10147.5 | 3808.2 | 13955.7 | 72.71 | 27.29 | 100.00 |

Rs. 1 crore = 10 million, NA = not available
Source: Compiled from Status of Microfinance in India–2009-2010, by NABARD.

The key point to remember here is that SIDBI's investments in MFIs—which included both debt[60] and equity[61]—served as the preliminary crucial foundation for the deployment of large-scale commercial funds by banks and commercial private equity investors. In other words, without SIDBI's facilitation, large-scale

---

57 See Appendix 4 for individual bank data with regard to MFI lending.

58 While there could be many reasons, I offer a couple of basic explanations: (i) maybe the personnel involved were responsible for this sea change and (ii) perhaps, perverse incentives had started to take over the entire credit-granting process as had happened in the global financial crisis.

59 While individually, the market share of the commercial banks has always been less than that of SIDBI, together, several commercial banks, typically, had between 70–75% market share of the MFI loan market during the same four years.

60 While year on year, SIDBI had increased its outstanding portfolio and disbursement, it is interesting to note that the growth was phenomenal during 2008–2009 and 2009–2010, both in terms of loans disbursed and loans outstanding. What makes SIDBI's loans even more powerful is that it is real long-term financing!

61 SIDBI investments in MFIs also include equity and quasi equity (a special product called transformation loans). These were extremely crucial in providing legitimacy for the MFIs concerned.

## Chapter 5: The Return of the Banker(s)

lending by commercial banks and the investment by commercial equity investors would not have occurred. In fact, based on Table 5.2 and the data given in Appendix 4, it can be said that SIDBI, HDFC Bank and AXIS Bank[62] are almost always among the top four ranked institutions with regard to lending to MFIs, irrespective of the criteria used, which could be: (i) loans disbursed to MFIs; and (ii) loan outstanding with MFIs. In other words, it can be inferred that these three institutions (definitely) played a major role in the rapid growth of the Indian microfinance sector, at least during the period 2006 to 2010.

That said, without any doubt, the single largest financier of the MFIs in the years preceding the 2010 AP crisis was SIDBI and the data given in Table 5.3 is very revealing. A close look at this data suggests that SIDBI had fully abandoned its slow growth trajectory somewhere in 2008–2009 (when its disbursements[63] had more than doubled that of the previous year). Thus, SIDBI had, in fact, started to push the Indian microfinance industry (into a very high growth path) by late FY[64] 2007 and early FY 2008. The data given here is self-explanatory.

| Table 5.3 SIDBI Microfinance Portfolio Outstanding Data | | | | | | | | | |
|---|---|---|---|---|---|---|---|---|---|
| Key aspects | 2002 | 2003 | 2004 | 2005 | 2006 | 2007 | 2008 | 2009 | 2010 |
| SIDBI MFI loan outstanding as of March 31 (in crores) | 44.31 | 56.01 | 90.93 | 137.76 | 339.00 | 550.00 | 950.38 | 2136.89 | 3808.20 |
| Yearly increase in SIDBI loan outstanding over previous year (in crores) | | 11.70 | 34.92 | 46.83 | 201.24 | 211.00 | 400.38 | 1186.51 | 1671.31 |
| SIDBI yearly portfolio increase as a proportion of previous year portfolio (%) | | 26.40 | 62.34 | 51.50 | 146.09 | 62.24 | 72.80 | 124.85 | 78.21 |
| Source: Compiled from official SIDBI documents, SIDBI presentations on the web and NABARD Annual State of Sector Reports. | | | | | | | | | |

Given these details, SIDBI's role deserves focused analysis and the same is done here. First, I must state that SIDBI has been a fair and conservative institution that always put low-income people first. That is why it is somewhat surprising to see that it experienced such burgeoning growth as given in these tables. It would therefore be good for SIDBI to introspect and understand the motivations for such unbridled growth in MFI lending during the years preceding the 2010 AP microfinance crisis—especially because its partner MFIs caused significant devastation on the ground in terms of enhancing indebtedness of poor and vulnerable people. The SIDBI board and senior management would certainly need to look into the processes/methods of sanctioning and disbursing loans to MFIs in the light of the above. Further, given that SIDBI had not been able to spot the over, multiple and ghost lending spree in Indian microfinance (and

---

62 ICICI Bank also comes into this group but not consistently across the three years. Possibly, there has been an impact of the Krishna 2005–2006 crisis on the bank's policies.
63 SIDBI's disbursements in 2007–2008 stood at Rs.695.80 crore, whereas it more than doubled to Rs. 1686.75 crore in 2008–2009.
64 FY 2007 = 2007–2008; FY 2008 = 2008–2009.

the associated indebtedness) is surely something for its management to reflect upon and analyze from a systems perspective.[65]

Second, SIDBI is investing in many MFIs as a social equity investor and the impact of its investments is such that it gives tremendous legitimacy to the concerned MFI. In other words, apart from the quantum of investments, the real additionality of SIDBI's equity investments in MFIs lies in associating its well-established and highly regarded brand name with the concerned MFIs. Therefore, its nominee directors are under serious obligation to diligently perform their roles—as independent directors (IDs)—in a professional and objective manner.

The fact that SIDBI's nominee director remained a mute spectator when the founder-promoter-MD of a large MFI gave himself a huge loan to buy shares in the same MFI is indeed cause for concern. That action is certainly unacceptable in any financial institution and is unquestionably an act of not-so-good governance. That the SIDBI nominee director again remained silent about the hurriedly convened board meeting of a large MFI—that too on a Sunday—to sack an immensely successful CEO who led the MFI through a spectacular IPO is again worrisome. Without question, as a social investor, SIDBI is expected to ensure appropriate and good governance at its partner MFIs and, more so, among the ones where it has invested (its funds as well as its brand name) and has a nominee director on board. These clearly call for a serious review of the process by which SIDBI: (i) makes equity investments into MFIs; (ii) appoints nominee directors to MFIs; and (iii) ensures the accountability of these nominee directors. This is another issue that requires deep introspection by SIDBI's management.[66]

Going forward, it would be important to ensure that SIDBI provides the right kind of leadership for responsible microfinance—after incorporating lessons from the 2010 AP crisis and building necessary safeguards against any real and/or potential conflicts of interests. These issues become relevant as institutions such as SIDBI intermediate (a large amount of) public funds and, having seen the *havoc* that microfinance agents have caused on the ground, I cannot help but raise these issues. I hope SIDBI's management takes these in the right spirit[67] and introspects with integrity. That alone should be able to provide practical guidance to the institutions such as SIDBI and the various development projects being implemented. In fact, the time is now surely ripe for *SIDBI, as an institution, to prepare and release a white paper on its role in the Indian microfinance industry,*

---

65 SIDBI officers (and other stakeholders hired by SIDBI) are supposed to perform due diligence checks with regard to end use of (client) loans. This involves a physical visit to the MFI field areas and meetings with their clients who have already received a loan from SIDBI's previous loan (tranche) to MFI. These stakeholders are also said to inspect MFI records. Additionally, certain companies were given contracts of loan portfolio audits to be performed on SIDBI's partner MFIs. How could the multiple, over-and ghost lending escape all these checks is something that still continues to baffle me very much.

66 Another aspect with regard to SIDBI's role in Indian microfinance deserves further mention. When I was traveling in the field, through the 2010 AP microfinance crisis, and observing firsthand the havoc caused by the agent-led fast-tracked decentralized microfinance model in India, and especially in the near microfinance saturated states, I was confronted by some basic questions: *(i) where did the MFIs get the funds to grow as fast they did?; (ii) how did wholesale financiers (DFIs such as SIDBI and banks) provide so much funds to MFIs and yet allow the kind of not-so-good practices that were prevalent on the ground?; and (iii) were they in some ways responsible for the kind of (not-so-good) practices (such as use of agents), found in Indian microfinance?*

67 The idea is not to blame anyone or find fault with any institution. The objective solely is to learn from past experiences and ensure that similar things do not happen on the ground again in the future.

pre- and post the 2010 AP crisis. This paper would be an extremely valuable learning tool for all concerned.

Lastly, the Government of India is channelizing a lot of equity through SIDBI, especially for MFIs. While it is a positive development, there are in fact several lessons and issues that need to be considered while facilitating equity investment in MFIs. I hope the concerned people have asked the right questions and done the required homework while establishing such initiatives. Again, the purpose here is not to be critical of any institution, but rather to learn valuable lessons from the past. The following specific learning points may be useful for SIDBI's board and senior management and other such DFIs that are involved in equity investment in microfinance.

One, SIDBI's track record in carrying out its obligations as an equity investor is rather poor. The case of SKS Microfinance is an excellent example, where a senior SIDBI officer on the board permitted the founder/promoter to lend a substantial sum of money to himself to enable him to buy shares of the same company (SKS Microfinance[68]). This huge related-party transaction can be viewed as the starting point of the current problems in Indian microfinance.

Two, the aspect of providing equity does not stop with merely making the investment, especially when it is valuable government money (in effect, public money) that is being channelized. Along with it comes the solid obligation to ensure that the MFIs that are recipients of this "special" equity investment are indeed worthy of the same and continue to stay worthy of the same—in terms of their practices in several areas including governance, management systems, and the like—and are more importantly, held accountable for their accessing these privileged funds.

Three, given the past experiences where related-party transactions and other not-so-good practices were perhaps (implicitly) authorized[69] by institutional nominee directors, it becomes important to strengthen and streamline the processes by which such nominee directors report back to their parent organizations. It may be useful to ensure that they mandatorily write physical reports and submit them as part of their obligation to serve on the boards of these MFIs. There must also be a process of vetting these reports and making these nominee directors accountable. Such directors must also not sign minutes with regard to issues that have not been deliberated upon—this continues to be common practice in the Indian microfinance sector.

Four, there is a tendency for such nominee directors to encourage vast amounts of borrowing from the parent organizations and this again causes the devastating supply-side growth. In short, these officer-nominee directors appear to be more loyal to the task of encouraging greater loan off-take from their parent organization by the concerned MFIs (and thereby causing huge supply-led growth) rather than ensuring responsible and appropriate growth of the MFI, commensurate with its systems and governance and actual client demand on the ground. This conflict of interest must be guarded against. Take the reckless and mindless growth of the microfinance sector between April 2008 and March 2010, for which SIDBI has to hold itself largely, if not completely, responsible. There is reasonably good evidence

---

68  SKS Microfinance was then called as SKS Microfinance Private Limited. The name SKSML came in later.
69  Their lack of open *dissent* has to be interpreted as implicit consent for the wrong action/practice.

to suggest that SIDBI's nominee directors at various MFIs were more interested in pushing loans from SIDBI to partner MFIs than carrying out their fiduciary, strategic and other responsibilities as (nominated) board members at the MFIs concerned.

These are some of the key issues that need the attention of all concerned with regard to equity investment. Otherwise, we will again see the use of equity (and bank funds leveraged on the basis of this equity) resulting in problems for the microfinance industry and its clients. These aspects will become clearer as you read the next chapter, which provides an overview of the unprecedented growth in Indian microfinance that eventually led to the AP crisis in 2010.

# Chapter 6:
# The General Growth Story of MFIs

As noted in the earlier chapters, with the resource support from equity investors and bankers, many MFIs (especially the large ones) were back to their old ways and experienced burgeoning growth from April 2008 to March 2010, adding the largest number of active borrowers and disbursing the largest loan amounts in global microfinance history (at least until then). Therefore, in many ways, these two financial years represent a watershed for Indian microfinance, and I believe the seeds for the 2010 AP microfinance crises were sown then or thereabouts. That this phenomenal growth occurred just 1 to 2 years after the 2005–2006 Krishna crisis is interesting, and I think the remarks of Mr C. S. Reddy, CEO, APMAS, (quoted from the CGAP blog, 'Crisis or Opportunity') put the various happenings in proper perspective:

> "For almost six years, the MFIs have been asked to improve their practices on the ground. However, there is no improvement. After the 2005-06 crisis, the MFIs came up with the voluntary code of conduct (CoC). Its implementation is yet to begin. The SHGs and their federations suffered a great deal due to the exponential growth of the MFIs without any regard for the SHGs.
>
> In 2005-06, MFIs made several commitments like reducing the interest rates, not indulging in multiple lending and that the recovery practices would not be coercive. None of those commitments were acted upon. They did not seem to learn any lessons from the previous experiences. MFIs have pushed a lot of credit resulting in many households in a debt trap.
>
> MFIs have to demonstrate that they "walk the talk". Those that seem to make comments in support of the MFI practices need to understand the practices on the ground. Responsible microfinance does not exist in practice."[70]

The growth patterns in terms of the clients and GLP added by the top 14 largest MFIs (during 2006–2008 and 2008–2010) is given in Appendix 5. The data establishes the fact that much of the growth in

---

70 Quoted from the CGAP blog, 'Crisis or Opportunity.'

microfinance occurred because of the six large AP-headquartered MFIs[71] (all NBFCs) that added as many as 9,757,489 clients during 2008–2010 in comparison to the eight other state-headquartered MFIs that added just 4,519,865 clients. In other words, the six large AP-headquartered NBFC MFIs added more than twice as many clients as the eight non-AP-headquartered MFIs (seven NBFCs plus one Trust).

Likewise, in terms of GLP addition during April 2008–March 2010, the six large AP-headquartered MFIs increased their GLP by US $1,911,680,234 as compared to the eight other state-headquartered MFIs whose GLP increased (during the same two years) by a mere US $701,154,992. In other words, the eight other state-headquartered MFIs added just about 1/3$^{rd}$ of the GLP increased by the six AP-headquartered NBFC MFIs.

Thus, it is clear that the six large AP-headquartered NBFC MFIs caused a huge impact in driving the burgeoning growth during 2008–2010. Likewise, it is very clear from the data that the growth of NBFCs in the top 14 MFIs far outstripped the growth of the nonprofit MFIs, both in terms of clients added and GLP enhanced. In fact, there were 13 NBFC MFIs in the top 14 MFIs and just one nonprofit MFI (i.e., a Trust)

Likewise, Appendix 6 portrays the growth of the six large AP-headquartered NBFC MFIs in comparison to all the AP-headquartered MFIs.[72] The data from this table reveal the following trends.

1. *Growth during April 2006–March 2010:* All AP-headquartered[73] MFIs added nearly 12,766,583 clients (12.77 million) in April 2006–March 2010, and, of this, as many as 12,199,342 clients (12.19 million) were added by the six large AP-headquartered MFIs. In other words, the clients added by the six large AP-headquartered NBFC MFIs accounted for nearly 95.56% of the total clients added by all AP-headquartered MFIs during April 2006–March 2010.

All AP-headquartered MFIs increased their GLP by nearly $2,539,558,896 ($ 2.54 billion) during April 2006–March 2010 and, of this, an increase of $ 2,412,765,614 ($ 2.41 billion) was due to the six large AP-headquartered NBFC MFIs. In other words, the six large AP-headquartered NBFC MFIs accounted for nearly 95.01% of the total GLP increased by all the AP-headquartered MFIs during April 2006–March 2010.

From this, it is clear that the six large AP-headquartered NBFC MFIs (SKSML, SPANDANA, SHARE, ASMITHA, BASIX, and TRIDENT) were the major growth drivers among the MFIs headquartered in AP (the nerve center of the 2010 microfinance crisis).

---

71 SHARE, SPANDANA, BASIX, ASMITHA, SKS AND TRIDENT.

72 There were 38 AP-headquartered MFIs that reported to the Mix Market and the six large AP-headquartered NBFC MFIs (SHARE, SPANDANA, BASIX, ASMITHA, SKS and TRIDENT) were part of this group.

73 It is presumed and perhaps correctly that AP–headquartered MFIS will have their largest concentration in their home state and the same analogy is consistently applied for other state-headquartered MFIs. This seems fine from the overall perspective of understanding growth of MFIs.

2. *Growth during April 2008–March 2010:* It is also pertinent to note that the six large AP-headquartered MFIs added a significant number of active borrowers during April 2008–March 2010—that is, they added 9.76 million clients, while their other AP-headquartered peers added just 0.43 million clients. Likewise, the six large AP-headquartered MFIs increased their GLP significantly during the same period—$1,911.68 million (1.91 billion), while their other AP-headquartered peers added just $87.38 million.

3. *Active borrowers and GLP as at end March 2010:* In fact, the six large AP-headquartered MFIs accounted for 94.66% of the number of active borrowers of all AP-headquartered MFIs in 2010 and 94.45% of the GLP (in US dollars)-which reveals their dominance among all AP-headquartered MFIs.

What is very interesting to note is that all of the six large AP-headquartered MFIs are NBFCs that are regulated and supervised by the RBI, under its regulatory framework, through the department of non-bank supervision. This aspect needs to be noted carefully and, it is these six NBFC MFIs that have to take the major blame for the 2010 AP crisis as they have been the most dominant and fastest growing among all the MFIs in AP.

Let us now look at the bigger picture (data in Table 6.1) with regard to the six large AP-headquartered MFIs. The data clearly show that the high levels of equity investment combined with high levels of commercial bank/DFI financing led to the disastrous and irresponsible growth—both in terms of GLP enhanced and active clients added—during (between April 2008 and March 2010) which, ultimately led to the (infamous) 2010 AP microfinance crisis.

| Table 6.1 Summary Data for Number of Clients and GLP Added by MFIs, Incremental Equity Investment into MFIs and Increase in DFI/Bank Outstanding in Indian Microfinance Across Two Reference Periods | | | |
|---|---|---|---|
| Description | April 2006–March 2008 | April 2008–March 2010 | Number of times increase across two reference periods |
| Total active clients added by six large AP-headquartered MFIs | 2,441,853 | 9,757,489 | 4.00 |
| Total gross loan portfolio enhanced by six large AP-headquartered MFIs (in million dollars) | 501,085,380 | 1,911,680,234 | 3.82 |
| Total equity investment into Indian microfinance (in million dollars) | 144.53 | 486.58 | 3.37 |
| SIDBI loan outstanding (in crores) | 611.38 | 2857.82 | 4.67 |
| Bank loan outstanding (in crores) Unable to calculate as 2006 outstanding data is not available for all commercial banks. End March 2007 outstanding is used | 1584.48 (end March 2007) | 7398.66 | Should be greater than five times (as even with March 2007 data, the increase is about 4.66 times) |

Thus, it is clear that SIDBI and commercial banks helped these six large AP-headquartered MFIs[74] leverage their burgeoning equity[75] investments several fold. In fact, this combination of equity and leveraged DFI/bank funds[76] provided these six large AP-headquartered MFIs with an unusually high quantum of money that they used to turbocharge growth, during April 2008–March 2010 and especially in AP, thereby creating the largest microfinance crisis in history (until then at least).

Given the facts, the next logical question is what were the real motivations? Specifically, in my opinion, there seemed to have been four major motivations for the burgeoning growth of the microfinance industry in AP and, together, their synergistic impact resulted in the catastrophic crisis of 2010.

- *Motivation 1: MFIs grew because they wanted greater investment, better valuation, were keen to tap capital markets, and create significant wealth for themselves and their promoters/investors.* The MFIs grew because they wanted to attract more equity at higher than normal valuations and, ultimately, tap the capital markets (through an IPO, etc.) and create wealth for themselves and their stakeholders (including promoters, lenders, investors, etc). For the years in question (April 2008–March 2010), the actual level of equity investment into Indian microfinance compared with previous years, both in terms of the volume of the transactions (deals) as well as the valuations paid, clearly illustrate this.

- *Motivation 2: The financial inclusion drive by policy, donors, and international agencies resulted in MFIs growing at a scorching pace.* MFIs grew (at the pace they did) because of the drive by policy makers (RBI, etc.) and/or specialized donors/international agencies (CGAP, etc.) toward financial inclusion. The specific policy/vision pronouncements (financial inclusion directive of RBI, etc.) can be traced to the above-mentioned periods (from 2005 onward) and the relative impact of these in accelerating the growth of microfinance in the subsequent years should *not* be underestimated.

- *Motivation 3: Commercial banks pushed MFIs to grow at a burgeoning rate so that they (the banks) could achieve the mandatory priority sector lending targets and also make safe/huge profits through the bottom of the pyramid (BoP) paradigm.* The MFIs grew because the commercial banks, in turn, pushed them so as to meet/satisfy PSL norms and/or acquire a larger portfolio, get better returns and make higher profits from a captive pro-poor market. The data indicates that many banks (HDFC Bank, AXIS Bank, and ICICI Bank especially) increased their microfinance portfolio very significantly during the concerned years. It is also clear that policy pushed the commercial banks

---

74 As well as other MFIs.

75 A very large proportion of the equity investment went to the six (and especially, five) large AP-headquartered NBFC MFIs, for the periods under consideration.

76 A very large proportion of the funds of SIDBI and banks went to the six (and especially, five) large AP-headquartered NBFC MFIs, for the periods under consideration.

to cater more to microfinance, with a view to enhancing financial inclusion and satisfying PSL targets.

- *Motivation 4: Investors who paid a huge premium sought commensurate returns ASAP and caused MFIs to grow rapidly.* Without any doubt, the investors—who had perhaps paid larger-than-normal valuations and were eager to get their commensurate returns as soon as possible (ASAP)—also made the MFIs grow at a rapid pace. The various equity deals that took place in the sector during April 2008–March 2010, the respective valuations, and the subsequent growth achieved clearly point to this hard fact.

To summarize, it appears that the six large AP-headquartered MFIs and their fast growing newly established professional peers (with the support of banks, equity investors, and policy makers)—sensing a great opportunity to attract more investment and create significant wealth (from a captive market of poor people), that too, alongside the noble cause of enhancing financial access for the world's poor—started to invest (and deploy) a majority of their newfound financial resources as loan assets to microfinance and other clients. This is reinforced by a Mix Market article, which says that in FY 2010 (April 2009–March 2010), many of these MFIs had deployed almost 90% of their assets as loans to clients—a phenomenally high percentage for any financial institution. As the article notes, "In the aggregate, Indian MFIs have gone from investing roughly 80 percent of their funding into the loan portfolio in 2006 to closer to 90 percent by 2010. This change has also been a driver of growth for the largest Indian MFIs."[77]

And the best part is that all these happened in the wake of an extremely supportive policy environment, which, among other things, called for turbocharging financial access and inclusion. Two mainstream Government of India committees—one on *financial inclusion* (chaired by Dr Rangarajan[78]) and the other on *financial sector reforms* (Dr Raghuram Rajan[79])—made out strong cases for speeding up financial access/inclusion efforts and financial sector reforms (respectively) to enable the greater/faster inclusion. Mr Vijay Mahajan, founder and CEO of BASIX, was part of both committees and it is certain that he played a significant role in shaping the overall thrust of the committee reports to build a strong and supportive enabling policy environment for MFIs.

And the fact that the stupendous growth was caused primarily by the NBFC MFIs[80] clearly shows failure in terms of regulation and supervision of NBFC MFIs by the RBI.[81] What is really startling is that the RBI did not even feel alarmed by this stupendous and unnatural growth (of NBFC MFIs registered

---

77 http://www.themix.org/publications/microbanking-bulletin/2010/11/how-has-growth-indian-microfinance-been-funded.
78 Chairperson of the committee on financial inclusion.
79 The Committee on Financial Sector Reforms was chaired by Dr Raghuram Rajan.
80 Thirteen of the fastest growing 14 MFIs were NBFCs and the six large AP-headquartered NBFC MFIs were part of this group. All NBFC MFIs were registered with the RBI.
81 See Chapter 28.

with it). This clearly points to some kind of regulatory/supervisory indifference and dereliction of duty as well. Therefore, in a sense, serious regulatory failure also perhaps led to the 2010 AP crisis as it did not nip the irresponsible growth of NBFC MFIs (especially during 2008–2010) in the bud, despite many warning signals including the Kolar microfinance crisis. We look at these dress rehearsals and related events in the next chapter as a run-up to the 2010 AP microfinance crisis.

# Chapter 7:
# Intervening Events from March 2009 to March 2010

Following the Kolar crisis in 2009, the MFIs had to slow down a little and the Microfinance Institutions Network (MFIN) was formed. Two issues again gained prominence: (i) a new CoC was drafted; and (ii) the idea of a credit bureau also started taking shape. However, issues of multiple lending, cartel-like competitive practices (multiple lending to shared clients and JLGs), over-indebtedness, aggressive growth, and coercive collection were still prevalent.

With the Kolar crisis somewhat tackled and no serious lessons learnt, the MFIs continued to grow and many of them received significant equity investments and PSL and other funds from banks/DFIs, post Kolar. If you look at the equity investments and funds from banks/DFIs in the subsequent year, you will understand what I am saying. And of course, the resultant growth, post Kolar, can be seen from the data given here.

| Table 7.1 Summary Data for Number of Clients and GLP Added by MFIs, Equity Investment into MFIs, and DFI/Bank Outstanding in Indian Microfinance, Post Kolar | | | |
|---|---|---|---|
| Description | April 2008–March 2009 (A) Pre/During Kolar | April 2009–March 2010 (B) Post Kolar | Number of times increase across two reference periods |
| Total active clients added for top 14 MFIs (13 NBFCs+1 Trust) | 5,869,251 (5.87 million) | 8,408,103 (8.41 million) | 1.43 |
| Total GLP (in US$) added for top 14 MFIs (13 NBFCs+1 Trust) | 757,570,103 (757.57 million) | 1,855,265,123 (1,855.27 million) | 2.45 |
| Total equity investment into Indian microfinance (in US$) | 141.33 | 345.25* | 2.44 |
| SIDBI loan outstanding (in crores) to MFIs | 2136.89 | 3808.2 | 1.78 |
| Bank loan outstanding (in crores) to MFIs | 5009.09 | 10,147.5 | 2.03 |
| * The equity investment from April 2009–July 2010 = US $ 387.30 | | | |

Thus, it is clear that despite Kolar, the MFIs grew at a fast pace and thereby attracted greater equity investment as well as larger amounts of DFI/bank (PSL) funds and used these to grow irresponsibly. An interesting point here is that while the top 14 MFIs increased their clients by 1.43 times across the two reference periods, they increased their GLP by nearly 2.45 times. This indicates, *ceterus paribus*, that these top 14 MFIs deepened their portfolio in 2009–2010. This also provides some surrogate evidence regarding the increasing loan sizes and multiple lending in 2009–2010.

As noted earlier, in between, MFIN was formed (December 2009) and its stated objective was to work with regulators to promote microfinance, enhance responsible lending, and institutionalize the process of credit information sharing. MFIN had also designed a CoC to be observed by its members.

As noted by Mr Vijay Mahajan, MFIN Chairman:

> "Proper enforcement of the code of conduct (CoC) would lead to greater financial inclusion. The aim is to stop multiple lending, which leads to delinquency. ...Communication of all terms and charges to clients is thus an important component of pricing transparency. This includes some specific parameters, such as making sure that the client has all this information in writing, and preferably in their local language. Not only is communication of pricing included in the MFIN Code of Conduct, it also has to be practiced by member MFIs internally."[82]

On June 28, 2010, after MFIN had been in operation for several months, I came across an interesting piece in the *Economic Times* by Mr Mahajan. The article[83] said MFIN was committed to exposing the black sheep and truly implementing its CoC. In fact, the truth was that, ironically, several of MFIN's own members were guilty of all the wrong practices that Mr Mahajan listed in his article and yet no action had been taken against them. Put differently, there had not been a single case of action by MFIN as on that date (June 2010). Mind you, all the damage had been done in AP but the cat was yet to come out of the bag.

That apart, you will find it very interesting to note that one of MFIN's most important members and Mr Mahajan's key MFIN aide, Mr Ajay Verma (of the infamous Sahayata[84] Microfinance) was suspended by his own board on several serious counts. It is entirely another matter that Mr Ajay Verma was used as the poster boy to propagate against multiple lending and several issues other (at the Microfinance India Summit 2011[85])-all of which he himself was (subsequently) found guilty of, as noted earlier. It is also another matter that reputed consulting organizations used Mr Ajay Verma as their poster boy to speak about data integrity and audits in a video.[86]

Interestingly, on June 29, 2010, a day after reading Mr Mahajan's article, I heard from my own sources that SKSML had received SEBI clearance for its IPO, despite many issues raised in the public domain via Prof. Sriram's EPW[87] paper. At around 10 p.m. on June 30, 2010, I contacted Mr Suresh

---

82 *Source*: Quoted from 'Aligned Objectives of MFIN & MFT,' by Ruchita Sharma, *MF Transparency*, October 7, 2010.
83 *Source*: Quoted from 'MFIs as engine of inclusive growth' by Vijay Mahajan, The Economic Times, June 28, 2010.
84 Award winning Sahayata Microfinance is the latest to go astray–http://moneylife.in/article/award-winning-sahayata-microfinance-is-the-latest-to-go-astray/21549.html
85 http://www.youtube.com/watch?v=OZ3JLwXR-Mw&feature=player_embedded
86 http://www.youtube.com/watch?v=ChKgQrDQUk8
87 Commercialization of Microfinance in India: A Discussion of the Emperor's Apparel by Prof. M. S. Sriram, Economic and Political Weekly (EPW), June 12, 2010 – Vol: XLV No: 24.

Gurumani,[88] who confirmed the same. And all along the AP crisis had been simmering, with more multiple/sequential loans being made to shared clients in shared JLGs. Yet, there was also complete calm on the AP front, but it seemed to be the calm before the storm. I sensed that the breaking point was close and all that was needed was a trigger. And I must confess that I had an inkling (then) that the IPO could perhaps be the trigger for the simmering crisis in AP. Once the IPO was announced, I read Prof. Sriram's article again. I also tried to look at the public domain information available about SKSML and answer questions regarding the issues raised by him. What followed was a paper titled, "The First Indian Micro-Finance IPO: Corporate Governance Issues and Key Questions for Stakeholders?" by Ramesh S Arunachalam, July 23, 2010. The same was sent to many stakeholders and the entire board of the RBI including the Governor, Deputy Governors, Board Members, and others. It is extremely sad that no tangible action was taken by the RBI and/or the regulators concerned. A look at the e-mails[89] clearly shows the indifference and apathy of the regulators—especially, the RBI and SEBI—as well as other industry stakeholders.

Especially, the indifference of SEBI comes out because while I wanted to meet the Chairman or the whole-time members of SEBI and give them an extensive overview of the wrongdoings in (Indian) microfinance, SEBI's response was not enthusiastic (to say the least). And I was asked to meet people who had approved the IPO in the first place. In my opinion, going back to the very same people who ignored issues in the public domain (Prof. Sriram's EPW article) was pointless and that is why I wanted to meet the Chairman or the whole-time members, which, sadly, did not materialize.

The rest is history, as SKSML made its spectacular debut to be followed by a historic fall in its shares, thereby impacting large numbers of individual and institutional investors—something that could have been avoided if only SEBI had been proactive. It is also ironical that SEBI initiated proceedings against SKS Microfinance Limited subsequently.[90] Anyway, bygones are bygones and let us now turn our attention to the SKSML IPO and subsequent events in the following chapters as we lead up the 2010 AP microfinance crisis.

---

88  This author received an SMS from Mr Gurumani, CEO and MD (on 10th July) confirming that the IPO had indeed been cleared by SEBI and the listing was likely by August 17, 2010.

89  Refer Appendix 7.

90  SKS Microfinance ready for SEBI probe into fall in share price
(http://www.thehindubusinessline.com/markets/sks-microfinance-ready-for-sebi-probe-into-fall-in-share-price/article2003432.ece), May, 2011.

# Chapter 8:
# The Run-up to the First Indian Microfinance IPO

With their soaring growth and profitability graph, especially in the years following 2006, some MFIs started to bring in radical changes in managerial compensation. Promoter, CEO, and/or senior management compensation at MFIs (including stock options) skyrocketed and microfinance began to be hailed as the industry of the future (just as IT was about two decades ago). As Mr Vijay Mahajan noted, "Much has changed in the past two decades and microfinance has evolved into a thriving sector."[91] Some MFIs, encouraged by investors (who perhaps wanted a quick exit) and banks who were chasing them as the new messiahs, even readied for an IPO. Meanwhile, as Prof. Sriram argued,[92] some of the MFI promoters/CEOs and senior management cashed in on their newfound wealth rather quietly. Thus, microfinance, as an industry, appeared to have arrived in India by June/July 2010.

The sector's burgeoning growth (from 2006 onwards until 2010) was testimony to the fact that a large number of private and commercial stakeholders had started embracing microfinance. While increased growth and interest in the sector were welcome signs, this growth was not uncontroversial—problems including issues of ghost clients, ghost branches, and ghost staff as well as operational problems such as inability to manage growth, supply-led lending, higher levels of delinquency, coercive repayment collection, operational frauds, and the like were repeatedly highlighted by various stakeholders.[93]

Despite these problems the rapid growth continued, followed by the more practical issue of the lack of sufficient capital. The MFIs thus started to look at ways to tap the primary markets. And when the news of SEBI's approval for the SKS IPO became public in end June/early July 2010, the industry was ecstatic and there was euphoria all around. Many other MFIs started building IPO dreams. Indeed, June/July 2010 represented a watershed in Indian microfinance, just as SKS was preparing for its IPO to open on July 28, 2010.

---

91 *Source*: Quoted from MFIs as engine of inclusive growth by Vijay Mahajan *The Economic Times*, June 28, 2010.

92 Commercialization of Microfinance in India: A Discussion of the Emperor's Apparel by Prof. M. S. Sriram, *Economic and Political* Weekly (EPW), June 12, 2010 – Vol: XLV No: 24, and Commercialization of Microfinance in India: A Discussion on the Emperor's Apparel by Prof. M. S. Sriram, W.P. No. 2010-03-04, March 2010.

93 Refer to Market Failures and Microfinance, Dr. Thorat and Ramesh S. Arunachalam (2005), paper presented at the NABARD High-Level Policy Conference in New Delhi.

## Chapter 8: The Run-up to the First Indian Microfinance IPO

On July 14, 2010, CARE assigned a "CARE IPO Grade 4" to the proposed IPO of SKSML. According to the CARE report:

> "CARE IPO Grade 4 indicates Above Average Fundamentals. CARE assigns IPO grades on a scale of Grade 5 to Grade 1, with Grade 5 indicating strong fundamentals and Grade 1 indicating poor fundamentals. …The grade assigned to any individual issue represents a relative assessment of the 'fundamentals' of the issuer. The grading reflects SKSML's position as one of the largest players in the Indian microfinance industry having pan India operations with a well-diversified portfolio. The grading takes into account track record of the promoters, experienced board of directors and strong management profile. The grading also takes into account good corporate governance practices[94] adopted by the company including presence of various committees and independence of the board. The grading considers the strong financial position with healthy margins including good asset quality, comfortable capital adequacy ratio, comfortable liquidity position and access to diverse sources of institutional funding. The grading also considers the strong industry growth in recent period with good prospects for future growth on account of large unmet potential demand."[95]

The run-up to the SKS IPO[96] was interesting. There appeared to be positive sentiments about the IPO, for example, with Quantum picking up around three lakh shares in the company from existing shareholder Yatish Trading Company Pvt. Ltd. Reports also pegged the price band of the issue between Rs. 650 and Rs. 700 per share, suggesting that the IPO might mop up anywhere between Rs. 1090 crore and Rs. 1175 crore. The IPO was slated to open on July 28 and close on July 30 for qualified institutional buyers and on August 2 for others.

However, the IPO was not without its critics. In the *Economic and Political Weekly* (EPW)[97] dated June 12, 2010, Prof. Sriram [formerly Professor, Indian Institute of Management, Ahemadabad (IIMA)] had raised several aspects, including two major corporate governance issues, in the context of the SKS IPO and these are briefly highlighted here:

- *Governance in SKS, the company:* "Such general preferential allotment (outside of the ESOP-ID) made to board members, or amounts lent by the company to its directors in order to purchase shares in the same company…, would be seen as serious breach of governance. Governance that is laced with conflict of interest of this nature—a reward system that puts the independence at stake, does not appear suitable for a company, particularly for one with a lofty mission statement."

---

94 The credit rating mechanisms in the microfinance industry have also, by and large, given positive ratings for SKS over the years.
95 *Source*: Quoted from CARE Assigns 'CARE IPO GRADE 4' to the proposed IPO of SKS Microfinance LTD by CARE Ratings – Press Release, July 14, 2010.
96 George Soros' Quantum Picks Up Stake In IPO-Bound SKS For Rs 19Cr, July 21 2010, 11:02:20 IST | MADHAV A. CHANCHANI, at http://www.vccircle.com/500/news/george-soros-quantum-picks-up-stake-in-ipo-bound-sks-for-rs-19cr
97 Commercialization of Microfinance in India: A Discussion of the Emperor's Apparel by Prof. M. S. Sriram, Economic and Political Weekly (EPW), Vol: XLV No: 24, June 12, 2010.

- *Governance of mutual benefit trusts (MBTs):* "Given that the MBTs own around 16% of the pre-issue capital at 1.04 crore shares, and assuming they would fetch a price of Rs. 636, which was the last price paid by Treeline, they are worth around Rs. 650 crore. This is a large amount of corpus to be controlled.... Given the nature of the fund and the purpose to which it can be put, the sudden changes in the governance of MBTs need to be examined. Each MBT had five trustees comprising three employees and two beneficiary members from the regions. In November 2009, SKS trust advisors was designated as the sole trustee of each SKS MBT. From broad-based governance (which included having women beneficiaries) to a concentrated control of two persons is a development that needs to be viewed carefully. Not only is this development of 'taking charge' of the MBTs worrying, but also the pattern of changes[98] in the board of SKS trust advisers is a matter of concern from the perspective of governance of public purpose funds. The DRHP states that the governance of SKS trust advisors is expected to be broad-based. However the quick turn of events and the churn in the board seems to indicate the narrowing down of control from a broad base. The speed at which some fundamental changes have taken place in the governance structure of the MBT funds have not been articulated clearly anywhere."

Thus, while the idea of MFIs tapping primary markets was indeed fascinating, in the light of the counterarguments made by Prof. Sriram, this chapter analyzes corporate governance and other issues related to SKSML. Much of the analysis is based on published material, available in the public domain.

## A. Corporate governance in SKSML

*Issue 1: Interest-free loan to the then promoter MD from the NBFC*

> *Prof. Sriram in his paper[99] (Page 70) states that, "From a governance point of view, what appears even more unusual is the fact that SKS Microfinance lent him an interest-free loan of Rs. 1.6 crore."*

*Facts and arguments:* From a perusal of the published documents, it is clear that an interest-free loan of Rs. 1.636 crore was indeed granted by the MFI/company (predominantly owned by the poor clients through MBTs) to its then managing director and promoter. See relevant exhibit[100] given here, reproduced from the audited statements (year ending March 2007):

---

98 The details of the changes are elaborated in Prof. Sriram's EPW articles referred to earlier.
99 Commercialization of Microfinance in India: A Discussion of the Emperor's Apparel by Prof. M. S. Sriram, (*Economic and Political Weekly* (EPW), Vol: XLV No: 24, June 12, 2010.
100 Also refer Schedule 1, Loan and Advances, on Page 151 in the Draft Red Herring prospectus, downloaded from the SEBI website.

## Chapter 8: The Run-up to the First Indian Microfinance IPO

**Exhibit 8.1 Reproduced Portion of Balance Sheet, Audited Statement 2007**

| B. Other Loans and Advances | 2007 | 2006 | |
|---|---|---|---|
| **Secured, considered good** | | | |
| Loans to Employees | 9,845,217 | 1,186,836 | Loans to Promoter MD |
| **Unsecured, considered good** | | | |
| Loans to Directors (Maximum amount outstanding Rs.16, 361,380 (Previous Year Rs. Nil) | 16,361,380 | - | |
| Loans to SKS Microfinance Employees Benefit Trust (Refer Note 16 of Schedule 19) | 8,231,800 | - | |
| Advances Recoverable in Cash or Kind or Value to be received Deposits | 5,993,882 | 3,167,079 | |
| Deposits | 3,131,789 | 708,902 | |
| Advance Income Tax (Net of Provisions) | - | 2,358,551 | |
| Interest Accrued and Due | 746,319 | - | |
| Others | 25,545,195 | 3,135,669 | |
| **Unsecured, considered doubtful** | | | |
| Advances Recoverable in Cash or Kind or Value to be received | 1,099,692 | - | |
| Less: Provision for Doubtful Advances | (1,099,692) | - | |
| Total (B) | 69,855,582 | 10,557,037 | |
| Total (A+B) | 2,711,778,947 | 768,204,728 | |

*Source: SKS Audit Financial Statement March 2007, Schedule 8B, Page 12*

*Legal perspective on loans to directors in a finance company:* On the aspect of credit facilities to the directors,[101] the RBI circular on corporate governance for NBFCs notes that, "in order to obviate conflict of interest in the lending operations of the NBFC, it should not grant any loan, advance, or non-fund-based facility or any other financial accommodation/facility to:

a. its directors or their relatives;

b. any firm in which any of its directors is interested as partner, manager, employee or guarantor;

c. any individual in respect of whom any of its directors is a guarantor;

---

[101] RBI "Guidelines on Corporate Governance," 2007, kept in abeyance (as at July 2010) for some reason. The guidelines were not to be practiced until further notice from the RBI. It is interesting to note that it is yet to be implemented, as on date.

d. any company of which, or the subsidiary or the holding company of which, any of the directors of the NBFC is a director, managing agent, manager, employee or guarantor or any firm in which he holds substantial interest;

e. any entity, whether incorporated or not, which uses as a part of its name or in connection with its business, the name of the NBFC or any such word as would show its association with the NBFC."[102]

Likewise, the spirit of the Companies Act (1956) prohibits companies from directly buying their own shares and/or indirectly financing directors to buy the same. A wider interpretation suggests that the term "indirectly" applies to companies using (and financing) their own directors to purchase shares in the company. Simply put, it states that a company cannot directly buy its shares or finance its employees to do the same. The only option is for employees (and directors in case they are employees) to buy shares through a proper scheme for which finance can be made available and/or facilitated, up to a maximum of six months of the concerned employee's salary. However, the share transfer will have to be routed through a trust administering the scheme and the shares must be in the name of the trust and transferred to the concerned individual after the repayment and the minimum period specified.

In this case, it must be noted that, as evident in the previous as well as next section, the interest-free loan to the promoter MD was towards purchase of shares in the same company, for an amount much greater than his six months' salary. Also, neither was this administered through a trust nor the shares issued in the name of the trust. Further, while the approval was (supposedly) for ESOPs, shares were directly allotted.

As per the prevailing laws,[103] what had been done at SKSML may not have been strictly illegal, but I am not sure that it is appropriate practice for a company, supposedly lending to the poor and registered as an NBFC with RBI and using public deposits (by way of accessing bank loans and PSL funds), to lend to its director, without being seen as a "misgoverned" company.

This practice raises the following major questions:

- On what basis did the company authorize the lending to the then promoter MD? Who were the people involved in making this decision? Were there conflicts of interest in the Board and/or company, at that time?

- Was this a correct practice given that the company was/is a financial institution registered under the Companies Act, 1956, and with the RBI as an NBFC, with the primary purpose of lending to low-income people?

---

102 http://rbi.org.in/scripts/NotificationUser.aspx?Id=3499&Mode=0
103 SKSML has all along maintained that these provisions of the Company's Act did not apply to private limited companies, which is what SKS was in 2006–2007.

- Was this correct practice from a shareholder perspective? Specifically, was this interest-free lending (to the promoter MD) appropriate given that the company had been originally established to provide loans to low-income people[104] and there were significant development funds in the company, and, as at the time of granting the loan, about 54% of the company was together owned by the MBTs[105] and DFIs such as SIDBI?

- What was the source of funds from which this loan was made to the promoter MD? This needs to be transparently understood in terms of whether the so-called "Priority Sector Funds" and/or "Soft Development Funds" were used to provide this loan.

- How does this practice of lending to the promoter MD relate to extant regulations and norms—RBI NBFC Corporate Governance notification of May 2007, other RBI regulations, SEBI rules and norms, Companies Act Guidelines, and all other relevant laws of the land—both in letter and in spirit?

- *Ceterus paribus* (all other things being equal), is this a correct practice of corporate governance, especially in a financial institution?

The implications of these for corporate governance cannot and should not be underestimated. Failure to look at these issues is tantamount to being negligent regarding serious corporate governance issues (that are in the public domain[106] and) that have the potential to further impact hundreds of public investors.

## *Issue 2: The use of the loan by the promoter MD to buy shares in the NBFC*

> *Prof Sriram, in his paper,[107] (Page 70) argues that, "In 2007, the founder was allotted shares worth Rs. 1.6 crore at par; ...From a governance point of view, what appears even more unusual is the fact that SKS Microfinance lent him an interest-free loan of Rs. 1.6 crore. It does not take too many dots to connect this loan to the purchase shares in the same company."*

*Facts and arguments:* An analysis of the financial statements[108] reveals the following entries.

The loan given to key management personnel indicated the key management personnel as the promoter MD and the identical amounts can be found against loans given and the shares issued.

---

104  There is an additional question here: For what stated purpose was this loan given (by the company) to its promoter MD? What were the terms of the loan and why was the loan made interest-free? What documentation is available with regard to this loan?

105  Despite the MBTs holding 47% of the shares, they appear to be weak shareholders and/or minority shareholders from the arguments detailed earlier.

106  See the following: (i) Prof Sriram's paper's given earlier; (ii) Draft Red Herring Prospectus of SKS Microfinance on (March 2010), and also news items in *The Economic Times* on various dates from January to July 2010.

107  Commercialization of Microfinance in India: A Discussion of the Emperor's Apparel by Prof. M. S. Sriram, (*Economic and Political Weekly* (EPW), Vol: XLV No: 24, June 12, 2010.

108  Notes No: 7b from "SKS Microfinance Ltd Audited Financials for the year of March 2008." The relevant entries are also available in financial statements for year ending 2007. While it is also there in DRHP, it does get lost amidst the huge pile of information.

## Exhibit 8.2 Notes to Related-Party Transactions

**b. Related Party Transactions**

|  | KEY Management Personnel ** | | Relatives of Key Management Personnel | | Entities holding Substantial Interest | |
|---|---|---|---|---|---|---|
|  | March 31, 2008 | March 31, 2007 | March 31, 2008 | March 31, 2007 | March 31, 2008 | March 31, 2007 |
| Issue of Equity Shares (including share premium) | - | 16,361,380 | - | - | 537,371,924 | 270,274,392 |
| Loans given # | - | 16,361,380 | - | - | - | - |
| Rent expense | - | - | 875,000 | 900,000 | - | - |
| **Balances as at year end** | | | | | | |
| Share Capital | 16,361,380 | 16,361,380 | - | - | 130,344,290 | 54,304,680 |
| Loan Balance Outstanding | - | 16,361,380 | - | - | - | - |
| Rent Payable | - | - | - | 63,525 | - | - |

→ Identical Amounts of Loan and Investment

** *Remuneration paid to Managing director is disclosed in note 12 below.*
# *Loans given to Key Management Personnel was interest free.*
*Source*: SKS Audited Financials, 2008, Auditor's Note No. 6.

Given these, it seems reasonable to make the assertion that the interest-free loan of Rs. 1.636 crore was used[109] (by the then promoter MD[110]) to buy 1,636,138 shares at Rs. 10 per share paying a total of Rs. 1.636 crore. The date of share allotment was March 31, 2007. The above sequence is summarized below.

- Loans increase—as the promoter MD is given an interest-free loan of Rs. 1.636 crore.

- Capital increases—as the promoter MD immediately invests an identical amount of Rs. 1.636 crore in the company.

---

109 In case the promoter MD and/or company argue that this was not the case, then they need to answer four questions in a transparent and clear manner: (i) why did the promoter MD take a loan for the identical amount of Rs. 1.636 crore invested in shares, in the first place?; (ii) what were the sources of funds for the promoter MD to make his investment?; (iii) how was the loan taken by the promoter MD utilized by him?; and (iv) when was the loan repaid and through what mode? This certainly calls for a close look into the transactions concerned.

110 According to the DRHP, the related party was listed as the promoter MD.

- Year-end balance sheet shows an increased capital of Rs. 1.636 crore—when in reality the company's own funds (may) have been used to bolster their own capital (through the above-mentioned loan given to the promoter MD).

- From this, it can be said that *ceterus paribus* (all other things being equal), there has been no serious change in the company's financial condition.

- However, the above-mentioned capital increase (of Rs. 1.636 crore) is therefore perhaps a misstatement, as also the associated leverage increase (of approximately Rs. 6 crore, assuming a 1: 4 ratio).

This is a serious aspect and the root transactions have to be checked for amounts and dates and modes of payment. An observation is that such a practice of taking a loan to buy shares in the same company would not have been necessary in the SKS society as there are no shares to buy. *Ironically, again, the commercialization of microfinance seems to have motivated the creation of such tautological transactions that are neither acceptable (as part of the larger corporate ethics and governance framework) nor valid in an accounting sense (as they result in the financial statements being misstated).*

The major questions that need to be addressed here are as follows:

- Was it correct practice to use the company's money (through a loan to the promoter MD) to buy shares in the same company? Is this correct practice from a shareholder perspective? Specifically, was this lending to the promoter MD appropriate given that the company had been originally established to provide loans to low-income people[111] and there were significant development funds in the company, and, as at the time of granting the loan, about 54% of the company was together owned by the MBTs and DFIs such as SIDBI?

- Are not the consequent increases in capital and the associated leverage (without any change in the company's true financial condition) serious misstatements of the financial condition? Irrespective of the quantum of misstatements, the practice is perhaps what is most damaging and questionable, from a perspective of corporate governance.[112]

- Is the above a correct practice, especially given that the company was/is a financial institution registered under the RBI NBFC regulations and Companies Act, 1956, with the primary purpose of lending to low-income people?

---

111 There is an additional question here: For what stated purpose was this loan given (by the company) to its promoter MD? What were the terms of the loan and why was the loan made interest-free? What documentation is available with regard to this loan?

112 It must be mentioned that all things begin small and eventually snowball.

- How does this misstatement of the financial condition relate to extant regulations and norms—RBI NBFC corporate governance notification of May 2007, other RBI regulations, SEBI rules and norms, Companies Act guidelines, and all other relevant laws of the land—both in letter and in spirit?

- Having heard everything, is the above a correct practice of corporate governance, given that the company was likely to become India's first listed micro-lender?

The implications—of ignoring this aspect while assessing a financial institution—are very serious, as the following arguments suggest. The question here is how could the authorities, who apparently approved the SKS IPO, and CARE, which rated the IPO as 4/5, ignore the corporate governance issues at SKS?

## Issue 3: Lack of transparency in allotment of shares in the NBFC

> A third issue raised by Prof. Sriram in his paper is the apparent *lack of transparency* in the process of share allotments.

Commenting on share allotments and related issues, he notes[113] as follows (EPW, Page No. 70):

- "In 2007, the founder was allotted shares worth Rs. 1.6 crore at par; all other employees together were allotted shares worth Rs. 81.8 lakhs (about half of what the founder received) in an employee share purchase scheme (ESPS). On the same day other investors, including the investors of the first tranche paid Rs. 49.77 per share.

- What appears even more unusual is the fact that SKS Microfinance lent founder an interest-free loan of Rs. 1.6 crore to purchase shares in the same company. This allotment of shares was outside of the ESPS – a special allotment.

- In 18 months from getting this allotment, he sold them out for a price of Rs. 103.91 – a gain of Rs. 15 crore on an investment (financed by an interest-free loan from the same company) of Rs. 1.6 crore.

- This is followed by a stock option allotted under the employee stock option plan (ESOP) of 2007 exercised in the month of December 2009 and sold in February 2010 (in the run up to the filing of the DRHP). The exercise of options was at a price of Rs. 49.77 per share, while the sale to Treeline Asia Master Fund was at a price of around Rs. 636 per share indicating a profit of around Rs. 55 crore in about three months."

---

113 *Source*: Commercialization of Microfinance in India: A Discussion of the Emperor's Apparel by Prof. M. S. Sriram, *Economic and Political Weekly* (EPW) Vol: XLV No: 24, June 12, 2010.

# Chapter 8: The Run-up to the First Indian Microfinance IPO

Reacting to this, SKS sent a rejoinder through Sa-Dhan,[114] which then sent it via e-mail to the various stakeholders. The rejoinder remarks that:

> "The allotment of shares to Vikram in March 2007 was not a sudden decision but had been agreed and approved by shareholders and the Board a year earlier in March 2006. Although Vikram's share allotment was approved and documented—and originally intended to be an Employee Stock Option Plan (ESOP) to take effect back in March 2006-the final form of the allotment was finalized, based on tax advice from KPMG, as an Employee Share Purchase Scheme (ESPS) -- a legally permissible variant of an ESOP -- in March 2007. There was no discount. Over the course of the year, as SKS grew and strengthened, the value of shares rose from Rs. 10 to Rs. 49 by March 2007, when the second round of investment took place. It was 18 months after that Vikram sold his shares at Rs. 103.91, a full 30 months after the initial allocation at Rs. 10 per share. The increase in value of the shares was the result of the stellar performance of SKS."

*Facts and arguments:* The following are the facts from SKS published documents (DRHP; Pages 27, 28) and several issues raised here are confirmed from the following, in terms of data and events.[115] Several new issues and concerns are also evident from the data and analysis given hereafter:

**Exhibit 8.3 Equity Shares Allotted on March 31, 2007, to the Promoter MD and Others**

| Date of Allotment and when made fully paid up | Number of Equity Shares | Nature of Consideration | Face value (Rs.) | Issue Price (Rs.) |
|---|---|---|---|---|
| March 31, 2007 | Allotted 818,000 Equity Shares under ESPS 2007 to the employees | Cash | 10.00 | 10.00 |
| | Allotted 1,636,138 Equity Shares to Dr. Vikram Akula | Cash | 10.00 | 10.00 |
| | Allotted 10,281,739 Equity Shares to: (i) MUC - 1,319,069 Equity Shares (ii) Mr. Vinod Khosla - 1,319,069 Equity Shares (iii) SKS Capital - 1,319,069 Equity Shares (iv) SCI II - 5,430,468 Equity Shares (v) Odyssey Capital Private Limited - 894,064 Equity Shares | Cash | 10.00 | 49.77 |
| November 20, 2007 | Allotted 514,250 Equity Shares under ESPS 2007 | Cash | 10.00 | 49.77 |
| *Source: DRHP, Page Nos. 28 and 29.* | | | | |

**Key Question:**
1) Under what scheme was allotment originally and subsequently made and is that appropriate and legal?
2) What is the rationale for the terms and conditions?

**Key Question:** Is it appropriate to directly allot the shares and are there any laws that are violated?

---

114 This was an unsigned note and was mentioned by Sa-dhan as a rejoinder sent by the then SKS chairman Mr Gurcharan Das.
115 The inferences made by Prof. Sriram with the above data and events, by and large, also seem logical and valid.

The following concerns need to be flagged, with regard to the allotment process:

- *Issues of discrepancy in the process:* It seems necessary to better understand the whole process in terms of what was approved: (i) in the board; and (ii) by the shareholders and compare the same with filings done with the Registrar of Companies (ROC) as there seem to be discrepancies. The DRHP is replete with discrepancies[116] on the share allotments.

- *Concerns with ESOPs:* It appears that all approvals were for ESOPs to be issued to Dr Akula and others like Mr Rao, the COO, in February 2007. However, in reality, it is clear that ESPS were issued to Mr Rao and shares were issued to Dr Akula. The question is how could this be done when the approval was for ESOPs? Therefore, a clear legal view on whether there were any discrepancies would be required, especially because the shares allotted to Dr Akula were fully sold out while those given to Mr Rao had been partially liquidated (as at the time just prior to the IPO).

- *Concerns with ESPS:* It appears that the company had a scheme where employees would be issued shares when they join, which were to be vested over a period of four years. The company was to give a loan to a trust, which was to lend the same money to employees to buy these shares. In turn, the employee would enter into a financing arrangement with the trust and the company. Under this, the shares would be directly either freshly allotted to the employee or, in the event of any available shares in the pool, they would be transferred to the employee's name. This arrangement of giving any amount of loan and allotting or transferring the shares directly in the name of the employee may be in contravention of Section 77(3) of the Companies Act.[117] As per this section, shares cannot be allotted in the employee's name directly and the loan amount cannot exceed six months' salary of the employee. It is not clear if the company was violating these conditions, but this has to be looked into from the perspective of the Companies Act and the extant NBFC regulations.

- *Founder having nil equity as at filing of DRHP:* Likewise, from Exhibits 8.4 and 8.5a, there seems to be reasonable evidence for the assertion that as the company was to enter the primary market and approach retail investors, the founder held zero equity and it is his unexercised options that had a

---

116 A set of shareholders (MUC, SKS Capital, and Mr Vinod Khosla – each 1,319,069 equity shares along with Odyssey Capital Private Limited – 894,064 equity shares and SCI II – 5,430,468 equity shares) came into the company on March 29, 2007, as mentioned in one place in the DRHP. At another place in the DRHP, the same set of shareholders is shown to have come on board on March 31, 2007. Either way, the fact is that this set of shareholders could not have participated in the key decision making in the company during 2006–2007.

117 The section also says that, "provided that nothing in this subsection shall be taken to prohibit, the making by a company of loans, within the limit laid down in sub-section (3), to persons (other than directors, or managers) bona fide in the employment of the company with a view to enabling those persons to purchase or subscribe for fully paid shares in the company or its holding company to be held by themselves by way of beneficial ownership." Subsection (3) states that, "No loan made to any person in pursuance of clause of the foregoing proviso shall exceed in amount his salary or wages at that time for a period of six months."

three-year lock-in period. In fact, in the DRHP table, the founder's name is not mentioned under the promoters group and as the fine print indicates, most of the key employees had sold out/were selling off before the IPO-a trend that continued even after the listing and one which perhaps prompted SEBI to order an enquiry on May 6, 2011.[118]

**Exhibit 8.4 History of Equity Shares Held by Founder Promoter**

| Sr. No. | Date of Allotment/ Transfer | Nature of consideration | No. of Equity Shares | Face Value (Rs.) | Issue/ Acquisition Price (Rs.) | Percentage of Pre-Issue Paid-up Capital | No. of Equity Shares pledged | Percentage of Equity Shares pledged |
|---|---|---|---|---|---|---|---|---|
| Dr. Vikram Akula | | | | | | | | |
| 1. | September 22, 2003 | Cash | 5,000 | 10.00 | 10.00 | 0.01 | - | - |
| 2. | May 8, 2004 | Cash | (5,000)[(1)] | 10.00 | 10.00 | (0.01) | - | - |
| 3. | March 31, 2007 | Cash | 1,636,138 | 10.00 | 10.00 | 2.5 | - | - |
| 4. | September 30, 2008 | Cash | (1,636,138)[(2)] | 10.00 | 103.91 | (2.5) | - | - |
| 5. | December 24, 2009 | Cash | 945,424 | 10.00 | 49.77 | 1.5 | - | - |
| 6. | February 10, 2010 | Cash | (945,424)[(3)] | 10.00 | US$ 13.67 | (1.5) | - | - |
| | Total | | Nil | | | | | |
| *Source: DRHP, Page No. 31.* | | | | | | | | |

Nil shares with promoter as at filing of DRHP

- *Lock-in is for unexercised options:* Regarding the issue of lock-in, according to the DRHP, it must be mentioned that 945,424 shares resulting from the exercised options were transferred to Treeline, 50 days before the DRHP was filed. The options were granted under ESOP 2007, at an acquisition price of Rs. 49.77 per share, and the same was sold at $13.67 (Rs. 636) per share. It must be mentioned that none of the options exercised remained with Dr Akula and the outstanding (unexercised options) of 906,734 shares were what he had consented to lock-in (DRHP, Pages 38, 39). Exhibit 8.5a highlights the same. Likewise, as per Exhibit 8.5b, the unexercised options from ESOP 2008 Tranche I were 1,769,537 and they had been locked in by the founder. Thus, without question, as Prof. Sriram argued, what remained were unexercised options and Dr Akula had consented to lock in the same for a period of three years—these include 906,734 from ESOP 2007 and 1,769,537 from ESOP 2008, Tranche I as per data in DRHP, Page No. 42. Thus, the fact

---

118 Quoted from "Will welcome any probe into share fall: SKS Microfinance", The Economic Times May 9, 2011 (http://articles.economictimes.indiatimes.com/2011-05-09/news/29525035_1_sebi-probe-breach-of-insider-trading-trading-volumes).

that he had nil shares in the company,[119] just prior to the IPO (and at time of filing of the DRHP), becomes absolutely clear.

### Exhibit 8.5a Details Regarding Options to Directors, 2007

Details regarding options granted to Directors and key managerial employees are set forth below:

| Name of Director/key managerial personnel | Total No. of options granted under ESOP 2007 | No. of options exercised under ESOP 2007 | Total No. of options outstanding under ESOP 2007 | No. of Equity Shares held | Plan |
|---|---|---|---|---|---|
| Dr. Vikram Akula | 1,852,158 | 945,424* | 906,734# | - | ESOP 2007 |

\* Equity Shares resulting from these stock options were transferred to Tree Line pursuant to a Share Purchase Agreement dated December 10, 2009, subject to certain stipulations set out therein.

\# Dr. Vikram Akula has consented to lock-in the stock options of the Company held by him for a period of three years.

*Source*: DRHP, Page No. 38.

### Exhibit 8.5b Details Regarding Options to Directors, 2008

Details regarding options granted to Directors and key managerial personnel are set forth below:

| Name of Director/ key managerial personnel | Total No. of options granted under ESOP 2008 | No. of options exercised under ESOP 2008 | Total No. of options outstanding under ESOP 2008 | No. of Equity Shares held | Plan |
|---|---|---|---|---|---|
| Dr. Vikram Akula | 1,769,537# | - | 1,769,537# | - | ESOP 2008-Tranche I |

*# Dr. Vikram Akula has consented to lock-in the stock options of the Company held by him for a period of three years from the date of Allotment in the Issue.*

*Source*: DRHP, Page No. 42.

- *Selling before IPO:* Therefore, at the time of the IPO, it is clear that Dr Akula did not hold any shares in the company. Likewise, the key personnel had either sold and/or were in the process of selling off their shares. Hence, it is clear that the founder held no real stake in the company in a true sense (when filing the DRHP) and that many of the key management personnel had transferred or were in the process of transferring their shares.

---

119 Also, do recall that 1,636,138 shares allotted on March 31, 2007, were already sold at Rs. 103.91 per share.

## Chapter 8: The Run-up to the First Indian Microfinance IPO

Commenting on this issue, Prof. Sriram stated:

- ✓ "The current CEO was appointed in December, 2008. He was granted a one-time bonus of Rs. 1 crore in April, 2009 and earns a salary of Rs. 1.5 crore per annum, along with a performance bonus of another Rs. 1.5 crore and stock options. In the run-up to the public offering, the CEO who had exercised his option to purchase 2,25,000 shares at a price of Rs. 300 on 23rd March 2010 already had an agreement with Treeline dated 27th January 2010 to sell his shares for a consideration for Rs. 14.32 crore – a profit of Rs. 7.5 crore.

- ✓ The senior management comprising the chief operating officer, the chief financial officer, and other employees had cashed out in the run-up to the public issue, selling all their allotments under both the stock option and stock purchase plans at a significant premium through a common agreement with Treeline. While there is nothing legally wrong in the encashment process, it does raise a larger question about the signaling of commitment on the eve of a public issue which needs to be considered.

- ✓ The argument that the unexercised portion has been locked in for the future is unconvincing, as the option not to exercise the "option" exists with the management, thereby offering only the upside and protecting them from the downside of the market vagaries. As the company is asking newer investors (including retail investors) to invest in the company, all the senior executives are encashing their own stakes indicating – as investors – that this is a good price to exit from the company."[120]

- *ESOPs for Independent Directors (IDs):* As noted in the table hereafter (reproduced from Page 30 of DRHP), Mr Tarun Khanna, ID, was allotted 8080 equity shares.[121] Even if it was permitted by the then prevailing regulations, this is indeed a questionable practice of corporate governance as it may take away the independence of the independent directors (ID). History is replete with examples of corporate governance failures when the "independence" of "independent directors" is compromised in such a manner.

Thus, ESOP 2008 (ID) does not seem appropriate from a corporate governance standpoint and again, it may be useful to examine whether this practice, in reality, affected the independent functioning of the "independent directors," especially in view of the fact that the same (ESOP compensated) independent director (ID), headed the remuneration and compensation committee (formed in 2010), and was to look into such schemes in the future.

---

120 *Source*: Commercialization of Microfinance in India: A Discussion of the Emperor's Apparel by Prof. M. S. Sriram, *Economic and Political Weekly* (EPW) Vol: XLV No: 24, June 12, 2010.
121 It must also be mentioned that sitting fees had been paid to this independent director.

## Exhibit 8.6 Equity Shares Allotted to Independent Directors

| Date of Allotment and when made fully paid up | Number of Equity Shares | Nature of Consideration | Face value (Rs.) | Issue Price (Rs.) |
|---|---|---|---|---|
| August 18, 2009 | Allotted 8,080 Equity Shares to Dr. Tarun Khanna | Cash | 10.00 | 300.00 |

*Source*: DRHP Page No. 30.

Prof. Sriram[122] argues this key issue as follows:

> "While independent directors are to be compensated, offering them stock options and setting their incentives on par with the management of the company is actually taking away their independence and aligning rewards to the performance of the company in the stock market and not on fundamentals. This instrument, which seems to provide an unlimited upside but a zero down side, is to be questioned–not only in case of SKS, but as a general practice. Governance that is laced with conflict of interest of this nature–a reward system that puts the independence at stake, does not appear suitable for a company, particularly for one with a lofty mission statement."

In summary, there were three major issues and they are highlighted here:

- *ESOP/ESPS schemes need to be SEBI compliant:* In fact, the aforementioned questions apply to the subsequent allotments as well, and it needs to be examined whether the allotment process, including decision makers involved, basis for allotment, the quantity of allotment, price and terms for allotment, and so on, were in conformance with relevant existing laws and regulations. This is more important, given that the company in question was then a large fast- growing MFI, intermediating increasingly large resources and one that was well on its way to becoming India's first listed MFI. Also, given that unexercised lock-in options still existed from many of these schemes and that SKS subsequently got listed, this aspect certainly needed a critical look, as there may have been some serious legal issues and violations.

See the e-mail reproduced,[123] which clearly shows that the founder even paid for options granted to a consultant and I am not sure that this was legal.

---

[122] Commercialization of Microfinance in India: A Discussion of the Emperor's Apparel by Prof. M. S. Sriram, (*Economic and Political Weekly* (EPW), Vol: XLV No: 24, June 12, 2010.

[123] See Appendix 8.

- *Selling in before public issue suggests an agency problem:* Expecting the public to invest when neither the promoter nor the key employees hold any/significant stake in the company is tantamount to giving "a postdated cheque on a crashing bank."[124] Agreed that the promoters and employees may have done hard work and need their due rewards. And, precisely, their most fitting reward would be through a successful public issue, in which part of their stake (as with that of others) is shared with the public. However, when all the key personnel sell their stake/options before the IPO, one cannot help but think that this exit is strategic, based on superior (inside) information available with the key management personnel.

  These apart, there are serious ethical and moral issues involved and it seems important to flag them. First, this issue of selling off stake before the IPO leaves the existing investors, including MBTs, exposed. Second, another relevant issue is when all other shareholders were allowed to divest (barring SIDBI who voluntarily perhaps did not do so), why were the MBTs not allowed to sell their 40% through the IPO? I am sure it is within the rights of these minority shareholders to decide to liquidate their stake and live with the wealth created. Two points are in order here: (i) it will be interesting to note who made that decision on behalf of the MBTs and (ii) even if the MBTs endorsed this decision, whether it was indeed an informed and fully voluntary decision and in the interest of the MBT (minority) shareholders (which is what a trustee is expected to do). These are questions that still need to be answered.

- *Independent Directors (IDs) need to be truly independent:* In fact, the Satyam fiasco looms large with regard to what happened when IDs were not truly independent and this issue needs to be carefully looked into. While the letter of law may not have been contravened, what needs close examination is whether the spirit of the law was being undermined. IDs are the backbone of good governance and any attempt to take away their independence must be viewed with utmost caution and highest suspicion. I hope that SEBI and RBI keep these issues in mind when other MFIs approach the market regulator for approval of an IPO.

## B. Governance and operational aspects of mutual benefit trusts

SKS uses the NBFC structure coupled with what are called MBTs. There are several serious questions with regard to the MBTs and their governance and operational processes that need to be looked at. All these are matters on which there seems little clarity, both in the financial statements and the DRHP. It would be helpful to understand the same with transparency. The implications for corporate governance are huge, without any doubt, and, given that SKSML became India's first listed MFI, the

---

124 *Source*: Adapted from The Speeches of the Father of the Nation, Late Mahatma Gandhi JI.

following issues assume greater importance and cannot, and should not, be ignored by the concerned authorities.

*Legality of MBTs:* Are the (SKS) MBTs legal bodies? Are they registered as per appropriate laws? This needs to be examined because the MBTs are (said to form) among the key promoters listed in the DRHP. The entire operations of the MBTs and their financial transactions, including the loan received from Silicon Valley Bank, need to be understood transparently from the perspective of the existing legal framework including the Foreign Regulation (Contribution) Act (FCRA), Income Tax Act, Foreign Exchange Management Act (FEMA), and the like.

*MBT ownership and changes:* Who owned the SKS MBTs at the time of the filing of the DRHP? Has there been a change in the ownership pattern—since inception? What were the implications before and after the IPO for the poor clients (for whom the MBT was originally established) as well as for SKSML?

*MBT governance:* What was the governance structure of the SKS MBTs at the time of the filing of the DRHP? Has there been a change in the governance pattern—subsequently? What are the pre- and post-IPO implications for the poor clients as well as for SKSML?

*Specific change in governance structure:* In the case of SKS MBTs, on what basis was the decision to convert the governance structure of the five MBTs (with community representatives) to a "trusteeship company" (currently having only two members on the board) made?

Commenting on this, Prof. Sriram stated:

> "From broad-based governance (which included having women beneficiaries) to having a concentrated control of two persons is a development that needs to be viewed carefully and as a questionable governance practice. The DRHP states that the governance of SKS Trust Advisors is expected to be broad-based. However the quick turn of events and the churn in the board seems to indicate the narrowing down of control from a broad base. The speed at which some fundamental changes have taken place in the governance structure of the MBT funds have not been articulated clearly anywhere and it would be useful to examine whether that again is a practice of good governance?"[125] (EPW Page Nos. 71 and 72).

According to Daniel and Vikash:

---

[125] *Source:* Commercialization of Microfinance in India: A Discussion of the Emperor's Apparel by Prof. M. S. Sriram, *Economic and Political Weekly* (EPW) Vol: XLV No: 24, June 12, 2010.

## Chapter 8: The Run-up to the First Indian Microfinance IPO

"The SKS Mutual Benefit Trusts (MBTs) have been a core component of SKS since it began its transformation to a for-profit entity. In essence, the MBTs are the link between SKS Society (the NGO) and SKS Microfinance (the NBFC). In 2003, these five private for-profit trusts were formed by SKS Society with the objective of promoting and enhancing the social and economic welfare of their members. At their inception, these trusts consisted of 500 *sangams* (SKS village-level groups) in Andhra Pradesh, representing about 16,600 women. In March 2010, the Trust deeds of the MBTs were revised to include 220,000 *sangams* that are currently part of the SKS network that will eventually represent some 6.8 million women."[126]

Prof. Sriram raised two issues in this regard.

"First, the funds technically belong to the five MBTs. Second, it is not clear if the larger community was informed of the impending public issue, explained the implications of not only expanding the benefits of the MBTs from the original five regions to all the clients of SKS but also that a fair amount of the investments made in the name of the poor would actually be locked in for another three years."[127]

Therefore, the key question is whether the "members" of each of the SKS MBTs had resolved to voluntarily hand over the management of these resources to the company? If so, what process was followed to obtain this consent? Were the members aware of what they were doing? Did they actually know that their money would be used not only to benefit themselves but also several other new and growing membership of the company, or better still, nonmembers who may have been ultra poor or even those who were not poor but getting included in a financial sense?

*MBT regulation and supervision:* How are the SKS MBTs regulated and supervised? Given that some of the MBTs are sitting on large sums of money (at least in SKS), are the present arrangements to regulate and supervise them sufficient? What are the implications for corporate governance in SKS, pre- and post-IPO?

*Source of funds for MBTs:* The SKS MBTs continue to hold significant stake in the NBFC. Not only do the MBTs hold shares but they have also been supposedly allotted shares twice, in the past few years for which they have (themselves) subscribed. What was the source of funds for the same and where did the MBTs get the money for subscribing to the shares? *This is again a critical issue.*

*MBT membership:* What kind of people are members in the SKS MBTs? Are the so-called poor still a part of the MBTs? What other people are part of the MBTs and what can be said about their demographic characteristics? *This is particularly relevant given that many of the MBTs were used to route the money of the nonprofit MFIs (based on donations and grants) to the for-profit MFIs.*

---

126 *Source*: Quoted from "SKS Microfinance journey to IPO–An inside story" by Vikash Kumar & Daniel Rozas, May 2010.
127 Commercialization of Microfinance in India: A Discussion of the Emperor's Apparel by Prof. M. S. Sriram, (*Economic and Political Weekly* (EPW), Vol: XLV No: 24, June 12, 2010.

*Day-to-day functioning of MBTs:* How do these SKS MBTs function on a day-to-day basis? Was it an informed choice of the clients (who were a part of the SKS MBTs) that they actually received the donations and voluntarily invested in SKS, the company? And specifically, through what process did they take a call on whether (or not) it was a good time to exercise equity options they had and/or alternatively, to sell the options and exit. *Who guides the so-called SKS MBT "clients" on such complex decisions and are there any conflicts of interest, real and/or potential?*

*MBTs, value of their shares, and the future:* Arguing on the above, Prof. Sriram stated:

> "Given that the MBTs own around 16% of the pre-issue capital at 1.04 crore shares, and assuming they would fetch a price of Rs. 636, which was the last price paid by Treeline, they are at least worth around Rs. 650 crore. This is a large amount of corpus to be controlled. The question is how would this amount be used in the future? Who would be responsible for its management in the ultimate analysis and how are the funds to be governed? Given the nature of the fund and the purpose to which it can be put, are not the sudden changes in the governance structure of MBTs seriously questionable?"[128]

Thus, Prof. Sriram's fears may not be unfounded, and in the light of the above, it may be useful to look into the future governance of MBTs. This is especially critical given the fact that the MBTs are still sitting on large sums of money (despite the current low share value of the SKS stock).

## C. Approval of SKS IPO despite easily available public domain material on governance issues in SKS

This is indeed a very serious issue and the concerned stakeholders,[129] who approved the SKS IPO to the Indian public, need to provide the necessary rationale and educate the various stakeholders.

In the light of these discussions, there are several questions that need to be answered.

- On what basis was the SKS IPO apparently approved[130] despite serious shortcomings in governance of SKSML and much of this information being available in the public domain?

- What process was followed, who were involved, and how did they reach this decision?

- What due diligence was done, and when, and what were the findings?

---

128 *Source*: Quoted from Commercialization of Microfinance in India: A Discussion of the Emperor's Apparel by Prof. M. S. Sriram, (*Economic and Political Weekly (EPW)*, Vol: XLV No: 24). Page: 71, Para: 9, June 12, 2010.

129 Note that one is not questioning the authorities, but rather one is highlighting the fact that there is a responsibility to educate the public.

130 As a stakeholder remarked, "Put differently, the same question can be rephrased as follows: Given that the shortcomings that are so evident from two papers by Prof. Sriram (Formerly of IIM-A), News/Stories in *The Economic Times*, a deep analysis of the SKS published documents (Draft Red Herring Prospectus (DRHP) and Financial Statements), how indeed was the SKS IPO approved?"

- Why did not the authorities unearth serious governance failures, which were so apparent from the DRHP[131] filed by SKS?

- Given that the SKS IPO was the first in the Indian microfinance industry and also given that Prof. Sriram's papers and other public domain material had clearly brought out the issues on corporate governance and related aspects at SKS, what specific actions had been/were taken by the authorities to ascertain facts in an objective manner and come to fair and reasonable conclusions? This is especially critical given that there was perhaps insufficient domain knowledge, in the capital market space, regarding microfinance.

- Given that SKS was an NBFC regulated by the RBI, what coordination did SEBI have with the country's prime financial services regulator in this regard? Did it seek or request any information or opinion? Did the RBI play a proactive role in sharing information voluntarily, especially given the fact SKSML was registered with it as an NBFC, under direct supervision of its non-bank supervision department?

- Which of the various parties—the company, investment banker, market regulator, financial regulator and others—did not perform their roles to the optimum and what lessons can be learnt going forward?

To summarize, the following final questions need to have been answered by the concerned stakeholders and authorities, while recommending the first ever microfinance IPO in India:

- Was investing in such a company, where even the most basic corporate governance norms are violated, a safe proposition for the ordinary retail investor?

- Was a retail investor's money safe in such an NBFC, where the most basic of norms in financial intermediation—*that of not granting any loan, advance or non-fund-based facility or any other financial accommodation/facility to its directors or their relatives*—were violated and there were serious conflicts of interest?

- How could a retail investor be sure that the NBFC would not (in the future) engage in any such redundant/spurious transactions—such as buying of its own shares, through financial assistance to directors or others, in the future—either for personal gain or for boosting the company's share prices or enhancing borrowing (leverage) capacity and/or other reasons?

---

131 The DRHP is a key document for the IPO.

- Given that the founder and key personnel of the to-be-listed company were selling their shares, was there an unknown long-term risk in this business of microfinance that stakeholders and the public ought to have known?

- How would this NBFC have been able to service the retail shareholder when it violated the most basic principles of corporate governance required in financial institutions?

*Without doubt, India and its citizens, the Indian microfinance sector, its various stakeholders, and all others await a convincing answer to these questions. That it has not yet been provided, even as late as December 2013, is clearly there for everyone to see.*

Thus, while the antecedents to the SKS IPO did *not* certainly look good, the (controversial) IPO by itself turned out to be a phenomenal success, as the next chapter articulates.

# Chapter 9:
# The Runaway Success of the SKS IPO

The SKS IPO proved a huge success and was oversubscribed at least 18 times, with the shares first listing at Rs. 980 and then going on to touch Rs. 1450 in September 2010. The mood in the Indian microfinance industry was extremely upbeat and many MFIs started looking at an IPO issue as a good means to infuse capital. Thus, many MFIs had begun to count their chickens even before the eggs had hatched. International bodies such as the CGAP, which brought out a special paper (focus note) on the SKS IPO, were equally gung-ho about this commercialization. This prompted some stakeholders to argue that IPOs and the commercialization of microfinance were indeed inevitable and perhaps even irreversible.

The CGAP focus note was interesting for several reasons. It brought out many of the success factors for the SKS IPO, while bypassing some of the weaknesses of SKS as pointed out by experienced professionals like Prof. Sriram.[132] In fact, both papers that Prof. Sriram had brought out in 2010[133] did not even find a mention in the CGAP paper, despite their being extremely relevant and available in the public domain.

Even as the CGAP paper was being discussed and debated, I continued to travel in the field. By then, I had started to notice increasing defaults at the field level in AP and also heard several complaints from clients regarding coercive repayment. Therefore, I kept posting on the Development Finance Network (DFN) and Microfinance Practice (MFP) e-groups[134] on the worsening ground situation in AP, but it did not capture the attention of the concerned stakeholders in India or elsewhere. I then wrote a response to the CGAP paper on the SKS IPO and posted it on their blog as well as sent it by e-mail to their senior officials overseeing the India and Asia regions. I reproduce my note here and leave it to you, as a reader, to judge the relevance and seriousness of the issues raised. I am sure you will be able to connect to a lot of issues that subsequently emerged during the AP crisis.

In my critique of the CGAP focus note, I wrote:

---

132 Formerly of The Indian Institute of Management (IIM), Ahmedabad.

133 Commercialization of Microfinance in India: A Discussion of the Emperor's Apparel by Prof. M. S. Sriram, (*Economic and Political Weekly* (EPW), June 12, 2010—Vol: XLV No: 24) and Commercialization of Microfinance in India: A Discussion on the Emperor's Apparel by Prof. M. S. Sriram, W.P. No. 2010-03-04, March 2010.

134 These are two electronic discussion groups for development finance and microfinance practitioners/professionals.

1. The growth and financial success of SKS and its IPO are well covered in the CGAP article,[135] *Indian Microfinance Goes Public: The SKS Initial Public Offering.*

2. However, there appeared to be several issues—based on data in the public domain (Prof. Sriram's article in EPW dated June 12, 2010, and his earlier working paper, published financial statements of SKSML, the (D)RHP filed by SKSML, newspaper advertisements and reports, etc.)—especially pertaining to the corporate governance processes (at SKSML) that should not have been ignored.

3. Despite the acknowledgement of the heightened importance of corporate governance, I would like to state that the CGAP article had not adequately addressed some of these crucial issues (already in the public domain)—which are an integral part of the phenomenal growth strategy of SKSML culminating in its IPO and subsequent listing. As these issues had significant (future) implications for the orderly growth, development, and commercialization of the microfinance industry globally, I raised them, as questions (not exhaustive[136]) for CGAP to address, in the future. The same are reproduced here and it would have been very appropriate if the CGAP paper had focused on the following:

    a. Who authorized the lending[137] of Rs. 1.636 crore (as an interest-free loan) by SKSML to its founder to enable him to buy 1.636 million SKSML shares at Rs. 10 per share? Was it an individual at SKSML? Was it the board? Was it the shareholders? Under what powers was this related-party transaction authorized? *What is CGAP's perspective on the process of approval and authorization from a best practices standpoint? Why was this not discussed in the CGAP paper?*

    b. *If it were the board of SKSML that authorized the transaction and/or approved the authorization provided by other stakeholders, who were the board members present when it voted to give an interest-free loan to its founder director to enable him to buy shares in the same company? Is this transaction an arm's length one?* Were there any conflicts of interest in the board and were these declared? What are the implications of this and other related-party transactions at SKSML for corporate governance in microfinance? *Would CGAP recommend special safeguards against such potential conflicts of interest at MFIs?*

    c. How appropriate was it for a financial services institution such as SKSML—especially one that was established to service poor clients and one, that had significant public money (SIDBI's[138] investments) and client money (MBTs)—to lend (interest-free) to its own founder director to buy shares in the same company? Was this a good practice of corporate governance? Would the

---

135 http://www.cgap.org/p/site/c/template.rc/1.9.47613/.
136 There are several other questions, including those on MBTs and their transactions, that are yet to be answered from a pure legal and policy perspective.
137 See paper by Prof. M. S. Sriram, EPW, June 12, 2010, SKS audited statements, DRHP, and SKS Advertisement dated July 28, 2010—all of which suggest that SKSML lent Rs. 1.636 crore to the founder to enable him to buy an equivalent number of SKSML shares at Rs. 10 per share.
138 SIDBI is one of India's major DFIs. It is government owned and has been at the forefront of the MFI model in India.

investors and donors who are a part of CGAP have approved this practice of MFI owners lending to themselves to buy their own (MFI/company) shares as a good practice? Would investors/banks who are investing/lending to MFIs have recommended this as good practice? *What is the CGAP's position on such related-party transactions in microfinance, especially from the perspective of the best (good) practices paradigm that CGAP has been prescribing (over the years) in microfinance?*

d. What was the impact of the above-mentioned related-party transaction on the financial condition of SKSML, the MFI? Did it result in a misstatement of the true financial condition? If so, were the shareholders (mis)informed? What were the implications of this under the various Indian laws, including the Indian Penal Code (IPC) and other acts as may be appropriate? *In the CGAP's opinion, from a good practices perspective, in case of such related-party transactions, should adjustments be done by MFIs to reflect the true financial condition? If so, what methodology should they follow and how should they present the results?*

e. Can this action by the SKSML board (in which public institutional investors and MBTs held significant shareholding) be termed as being in the interest of the shareholders, especially the minority shareholders? While the MBTs held a lot of shares in aggregate, in reality they were individual minority shareholders. Who on the board protected the interest of these minority shareholders? *In the CGAP's opinion, was this transaction in the interest of the minority stakeholders—that is, members in MBTs? What should be done to protect the interests of such minority stakeholders in future?*

f. Were there nominee directors of the institutional investors (like SIDBI) on the SKSML board when this happened? If so, how did they react and/or even permit this? What were they doing on the board of SKSML when norms/rules of corporate governance were seemingly not followed? Did they object to or express reservations on this related-party transaction and other such happenings? If so, did they inform the institutional investors officially? If they were silent, was there any conflict of interest? How did they make themselves accountable to the institutional investors for being their nominees on the board, safeguarding their investment and (public) funds? *What are the CGAP's suggestions for enhancing the accountability of the nominee directors—both in terms of the reporting to be done by them and also the processes to be followed by investors while appointing them?*

g. Institutional investors have the moral and legal responsibility to ensure that such corporate misgovernance does not occur, at least, in MFIs/companies where they have made investments and where they also have a responsible officer as a nominee on the board. In this case, did the institutional investors have any procedure to review the performance of their nominee directors and/or the functioning of the board in MFIs where investments had been made? *In the CGAP's opinion, what safeguards should be built to ensure that nominee directors really act in the interest of their investors, while upholding the highest standards of corporate governance?*

h. Given that some MFIs (there are a few that have done this to a varying degree) have been in the habit of lending to their own directors (and none of these can be described as an arm's length transaction) to buy their own shares, *were they* entitled to access PSL funds?[139] Was this practice of lending to directors (to buy own company shares[140] and for other reasons) in consonance with norms for PSL? What are the implications for policy in India? *What is the CGAP's position on the (mis)use of PSL and what are its prescriptions for policy in India regarding the same?*

i. SKSML had publicly mentioned in an advertisement dated July 28, 2010, that its (related-party) transaction in lending to its own founder director to buy shares in the same company did not represent a violation of the Companies Act and RBI circulars. While this may be legally tenable, the key question is whether it is right from a moral/ethical standpoint? Especially when one considers the IPC under which other companies have been implicated for presentation of wrong information to shareholders? What is the actual position of policy (RBI, Ministry of Corporate Affairs, Ministry of Finance, and other relevant authorities in India) on this, especially in the wake of the global financial crisis and the Satyam fiasco? *What are the CGAP's suggestions to Indian policy makers, as per its good practices paradigm, on the aspect of dealing with such related-party transactions in microfinance?*

4. Several concerns were raised regarding compensation aspects and process of allotment of shares at SKSML. Much of this material is already in the public domain (Prof. Sriram's article, SKS' supposed rejoinder to Prof. Sriram's article sent via Sa-Dhan by e-mail, and other documents). There are several issues here and *it would have been useful to have had CGAP's input on whether the compensation and allotment processes followed at SKSML were indeed transparent, as per good practices norms and also legally correct:*

   a. Regarding the process of allotment of shares at SKSML, it would be good to know what was approved by the board and by the shareholders, and compare the same with filings done with the ROC since the documents *in the public domain seem to indicate discrepancy.*

   b. It appears that all approvals were provided for ESOPs to be issued to the founder and others [such as the then Chief Operating Officer (COO)] in February 2007. However, in reality, it seems that ESPS (shares) were issued to the COO and shares were issued to the founder.[141] *The question*

---

139 It would be interesting to get a CGAP perspective on PSLF because a committee appointed by the RBI is looking into PSLF-related issues at the moment and a draft report is likely to be submitted shortly.

140 Given that many of the MFI promoters in India are from social backgrounds, they may not have the initial funds to invest in ESOPs/ESPSs that they receive from their MFI for their work and contribution. It would be useful to know whether the CGAP can suggest a special loan product (from special DFIs/banks) to enable such MFI promoters (without investment funds) to invest their MFIs? It would also be appropriate if the CGAP suggests the norms and guidelines for developing ESOPs/ESPSs, tailored to the microfinance context.

141 The supposed rejoinder from SKS notes that the fact that the founder's share allotment was originally approved and documented to be an Employee Stock Option Plan (ESOP), whereas in reality the final form of allotment was through the ESPS—see quote attached— *"Although Vikram's share allotment was approved and documented—and originally intended to be an Employee Stock Option Plan (ESOP) to take effect*

*here is how could this have been done when the approval was for ESOPs—stock options?* Therefore, a clear understanding of the above—on whether there were any discrepancies—would be required, especially in view of the fact that shares allotted to the founder had been fully sold out before the IPO, whereas those given to the COO had been partially liquidated.

c. Regarding ESPS, it appears that the company had a scheme where employees would be issued shares when they join, to be vested over a period of four years. The company was to give a loan to the trust, which was to lend the same money to employee to buy these shares. In turn, the employee would enter into a financing arrangement with the trust and the company. Under this, the shares would be directly either freshly allotted to the employee or if there were any shares in the pool available, they would be transferred to the employee's name. *This arrangement of giving any amount of loan and allotting or transferring the shares directly in the name of the employee appears to have been in contravention of Section 77 (3) of the Companies Act.*[142] As per this section, shares cannot be allotted in the name of the employee directly and also the loan amount cannot exceed six months' salary of the employee. Prima facie, it appears that the company was violating the above conditions.

d. There seems to be reasonable evidence to the assertion made in Prof. Sriram's paper that at a time when the company was attempting to enter the primary market and tap retail investors, *the founder indeed held zero equity,* and it was his unexercised options that had been subjected to a three-year lock-in period. In fact, in the DRHP table, the founder's name was not there under the promoter's group and some of the key employees were selling off their exercised options before the IPO.

e. There appear to have been several other issues, including the following—that the vesting period for some schemes were not satisfied, specific schemes were perhaps SEBI noncompliant, and high bonuses had been granted to senior management.

f. Therefore, it would have been appropriate if the CGAP had looked at these issues and developed some lessons for MFIs on how to tackle compensation aspects (including composition and the role of a compensation committee) from a good practices perspective. The CGAP's comments on one of the key aspects in the compensation debate—*that is, whether the process and outcomes related to compensation were in line with the medium and long-term risk inherent in the microfinance industry* —would also have been extremely useful from an industry-wide perspective.

---

back in March 2006—-the final form of the allotment was finalized, based on tax advice from KPMG, as an Employee Share Purchase Scheme (ESPS)—a legally permissible variant of an ESOP—in March 2007." (Sa-Dhan Circulated Rejoinder Note from SKS received by e-mail). The CGAP article also acknowledged that this discrepancy occurred.

142  The section also says that, "provided that nothing in this sub-section shall be taken to prohibit, the making by a company of loans, within the limit laid down in sub-section (3), to persons (other than directors or managers) bona fide in the employment of the company with a view to enabling those persons to purchase or subscribe for fully paid shares in the company or its holding company to be held by themselves by way of beneficial ownership." Subsection (3) states that, "No loan made to any person in pursuance of clause of the foregoing proviso shall exceed in amount his salary or wages at that time for a period of six months."

5. It should be noted that after[143] the IPO, Dr Akula became the executive chairman of SKSML and Mr M. R. Rao the deputy CEO. Thus, it was clear that key people and positions were being changed in the SKS group of institutions at will—one day, there was a trust with several members looking after the interest of the MBTs, then another day, most members of the trust resigned and there were just two people including the founder. The founder then suddenly became the executive chairman, post IPO. Just as I was finishing the CGAP note, there was an announcement from the Bombay Stock Exchange (BSE) that SKSML had terminated the services of Mr Gurumani, its CEO, whom it had appointed for a period of five years from 2009.

6. This again raised serious questions about the effectiveness of corporate governance at SKSML; the market did react, with SKSML shares going down by almost 5.81% at around 3.20 p.m. on October 4, 2010. Therefore, it would be useful to get the CGAP's opinion, on the *frequent and sudden changes in the board and senior management structure of SKSML* and related institutions from a corporate governance perspective and provide lessons for the MFIs, so as to enable them to maintain their valuations, in case they tap the primary market.

7. And before I wrap up the discussion on this aspect of corporate governance, I would like to quote an experienced and senior microfinance practitioner, Ms Shashi Rajagopalan, who, while commenting[144] on the CGAP SKS paper, stated:

> "Notwithstanding the sleight of hand by which large numbers of women are shown to be shareholders through MBTs, many NBFC MFIs are closely held companies, and, in my view, statistics quoted by such closely held companies are hard to ascertain. It appears to be in everyone's interest to pretend that these companies are indeed growing at the rates claimed and that their default rates are indeed the rates claimed. Anyone buying into these figures, has either never given and collected credit, or, is either incredibly naive, or has a stake in pretending that this is indeed a wonderful gift to the low income group. CGAP is gung-ho about things that it ought to be much more discerning on, if indeed it wants people with low income to truly benefit from regular access to genuine and usable credit."

8. Journalist M. Rajsekhar, of *The Economic Times* (June 27, 2010) concurred with this and further added:

> "Even the regulators have their concerns. For instance, RBI deputy governor Usha Thorat flagged possible risks like conflicts of interest, co-mingling of MFI and bank funds, misrepresentation and other agency-related risks recently in her talk at a seminar co-hosted by the US Federal Reserve, IMF and the World Bank in early June. ...Today, some of India's leading MFIs face charges of both corporate mis-governance and lending irregularities—like coercive repayment techniques and harsh repayment schedules

---

143 On September 7, 2010.
144 Comment sent by e mail to the author

that result in women taking fresh loans to settle existing debt. Any regulatory framework chosen must check corporate mis-governance and ensure microfinance doesn't degenerate into predatory lending."[145]

9. Last but not the least, I would like to make the point that:

*"Commercialization of microfinance may be a necessary trend and this critique of the CGAP SKS article should not be taken as an argument against commercialisation. However, to be welcome, commercialization must be executed in a proper and legally tenable manner. Without question, the means are as important as the ends and only commercialization that is achieved through legally tenable methods and means should be supported—as that alone can have a positive impact on people with low income."*[146]

There was no proper response from the CGAP to my comments posted on their blog and also sent by e-mail to several officers looking after the South Asia region.

The rest is history as, thereafter, the AP government, in response to the mounting suicides, enacted the AP MFI Ordinance and also made it mandatory for MFIs to register to operate/continue their business in AP. The ordinance crippled the MFIs with its stringent use of regulation, and microfinance in AP, as we knew of it before 2010, had died. Even today, there is little loaning and recovery on the ground in AP, which once was hailed as the 'Mecca' of 'Indian microfinance.'

In fact, I had been writing to the bankers' forum under the SIDBI responsible microfinance project even before the ordinance was enacted to alert them on the deteriorating ground situation. I wrote several times but I got no serious response from SIDBI or any of the other bankers officially. A perusal of the e-mail given[147] will serve to set the record straight. While my initial reaction to their lack of response was one of surprise (as I felt that any genuine bank would want to know ground level reality), I am now clear that the bankers played a very important role in the build up to the 2010 AP microfinance crisis. Therefore, in retrospect, their lack of response to my e-mails (below) should have been anticipated.

That said, let us now examine how the situation on the ground actually deteriorated in September/October 2010 and also look at the response of various stakeholders such as the AP government, MFIs, banks, investors, MFI associations, RBI and other regulators, media and others to the fast unfolding drama. This is done in the next few chapters.

---

[145] Quoted from "Disciplining the MFIs: Adopting right regulatory framework to be crucial", (http://economictimes.indiatimes.com/opinion/policy/disciplining-the-mfis-adopting-right-regulatory-framework-to-be-crucial/articleshow/6221439.cms), by M Rajshekhar, 27 July, 2010.

[146] Reproduced from note sent by the author to CGAP as a response to their focus note on SKSML.

[147] See Appendix 9.

# Chapter 10:
# Andhra Pradesh Crisis and Microfinance as India's Subprime

In September/October 2010, the crisis in AP took a turn for the worse and the *Society for Elimination of Rural Poverty* (SERP) released a list of over 50 suicides by microfinance clients. After this, I read an interesting paper[148] by Mr Aloysius (Al) Fernandez, who talked candidly about the prevailing situation and asked the question as to whether microfinance could be leading to a macro mess. He basically referred to:

> *"Microfinance as driven by pressures resulting from venture capitalists and other private investors which is characterized by quick growth, high profits, high cost (interest and remunerations especially for senior staff), IPOs and quick exits."*

But while the ground situation prevailing then was indeed a matter of grave concern to the microfinance movement and even threatened its very existence, it was not totally unexpected. In fact, as noted earlier, in 2005, Dr Thorat and I, in a paper[149] presented at the NABARD high-level policy conference in New Delhi, had suggested that the burgeoning growth of microfinance could result in a number of not-so-desirable practices being adopted. Commenting[150] on that, Mr Devarajan of *The Hindu Business Line* (Oct 1, 2010) argued that:

> *"MFIs have access to collateral free, soft interest loans that come with almost no conditionalities—on an unlimited scale today. The money mela of MFIs in the rural areas looks more than a trifle scary."*

Thus, when the AP crisis first appeared through media reports and SERP released its list of suicides, I immediately knew that the river banks had been breached and the floodgates would soon open. And

---

148 Is Microfinance Leading to a Macro Mess, The AP Ordinance, by Aloysius P. Fernandez, 2010, unpublished paper.
149 Regulation and Areas of Potential Market Failure in Microfinance, by Thorat, Y. S. P. and Ramesh S. Arunachalam (2005), paper presented at the NABARD high-level policy conference in New Delhi.
150 http://www.thehindubusinessline.com/2005/10/01/stories/2005100102220600.htm

# Chapter 10: Andhra Pradesh Crisis and Microfinance as India's Subprime

having seen the 2005–2006 Krishna crisis at very close quarters, I, for one, was sure that the many undesirable practices in the sector had resulted in this situation.

Commenting on the burgeoning growth in Indian microfinance in 2010 and the resultant situation, Adjunct Professor at IIM (A), Prof. M. S. Sriram,[151] had argued (in 2010) as follows:

> "This anxiety for growth is partly dictated by the fact that the investors in the market based models are impatient and look for returns. The more the investors put pressure on returns, the more the pressure is on fast growth and this in turn makes the organizations cut corners to achieve growth. The growth story of microfinance thus is giving enough cause for anxiety. In the process they are creating an unnecessary storm in the lives of the poor by offering them something that is difficult for them to digest in such a quick time. This, in the short run, will harm the interests of inclusion. The response of the state has not been in the desirable direction. Instead of harping on about caps on interest rates and threatening to remove microfinance out of the priority sector list, it is necessary for the State/RBI to look at specific instances and pull the delinquent organizations up. Nothing prevents the RBI from causing an audit of the end-use of the loans of MFIs, looking at their governance more carefully and advising the institutional representatives on the boards of these MFIs to exercise independence."

In fact, the overall situation in 2010 prompted Dr Y V Reddy, former RBI governor, credited with insulating the Indian financial system from the 2008 meltdown, to label *microfinance as India's subprime*.[152] *"Ultimately, it's something like subprime lending,"* he told *The Economic Times*[153] in an interview ahead of his book release. *"The same incentives are operating here, it was securitization and derivatives that operated in the US. Here it is the priority sector lending by banks."* "Yes, I agree with Mr Reddy when he says a lot of perverse incentives got aligned," said Mr Mahajan. "Here perverse incentives got aligned like in the US and in two years the sector went from helping the poor to preying on the poor."[154]

Dr Reddy, raising the issue of microfinance being India's subprime, certainly caught my attention even as many in the civil society began asking the same question—*was microfinance India's subprime*? And before I answer this crucial question, let us look at what constitutes subprime lending? Basically, it refers to loans extended to people with poor repaying ability that ultimately led to defaults. And as the same *Economic Times* article notes, the similarities do not end there: Indian microfinance and the US subprime have a lot more in common including *"opaque practices, high salaries and commissions inducing unethical business, leverage and several other issues."*[155]

---

151 The Anxiety of Growth in Microfinance, by Prof. Sriram is Adjunct Professor, IIM–A, unpublished paper, 2010.

152 http://economictimes.indiatimes.com/news/economy/indicators/Microfinance-in-India-is-like-subprime-lending-Y-V-Reddy/articleshow/6972903.cms

153 http://economictimes.indiatimes.com/news/economy/indicators/Microfinance-in-India-is-like-subprime-lending-Y-V-Reddy/articleshow/6972903.cms

154 http://economictimes.indiatimes.com/news/economy/indicators/Microfinance-in-India-is-like-subprime-lending-Y-V-Reddy/articleshow/6972903.cms

155 http://economictimes.indiatimes.com/news/economy/indicators/Microfinance-in-India-is-like-subprime-lending-Y-V-Reddy/articleshow/6972903.cms

In fact, even before the global financial crisis, in September 2005, the CGAP[156] observed that the increased attention to "microfinance could attract lenders that might not care as much about development objectives, and might even engage in predatory lending practices that take advantage of poor clients."

Likewise, as Rhyne[157] argued in 2010:

> "The blame for this unfortunate situation falls most squarely on the microfinance institutions, or MFIs, that failed to restrain aggressive growth even as the market became increasingly saturated. ... Investors must also swallow a big spoonful of blame. Because they paid dearly for shares in the MFI's, they need fast growth to make their investments pay off. Regulators share some responsibility, however. The public-sector policy environment has treated microfinance institutions as orphan children of the financial sector rather than helping them to build solid foundations."

Therefore, while experts were slowly but surely getting to identify conditions that could result in microfinance being heralded as India's subprime, it was time that we explored this in a detailed and objective manner. And this requires answering the following questions:

- Did clients have multiple loans and did they appear to be (over)indebted? Were they not in a position to repay loans from their known (legitimate) sources of income/cash? How widespread was this phenomena?

- Had institutions (for whatever reason) provided successive loans, despite knowing that the concerned clients could not repay existing (multiple) loans from the known (legitimate) sources of income/cash?

- Had clients used one loan to repay another? Was periodic refinancing required to provide sufficient liquidity to enable the client to service other/existing loans? Were additional loans provided midway through an ongoing loan and, especially, on easier terms? Had there been a series of delinquent payments and one equalizing payment (often from another loan), and was this pattern repeated?

- Were coercive repayment practices used to ensure better repayment? Had there been a lack of transparency with the product terms and the like, especially in terms of the effective interest rates as well as other issues?

- Had growth of institutions been unusually large and been supply led? Had MFIs grown this rapidly to show better operating results? To have greater returns? To pay higher salaries and commissions to staff/management? To get better valuations? To tap capital markets at a premium, and so on?

---

156 http://www.microfinancegateway.org/p/site/m/template.rc/1.26.7211/
157 http://www.nytimes.com/2010/11/26/opinion/lweb26microfinance.html

- And most importantly, had there been policy as well as regulatory/supervisory failure, in one sense or another?

The lessons from the 2010 AP crisis clearly provide a resounding 'YES' to all of these questions and thereby position microfinance as indeed India's subprime.

Without question, a lot of stakeholders including regulators will have to (satisfactorily) explain to the public and civil society as to how and why this happened. And of course, regulation would no longer be able to use a hands-off approach to microfinance, which has been treated as an orphaned child (in a regulatory sense) for several years now. That, sadly, was the prevailing situation even as of December 2013. In fact, despite the Ordinance (Act) enacted (passed) by the Government of AP, the only national regulatory framework currently available are the RBI's guidelines based on the MCR—which incidentally represented a good beginning but in my opinion, lacked the sufficient depth and required detail to tackle the real causes of the 2010 AP crisis. All of these (including the ordinance and the MCR) are discussed in the next chapter, which I am sure you will find interesting.

# Chapter 11:
# Responses by the State Government, RBI, and Microfinance Associations to the Andhra Pradesh Crisis

The AP government, finding itself in a rather precarious situation, claimed to have no choice but to try and reign in the MFIs. To that effect, it enacted a hastily put together ordinance (October 15, 2010). The ordinance was not necessarily the best drafted from a legal perspective, but one that seemed sufficient to stem the rot (at least for that moment). After the enactment of the ordinance, the repayments came down considerably and MFIs also claimed that they were facing a resource (liquidity) crunch. It must also be noted that the ordinance subsequently became a full-fledged bill (December 10, 2010) and as on date (December 2013), the bill is still in force and being implemented.

While we can argue on the merits of whether the government was justified in enacting an ordinance first and subsequently converting it into a bill, the fact remains that state governments have the right to protect their subjects, and that cannot be questioned. While banking is a central subject, money lending is a state subject and given the manner in which many of the (NBFC) MFIs operated—using multiple lending to shared clients in shared JLGs with coercive repayment collection—I am inclined to believe that they were engaged in nothing but organized money lending.

In fact, people like Dr Y. V. Reddy strongly emphasized this point and argued that, "Profit-seeking MFIs ...are no better than money lenders."[158]

That said, having been a part of the industry for over two decades, I can vouch for the fact that when it started out, at least in the initial years (and before the hardcore commercialization drive came in), microfinance was nowhere close to money lending. I can recount innumerable stories from several places and districts on how microfinance had positively impacted the lives of poor people. Therefore, in its original *avatar*, microfinance could have been regulated either directly through the RBI or via a specialized microfinance regulator. However, given that most NBFC MFIs behaved like money lenders, the AP ordinance and bill appear rather justified. As far as the AP ordinance and bill are concerned, I see it as an exercise in client protection by the state. However,

---

[158] *Source*: Quoted from MFIs no better than money lenders, must be regulated: YV Reddy, by Press Trust of India, November 22, 2010 (http://articles.economictimes.indiatimes.com/2010-11-22/news/27622214_1_mfis-finance-institutions-money-lenders).

# Chapter 11: Responses by the State Government

I am sure that if enabling client protection measures are included in any central regulation, then, convincing the AP government to revoke the ordinance/bill could be attempted, although these efforts would certainly need to be backed by credible operational (ground level) changes to MFI operations as well.

Meanwhile, the growing public outrage against MFIs, coupled with the virtual halt of MFI operations in AP after the ordinance, had resulted in the RBI appointing a board subcommittee on October 28, 2010, to look into the AP microfinance crisis.[159]

Once the committee had been appointed, the expectations with regard to the report of the RBI board subcommittee—looking into the microfinance industry and its working—started rising, with even Mr Pranab Mukherjee (the then Finance Minister of India) stating that he was waiting for the RBI report to finalize the regulatory structure for MFIs.

Meanwhile, the ground situation was deteriorating day by day. And given the turmoil in microfinance—which started with the controversial SKS IPO and was followed by the serial suicides in AP, the unearthing of multiple lending by MFIs to shared JLGs and clients, the promulgation of the AP ordinance, and the aftereffects of these—the future of the industry appeared bleak. So much so that, even stalwarts such as Mr Mahajan started talking of the creative destruction of the current growth and consumption loan–oriented MFI model in favor of livelihood financing. See Mr Mahajan's quote from *The Economic Times*, November 12, 2010:

> "I believe in Schumpeterian creative destruction. Its time has come. The present MFI model has to go," predicts Mahajan, considered the high priest of Indian microfinance. Mahajan, ironically, also presides over the Microfinance Institutions Network (MFIN), an industry coalition, and is currently engaged in dousing the fire in Indian microfinance - cajoling bankers, assuaging governments, building confidence and seeking a shift in stratagems."[160]

In fact, by December 2010, the happenings in Tamil Nadu[161] suggested that the contagion had spread to places outside of Andhra Pradesh. There was also consensus on the fact that the crisis was due to the irresponsible growth and client acquisition strategies pursued by the NBFC MFIs during the period 2006–2010 and especially the six large AP-headquartered MFIs during 2008–2010. Given the large-scale ramifications of such situations, the key question was who was responsible and who needed to be held accountable?

Indeed, as I wrote in blog, "there were several stakeholders, including the following, who needed to answer for this mess created in India's rural and urban low-income economy:

---

159 http://www.microfinance-in-india.blogspot.in/search/label/AP%20Micro-Finance%20Crisis

160 Source: How to fix flaws in the present microfinance model by Naren Karunakaran, *The Economic Times*, (November 12, 2010), (http://articles.economictimes.indiatimes.com/2010-11-12/news/27585259_1_indian-microfinance-mfi-basix).

161 http://www.microfinance-in-india.blogspot.in/search/label/Tamilnadu%20Micro-Finance%20Crisis

- *Large and fast-growing MFIs* who wanted unnatural profits and artificial growth numbers to attract equity investments at a premium and create wealth for themselves and their investors.

- *Investors* who paid a premium and, hence, perhaps pushed MFIs to grow recklessly, using the bait of further and larger equity investments to get MFIs to show consistently better results and offer artificially high returns.

- *Banks* that made excellent profits from microfinance and satisfied their priority sector obligations. Without question, the banks, ably led by SIDBI, irresponsibly threw around their (public deposit) money in the garb of financial inclusion, knowing well that greening and other strategies were being used to repay loans. That they need to shoulder much of the blame, is an issue beyond doubt.

- *International agencies such as CGAP and others* who strongly pushed the agenda of hardcore commercialization without even thinking once on whether (or not) inclusive access to finance was being implemented as envisaged and/or whether (or not) it was making any tangible difference to the lives of clients on the ground.

- *Policy makers* who enthusiastically pushed the vision of financial inclusion without realizing that this concept primarily translated into small consumption credit (and perhaps some small production credit) being channeled to the very same borrowers multiple times.

- *The so-called self-regulatory organizations* (SROs)—mainly MFI associations—that were not able to bring order to the chaotic growth of the microfinance industry in several years, despite their well-intentioned CoCs."

Yet, despite several months of crisis, there had been no serious response from the microfinance industry or other stakeholders to the poorest clients who had been affected so badly on the ground. Everyone was waiting, I guess, for the Malegam Committee Report (MCR), which finally got submitted on January 20, 2011. A complete summary of the recommendations are summarized elsewhere.[162] Commenting on the MCR, I wrote in my blog as follows:

> "At the outset, I must mention that the MCR is laudable because it is the first committee report of (some) significance to attempt the creation of a (national) regulatory framework for microfinance in India. The report must be appreciated because it seeks to legitimize microfinance as an integral part of the financial sector. By recommending the creation of a new category called NBFC MFIs (with associated conditions that are perhaps open for discussion), the report *has* clearly positioned and mainstreamed microfinance

---

162 The Malegam Committee Report on Microfinance: What's on the Platter?
(http://microfinance-in-india.blogspot.in/2011/01/malegam-committee-report-on-micro.html).

within the framework of the larger financial sector. This ensures that microfinance will come under the RBI's purview and can no longer be treated as a fringe activity or as an orphaned child.

A second aspect that deserves appreciation is that while the report *has* recommended continuation of priority sector funds for MFIs, it was however made *conditional* on MFIs meeting certain standards and requirements, especially after recognizing some of the key problems (such as ghost lending, multiple lending, and over-lending) and outlining some measures to tackle them (which again are open to discussion).

Third, the report has recognized and stressed the importance of off-site and on-site supervision of NBFC MFIs (including systemically important ones), while alluding to the need for *significantly* enhancing the supervisory capacity of RBI with regard to microfinance. This is especially crucial.

Fourth, the emphasis on corporate governance is noteworthy and, specifically, the committee has suggested that corporate governance rules will have to be specified (encompassing several issues) for NBFC MFIs by the regulator. *A very critical aspect indeed."*

Meanwhile, the RBI broadly accepted the various recommendations of the MCR. And I quote from the monetary policy document of the RBI,[163] which is reproduced here:

"92. In the wake of the Andhra Pradesh micro-finance crisis in 2010, concerns were expressed by various stakeholders and the need was felt for more rigorous regulation of non-banking financial companies (NBFCs) functioning as microfinance institutions (MFIs). As indicated in the Second Quarter Review of November 2010, a sub-committee of the Central Board of the Reserve Bank (Chairman: Shri Y. H. Malegam) was constituted to study issues and concerns in the MFI sector. The Committee submitted its report in January, 2011, which was placed in public domain.

The committee, *inter alia*, recommended (i) creation of a separate category of NBFC-MFIs; (ii) a margin cap and an interest rate cap on individual loans; (iii) transparency in interest charges; (iv) lending by not more than two MFIs to individual borrowers; (v) creation of one or more credit information bureaus; (vi) establishment of a proper system of grievance redressal procedure by MFIs; (vii) creation of one or more "social capital funds"; and (viii) continuation of categorization of bank loans to MFIs, complying with the regulation laid down for NBFC-MFIs, under the priority sector. The recommendations of the committee were discussed with all stakeholders, including the government of India, select state governments, major NBFCs working as MFIs, industry associations of MFIs working in the country, other smaller MFIs, and major banks.

---

163 http://www.rbi.org.in/scripts/NotificationUser.aspx?Id=6376&Mode=0

In the light of the feedback received, it has been decided:

- to accept the broad framework of regulations recommended by the committee;

- that bank loans to all MFIs, including NBFCs working as MFIs on or after April 1, 2011, will be eligible for classification as priority sector loans under respective category of indirect finance only if the prescribed percentage of their total assets are in the nature of "qualifying assets" and they adhere to the "pricing of interest" guidelines to be issued in this regard;

- That a "qualifying asset" is required to satisfy the criteria of (i) loan disbursed by an MFI to a borrower with a rural household annual income not exceeding 60,000 or urban and semi-urban household income not exceeding 1,20,000; (ii) loan amount not to exceed `35,000 in the first cycle and 50,000 in subsequent cycles; (iii) total indebtedness of the borrower not to exceed 50,000; (iv) tenure of loan not to be less than 24 months for loan amount in excess of 15,000 without prepayment penalty; (iv) loan to be extended without collateral; (v) aggregate amount of loan, given for income generation, not to be less than 75 percent of the total loans given by the MFIs; and (vi) loan to be repayable by weekly, fortnightly, or monthly installments at the choice of the borrower;

- That banks should ensure a margin cap of 12 percent and an interest rate cap of 26 percent for their lending to be eligible to be classified as priority sector loans;

- That loans by MFIs can also be extended to individuals outside the self-help group (SHG)/joint liability group (JLG) mechanism; and

- That bank loans to other NBFCs would not be reckoned as priority sector loans with effect from April 1, 2011.

93. Detailed guidelines in this regard will be issued separately."

A bill to regulate microfinance—The Microfinance Institution Development and Regulation Bill (2012), MFIDRB (2012)—was also introduced in the Lok Sabha in May 2012. The same was referred by the Speaker of the Lok Sabha to the Parliamentary Standing Committee on Finance (PSCF), which rejected the bill in 2014 and sent it back to the Department of Financial Services, Ministry of Finance, Government of India for redrafting and presentation, as per suggestions outlined in the PSCF report.[164]

---

164 http://164.100.47.134/lsscommittee/Finance/15_Finance_84.pdf

## Chapter 11: Responses by the State Government

Thus, various stakeholders (RBI, Ministry of Finance, PSCF and others) are still now involved in developing a robust regulatory and supervisory architecture for Indian microfinance. Having thus described the antecedents and pathways to the 2010 AP microfinance crisis and the responses of the various stakeholders including the RBI, MoF, and others, I now try to share critical issues and lessons that I have learnt from the 2010 crisis and thereafter for the larger benefit of various stakeholders including those developing the regulatory architecture. I am sure that all of you will find this flight even more interesting!

# PART - III

# Chapter 12:
# Does a Five-Star Board Always Guarantee Good Corporate Governance?

Often, people look at the high-profile membership of the board as a surrogate for good corporate governance, and microfinance is no exception. But despite having the equivalent of five-star boards, many (NBFC) microfinance institutions (MFIs) in India have come under attack for various weaknesses in governance.[165] Interestingly, much of this is said to have happened despite many of these (NBFC) MFIs having, what bystanders would often call as, a five-star board—that is, a board packed with well-known personalities from within and outside the industry. And indeed, this is where a common judgment made with regard to corporate governance has, often repeatedly, proved costly, both in microfinance and the broader corporate sector.[166] In fact, if you look at the credit rating reports of some of India's largest (NBFC) MFIs, this is apparent. These reports[167] use the presence of a five-star board to claim that governance in these MFIs is very good. Yet, as the past several years have shown, there were several controversial governance-related issues[168] in these MFIs, as espoused by the following:

a. *Inadequate checks and balances over executive decision making and whimsical behavior by the board and/or senior management.* For example, take the case of the sudden removal (in October 2010) of the chief executive officer (CEO)—Suresh Gurumani of SKSML—who had just led the company through a spectacularly successful IPO. Interestingly, the same CEO had received a huge bonus/raise[169] a few months earlier.

b. *Insufficient transparency about ownership/control and related-party transactions.* One key example should suffice here—that is, the granting of a loan of Rs. 1.636 crore to the founder managing director

---

165  There are some exceptions, but several MFIs exhibit such characteristics.
166  The case of Satyam Computers and Ramalinga Raju.
167  While I can quote several examples from these credit rating reports, the idea is not to embarrass anyone and so I have refrained from quoting these reports.
168  These have been witnessed in some large MFIs, not all of them always.
169  "More to SKS script than meets the eye" by M. Rajshekhar and M. Anand, *The Economic Times*, October 8, 2010.

## Chapter 12: Does a Five-Star Board Always Guarantee Good Corporate Governance?

(Vikram Akula) of SKS Microfinance Private Limited[170] to enable him to buy 16.36 lakh shares (of Rs. 10 par value) in the same MFI.[171] The most interesting part is that an institutional nominee (of SIDBI) was part of the SKS board that made this decision.

c. *High stake acquired by promoters' friends/well-wishers/families in order to maintain control over the MFI.*[172] Jan Postmus writes about the huge sweat equity given to the promoter of Asmitha Microfin and I quote:

"A fourth contradiction is the remuneration of... promoters. We now know that the promoters of Compartamos have become millionaires. India also has welcomed its first microfinance millionaires. The pattern is the same. The promoters either buy the shares at par value in an early stage or get the shares allotted as 'sweat equity', which has become one of the standard conditions from mfi promoters in their negotiations with private investors. As an example, the promoter of Asmitha got sweat equity allotted worth USD 2.5 million at the time of investment of Blue Orchard. Now, this is not fair to the clients who are served by mfi's. Exorbitant promoter(s) enrichment vis-à-vis the financial situation of the poor clients, is in my view unethical and furthermore a clear deviation from the social mission. Mr. Vijay Mahajan is also very clear about this. He said[173] 'the key obstacle that an mfi faces in raising equity is what it does to the poor.... f.e. let us take Compartamos – its founders have personally become multimillionaires. Presumably this will attract more capital but on what terms to the ultimate users? Is this what we set up this sector for? If this if microfinance than I repudiate the field.'" [174]

Likewise, Jan Postmus talks about the case of SHARE Microfin, which came under the same group as Asmitha:

"SHARE was one of the First Grameen replicators in India. Like Grameen it was seen as follower of the welfarist approach. The vision of SHARE was 'to improve the quality of life of the poor by providing access to financial and support services. To be a viable **community-owned** institution developing sustainable communities.' It is not so long ago that Van Maanen (2004) glorified SHARE for following the 'development school approach'. In 2006 as a result of the AP crisis wherein SHARE got caught in political accusations of lending at usurious rates to its clients, SHARE decided to focus on institutional sustainability. Client ownership was now seen as the weakest link to gain institutional sustainability. SHARE argumented that the AP crisis has learnt that if clients can be influenced so

---

170 SKS was a private limited company then, also registered as an NBFC with the RBI.
171 Commercialization of Microfinance in India: A Discussion of the Emperor's Apparel by Prof. M. S. Sriram, *Economic and Political Weekly* (EPW), June 12, 2010–Vol: XLV No: 24.
172 Microfinance at a Crossroads—The Need for Social Equity by Jan Postmus, unpublished paper (2010).
173 Microfinance Insights, Vol 3, June 2007.
174 Source: Quoted from "Microfinance at a Crossroads—The Need for Social Equity" by Jan Postmus, unpublished paper (2010), Page 21.

easily by external parties like the government, it is better not to have them as owners. SHARE bought back all the shares from the clients and changed the vision to: 'to improve the quality of life of the poor by providing access to financial and support services and to be a viable **financial** institution developing sustainable communities.' A subtle but crucial change. The promoters of SHARE bought back the shares at PAR value from the clients and a few years later the shares were sold at high premium to Legatum, a private equity investor who acquired a majority stake in the company. The promoter of SHARE became a multi-millionaire."[175]

The case of SHARE was also highlighted by a brilliant article in economic times.[176] Besides, there is the case of a (married) couple, each of whom were listed as key promoters in two different and large NBFC MFIs in the same group—Asmitha Microfin and SHARE Microfin.

d. *Lack of truly independent and nominee directors[177] and board nomination subcommittees, conflicts of interest at board, senior management and operational level, and other such aspects.*[178] That SIDBI's representative nominee director remained a mute spectator to a huge interest-free loan given to the promoter MD of SKS Microfinance Private Limited is one example. That SIDBI's representative nominee director did not raise objections to the hastily convened board meeting of SKSML on a Sunday for sacking an immensely successful CEO after he had led SKSML through a spectacular IPO is another case in point. There have been some cases of institutional nominee directors being offered stock options[179] and this creates a conflict of interest. Also, oftentimes, nominee directors are very keen on enhancing loan off take by the MFI from their parent institutions. This again creates a huge conflict of interest, especially if the MFI is a large one and has the potential to become an important borrower (client) for the parent lending institution (which could be a bank or DFI).

e. *Lack of transparent reporting to the outside world.*[180] The case of Sahayata Microfinance is a good example here but there are many more. And what makes the case of Sahayata very interesting is the fact that Ajay Verma, its MD (who was subsequently suspended[181]) was a board member of MFIN

---

175 Quoted from "Microfinance at a Crossroads—The Need for Social Equity" by Jan Postmus, unpublished paper (2010), Page 15, Box 1: The Case of SHARE.

176 SKS Microfinance: Promoters got the better of poor women borrowers (http://articles.economictimes.indiatimes.com/2011-01-31/news/28423452_1_sks-microfinance-poor-women-trust-deed), by John Samuel Raja D and M Rajshekhar, *The Economic Times*, January 31, 2011.

177 Institutional nominee directors.

178 The case of Suresh Gurumani given earlier in point a.

179 I am not sure that the nominating institution concerned has permitted them to take the options. An RTI query to ascertain this can be filed and I can provide specific details if someone is interested in doing so.

180 The case of Sahayata Microfinance is a good example here but there are many more.

181 See Award winning Sahayata Microfinance is the latest to go astray (http://moneylife.in/article/award-winning-sahayata-microfinance-is-the-latest-to-go-astray/21549.html), by Ramesh S Arunachalam November 18, 2011.

## Chapter 12: Does a Five-Star Board Always Guarantee Good Corporate Governance?

and he had preached the following at the Microfinance India Summit 2010[182] at the height of the AP crisis. Speaking at that summit, Mr Verma touched on three themes:

"1) *Managing multiple lending:* He said that multiple lending can only be managed if organizations themselves drive their credit policy very hard. He said the key is to have a (good) credit policy, adhere to it and build systems to check that the credit policy is working. He also stated that the proposed industry efforts for a credit bureau will help reduce multiple lending. And he also argued that the high (annual) growth of 100–300% can be better managed if multiple lending is managed as this will then taper down the growth.

2) *Have engagement at all levels:* Here he stressed employee engagement through good training—where there would be emphasis of organizational core values and code of conduct— within the institution. He said that MFIs (microfinance institutions) must have a strong and solid agenda to engage with their employees as it is employees who can create engaged customers. He also said that customer engagement must be absolutely transparent and they must be given complete information on products, charges, fees, etc. He cautioned that it would not be enough to merely provide information to customers but rather more importantly" to ensure that they understand various facts clearly. For this, he said that engagement through financial literacy would be necessary so that low-income clients are educated on the dangers of debt trap and the need to invest borrowed money in income generation ventures. He further stressed for open engagement with the local authorities, stakeholders, and funders so that information can flow transparently to them.

3) *Focus on product innovation:* He said that 99% of the industry is on a single product and he said that a life-cycle approach must be used to have product innovation. He argued for starting with basic loan and as client income grows, he suggested that MFIs look at education loans, housing loans, etc."

What makes his case even more interesting is the fact that reputed consulting institutions *used him to promote concepts like various kinds of audit. See Video*[183] *and transcripts of the same, which are given here:*

"The Internal Audit (IA) function is designed to check, whether the internal controls in the MFI are functioning as intended? Internal controls are designed to provide reasonable assurance regarding the efficiency and effectiveness of operations, the reliability and completeness of financial and operational information, and the compliance with applicable laws and regulations.

---

182  Source: http://www.youtube.com/watch?v=OZ3JLwXR-Mw and What is said at conferences is very different from what is implemented in practice.
(http://www.moneylife.in/article/what-is-said-at-conferences-is-very-different-from-what-is-implemented-in-practice/22124.html), by Ramesh S Arunachalam December 12, 2011 and http://www.moneylife.in/article/award-winning-sahayata-microfinance-is-the-latest-to-go-astray/21549.html, by Ramesh S Arunachalam November 18, 2011.
183  The same came be provided if it is not available at the link specified—Source: http://www.youtube.com/watch?v=ChKgQrDQUk8

*Ajay Verma, CEO, and Sahayata:* In terms of internal audit and controls, you need to very clearly define what is auditable and what is not auditable. Like what we have done, we have three types of audit. One is the process of audit which happens in the field, then second is the branch audit. We audit all the branch documentation, which the loan officers have to do and the branch manager has to do; and third one is the cash and the finance audit which happens on the branch and the head office levels."[184]

That he did not practice what he preached is very clear from the fact that he was suspended in November 2011 for various aspects including data misrepresentation, false reporting and the like.[185]

f. *Manipulation of processes regarding board functioning.* Look at this e-mail conversation between a director of the board in a large NBFC MFI and its managing director. The mail was supposedly received on Wednesday, September 23, 2009.

"I noticed something in the AGM notice that I had not seen before and specifically raised it to person YYY. The agenda item is a supposed discussion on a NNN year contract for ZZZ person (to be filed with GoI for concurrence) and that this was approved by the compensation committee, on which I also happen to sit. I spoke with CCC and BBB, both of whom are members of the same committee with regard to this and they have absolutely no recollection of such a proposal. Hence, I have asked for some clarification on this and I also thought that I should also keep you posted of the various happenings."[186]

The same director further wrote (Wednesday, September 23, 2009):

"I am sure there is a reason behind it but it was not something some of us had seen before. Prior to your joining, there was pattern of resolutions and other matters being placed in the Board minutes, EGM resolutions, and AGM resolutions that were not discussed etc.. Mr. YYYYYYYYYY, among others, had issues with this. Seeing this matter in the minutes reminded me of this issue. As you would agree, we must adhere to the highest standards of corporate governance and so issues that have not been fully vetted or discussed should not be put into the minutes just for the purposes of administrative convenience. Either we should be better prepared for this meeting or we should schedule a separate meeting etc...

My only point is that we should discuss things before they go into official minutes or documents. If not, at least send an explanatory note which explains the background behind the proposal. I do not believe that the explanation you are providing was highlighted to us nor was it provided in the document."

---

184 Source: http://www.youtube.com/watch?v=ChKgQrDQUk8.
185 Award winning Sahayata Microfinance is the latest to go astray (http://moneylife.in/article/award-winning-sahayata-microfinance-is-the-latest-to-go-astray/21549.html), by Ramesh S Arunachalam November 18, 2011.
186 Names have been withheld as the idea is not to embarrass any individual MFI; but the original e-mail can be provided if required!

g. *Nontransparency in process of allotment of shares/options.* The process of allotment of shares to SKS Microfinance Private Limited managing director (Vikram Akula) and its pricing has been commented upon by Prof. Sriram:

> "In 2007, the founder was allotted shares worth Rs. 1.6 crore at par; all other employees together were allotted shares worth Rs. 81.8 lakhs (about half of what the founder received) in an employee share purchase scheme (ESPS). On the same day other investors, including the investors of the first tranche paid Rs. 49.77 per share. What appears even more unusual is the fact that SKS Microfinance lent founder an interest-free loan of Rs. 1.6 crore to purchase shares in the same company. This allotment of shares was outside of the ESPS – a special allotment. In 18 months from getting this allotment, he sold them out for a price of Rs. 103.91 – a gain of Rs. 15 crore on an investment (financed by an interest-free loan from the same company) of Rs. 1.6 crore. This is followed by a stock option allotted under the employee stock option plan (ESOP) of 2007 exercised in the month of December 2009 and sold in February 2010 (in the run up to the filing of the DRHP). The exercise of options was at a price of Rs. 49.77 per share, while the sale to Treeline Asia Master Fund was at a price of around Rs. 636 per share indicating a profit of around Rs. 55 crore in about three months."[187]

See the following that is a supposed apparent rejoinder (from SKS Chairman in 2010) to Prof. Sriram's articles and this was circulated by Sa-Dhan[188] through e-mail:

> "The allotment of shares to Vikram in March 2007 was not a sudden decision but had been agreed and approved by shareholders and the Board a year earlier in March 2006. Although Vikram's share allotment was approved and documented—and originally intended to be an Employee Stock Option Plan (ESOP) to take effect back in March 2006-the final form of the allotment was finalized, based on tax advice from KPMG, as an Employee Share Purchase Scheme (ESPS) -- a legally permissible variant of an ESOP - in March 2007. There was no discount. Over the course of the year, as SKS grew and strengthened, the value of shares rose from Rs. 10 to Rs. 49 by March 2007, when the second round of investment took place. It was 18 months after that Vikram sold his shares at Rs. 103.91, a full 30 months after the initial allocation at Rs. 10 per share. The increase in value of the shares was the result of the stellar performance of SKS."

The following concerns need to be flagged, with regard to the allotment process:

- *Issues of discrepancy in the process:* It seems necessary to better understand the whole process in terms of what was approved: (i) in the board, and (ii) by the shareholders, and compare the same

---

187 Source: Quoted from "Commercialization of Microfinance in India: A Discussion of the Emperor's Apparel" by Prof. M. S. Sriram, *Economic and Political Weekly* (EPW) June 12, 2010–Vol: XLV No: 24.
188 This was an unsigned note and was mentioned by Sa-Dhan as a rejoinder sent by the then SKS chairman Mr Gurcharan Das.

with filings done with the Registrar of Companies (ROC) as there seem to be discrepancies. The DRHP is replete with discrepancies[189] on the share allotments.

- *Concerns with ESOPs:* It appears that all approvals were for ESOPs to be issued to Dr Akula and others like Mr Rao, the COO, in February 2007. However, in reality, it is clear that ESPS were issued to Mr Rao and shares were issued to Dr Akula.[190] The question is how could this be done when the approval was for ESOPs? Therefore, a clear legal view on whether there were any discrepancies would be required, especially because the shares allotted to Dr Akula were fully sold out while those given to Mr Rao had been partially liquidated (as at the time just prior to the IPO).

- *Concerns with ESPS:* It appears that the company had a scheme where employees would be issued shares when they join, which were to be vested over a period of four years. The company was to give a loan to a trust, which was to lend the same money to employees to buy these shares. In turn, the employee would enter into a financing arrangement with the trust and the company. Under this, the shares would be directly either freshly allotted to the employee or, in the event of any available shares in the pool, they would be transferred to the employee's name. This arrangement of giving any amount of loan and allotting or transferring the shares directly in the name of the employee may be in contravention of Section 77(3) of the Companies Act.[191] As per this section, shares cannot be allotted in the employee's name directly and the loan amount cannot exceed six months' salary of the employee. It is not clear if the company was violating these conditions, but this has to be looked into, both from perspective of the Companies Act and the extant NBFC regulations.

*Another instance* concerns a large NBFC and its ESPS (employees' stock purchase scheme) agreements with employees. This event apparently occurred in September 2009.

The last page in the ESPS agreement[192] with several employees was supposedly changed because the auditors suddenly noticed (in September 2009) that payments from employees were due by end

---

189 A set of shareholders (MUC, SKS Capital, and Mr Vinod Khosla—each 1,319,069 equity shares along with Odyssey Capital Private Limited—894,064 equity shares and SCI II—5,430,468 equity shares) came into the company on March 29, 2007, as mentioned in one place in the DRHP. At another place in the DRHP, the same set of shareholders is shown to have come on board on March 31, 2007. Either way, the fact is that this set of shareholders could not have participated in the key decision making in the company during 2006–2007.

190 The rejoinder from SKS notes that the founder's share allotment was originally approved and documented to be an Employee Stock Option Plan (ESOP), whereas, in reality, the final form of allotment was through the ESPS—see quote attached—*"Although Vikram's share allotment was approved and documented—and originally intended to be an Employee Stock Option Plan (ESOP) to take effect back in March 2006—the final form of the allotment was finalized, based on tax advice from KPMG, as an Employee Share Purchase Scheme (ESPS)—a legally permissible variant of an ESOP—in March 2007."* (Unsigned Sa-Dhan Circulated Rejoinder Note), supposedly from the then SKS chairman Mr Gurcharan Das.

191 The section also says that, "provided that nothing in this subsection shall be taken to prohibit, the making by a company of loans, within the limit laid down in subsection (3), to persons (other than directors, or managers) bona fide in the employment of the company with a view to enabling those persons to purchase or subscribe for fully paid shares in the company or its holding company to be held by themselves by way of beneficial ownership." Subsection (3) states that, "No loan made to any person in pursuance of clause of the foregoing proviso shall exceed in amount his salary or wages at that time for a period of six months."

192 See Appendix 10.

## Chapter 12: Does a Five-Star Board Always Guarantee Good Corporate Governance?

March 2009 and had not been deducted and/or collected. However, because they did not notice it until September 2009 (when they would have had to list it as an overdue), the last page of several such agreements was supposedly changed to reflect a new (future) due date for repayment of the ESPS loans owed (to the trust) by the various employees. This enabled the ESPS loans to be not shown as an overdue.

Yet another instance concerns a laundry list,[193] provided by a member of the senior management team to the MD of a large NBFC MFI. As evident from this exhibit, these were violations in a large supposedly well-governed company with a solid five-star board. God alone can imagine what corporate governance violations exist in other NBFC MFIs that (supposedly) did not have five-star boards.

h. *Insufficient transparency about the (MFIs/group's) operational strategies and overall financial position.* The turbocharging of growth and tweaking of MFI performance through multiple, over-lending and ghost lending to attract equity investment at a premium and build wealth for the promoters, directors, senior management, shareholders, and so on (the available evidence seems to suggest this) is a case in point here. Several researchers have provided evidence toward the presence of multiple lending and MFI financial statements have themselves admitted nonexistent clients and ghost lending.[194] For example, see the 2011 financial statement of SKS Microfinance (where the auditors claim that frauds due to nonexistent clients and clients with false identity run into crores). Also, see the following quotation that lends credence to this fact:

> "That (following sound lending practices) is where we failed," says Sajeev Viswanathan, CEO of Basix, which is an MFI. "MFIs lent liberally to individuals who didn't have the corresponding ability to repay. The mismatch had to hurt sometime..."[195]

The cornerstone of this argument is essentially this. Many (NBFC) MFIs engaged in multiple and over-lending for consumption purposes and they often granted loans without assessing the loan absorption capacity of the clients. Implied in this statement is the fact that these MFIs have pushed loans indiscriminately to low-income clients for consumption purposes without any sensitivity to their debt-servicing ability and they tried to grow (quickly) in this manner and make unnatural profits.

Again, as with the above, it is more and more clear that these (NBFC) MFIs (perhaps) tried to grow fast (with high profitability) to attract capital at high valuations and, thereafter, had to justify these high valuations by providing better returns to investors. And investors likewise, as they had paid huge premiums, wanted to recover their investment fast and perhaps pushed these MFIs to grow faster.

---

193 See Appendix 11.
194 Refer to the following link for an overview of frauds in microfinance: http://microfinance-in-india.blogspot.com/2010/11/has-burgeoning-growth-caused-increasing.html and a later chapter on the same topic.
195 "Microfinance: What's wrong with it," by M Rajshekhar, *The Economic Times*, (November 11, 2010).

Therefore, as illustrated in the chart, there appears to have been a mutually reinforcing cycle of multiple/over-lending/ghost lending, fast growth, high profits, very high share valuation, equity investments, faster growth, greater profits, more returns, turbocharged growth, and so on. *And the onus for all of this perhaps lies with the manner in which many of these NBFC MFIs were being (mis)governed.*

**Figure 12.1 Mutually Reinforcing Cycle of MFI Growth**

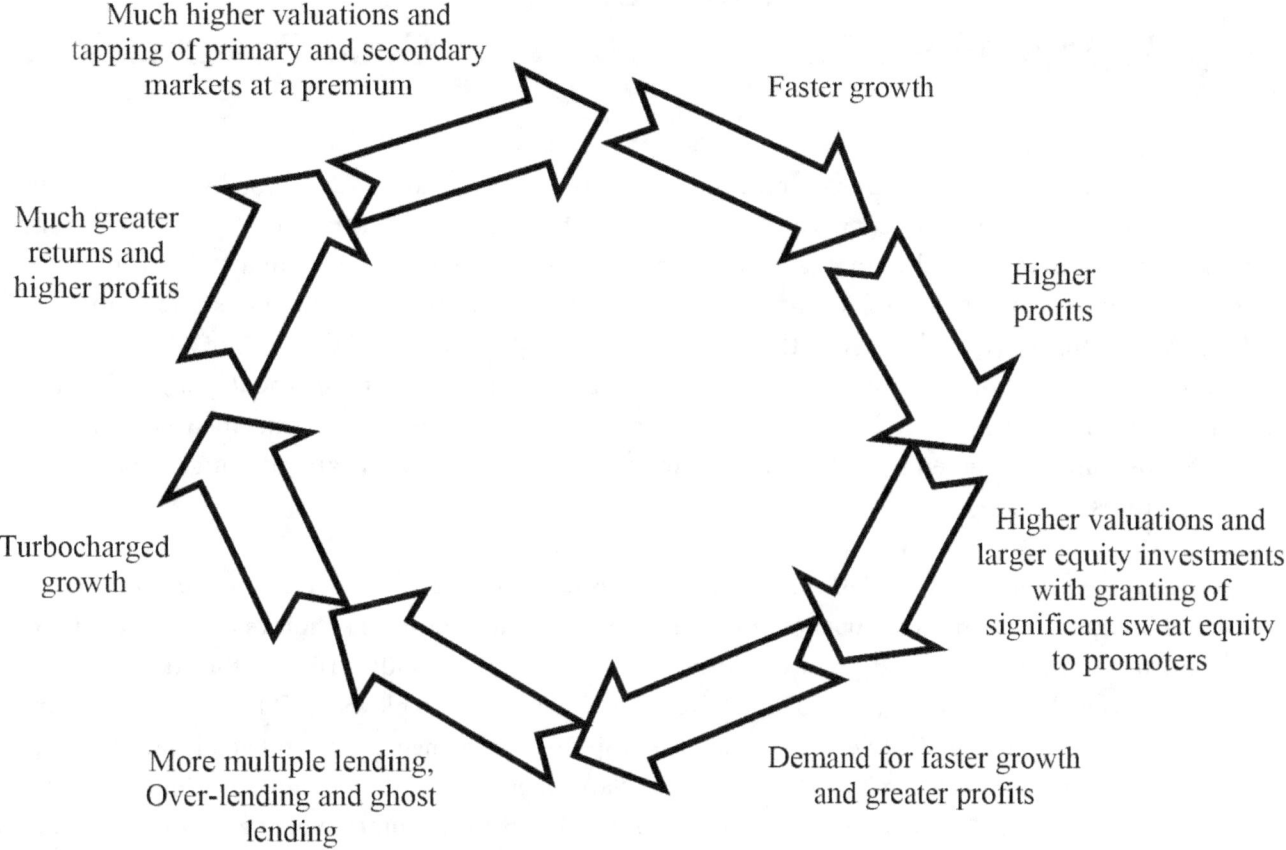

Therefore, with the mere presence of a five-star board, it cannot be assumed that there is good corporate governance at the MFI. The regulatory architecture must provide sufficient incentives for facilitating good corporate governance, while at the same time creating disincentives for bad governance. *This point needs strong emphasis and needs to be noted by all stakeholders including those developing the regulatory architecture for Indian microfinance.*

# Chapter 13:
# Can Independent Directors Promote Good Governance?

What is really interesting to note is that all of the corporate governance violations listed in the earlier chapter happened despite the concerned (NBFC) MFI boards having so-called strong institutional[196] representation on their boards. For example, a senior officer of a development finance institution[197] was part of the board that sanctioned an interest-free loan to the promoter for buying shares in the same (NBFC) MFI. This was also the case with the board[198] that suddenly sacked the CEO of a large MFI after awarding him a huge bonus earlier. *Therefore, using board membership as a surrogate for good corporate governance is fraught with danger.* I hope that credit rating companies do not continue to use this in the future as the damage created by the use of this inappropriate surrogate is already huge, as the Satyam saga, illustrates.

> **"Satyam's five-star board of directors—as onlookers liked to call it—had just the right number of independent directors with just the right credentials, eminent scholars and administrators.** Also, Satyam had PricewaterhouseCoopers (one of the big four audit firms) as the statutory auditor. All was well with Satyam's world, or so everyone thought. ...Two blows dealt to the company's image within a span of one month ended Satyam's high-prized innocence, the fateful and insane board decision taken on 16th December, 2008, and then Satyam chairman Mr Ramalinga Raju's confession of false invoicing of 7th January 2009. ...Never in the history of corporate India has a company fallen so hard and so fast. And everyone, from investors to experts, attributes this to the failure of the company's corporate governance controls. In fact, all events surrounding the scam (the aborted Maytas bid, the World Bank barring the company from all bank contracts) were being linked to the way Satyam was governed."[199]

---

196 SIDBI normally appointed nominee directors to boards of MFIs that it invested in (in terms of debt, quasi-equity and equity).
197 SIDBI's nominee director was on the board of SKS Microfinance Private Limited in 2006–2007.
198 The board of SKSML met on October 3, 2010 to sack its highly successful MD Suresh Gurumani.
199 "The Satyam Saga" by Bhubesh Bhandari, Prashanth Reddy Chintala, Vandana Gombar, Latha Jishnu, Shyamal Majumdar and Aanand Pandey, (2009), *Business Standard Publication*.

Now, when one considers the (huge) volume of money[200] being intermediated by many of the (NBFC) MFIs and given that much of this money comes from the banking system in India (and, therefore, are in some ways, public deposits), *corporate governance becomes a very important aspect and in fact that is where the buck really stops.* Whether multiple lending, or client harassment, or ghost lending, or coercive recovery, the onus is on the board of directors in MFIs, who are ultimately responsible for all of this and more, as part of their corporate governance obligations. We need to be clear on that!

In fact, currently there is no serious guiding corporate governance framework for nonlisted MFIs[201] and this includes many of the (NBFC) MFIs as well. To the best of my knowledge, the RBI circular on corporate governance for NBFCs, although issued in May 2007, is yet to be fully implemented (on the ground) in terms of many provisions (such as loans to directors and similar related-party transactions). Therefore, it becomes absolutely necessary to build safeguards against governance weaknesses and failures, such as those described in the earlier chapter by providing adequate and workable corporate governance directives. *And I sincerely hope that the various stakeholders involved in developing a new and robust regulatory architecture for microfinance—the RBI,* which is supposedly preparing detailed guidelines for NBFC MFIs based on the Malegam Committee Report as mentioned in its circular dated May 11, 2011, *the Parliamentary Standing Committee on Finance (PSCF),* to whom the Microfinance Regulation and Development Bill, 2012, has been referred, and *the Union Ministry of Finance,* which is engaged in promoting access to finance for excluded and low-income people—*do take these critical aspects into consideration.*

That said, while it is always easy to provide directives for good corporate governance, a second and more crucial issue that must be considered by the above stakeholders is how to ensure the implementation of these guidelines on the ground. *That is a critical aspect and one where the so-called independent directors (including nominee directors) will have to play a major and catalytic role.* In fact, the very premise of good corporate governance hinges on the ability of independent and nominee directors to act impartially, objectively and with prudence, keeping in mind the overall vision of the MFI and its duty to all of its shareholders.

And sadly, this did not happen in the microfinance sector in India, as independent directors in many of the (NBFC) MFIs lacked accountability and true independence in their functioning. Some of them were even compensated for by way of stock options and the like—instruments that compromised their independent functioning. Further, as many of them owed their appointments to the promoters/CEOs, this perhaps seriously limited their ability to function independently. Strangely, even directors nominated by institutional investors were quiet and, sometimes, they did not even write a dissent note when the board norms and procedures were seriously violated. As an aside, it must be noted that the current procedures adopted by institutional investors to ensure the accountability (and effective functioning) of their nominee directors, also appear rather weak. I will not get into the specifics, but there are numerous examples of situations (at MFIs) that could have been salvaged, had the independent (and nominee) directors acted

---

200 We are talking of over Rs. 20,000 crore and this is no small amount. Also, because much of this money comes from the banking system, these funds are, in many ways, public deposits. Therefore, safeguarding them becomes very important.

201 Neither are the SEBI directives on Corporate Governance followed in letter and spirit—as the case of the Ramalinga Raju-led Satyam Computers Ltd has strongly demonstrated.

independently and truly in the interest of the (minority) shareholders. The fact of the matter is that the image of microfinance has taken a beating and this could have been avoided if only the independent and nominee directors had acted in a fair and swift manner.

Never mind, and let bygones be bygones. But going forward, the various stakeholders involved in building a regulatory architecture for microfinance in India, would do well to ensure that there are clear regulatory (supervisable) standards with regard to appointment, roles, compensation, and evaluation of independent directors, so that corporate governance in MFIs does not exist merely on paper. This is one place where the regulatory reform for responsible microfinance could begin in right earnest. *The various specific issues that would have to be looked into by them are highlighted here:*

- ✓ *Practice of CEO hiring board/independent directors in many MFIs*: First, in many MFIs, the promoter who is (often) also the CEO hires the board and this practice needs to be questioned from the perspective of implementing corporate governance directives on the ground. The key question here is whether a board hired by the promoter/CEO (of an MFI) can really be independent in terms of its functioning? And the related issue is how such boards can be expected to perform the roles that they are supposed to in terms of safeguarding the interests of various stakeholders, including minority shareholders. So, this is an aspect worthy of regulatory attention, especially given the peculiar aspect of promoters being CEOs in many MFIs.

- ✓ *Definition of an independent director*: Second, there is lack of clarity on who is an independent director in terms of objective criteria such as age, expertise, and experience (especially related to microfinance) as well as having had past relationships with the same MFI (which can result in significant conflicts of interest). Therefore, regulatory guidelines[202] regarding the definition of independent directors would be very useful.

- ✓ *Appointment of independent directors*: Third, it seems appropriate to vest the powers of appointment of new, independent and executive directors in board nomination committees (at MFIs), which must hereafter become a mandatory requirement for all types of MFIs. These committees should follow a transparent process and lay down clear steps and criteria for selecting board members. Further, an independent director must chair the board nomination committee so that 'truly' independent candidates are hired to the MFI board, and the climate for their 'real' independent functioning is ensured. This is another aspect that could be looked into as part of the ongoing work to create a regulatory architecture for microfinance.

- ✓ *Time spent by independent directors on work at MFIs*: Fourth, is the issue of whether the independent directors should be mandated to spend a certain minimum time on work at the MFI and

---

202 See Appendix 12 for some ideas.

especially, in the field at the grassroots. As an industry observer argues that *'independent directors should be made to devote a certain minimum number of hours every quarter (or regular period) so as to understand the business of microfinance and gain insights about the MFIs in which they are serving as directors. This will enable them to examine the risks being taken and the appetite of their MFI to take such risks as well as understand and provide guidance on other strategic aspects, as may be required.'* This again could be looked into as part of the regulatory architecture being developed.

- ✓ *Number of MFI boards on which an independent director can serve concurrently*: Fifth, a related aspect is the amount of time spent by independent directors on board meetings at MFIs annually. When there are people who, at any one point in time, serve as independent directors on several MFI boards, the quality of directorship is naturally likely to suffer. This is especially true of microfinance. It may therefore be appropriate for the *regulatory architecture*[203] to recommend a threshold level for the number of MFIs in which people (professionals) could serve as independent directors. This is a very critical aspect indeed.

- ✓ *Peer appraisal of independent directors must be made mandatory*: Sixth, peer appraisal of independent directors is an option for enhancing their effectiveness in working, and this, again, needs to be examined from the perspective of independent directors in MFIs. While such an appraisal process would need to be managed with associated sensitivities, board members should also view this as an opportunity for continuous learning and improvement. Traditional methods of evaluation (in terms of share valuations/prices and strategy initiatives) would perhaps need to be augmented by a formal and objective appraisal of the independent directors' performance with regard to governance (in terms of various parameters). Such an appraisal should enable identification of gaps in governance, enhance the decision-making process and improve effectiveness of board meetings and various processes at the MFI. This is also an aspect that could be looked at, in the context of MFIs by the concerned stakeholders.

- ✓ *Capacity building of first-time (independent) directors*: Seventh, another critical area often ignored is the need for continuous education programmes for independent directors, especially for entry or first-time (independent) directors. This is critical for microfinance, which is a nascent field, and especially, if we have to ensure that the same people do not serve on the boards of too many MFIs (as this also creates a conflict of interest). This capacity-building support could be offered through IIMs, or College of Agricultural Banking, or other appropriate institutions. This is a critical issue and should be examined as part of the mandate to develop a robust regulatory framework for microfinance in India, which is still lacking.

---

[203] *Microfinance* Institutions *(Development and Regulation) Bill and other such efforts like RBI detailed guidelines for MFIs, the Union Ministry of Finance's (MoF's) financial inclusion initiatives and the like.*

## Chapter 13: Can Independent Directors Promote Good Governance?

✓ *Compensation of independent directors*: Eighth, the compensation of independent directors is a critical issue and there have been a lot of controversies[204] in recent years. Surely, there must be guidelines for the same so that the real independence of the independent directors is not compromised under any circumstances. One option would be to entrust this task to the board nomination committee and ensure that the promoters/CEOs do not interfere in setting and implementing norms of compensation for independent directors. While there could be other strategies, I think this is one of the most important issues that the regulatory architecture would need to address.

✓ *Protecting client interests on the MFI board*: Last, but not the least, the stakeholders should also examine whether there could be specially designated independent directors, representing client interests. We have directors in banks representing staff interest and the same could be done in microfinance to safeguard client interests. This is especially crucial in MFIs that have and use the Mutual Benefit Trust (MBT) structure, which is indeed a client owned body—recall that there have been many issues with regard to governance of MBTs in the past[205] and the extent to which their interests are being protected in the boards of MFIs. This should most certainly be explored as part of the process of building a regulatory architecture for microfinance and suitable recommendations should also be provided for practical implementation. Similar to compensation, this is an important issue in MFI governance.

Thus, while enhancing the quality of independent directors would surely enhance governance, there is also a right mindset aspect that we should not forget. As Mr Kris Gopalakrishnan,[206] Infosys, once said,

> "We may not be able to eliminate corporate frauds altogether. No amount of regulation will help to stop frauds. At the end of the day, corporate governance is a mindset issue. We need stricter, stronger and quick enforcement of law by regulatory agencies so that it will act as a deterrent for others."[207]

> Other observers agree. "As a rule rather than exception, MFIs need to practice good governance in order to sustain in *the long run. And for this, promoters and senior management must practice good governance at all times including, when faced with the most difficult of situations."*

---

204 See 'Share Microfin MD takes home Rs. 7.4 cr, more than double HDFC Bank MD's salary' by John Samuel Raja D & M Rajshekhar, *The Economic Times*, February 1, 2011. See Chapter 20 for more details.

205 See Chapter 8. Also refer to Chapter 12. Also see SKS Microfinance: Promoters got the better of poor women borrowers (http://articles.economictimes.indiatimes.com/2011-01-31/news/28423452_1_sks-microfinance-poor-women-trust-deed), by John Samuel Raja D and M Rajshekhar, *The Economic Times*, January 31, 2011.

206 Mr Kris Gopalakrishnan was then the CEO of Infosys.

207 Quoted from The Satyam Saga by Bupesh Bhandari, Prashanth Reddy Chintala, Vandana Gombar, Latha Jishnu, Shyamal Majumdar and Aanand Pandey, (2009), *Business Standard Publication*.

Therefore, while practicing good governance at all times is certainly a mindset issue, the least we can do is to incentivize good governance and, perhaps, penalize bad governance, and do this consistently and without fear or favor. For this, we need a practical guiding (regulatory and supervisory) framework pertaining to appointment, roles, responsibilities and compensation of independent directors in MFIs as noted earlier. And mind you, this is something that the Indian microfinance sector desperately needs as it is rather low on its governance quotient, because of the 2010 AP crisis and events related to the commercialization of Indian microfinance. So, this is yet another place where regulatory reform could begin to usher in responsible microfinance. Otherwise, the NBFCs (MFIs included) will simply get away by perhaps appointing all and sundry and "yes" men/women to the board—and then governance will sadly falter, despite the presence of even the so-called independent directors.

You may wonder why I have dwelt so much on the topic of independent directors. One of the most critical reasons for the importance attached to the topic of independent directors in any organization (including MFIs) relates to conflicts of interest. There are several issues here: (i) Conflicts of interest hinder judgment and affect decision making; (ii) judgment and decision making are what directors are asked to do; and (iii) directors must feel free to think, express, question, and decide in the interest of those they represent. And all of these apply very much to microfinance institutions as well who, during the past few years, have received a lot of (negative) publicity with regard to corporate governance, conflicts of interest and the role of independent directors on their boards.

In fact, the debate has now widened to encompass not only the roles of independent directors but also that of nominee directors from financial institutions, and several questions continue to be raised regarding real and potential conflicts of interest on the ground. For example, what was the nominee director of SIDBI on the board of SKS Microfinance Private Limited doing when an interest-free loan was provided to the founder MD to buy shares in the same company? There are other examples as well and perhaps all of these happened because of serious conflicts of interest[208] that existed on the ground with even the nominee institutional directors.

So, where does that leave us? I offer some ideas with regard to nominee directors and hope that the regulatory architecture issues some guidelines for lenders and others who appoint nominee directors on the boards of MFIs.

First, the aspect of appointing nominee directors must be streamlined and institutionalized. A separate department (or cell) must be created[209] for this purpose with a high-ranking official (at least at the

---

208 Imagine that you are the nominee director of a lender DFI and you suddenly start thinking as follows, "Gosh, I better not say anything against these wrong (board) practices as otherwise, it could result in my parent (lending) institution, whose interests I represent, losing out on a large NBFC MFI borrower." This is a classic conflict of interest issue. In fact, going by past experiences, some of the key issues here that need regulatory attention are: (i) Does a board need to have clear guidelines with regard to conflicts of interest that must be disclosed? (ii) Who discloses conflicts? (iii) To whom are conflicts disclosed? (iv) What happens if conflicts are not disclosed? (v) What if conflicts are disclosed later? (vi) What if all is not disclosed to the board and/or to shareholders? It would be very useful if the regulatory architecture explores these issues as well.

209 Or any existing department can be given this responsibility.

level of chief general manager or equivalent) at the helm. And nominee directors should be appointed on the boards of all systemically important MFIs and especially NBFC MFIs who are clients of the bank/DFI and have a gross loan portfolio outstanding greater than Rs. 100 crore. The nominee directors should exclusively represent their institutions on the boards of MFIs and must be staff from this institution and not less than a deputy general manager or equivalent by rank. This way, the work of nominee directors will become an integral part of the overall operations. The proposed department/cell should function like any other department of the bank with normal rotation of officers and the like. Outsiders may be appointed as nominee directors to boards of MFIs only as additional directors on MFI boards, wherein, because of the strategic importance and/or larger portfolio of the MFI concerned, the bank/DFI may aspire to have more than one nominee director.

Second, in terms of the officials who are to be nominee directors, at no time should any of them serve on the boards of more than three MFIs. Also, none of the nominee directors should have had a past (working or lending) relationship (for at least three years) with the MFIs on whose boards they are to serve. Microfinance is not rocket science and it should not be difficult for the nominee directors to gain reasonable expertise within 6 months or so through field visits at the MFIs concerned and other capacity-enhancing mechanisms. Of course, as a prerequisite, these nominee directors could be exposed to contemporary microfinance knowledge through available courses such as at the College of Agricultural Banking, Pune, and other institutions as appropriate.

Third, an important issue that is relevant here is that banks (or, for that matter, DFIs such as SIDBI), by nominating directors on the boards of MFIs, are giving tremendous legitimacy to the concerned MFI. In other words, apart from the quantum of loans given and/or investments made, the real additionality of their board participation lies in associating their well-established and highly regarded brand name with the concerned MFIs. Therefore, the nominee directors are under serious obligation to diligently perform their roles as directors in a professional and objective manner. And this is where we should not forget the fact that SIDBI's nominee director remained a mute spectator when the founder-promoter-managing director of a large MFI gave himself a huge loan to buy shares (at par value) in the same MFI. That the SIDBI nominee director again remained silent at the hurriedly convened board meeting of a large MFI, that too on a Sunday, to sack an immensely successful CEO who had led the MFI through a spectacular IPO, is again worrisome. These remain causes for great concern and are certainly not acceptable in any financial institution. They are unquestionably acts of not-so-good governance.

Fourth, while I can cite many more such instances where SIDBI's nominee directors turned a blind eye to the not-so-good governance and operational practices of several MFIs, the idea is not to single out SIDBI and/or blame them.[210] Let bygones be bygones, but the key point is that we should learn the lessons and make necessary changes. Thus, as representatives of banks (or other lenders), nominee directors are expected to ensure good governance and transparent operations of the MFIs on whose boards they serve. This, in turn, necessitates that banks (or other lenders): (i) establish a

---

210 They have done a lot of good work in microfinance but that does not absolve them of their responsibility in the 2010 AP microfinance crisis.

transparent and effective process of appointing nominee directors to MFIs; and (ii) have appropriate mechanisms for ensuring accountability of these directors including disincentives for irresponsible behavior and/or nonperformance.

Fifth, this also means that nominee directors should be given clearly identified responsibilities in a few areas that are important for public policy. The illustrative lists of these are: (i) financial performance of the MFI; (ii) payment of dues to lenders, governments, and other institutions; (iii) payment of government-tax-related dues—and where the MFI feels that a particular tax demand is unjustified, nominee directors should satisfy themselves about the *prima facie* reasonableness of the MFIs' case before action is recommended by the board; (iv) inter-corporate/group investment in and loans to or from associated companies, concerns and/or related parties in which the promoter group and/or senior management have significant interest; (v) all transactions in shares of any kind; (vi) expenditure being incurred by the company on management group including total cost to MFI; and (vii) policies relating to the award of contracts and purchases/sales of a significant amount.

Sixth, the nominee directors should also ensure that the tendencies of many MFIs toward inefficiency, extravagance, lavish expenditure, and diversion of funds are curbed. With a view to achieve this objective, the banks/lenders should also necessitate that the MFIs concerned have a formal audit subcommittee of the board of directors for the purpose of periodic assessment of expenditure incurred by the MFI. Their institutional nominee director will invariably have to be a member of these audit subcommittees.

Thus, while it is indeed welcome that banks and DFIs are now participating more on the boards of MFIs, they must (however) use their position and leverage to ensure good governance, transparent and efficient operations, and client responsiveness at the MFIs concerned. If that happens, we can surely begin to see light at the end of the long microfinance tunnel in India. This again is a task that can be appropriately structured and implemented through regulatory reform.

*Connected lending:* While on the topic of conflicts of interest, let us look at connected lending. Consider yourself as an institutional/retail investor in a micro-lender and you may have bought equity because you believe that MFIs provide access to finance for low-income people and enable them to have a better life. Alternatively, you could be a development finance institution (DFI)/bank that has provided a loan to an NBFC MFI as part of the priority sector obligations and/or other schemes. Or you could be a multilateral or bilateral institution that seeks to improve the lot of excluded and disadvantaged people in an emerging market through development of the private (financial) sector using institutions such as NBFC MFIs. How would you react when you hear that one such NBFC MFI, where you have either invested your hard-earned money or lent priority sector funds, has, in turn, lent to its own founder managing director, a huge sum of money to buy shares in the same MFI and especially, at par value?

Unbelievable but true. Such a transaction did take place at a large Indian NBFC MFI.[211] The incident first came to light through Prof. M. S. Sriram's paper,[212] in the *Economic and Political Weekly* (June 2010),

---

211 SKS Microfinance Private Limited in 2006–2007.
212 Commercialization of Microfinance in India: A Discussion of the Emperor's Apparel by Prof. M. S. Sriram (*Economic and Political Weekly*, June 12, 2010, Vol XLV No. 24, Page 70).

## Chapter 13: Can Independent Directors Promote Good Governance?

which noted that SKS Microfinance Private Limited had lent its founder and managing director Vikram Akula a sum of Rs. 1.636 crore to enable him to buy shares in the same company. From a perusal of the published financial statements of this NBFC MFI, it is clear that an interest-free loan of Rs. 1.636 crore, was granted by the MFI [which was supposedly predominantly owned by the poor clients through several Mutual Benefit Trusts (MBTs) and also had key institutions as shareholders[213]] to its then managing director and promoter to buy shares at par value. (*Read relevant exhibit reproduced from the MFI's audited statements for the year ended March 2007.*)

**Exhibit 13.1 Reproduced Portion of Balance Sheet, Audited Statement 2007**

| B. Other Loans and Advances | 2007 | 2006 | |
|---|---|---|---|
| **Secured, considered good** | | | |
| Loans to Employees | 9,845,217 | 1,186,836 | |
| **Unsecured, considered good** | | | |
| Loans to Directors (Maximum amount outstanding Rs.16, 361,380 (Previous Year Rs. Nil) | 16,361,380 | - | 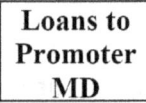 Loans to Promoter MD |
| Loans to SKS Microfinance Employees Benefit Trust (Refer Note 16 of Schedule 19) | 8,231,800 | - | |
| Advances Recoverable in Cash or Kind or Value to be received Deposits | 5,993,882 | 3,167,079 | |
| Deposits | 3,131,789 | 708,902 | |
| Advance Income Tax (Net of Provisions) | - | 2,358,551 | |
| Interest Accrued and Due | 746,319 | - | |
| Others | 25,545,195 | 3,135,669 | |
| **Unsecured, considered doubtful** | | | |
| Advances Recoverable in Cash or Kind or Value to be received | 1,099,692 | - | |
| Less: Provision for Doubtful Advances | (1,099,692) | - | |
| Total (B) | 69,855,582 | 10,557,037 | |
| Total (A+B) | 2,711,778,947 | 768,204,728 | |
| *Source*: SKS Audit Financial Statement March 2007, Schedule 8B, Page 12 | | | |

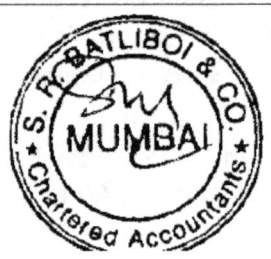

---

213 Development Finance Institutions.

Now, you may wonder whether this is legally permissible from the standpoint of corporate governance. In fact, I had a similar question and did some research on the matter and found that there is a Reserve Bank of India (RBI) circular that talks about this aspect of (not) providing credit facilities to the directors.[214] Specifically, the RBI circular on corporate governance for NBFCs, dated May 2007, states:

> "In order to obviate conflict of interest in the lending operations of the NBFC, it **should not grant any loan, advance or non-fund based facility or any other financial accommodation/facility** to: (a) its directors or their relatives; (b) to any firm in which any of its directors is interested as partner, manager, employee or guarantor; (c) any individual in respect of whom any of its directors is a guarantor; (d) any company of which, or the subsidiary or the holding company of which, any of the directors of the NBFC is a director, managing agent, manager, employee or guarantor, or any firm in which he holds substantial interest; and (d) any entity, whether incorporated or not, which uses as a part of its name or in connection with its business, the name of the NBFC or any such word as would show its association with the NBFC."

Likewise, further research led me to believe that the spirit of the Companies Act, 1956, typically prohibits companies from directly buying its own shares and/or indirectly financing its directors to buy the same. In the present case, it must be noted that the interest-free loan granted[215] to the promoter managing director was toward purchase of shares in the same company.

My views apart, as I got deeper into the legal aspects, I got to know an interesting aspect that the provisions relating to connected lending in the aforementioned RBI circular have been in abeyance[216] since July 11, 2007. Likewise, it appears that the concerned MFI also publicly stated (prior to its IPO) that there was nothing illegal in what it had done (insofar as the connected lending was concerned) and further that the said provisions of the Companies Act did not apply to private limited companies, which is what the NBFC MFI was when the said (connected lending) transaction took place.

Therefore, it seems prudent to conclude that as per the prevailing laws,[217] the connected lending that occurred at the NBFC MFI may not have been strictly illegal. However, I am not sure whether it is appropriate for a company—established, in the first place, *to provide access to finance to low-income and vulnerable people, and registered as an NBFC (with RBI) that was using public deposits (by way of*

---

214 RBI Guidelines on Corporate Governance 2007, kept in abeyance for some reason. The guidelines were not to be practiced until further notice from the RBI. This was as in July 2010.

215 It must also be noted that the loan amount was much larger than the total of six months of his (then listed) salary and apparently, this interest-free loan was also not administered through a trust. Likewise, it seems that the shares were also not issued in the name of the trust.

216 In fact, the circular on Corporate Governance (dated July 11, 2007) on the RBI site still contains the following with regard to 'connected lending': "The Bank has received suggestions in the matter with reference to paragraph 2 (vi) of the circular dated 28 May 2007 containing instructions on connected lending. The suggestions are being studied and the instructions contained in paragraph 2 (vi) of the said circular will become operational after final evaluation of the suggestions and modifications, if any considered necessary."

217 The concerned MFI has all along maintained that these provisions of the Companies Act did not apply to private limited companies, which is what the MFI was in 2006–2007.

*accessing priority sector bank loans)*—to lend to its promoter and managing director to enable him to buy shares in the same company at par value, without being seen as a "misgoverned" company. This is something that all of us need to take a call on.

**Exhibit 13.2 Notes to Related-party Transactions**

<u>b. Related Party Transactions</u>

|  | KEY Management Personnel ** | | Relatives of Key Management Personnel | | Entities holding Substantial Interest | |
|---|---|---|---|---|---|---|
|  | March 31, 2008 | March 31, 2007 | March 31, 2008 | March 31, 2007 | March 31, 2008 | March 31, 2007 |
| Issue of Equity Shares (including share premium) | - | 16,361,380 | - | - | 537,371,924 | 270,274,392 |
| Loans given # | - | 16,361,380 | - | - | - | - |
| Rent expense | - | - | 875,000 | 900,000 | - | - |
|  |  |  |  |  |  |  |
| **Balances as at year end** |  |  |  |  |  |  |
| Share Capital | 16,361,380 | 16,361,380 | - | - | 130,344,290 | 54,304,680 |
| Loan Balance Outstanding | - | 16,361,380 | - | - | - | - |
| Rent Payable | - | - | - | 63,525 | - | - |
| ** *Remuneration paid to Managing director is disclosed in note 12 below.* | | | | | | |
| # *Loans given to Key Management Personnel was interest free.* | | | | | | |
| *Source*: SKS Audited Financials, 2008, Auditor's Note No. 6. | | | | | | |

→ Identical Amounts of Loan and Investment

In my humble opinion, *granting of such a huge interest-free loan to a director* in a financial services company that is owned in majority by the poor clients in MBTs and DFIs (together, the MBTs and DFIs held 54% of the shares of the company then), and meant to service these poor clients in the first place, is not at all appropriate from a corporate governance perspective. Without question, this action of providing the loan to a director was certainly not, under any circumstance, in the interest of these shareholders, especially the minority (individual MBTs and/or individual women) shareholders. One can certainly put forth the argument that this may not have happened if there had been someone on the NBFC's board protecting the interest of the (minority) shareholders. *I am sure that whether an institutional/retail investor or a DFI/bank or a multi-/bilateral agency, you will certainly not approve of such connected lending transactions as examples of good practices in corporate governance.* In fact, the critical issue here is that this would have perhaps not happened if only the independent and nominee directors on the board of the concerned MFI had acted in a truly independent fashion.

Thus, without question, all of the issues mentioned in this chapter with regard to independent and nominee institutional directors need to be addressed in a fair manner through appropriate regulatory reform, and there can be no compromise with regard to that. And unless that is done, we will continue to see *colleagues, friends, associates, and relatives functioning as independent directors (with huge conflicts of interest)* and good corporate governance will remain an elusive dream. And if that happens, we could be making a 'blind date' with the next microfinance crisis (as the well-intentioned regulations will not be implemented on the ground) and responsible microfinance will continue to remain an illusion indeed!

# Chapter 14:
# What Can MFI Boards Do to Implement Corporate Governance in Practice?

While the earlier chapters highlighted corporate governance violations from the 2010 crisis with regard to (NBFC) MFIs and also outlined suggestions for stakeholders developing the regulatory architecture for microfinance, let us also remember that MFI boards can play a major role in fostering good governance on the ground.

*What then are the major issues that require the attention of MFI boards and what specific changes would be required?* These crucial aspects are dealt with hereafter.

First, a key requirement is for MFI boards to strike the right balance between independence and skills with regard to their directors. Boards will be able to effectively monitor senior management at MFIs provided their directors have the *skills, experience, time, willingness, objectivity, and independence* to do so. And this needs to be ensured in real time. An additional aspect here is that in order to safeguard the objectivity and independence of directors, it is imperative for the MFI to put in place clear policies for managing conflicts of interest. And given the diversity in MFI operations, directors must spend time in understanding the MFIs' specific operations so that institutional complexity does not come in the way of their effective functioning (an argument put forth by many so-called independent directors at MFIs during the 2010 AP crisis).

Second, it would be beneficial to review the level of *diversity* in the composition of MFI boards and ensure greater diversity (especially women, directors with different sociocultural and educational backgrounds, etc.). It is believed that diversity should contribute positively to the overall quality of the MFI board's actual working.

Third, in view of the increasing scale of MFI operations together with the enhanced complexity of microfinance activities, there is a critical need to enhance the *efficiency* of MFI directors. For example, one strategy could be to *limit* the number of MFI boards on which a director may sit—so as to ensure that they devote the time necessary for properly discharging their responsibilities.

Fourth, MFIs must put in place an appropriate procedure (using external and independent people) for *evaluating the performance of their board of directors*. These evaluations should also be shared with the shareholders and other stakeholders (including supervisory authorities)—so that there is formal and explicit understanding of the skills, capabilities, and effectiveness of directors serving on MFI boards.

Fifth, it is critical that responsibilities of the board (of directors) at MFIs—especially with regard to its *role in risk supervision*—be made more explicit and thereby strengthened. In other words, it would be prudent to consider creating *a specialised risk supervision subcommittee* within MFI boards. And it would also be critical for the MFI boards to publish their approval of the MFIs' overall risk strategy and profile through a transparent (public) document—this is the equivalent of a *risk control declaration* in common banking parlance. Such a public document should also contribute to prudent management and supervision of risks within MFIs and this is very important, given what happened in AP in 2010.

Sixth, in practice, there seems to be a lot of overlap with regard to decision making in many MFIs. Without any doubt, greater clarity is needed on what the respective roles and responsibilities (of the various stakeholders) are with regard to decision making within the MFI. And this is especially true with regard to the roles and responsibilities of the board vis-à-vis senior management. Therefore, MFI boards must ensure that clear accountability and responsibility structures are in place with regard to the entire institution including subsidiaries (if any), related group entities, regional/state offices, branches, and so on.

Seventh, where possible, MFI boards must seek and have increased cooperation with the supervisory authorities so that any substantial/systemic risks, similar to what happened in AP in 2010, are nipped in the bud.

And, last but not the least, apart from looking after shareholders' interests, MFI boards also need to take better account of other stakeholders' interests. And clients are especially important here. Especially, the creation of a specific subcommittee in MFI boards to take account of the interests of other stakeholders (such as clients and their protection) in their decision making ("*duty of care*") could go a long way in alleviating some of the key issues that emanated from the 2010 AP microfinance crisis.

The regulatory framework being developed must therefore get the concerned MFI associations to ensure that (NBFC) MFI boards take a proactive approach of putting into practice their stated governance principles in real time.

While we have discussed critical issues with regard to implementation of corporate governance in microfinance NBFCs in terms of what the regulatory framework can get them to do, it is also important to dwell on what these MFI boards can (themselves) do to improve the practice of corporate governance in reality. Here are some initial practical suggestions based on experience:

1. *Limit the number of MFI boards on which a director may sit to not more than three at any given point in time.* This will hopefully afford directors the time and space to understand how the MFIs, on whose boards they serve as directors, are actually performing on the ground. During and before the 2010 AP crisis in India, I had personally witnessed directors—who were on multiple MFI boards (often exceeding three)—jumping planes in a literal sense and having very little time to attend to their fiduciary and other responsibilities. Many of them could not even visit the field areas, even before the customary quarterly board review. Some of them who served on subcommittees were even more

Chapter 14: What Can MFI Boards Do to Implement Corporate Governance in Practice?

harassed for time. Therefore, it appears necessary to ensure that there is a limit—in tune with physical reality—on the number of MFI boards in which a director may sit. And three appears to be a good permissible number.

2. *Separate the functions of the chairman of the board of directors and MD (or chief executive officer or equivalent) in MFIs, where they are together and ensure that appropriate outsiders at least occupy one of those posts.* This is very critical and should result in dispersed power, especially when the founder promoter is the chairman and/or managing director. Much of the excessive risk taking (in the form of multiple, sequential, and larger loans being given to subprime-like clients) that occurred during the lead up to 2010 AP microfinance crisis happened primarily because there was no one on the board to seriously question the enthusiastic and entrepreneurial promoters, occupying one or both of these positions. Often, this was because the promoter had, in the first place, appointed these individuals to the board and this had caused a huge conflict of interest.

3. *Create a transparent board recruitment (or appointment) policy that clearly specifies the duties and profiles of MFI directors, including the chairman.* Such a policy must also ensure that directors have adequate skills and experience (apart from the availability of time to do their job). The policy must also ensure that the overall composition of the MFIs' board of directors is suitably diverse—including more women, youth, clients (or their interest groups), and individuals with the requisite skills (but possibly different backgrounds) in the board is perhaps a way to improve the boards' overall functioning and effectiveness. The policy must also ensure that conflict of interest issues are taken into account with regard to board appointments so that the independence of the directors is not compromised.

4. *Ensure that MFI boards develop (on their own) a formal conflict of interest policy and an objective set of compliance procedures and processes for implementing the same.* Such a policy should ideally include: (a) an MFI director's duty to avoid (if possible) all activities and transactions that could either create a conflict of interest or even the appearance of a conflict of interest; (b) a transparent set of processes and procedures for MFI directors to follow before they engage in certain types of activities (such as agreeing to serve on the board of another MFI or that of a lender or an investor etc.) so as to ensure that such activities will not create a conflict of interest; (c) an MFI director's duty to disclose any activity and issue that may result, or has already resulted, in a conflict of interest; (d) an MFI director's (voluntary) responsibility to abstain from voting on any matter where the director may have a conflict of interest or where the director's objectivity/ability to properly fulfill duties to the MFI may be compromised; (e) adequate procedures and clear norms for transactions and activities conducted with related parties on an arms-length basis; and (f) transparent procedures by which the MFI board will deal with the issue of any noncompliance with the (conflict of interest) policy. Ideally, it would be good for the policy to contain specific (conflict of interest policy) examples of where and how

conflicts of interest can arise when serving as an MFI board member. This should facilitate greater understanding of conflict of interest issues, with regard to microfinance in general and the MFI in particular.

5. *Have a compulsory formal evaluation of the functioning of the MFI's board of directors by an external independent evaluator.* This is a critical issue and the results of this evaluation should be made available to shareholders and supervisory authorities—officially publishing this evaluation (on their website) is an aspect that could also be considered by the MFIs concerned. Such a formal evaluation of the board should preferably be done in the absence of the CEO or managing director, so as to ensure that the exercise is a free, fair, and independent one. The services of independent evaluators—individuals and/or institutions who have not had (or do not have) a material relationship (as defined in common parlance) with the MFI—could be taken in this regard. Management institutes (such as IIMs) and others (like the College of Agricultural Banking, etc.) could also be actively involved in these (evaluation) processes.

6. *Suitably compensate MFI board members for their time but do not incentivize their working on the basis of stock options or other such mechanisms that invariably encourage undue or excessive "risk" taking as was witnessed during the 2010 AP microfinance crisis.* Even if the law permits, it seems prudent not to remunerate board members through stock options and the like as the independence of (independent) directors may be seriously compromised. Again, the happenings, in India, in the run-up to the 2010 AP microfinance crisis clearly demonstrate the fact that independent directors who had been so compensated had *not* performed their fiduciary and other duties appropriately. The key issue to note here is that much of the 2010 crisis occurred because board members and senior management were compensated heavily (in the short term), whereas the risks of their strategies could be known only in the medium/long term. This mismatch created a huge incentive for excessive risk taking, which, in turn, led to the 2010 AP microfinance crisis. The parallels with the US subprime can hardly go unnoticed.

7. *Make it mandatory for MFI boards to set up a risk committee and establish clear rules regarding the composition and functioning of this committee.* In addition, make it compulsory for one or more members of the audit committee to be a part of the risk committee and vice versa. Further, the chairman of the risk committee should always report to the AGM and outline the role that directors have played in shaping the MFI's risk profile and strategy. Also, the risk committee should frame a "risk control declaration," which should also be published so as to ensure its wider dissemination and use—both within and outside the organization.

8. *And last but not the least, create an obligation for a specific duty ("duty of care") to be established for the board of directors so that they take into explicit account the interests of various stakeholders (mainly, clients) during the decision-making procedure.* This is especially critical and the 2010 AP microfinance

crisis would (perhaps) not have occurred, if only boards of MFIs had exercised such a duty of care that explicitly looked after the interest of clients who were constantly over-indebted. The desire for better operating performance at many MFIs meant that the board of directors at these MFIs just did not bother about the impact of their turbocharged growth on clients and their well-being. Therefore, there is an explicit need to incorporate a duty of care—especially with regard to clients—among MFI boards.

To summarize, for the microfinance sector that has undergone a deep crisis in India, corporate governance has never been more important than now. Corporate governance is not just the responsibility of an individual MFI. Rather, it is the collective responsibility of all individuals who become directors on the boards of an MFI and serve together. While we can have great sounding norms and guidelines for corporate governance, unfortunately, they cannot be effectively enforced through regulation alone. They need to be practiced at all times (including difficult circumstances as is currently the case in Indian microfinance) and that is where the individual initiative of directors (serving on MFI boards) does really matter. And I sincerely hope that directors on MFI boards do ensure that this happens in real time on the ground—by enabling and facilitating their boards to reorient their functioning in the light of the suggestions made. If this happens, many of the ills plaguing the Indian microfinance sector and MFIs will slowly but surely start to vanish.

# Chapter 15:
# The Governance of Compensation at NBFC MFIs: Is There a Need for Serious Regulatory Reform?

*Regulating the compensation awarded to bosses of MFIs:* Compensation is indeed a very sensitive and critical aspect of governance in MFIs and let us now look at specifics with regard to compensation in large Indian NBFC MFIs. Data from a very interesting article in *Live Mint*[218] has been compiled in a table given here. The table lists the yearly compensation[219] (for FY 2009–2010) of the chairman/managing director/chief executive officer (as applicable) at five large NBFC MFIs, with headquarters in Andhra Pradesh, the hotbed of the 2010 microfinance crisis.

| Table 15.1 Data on Compensation at Five Large AP-Headquartered NBFC MFIs | | | | | | |
|---|---|---|---|---|---|---|
| Rank of MFI in Top 10 MFIs as per salary drawn | Salary of Chairman or MD or CEO (in Rs. crores) as applicable | Net profit of MFI (in Rs. crores) | Total cash outgo for staff compensation (in Rs. crores) | Loan outstanding (in Rs. crores) | Salary to net profit (in %) | Salary of Chairman/MD /CEO/total cash outgo for staff compensation (in %) |
| SHARE | 7.41 | 176.24 | 72.99 | 1695.50 | 4.20 | 10.15 |
| Asmitha | 4.6 | 58.8 | 44.2 | 1082.80 | 7.82 | 10.41 |
| SKS | 2.44 | 174 | 216.37 | 4321.00 | 1.40 | 1.13 |
| Spandana | 1.4 | 200 | 114 | 3500.00 | 0.70 | 1.23 |
| Basix | 0.36 | 30.98 | 37.01 | 961.00 | 1.16 | 0.97 |

*Source of Data:* Tiny Loans, Not so Tiny Salaries, Compiled by Khushboo Narayan and Unnikrishnan (Live Mint, February 3, 2011).

As readers would recall, these top five MFIs headquartered in AP grew at a phenomenal rate between April 2006 and March 2010 (and especially, between the years April 2008 and March 2010) in the backdrop

---
218 Source: "Tiny Loans, Not so Tiny Salaries," Khushboo Narayan and Unnikrishnan, *Live Mint*, February 3, 2011.
219 Data taken from the *Live Mint* article, "Tiny Loans, Not so Tiny Salaries," Khushboo Narayan and Unnikrishnan, February 3, 2011.

# Chapter 15: The Governance of Compensation at NBFC MFIs: Is There a Need for Serious Regulatory Reform?

of the earlier Krishna (2005–2006) microfinance crisis. As per Mix Market data,[220] they are said to have added as much as over $2 billion in GLP and about 9.59 million clients, in the two-year period (April 2008–March 2010), which is indeed phenomenal by any standards. And a brief glance at the table (data on compensation) suggests that the compensation drawn by some of the CEOs[221] (at these NBFC MFIs) is rather unique, given that many of these NBFCs pride themselves on working with the "poorest/poor" and/or "excluded" to facilitate and enable their inclusion in the larger financial system. *Clearly, the promoters/senior management of these institutions, which claim to be serving the poor, received unusually high payments that appear not to have been determined through an explicit and transparent process.*

For example, as a very interesting article in *The Economic Times*[222] (February 1, 2011) commented:

> The "promoter of microfinance company Share Microfin draws a salary unmatched by any executive among listed banks. In 2009-10, he earned Rs. 7.4 crore as managing director of his own microfinance company. This is more than double what the highest-paid executive in all listed banks made that year-Aditya Puri, managing director of HDFC Bank, earned Rs. 3.4 crore. This is more than the limit set by the Companies Act, which regulates the operations of firms in India. Share Microfin is India's third largest microfinance company."

While I am not against anyone getting appropriate compensation for the work they do (provided it is legal and justifiable), I do think it is important for all of us to understand what work (done by the MFI bosses) justifies such exceptionally large salaries to them. This is especially critical given that these salaries are sometimes much higher than those offered even by listed (private) banks as noted in *The Economic Times* article mentioned earlier. We need to understand this phenomenon fair and square!

If compensation is an aspect worthy of closer understanding, so is the process by which equity (sweat or whatever) is allotted to the promoters. Recall Prof. M. S. Sriram's article[223] in the *Economic and Political Weekly* (June 12, 2010) that talked about a huge interest-free loan of Rs. 1.636 crore given by SKS Microfinance Private Limited (NBFC MFI) to its promoter and then managing director (Vikram Akula) to enable him to buy shares in the same company at a face value of Rs. 10.

Now, as the data (from the draft red herring prospectus filed with SEBI in March 2010 by SKS Microfinance) reproduced in the table here shows, as of March 31, 2007, 1,636,138 company shares with a face value of Rs. 10 were bought by the promoter managing director. The source of funds was the interest-free loan provided by SKS Microfinance Private Limited to its own promoter and managing director to enable him to buy its own shares. This is also evident from the financial statements of SKS Microfinance Private Limited given in a previous chapter.[224]

---

220  www.mixmarket.org.
221  They could be chairman, managing director, or CEO as applicable.
222  Source: Quoted from "Share Microfin MD takes home Rs. 7.4 crore, more than double HDFC Bank MD's salary" by John Samuel Raja D and M. Rajshekhar, *The Economic Times*, February 1, 2011.
223  Commercialization of Microfinance in India: A Discussion of the Emperor's Apparel" by Prof. M. S. Sriram, *Economic and Political Weekly*, June 12, 2010, Vol. XLV, No. 24.
224  Refer to Chapter 8.

| \multicolumn{8}{c}{Table 15.2 Equity Shares Allotted and Sold by Promoter MD of an NBFC MFI (SKSML, Formerly SKS Microfinance Private Limited)} |
|---|---|---|---|---|---|---|---|
| Sr. No. | Date of allotment/ transfer | Nature of consideration | No. of equity shares | Face value (in Rs.) | Issue/ acquisition Price (in Rs.) | Percentage of pre-issue paid-up capital | No. of equity shares pledged | Percentage of equity shares pledged |
| \multicolumn{9}{l}{Dr. Vikram Akula (Promoter MD)} |
| 1. | September 22, 2003 | Cash | 5,000 | 10.00 | 10.00 | 0.01 | - | - |
| 2. | May 8, 2004 | Cash | (5,000)$^a$ | 10.00 | 10.00 | (0.01) | - | - |
| 3. | March 31, 2007 | Cash | 1,636,138 | 10.00 | 10.00 | 2.5 | - | - |
| 4. | September 30, 2008 | Cash | (1,636,138)$^b$ | 10.00 | 103.91 | (2.5) | - | - |
| 5. | December 24, 2009 | Cash | 945,424 | 10.00 | 49.77 | 1.5 | - | - |
| 6. | February 10, 2010 | Cash | (945,424)$^c$ | 10.00 | US$ 13.67 | (1.5) | - | - |
|  | Total |  | Nil |  |  |  |  |  |

$^a$Transferred to Party I.
$^b$Transferred to Party II and Party II
(1) Transferred to Party III pursuant to a share purchase agreement dated December 10, 2009. For further details, see "History and Certain Corporate Matters – Material Agreements – Share Purchase Agreement dated December 10, 2009 between, Name YYY, Party III and the Company" on page 105 of this Draft Red Herring Prospectus.

Source: DRHP (March 25, 2010) filed by the NBFC MFI with SEBI.

Now, as is evident from the data in the table, the promoter managing director bought 1,636,138 shares (at a face value of Rs. 10) for a total outlay of Rs. 1.636 crore and sold the same in September 2008 (about 18 months later) for Rs. 103.91 per share. The total profit booked in this transaction was a huge Rs. 15.36 crore and profit per share was Rs. 93.91.

This clearly demonstrates personal enrichment of MFI promoters through the inappropriate and arbitrary provision of so-called sweat equity. Similarly, the example of Asmitha Microfin cited by Jan Postmus is equally relevant here and it demonstrates the arbitrariness in the share allotment process:

> "A fourth contradiction is the remuneration of mf promoters. We now know that the promoters of Compartamos have become millionaires. India also has welcomed it's first microfinance millionaires. The pattern is the same. The promoters either buy the shares at par value in an early stage or get the shares allotted as 'sweat equity', which has become one of the standard conditions from mfi promoters in their negotiations with private investors. As an example, the promoter of Asmitha got sweat equity allotted worth USD 2.5 million at the time of investment of Blue Orchard. Now, this is not fair to the clients who are served by mfi's. Exorbitant promoter(s) enrichment vis-à-vis the financial situation of the poor clients, is in my view unethical and furthermore a clear deviation from the social mission. Mr. Vijay Mahajan is also very clear about this. He said[225] 'the key obstacle that an mfi faces in raising equity is what it does to the poor.... f.e. let us take Compartamos – it's founders have personally become

---
225 Microfinance Insights, Volume 3, June 2007.

multimillionaires. Presumably this will attract more capital but on what terms to the ultimate users? Is this what we set up this sector for? If this if microfinance than I repudiate the field.'"[226]

Therefore, with all due respect, it is indeed important for the various stakeholders (as part of their work on developing the microfinance regulatory architecture) to study and understand the rationale, terms, and processes by which shares are allotted to promoters, CEOs, and others in NBFC MFIs, so that any existing/potential loopholes are plugged and the scope for irregularities removed. Again, I am not against promoters getting equity that they legally deserve but without question, the rationale, terms, and processes must be necessarily appropriate and surely above board.

These are just a few instances, and as we look at the 2010 AP crisis in Indian microfinance, there are several important lessons with regard to the governance of compensation in Indian MFIs that we all need to understand. I will try and articulate these here for wider benefit, in the hope that these will be factored into the (robust) regulatory framework that is still being developed for microfinance in India.

*Lesson 1: Lack of arm's-length decisions and negotiations:* The governance of remuneration and incentive systems seems to have (apparently) failed in some Indian MFIs because decisions and negotiations (carried out) have not been at arm's length. Conflicts of interest at various levels have aided such improper decision making and negotiation. And much of this is applicable to remuneration and incentive systems for a range of senior management personnel and not just the CEO or managing director or chairman of the board. While there are several examples from the Indian microfinance context, the earlier articles cited (*The Economic Times* and *Live Mint*) offer good factual insights.

*Lesson 2: Inordinate level of influence of senior management in establishing remuneration schemes:* In several cases that I have personally seen, senior management generally appears to have far too much influence over the level and conditions (including measures) set for performance-based remuneration. On the other hand, boards are often unable to or, sometimes, even incapable of exercising objective, independent judgment. Here again, there are serious conflicts of interest, which certainly exacerbate this whole issue—in fact, this has been one of the most important reasons for inaction by the board against inappropriate remuneration proposals of senior management at MFIs (especially, NBFC MFIs).

*Lesson 3: Medium-and long-term risks are not taken into account:* In some cases that I have closely observed, the relationship between performance and remuneration is rather tenuous. Sometimes, this linkage is even difficult to establish, especially given the nature of microfinance operations. A very critical aspect here is that medium-/long-term risks and the possibility of adversarial political action are rarely factored into the whole process—something that should have been done, given the nature of

---

226  Source: Quoted from "Microfinance at a Crossroads - The Need for Social Equity" by Jan Postmus, unpublished paper, 2010, Page 20.

microfinance and given what happened in Andhra Pradesh in 2010. Suresh Gurumani was apparently paid a hefty bonus in May 2010. Yet, he was summarily dismissed in October 2010 and stakeholders close to Vikram Akula have blamed Suresh Gurumani for the rapid growth and deterioration in SKS's portfolio, which was evident by 2010 October.[227]

*Lesson 4: Complicated and opaque remuneration schemes:* Some of the MFI remuneration schemes are fairly complicated and also opaque in terms of shrouding actual conditions in the operation of the scheme and the consequences. What I am saying is that these (operational conditions and terms) are perhaps not clear and obvious to the naked eye of an unassuming observer. These conditions also tend to encourage excessive and mindless (growth and) risk taking and especially with a short-term orientation. Suresh Gurumani's case is again a perfect example.

*Lesson 5: Mere disclosure is not transparency:* While transparency (in some cases) may exist in terms of disclosure, several MFIs couch the main characteristics of their performance-related remuneration programmes in verbose technical language and thereby make it very difficult for comprehension to the normal reader. Very rarely do we get information on the following:

a. The total cost of the remuneration programme to the MFI;

b. The specific performance criteria and measures along with their conceptual and operational definitions;

c. The manner in which remuneration has been adjusted for relevant risks—especially medium-and long-term risks as well as risk of political action (which is so relevant in microfinance). Without question, MFIs will surely need to have remuneration and incentive systems that focus and encourage at least the medium-term, if not long-term, performance. This, in turn, means that MFIs must choose to reward their senior management after significant actual performance has been realized and that has not usually been the case—there are several examples of high front-loaded one-time bonuses paid to senior management executives of large NBFC MFIs and the results are there for everyone to see.[228] In fact, just as in the firms that caused the global financial crisis, the focus on the short-term performance, incentives, and compensation has been excessive at Indian MFIs (much to their detriment). This certainly needs to be changed to reflect the medium- and/or long-term performance and operations.

Overall, remuneration does not seem to have been established through an explicit governance process where the roles and responsibilities of all stakeholders involved, including committee members,

---

227 More to SKS script than meets the eye (http://articles.economictimes.indiatimes.com/2010-10-08/news/27570919_1_ceo-suresh-gurumani-sks-microfinance-independent-directors), by M. Rajshekhar and M. Anand, *The Economic Times*, October 8, 2010.

228 More to SKS script than meets the eye (http://articles.economictimes.indiatimes.com/2010-10-08/news/27570919_1_ceo-suresh-gurumani-sks-microfinance-independent-directors) by M. Rajshekhar and M. Anand, *The Economic Times*, October 8, 2010.

# Chapter 15: The Governance of Compensation at NBFC MFIs: Is There a Need for Serious Regulatory Reform?

consultants, risk managers, and others, are clearly defined and separated (without conflict of interest). The roles given to nonexecutive independent board members in the process—although they may seem somewhat appropriate—again appear to be laden with serious conflicts of interest. And finally, while remuneration policies are sometimes submitted to the annual meeting and subjected to shareholder approval, much of this seems to be a routine matter, with minimal (informed) discussion because of aspects mentioned earlier. Read the instance given in the section on independent directors in a previous chapter[229] where a director of a large NBFC writes to the managing director of the same institution complaining about a similar happening. I can fully empathize with such directors as my own personal experience (as a board member of a large NBFC MFI) suggests that the same happens in other MFIs as well.

Thus, in my opinion, an aspect that stands out is the irrational and unusually high compensation to senior management, directors, founders, and promoters. Much of this seems to be similar to the practices observed in financial services companies during the subprime and global financial crisis. This apart, ad hoc bonuses, pay raises (followed by sudden termination), the grant of shares when options have been sanctioned, the nontransparent pricing of options, provision of (huge) interest loans to enable founders and board members to buy the shares of their own company, the nontransparent granting of sweat equity etc., are some of the other key remuneration issues in the Indian microfinance industry that need to be studied, analyzed, and factored in by those developing the new regulatory architecture. In fact, while I have observed many of these practices during the past few years, the seeds were undoubtedly sown much earlier.

Thus, given this situation, we, as stakeholders, need to continually ask a key question, "whether the compensation approaches being pursued are indeed consistent with the institutions' (MFIs) ethics of creating value for clients and its objectives, strategy and control environment as well as that of the overall microfinance industry." And we certainly need to keep looking for objective answers as well.

Therefore, as has been often mentioned, "Compensation is one factor among many that contributed to the financial crisis that began in 2007. Official action to address unsound compensation systems must therefore be embedded in the broader financial regulatory reform programme, built around a substantially stronger and more resilient capital and liquidity framework. Action must be speedy, determined, and coherent. Urgency is particularly important to prevent a return to the compensation practices that contributed to the crisis."[230]

I hope that the various stakeholders focus on this aspect as part of their exercise in developing a new microfinance regulatory architecture and ensure that the same compensation practices and incentives that (adversely) affected the global subprime do not negatively impact Indian microfinance (at least, in the future).

Accordingly, I suggest four strategies that these stakeholders should seek to have implemented at MFIs in the Indian microfinance industry. These practical strategies will ensure that processes in the governance of compensation at MFIs become transparent and are indeed perceived to be fair.

---

229 See Chapter 13. Also refer Chapter 12 for generic issues on Corporate Governance at MFIs.
230 Quoted from BIS paper on Compensation and Corporate Governance, 2010.

*Strategy 1: Enable boards to play a proactive role in the governance of compensation at MFIs and prevent the compensation system from being in the grip of the CEO/senior management.* First, the boards of MFIs can and must play a proactive role in establishing proper governance of remuneration and that is where the buck actually stops. It naturally follows that the board must also ensure that this compensation system is not primarily controlled by the chief executive officer and/or other members of the senior management team (CEO, CFO, etc.).

In fact, this has been a major problem with some MFIs in India. In cases where *the compensation system has tended to be firmly in the grip of the CEO and/or senior management team, it seems prone to nontransparent actions, related-party transactions, and whimsical payouts to CEO/senior management, without sufficient rationale or justification.* In fact, I see this as a major cause for the 2010 microfinance crisis in AP—as at these NBFC MFIs, the compensation decisions were laden with significant conflict of interest and questionable from a legal as well as ethical standpoint.

Therefore, the regulatory architecture being developed must facilitate the supervisor and related stakeholders to ask relevant questions as part of their day-to-day work and ensure course corrections in real time.

- Is the board of directors effectively taking overall responsibility for the MFI compensation system, including participating directly in the design and operation of this system?

- Has the board ensured that the CEO and/or senior management team at the MFI are not controlling the compensation system?

- Is the compensation policy aligned with the risk management framework of the MFI?

- Has the board of directors at the MFI approved and periodically reviewed the compensation policy?

- Has the board ensured that the compensation policy at the MFI does not provide incentives for excessive risk taking and also that it is aligned with medium/long term operations as well?

*Strategy 2: Ensure that the boards of MFIs have members with requisite compensation experience and real independence, so that they can effectively participate in the regulation of compensation.* It is crucial for the MFI to have board members with relevant expertise in compensation and perhaps risk management. More importantly, these members must have complete independence in dealing with the (design and operation) of the compensation system. In a way, this is the fulcrum of a fair compensation system where the board members not only have the requisite experience but are also able to use it in an independent and objective manner. This, in turn, implies that the boards of MFIs should not be filled with friends, relatives, and yes-men, as Mr M. Damodaran, the former SEBI chairman, has argued.

Again, as evident from the 2010 AP crisis, in a few cases, nominee directors and other independent directors seem to have been silenced and their independence compromised (on several occasions) with

# Chapter 15: The Governance of Compensation at NBFC MFIs: Is There a Need for Serious Regulatory Reform?

regard to matters of compensation and remuneration. This again, has left a very poor impression of the microfinance industry in India in the minds of the general public.

Here are some key questions in this regard for the supervisor and concerned stakeholders developing the regulatory architecture for microfinance:

- Is the board composed of independent, nonexecutive members, without any conflict of interest?

- Does the board have sufficient expertise (in terms of members) to assess risk management issues related to compensation?

- Does the board have (members with) the skill and experience to reach an independent judgment on the compensation policy?

- Are the relatives of the CEO and/or senior management on the board of the MFI? Are there close former associates and/or friends of the CEO/senior management, who are on the board of the MFI?

- Can the appointment of these members to the board of the MFI be justified in terms of their professional expertise? Or are these relatives/former associates/friends on the board primarily because of their (personal) relationship with the CEO/senior management?

*Strategy 3: Mandate the establishment of an independent board remuneration committee at each MFI to oversee design and implementation of the compensation system.* While the previous two strategies articulated the role and responsibility of the board of directors, the key question that arises is how best the boards of MFIs can accomplish this in real time. Neither can all members of the board spend their entire time on this nor can individual members of the board work on this in an ad hoc manner.

In other words, there is a critical "how to" with regard to the discharge of the above roles and responsibilities by the MFI board—that is, through the establishment of an appropriate independent remuneration committee[231] and defining its mandate. It is through such a committee that the board of directors can design, monitor, and review[232] the compensation system to ensure that it operates as intended. Therefore, it is critical that MFIs have a board remuneration committee as an integral part of their governance structure and organization, to oversee the compensation system's design and operation on behalf of the board of directors.

---

231 Sometimes the board may have people with requisite skills and experience and also independence. They, however, need to be appointed to the MFI compensation committee and there are cases, where this has not happened as the CEO/senior management have desired otherwise.

232 Two issues are relevant here. One is that the compensation system will need to have controls to ensure compliance and, in some ways, the committee itself is the main control available. Thus, the committee will have to also review the practical operation of the compensation system regularly for compliance with design policies and procedures. Compensation outcomes, risk measurements, and risk outcomes should also be regularly reviewed for consistency on intentions.

- The remuneration committee should be constituted in a way that enables it to exercise competent and independent judgment[233] on compensation policies/practices and the incentives created (at the MFI) for managing risk, capital, liquidity, and customer satisfaction.

- In addition, the committee should carefully evaluate practices by which compensation is paid for potential future revenues, whose timing and likelihood remain uncertain. This is a critical lesson from the 2008 global financial crisis as also the 2010 microfinance crisis in AP. And while doing so, the committee should demonstrate that its decisions are consistent with an assessment of the MFI's true financial condition and future prospects, including medium- and long-term risks.

- To this end, the remuneration committee must work closely with the MFI's risk committee in the evaluation of the incentives created by the compensation system.

- It should also ensure that the MFI's compensation policy is in compliance with global good practices and standards as well as the respective rules of the national regulatory authorities.

Here are some relevant questions for the supervisory authority and concerned stakeholders developing the regulatory architecture for microfinance.

- Are there controls in place to regularly oversee the compliance of the compensation system? What are these and how sufficient are these controls? Is the independent board remuneration committee one of the key controls?

- In order that the MFI board remuneration committee is able to operate independent of the senior executives, is it composed (at a minimum) of a majority of independent, nonexecutive (board) members without any conflict of interest?[234]

- Does the MFI board remuneration committee have (members with) the skill and experience to reach an independent judgment on the compensation policy?

- Do the terms of reference/charter of the board remuneration committee suggest that it has sufficient powers (mandate) to perform its functions independently?

- Is the board remuneration committee at the MFI responsible for the preparation of recommendations to the board regarding compensation, including those having implications for risk and risk management?

---

233 BIS paper on Compensation and Corporate Governance, 2010.
234 BIS paper on Compensation and Corporate Governance, 2010.

- Has the board remuneration committee at the MFI made recommendations to the board on the compensation to be paid to the highest paid employees, based on a predetermined materiality threshold?

- Does the board remuneration committee at the MFI have access to advice, either internal or external, that is independent of advice provided to senior management? What has been the process used for commissioning external advisers to advise the board on compensation policy? Do these advisers report directly to the board remuneration committee?

- Does the board remuneration committee at the MFI have unfettered access to information and analysis from risk and control function personnel (e.g., risk management, finance, compliance, internal audit, and human resources)?

- Does the board remuneration committee at the MFI engage appropriate control function personnel in its deliberations on compensation policy? Do control functions at the MFI have input in the structure and determination of compensation?

*Strategy 4: Mandate that MFI board remuneration committees ensure an annual external compensation review.* Last but not the least, the remuneration committee should facilitate an annual compensation review at the MFI and get it done externally. This review should be independent of any CEO/senior management interference and it should be submitted to the remuneration committee, board of directors, and regulator/supervisor. It should also be disclosed to the public. It goes without saying that such a review should, among other things, assess (legal) compliances with the applicable rules and standards promulgated by the relevant regulatory authority. For example, the *Economic Times* article by John Samuel Raja D./M. Rajshekhar, notes that 'SHARE Microfin's MD's salary is well beyond the limit stipulated by the Companies Act.'[235]

Some relevant questions in this regard for the supervisory authority and concerned stakeholders developing the regulatory architecture for microfinance include the following:

- Is there an external annual compensation review at the MFI?

- What is the process developed for conducting the annual compensation review? Is it an objective and fair process without (any) conflicts of interest?

- Does the annual compensation review assess the compensation policy's compliance with global principles/standards in the microfinance industry, as well as standards (if any) promulgated by the (national) regulators/supervisors?

---

[235] Paraphrased from: "Share Microfin MD takes home Rs. 7.4 crore, more than double HDFC Bank MD's salary" by John Samuel Raja D. and M. Rajshekhar, *The Economic Times*, February 1, 2011.

- Does this include ensuring that all material compensation plans/programs (including those for executives and employees, whose actions have a material impact on the risk exposure of the MFI), are covered?

- Does this include assessing the appropriateness of the compensation plans/programs relative to organizational goals, objectives, and risk profile of the MFI?

Without question, irrational and ad hoc compensation practices (at some MFIs) have been a major factor that appears to have contributed (in significant measure) to the 2010 AP microfinance crisis. Therefore, it is imperative that the various stakeholders—i.e., RBI, PSCF,[236] MoF,[237] and others from the microfinance industry—involved in developing the regulatory architecture undertake immediate and suitable action to address the issue of (such) unsound compensation systems prevalent at many (NBFC) MFIs. The urgency of this task should not be underestimated as I see this as one of the most important causes leading to the 2010 AP microfinance crisis.

Only that can keep future crisis situations at bay.

---

[236] *Parliamentary Standing Committee* on *Finance.*
[237] Ministry of Finance.

# Chapter 16:
# Can the Credit Bureau[238] Stop Multiple Lending?

Can a credit bureau for microfinance really work? Let me first look at what happened in the past before dwelling on this crucial topic. I go back in time to 2005–2006 when we had a similar, but not so severe, microfinance crisis in the Krishna and Guntur districts of AP. Some industry well-wishers had then argued strongly for the (Sa-Dhan) CoC, a concept on paper that was so very well intentioned but not implemented adequately on the ground. Others had mentioned the use of technology (for enhancing outreach) as a means to weed out the black sheep. Fast forward to the Kolar crisis (2009) and industry observers argued that the situation involved a different association but proposed a similar strategy and commensurate results—that is, MFIN and its CoC—again very well intentioned but not well implemented. And in the aftermath of the 2010 AP crisis (from September onward), industry experts suggested a solution that is "high tech"—that is, the proposed credit bureau to be facilitated by MFIN.

And as this game of musical chairs and relay continued, I wrote in my blog[239] that "the proposed bureau could be more of a red herring and less of a real solution for several reasons:

> First, despite the most sophisticated credit bureaus, the subprime crisis in the United States could not be avoided and, therefore, no credit bureau—irrespective of the manner in which it is designed and implemented—is likely to be a foolproof strategy with regard to avoiding such crises. Believing that a credit bureau could prevent such a crisis from recurring would be the height of naiveté, to say the least. There can be no replacement for sound lending, based on an objective assessment of a client's (likely) cash flows and his/her loan absorption capacity. Further, there can be no substitute for the relationship banking that most of us get, and, without any doubt, that microfinance clients also deserve.
>
> Second, when we talk of microfinance clients, there is so much information asymmetry with regard to their loans and lives and we are not sure that the proposed credit bureau would be able to acquire such

---

238 This chapter uses material previously posted on the blog, *"Candid Unheard Voice of Indian Microfinance"* and it was jointly written by Mr Ramesh S. Arunachalam and Mr Bhalchander Viswanath, CEO of United Prosperity.org.

239 http://www.microfinance-in-india.blogspot.in/

information. We do not have access to any reliable and valid information on informal sources of finance and getting them at the scale required for the proposed bureau would be next to impossible in the Indian context. We cannot also easily track the lending that an SHG does to its members—it could become cumbersome and a very difficult task from a record and data management perspective.

Third, when many MFIs (including the large ones) have not been able to set up and run appropriately designed and aggregated MIS across geographies, products, and states, at their own individual MFI level,[240] how can we expect them (and their association) to accomplish a more difficult task with significant complexity and scale? There are serious issues with record keeping, portfolio management, internal control, and finance/accounting systems in many MFIs and the integrity of the ground-level data is questionable. Therefore, expecting the MFI association to do something more advanced, when the basic foundation of record keeping and data management is itself weak, is going to be difficult.

Fourth, establishing a credit bureau even with limited functionalities takes an enormously long time. In India, with multiple models of microfinance—MFIs, banks, RRBs, SHGs, and cooperatives lending to clients, integrating information from all these entities and making them available with a reasonable degree of reliability will be an enormously complex project requiring significant investments. Note that huge investments in terms of money and effort would be required to build the central credit bureau and also implement it at the individual MFI level.

Fifth, studies on efficacy of credit bureaus indicate that they do run the risks of financial exclusion of the poorest clients. That needs to be noted and, before embarking on such an initiative, we need to mitigate the risks of financial exclusion due to new techniques that focus on impersonal means of making credit decisions.

> 'Credit bureau information allows MFIs to more effectively service the poor. Yet, they highlight that a number of poor individuals are initially screened out as credit bureau information is utilized. It is important that we understand which poor individuals are no longer offered loans.
>
> If they are indeed bad clients, in the sense that they are likely to default because they refuse to pay even though they have sufficient resources or because they make overly-risky investments, then there is little cause for alarm. However, if those who are screened out are individuals whose bad repayment record is a result of idiosyncratic shocks and not moral hazard, then MFIs must be careful in using credit bureau information.'[241]

---

240 See Chapter 17, which deals with MIS at MFIs.
241 *Source*: Quoted from Better Lending and Better Clients: Credit Bureau Impact on Microfinance, by Alain de Janvry, May 2006.

Sixth, there are also significant investment and operational costs involved in setting up a credit bureau. These include the following:

- Cost of setting up and maintaining the credit bureau.

- Cost of capturing additional information for credit bureau purposes and making changes to the MIS systems of participating organizations, which may have differing designs and standards (thereby, posing numerous problems for integration as well).

- Cost of training the staff.

- Cost of client education: clients who are poor should be able to get their credit status and report for free. They should be entitled to this information. They should also be educated on what a credit report means and what they need to do to improve their credit (rating or score). There should be also an independently monitored appeal process at no cost to the client so that clients are not inadvertently excluded because of improper credit approval systems.

- A robust financial model that takes all of these into account should be built so that it does not lead to additional costs for the client or handling fees for the MFI.

Seventh, the efficacy of setting up specialized microfinance credit bureaus has been questioned in a few studies in Latin America. It perhaps makes more sense to set up a general credit bureau through the main banking system (for the middle and upper middle classes) and extend the same to the lower middle class and the poor. The same could be done in India with already existing and operational credit bureaus, and that would also not burden the poor with bearing the costs of setting up the infrastructure of a credit bureau.

> 'The country case studies reviewed ... lead to the preliminary conclusion that it is unwise to develop very specialized credit bureaus that by their nature fragment the credit information market. Whether in El Salvador or Bolivia, the specialized sectarian bureaus do cater to their institutional subscribers, but their databases miss a wealth of information on clients who have not yet fallen under the purview of that particular sector. Efforts to create specialized MFI credit bureaus have been based on the assumption that the market niche of MFIs is completely separate from the market niche of other lenders. This assumption is proving to be false, at least in many Latin American countries, where microfinance clients access a variety of sources of financing, including the corner store.
>
> Pursuing quick-fix solutions, such as endowing an MFI association with equipment, software, technical assistance, and operating expenses to run a small MFI credit bureau, is tempting for donors. As has been illustrated by the cases of INFORED and FINRURAL, however, setting up a credit bureau

is not a simple matter. It requires superior technology, business marketing sophistication, and the ability to attract as subscribers large and multiple clients. With a large subscriber base, a bureau can have something useful to offer, in addition to securing its financial sustainability.'[242]

Eighth, microfinance (or rather micro-credit) is currently going through a phase of limited relationship building with the client. A credit bureau will depersonalize the client–loan officer relationship even more. What is needed is deeper involvement and knowledge of the client's life and business and building of stronger relationships with clients. A credit bureau may end up doing the reverse and thereby increase the risks to the sector.

Ninth, such a bureau should be mainstreamed and housed with an independent body, and MFIN should (perhaps) limit itself to playing the much-needed facilitating/coordinating role. This alone will enable the credit bureau to be viewed as a reliable and valid data source with regard to low-income people. It will also allay concerns of poaching of bank clients by MFIs and vice versa.

Therefore, while a credit bureau is a good medium-to-long-term solution, it is certainly not an immediate solution for the current set of issues. It has, and will continue to have, operational challenges for several years, if not decades, in the context of a country like India that has a huge variety and complexity of financial services. Let us not overburden it with unrealistic expectations—that would be a recipe for disaster. A credit bureau is a great idea by itself and it should be made to succeed. Let us incubate it in a more favorable environment rather than let it face baptism by fire."

At this point, I would like to set the record straight regarding my views on the credit bureau. I have not spurned the suggestion at any time. In fact, a credit bureau is a good tool but let us not put too much pressure on it, as it may then fail. *I also feel that a credit bureau is not a guarantee against multiple lending and will not eliminate it.* Further, as long as client acquisition occurs through agents, brokers, takeover/breaking of SHGs and other not-so-good means, and as long JLGs and clients are operationally shared by MFIs who hold meetings and disburse loans on successive days to shared JLG and clients, the problem of multiple lending will not go away. Thus, what I am saying is that while the credit bureau is a data solution, there has to be a physical solution on the ground. Also, a credit bureau gives you data based on what you feed in and given the various issues regarding the credibility of MIS[243] in MFIs this seems to be a huge task indeed.

Let us now turn our attention to the fact that it has been over 3 years since the 2010 AP microfinance crisis and, yet, a transparent use of the microfinance credit bureau appears to be nowhere in sight—at least for outsiders like me.

---

242 *Source*: Credit Bureaus: A Necessity for Microfinance? by Anita Campion and Liza Valenzuela. http://www.microlinks.org/ev_en.php?ID=7445_201&ID2=DO_TOPIC, Page 22.
243 See Chapter 17.

While the intentions of establishing the credit bureau may have been genuine and well founded, the lack of real-time implementation progress raises several important questions with regard to the process of establishing the (Indian microfinance) credit bureau in the first place.

In my opinion, the current delay could be due to several factors articulated below, and I would like the stakeholders developing the regulatory architecture for microfinance to take this fact into account while proposing the establishment of a credit bureau as an integral part of the overall regulatory architecture.

So, what then has caused the delay in establishment of the microfinance credit bureau? Here are some plausible reasons.

- *Lack of strong and committed leadership*—to ensure that the credit bureau is indeed functional within the stipulated timeframe. Several deadlines have gone by and we still keep hearing statements that the credit bureau is ready and will be operational soon. It has been getting ready from December 2009 and several years have already gone by and it is about time that we began objectively analyzing as to why these deadlines have constantly shifted. It would surely help us understand the real issues better in terms of why the delays are occurring (data availability and integrity, willingness of MFIs or microfinance institutions to walk the talk with regard to the credit bureau initiative, etc.,) and thereby pave the way for quicker and timely implementation on the ground.

- *The credit bureau initiative has no serious regulatory support whatsoever*—I have not seen a single statement from the RBI affirming the validity of the ongoing credit bureau efforts and wonder what role it will have in ensuring data integrity, especially given the proliferation of agents, multiple loans to shared JLGs and clients and also the lack of a unique ID for low-income clients. The MIS at many MFIs is weak and unless robust standards are created and enforced with regard to the MIS at MFIs by the regulator/supervisor, I doubt that any meaningful (reliable and valid) data will go into the credit bureau. I hope that the RBI looks into the various issues as soon as possible so that it is not caught on the wrong foot later when it becomes the sole regulator for microfinance.

- *Absolutely unrealistic targets, which means that quick wins and early results are not possible to show*—This gets further exacerbated by the microfinance industry's underestimation of data quality and information technology issues, which are dealt with below. Quick wins provide a great momentum and that has not been possible in the Indian scenario. This is what makes the credit bureau a real red herring! From December 2009, when MFIN was formed to date, I have seen a number of public statements on when the credit bureau is likely to be ready and used and I would like someone to go into the reasons for the shifting goalposts. I, for one, feel that this could be occurring because of lack of proper data at the grassroots mainly due to the use of the agent-led decentralized model at this level.

- *Lack of reliable ground-level data*—A number of issues affect data quality in microfinance, especially in India. There are both structural problems (agent-led models,[244] shared JLGs, shared clients) and bad credit-granting practices (over-lending, multiple lending, successive greening, ghost lending and frauds,[245] etc.). Among the data issues observed are lack of unique identifiers (several people in villages especially can have the same names and initials); lack of location identifiers (e.g., village/street names and building numbering, especially in rural areas are hugely duplicated); unavailability of key credit information (e.g., especially because of the highly prevalent agent-led model); and poor data quality of available information (e.g., errors in data entry, data conversion/manipulation, frauds as you have been reading of, etc.). Recall that when the Andhra Pradesh government requested data from MFIs, errors were reported in the media about wrong data conversion.

  Also, misreporting of data is always a real threat for any microfinance credit bureau and the case of Sahayata Microfinance[246] resounds strongly in memory. The key question here is what is the guarantee that the self-report data being provided by MFIs has not been tampered with by them (as has been alleged at Sahayata Microfinance)? As the *Business Standard* noted in the case of Sahayata:

  > *"The board questioned chief executive, chief financial officer and other senior managers on charges of serious misreporting and mismanagement.... While the chief executive was suspended with immediate effect, the CFO and head of operations were stripped of their duties immediately. They were subsequently suspended."*[247]

  Further, as clearly shown in exhibits given in various chapters of this book, many of the NBFC-MFIs have self-admitted to the existence of agents and the same has also been confirmed by several studies. The MFIN-sponsored NCAER study admitted to the presence of agents in AP and the SIDBI–World Bank–sponsored COCA reports have also provided evidence with regard to the presence of agents among the fast growing NBFC-MFIs.[248] When such agents are in charge and the last mile end user clients are not known, how reliable and valid (from a measurement viewpoint) is the data supplied to a credit bureau?

---

244 See previous *Moneylife* articles on microfinance agents—http://www.moneylife.in/article/how-and-why-did-microfinance-agents-become-a-part-of-the-indian-microfinance-business/19301.html, http://www.moneylife.in/article/implementation-safeguards-against-notorious-agents-are-an-imperative-for-the-proposed-microfinance-bill/19017.html and http://www.moneylife.in/article/proposed-microfinance-bill-has-to-look-at-the-re-leader-as-a-microfinance-agent/20019.html

245 See previous *Moneylife* article on frauds—http://www.moneylife.in/article/increasing-frauds-internal-lapses-at-mfis-need-to-strengthen-supervisory-arrangements-to-protect-the-poor/18309.html

246 See http://moneylife.in/article/award-winning-sahayata-microfinance-is-the-latest-to-go-astray/21549.html

247 Source: Quoted from "Sahayata microfin sacks top mgmt for irregularities", (http://www.business-standard.com/article/finance/sahayata-microfin-sacks-top-mgmt-for-irregularities-111111800061_1.html), by Abhijit Lele, November 18, 2011.

248 See Chapter 20 on Code of Conduct Assessments.

- *A range of information technology issues*—Different IT-related constraints prevent the smooth establishment of a credit bureau, and much of these constraints arise because of the remote physical spread of Indian microfinance. Among the IT issues observed are the lack of a standardized core MIS system at the MFI level; weak IT infrastructure within MFIs (branches not connected to headquarters, etc.); basic IT commodities are not available or not reliable (e.g., unstable power supply; slow or unreliable Internet connections); hardware and software provisioning issues (e.g., limited availability of hardware brands and models to ensure quick and efficient processing of very large volumes of small amounts of repetitive data that characterize microfinance); and lack of experienced service providers for infrastructure setup and maintenance.

- *Design of MIS at MFIs is not using accepted standardized best-practices*—The problem is further compounded because MIS at the MFI level is not up to commonly accepted standards. This means that consistency and integrity of data will continue to be a major issue in credit bureau implementation.[249]

- *The lack of focus on execution to overcome lack of implementation capabilities*—I also see no serious effort whatsoever by the microfinance industry to overcome the implementation bottlenecks. All I get to hear is, "the job is very difficult as this is a low-income financial services industry and therefore what the industry has achieved so far is commendable." But that is not a fair argument, as we are talking of commercial microfinance that seeks to become a part of the larger financial sector. Surely, under such circumstances, no handicap is permissible because the microfinance industry has always wanted to mainstream itself as an extended arm of banking and hence there can be no compromise whatsoever with regard to the quality of the MIS and related standards (accounting, internal control, etc.) that influence the integrity of data going into the MIS.

All of these issues do indeed make setting up a credit bureau in an emerging market such as India an extremely challenging task—if serious efforts are made, it could take at least 3 to 4 years (or maybe even 5 years) from initial discussions to regular use of the credit bureau (that produces transparent, reliable, and valid credit information reports and not just some reports). So, folks, it is time to tune down our expectations and I hope that the powers that be, who argue that a credit bureau will solve all problems in Indian microfinance, do look into the above and other issues of practical relevance. I would also like various stakeholders—DFIs (development financial institutions) like SIDBI (Small Industries Development Bank of India), commercial banks, international agencies like CGAP (Consultative Group to Assist the Poor), and donors supporting the credit bureau initiative—to come out and vouchsafe the integrity and quality of the data being supplied to the credit bureau by MFIs. This must be done in terms of data integrity, internal consistency, and physical compatibility with client existence and records, and these stakeholders (especially SIDBI and commercial banks) must

---

[249] See *Moneylife* article on MIS for MFIs—http://www.moneylife.in/article/establishing-standards-for-effective-management-information-systems-for-mfis/19655.html.

make themselves accountable and responsible for the quality and integrity of such data. Unless all these are done, the credit bureau will just remain another idea like the (multiple) codes of conduct, supposedly operational on paper in the Indian microfinance industry for a long time! I hope that the stakeholders developing the regulatory architecture for microfinance take these aspects into account while formulating a strategy for implementing a microfinance credit bureau in a serious, transparent and accountable manner.

Therefore, as a practitioner who has worked for more than two decades in many districts of India, it is my humble opinion that reliable ground-level data is seriously lacking in Indian microfinance and this is certain to affect the quality of the credit reporting to credit bureaus. Therefore, this aspect requires all the attention first and unless cleaning up takes place here, the credit bureau data cannot be called as reliable, valid, and suitable for making sound credit decisions. And this needs to be recognized and addressed by the various stakeholders (including IFC and Omidyar) involved in these efforts.

That said, even assuming that the credit bureau becomes fully operational sooner than later, what *else must be done to ensure the success of the great Indian microfinance credit bureau? Here are some suggestions in this regard.*

For better credit reporting (a precondition for the credit bureau to work effectively), 'the boards of MFIs' must be able to reorient their organizational vision to one of responsible finance—this means they will have to move away from their desire for 'super fast' unnatural growth and high profits (to gain better valuations in investment and go for an IPO, etc.) to balanced natural growth and normal profits. Much of the motivation for multiple lending, ghost lending, performance misreporting (as happened at Sahayata) appears to be related to the above and unless that vision is altered, no amount of technology can perhaps prevent multiple lending. Technology was touted as the solution in 2005–2006 after the Krishna crisis and you can judge for yourself what it has achieved so far. You may want to refer to the chapter on MIS in this book, which clearly shows that even the most basic issues with regard to an MIS still need significant attention in Indian microfinance—and even among the largest Indian MFIs (microfinance institutions).

Even when the boards take the call, the MFI's senior management must be willing and able to translate the above vision into action by bringing about changes in systems, policies, procedures, processes, staff attitudes, and so on. This is very critical as 'intended strategies' will otherwise remain on paper and realized strategies will be very different. It is like what Jack Welch, the famous CEO, commenting on the new breed of strategic planners in the 1980s, is supposed to have said:[250]

> *'There is no point in developing great plans with lot of effort when you are going to do something else on the ground. Oftentimes, organizations put these well-prepared plans in the shelf and lock them up and get around to doing what they are anyways doing.'*

---

250 This is a paraphrased quote.

Again, the case of what happened at Sahayata[251] should not be forgotten where its MD and CEO flattered to deceive by first espousing great concepts at the Microfinance India Summit 2010, only to be charged with serious misreporting a year later.

Therefore, once the MFI board and senior management have done what they have to do, then it may be possible to check multiple lending, provided:

(a) Internal control *systems have sufficient checks/balances to do so*—In other words, internal control systems must have sufficient checks/balances with regard to loan disbursement, loan collection, client selection, and so on, and these controls should properly work on the ground. Proper functioning also means that MFIs are willing and able to take action against errant staff/stakeholders in real time, as and when the frauds and exceptions are spotted. Ideally, systems should deter frauds/exceptions, failing which they must at least swiftly and appropriately punish staff/stakeholders who have caused these frauds in the first place.

(b) Internal audits *spot multiple and ghost lending exceptions as and when they occur and recommend/ensure immediate corrective action*—Internal audits must spot multiple lending exceptions as and when they occur and recommend/ensure immediate corrective action on the ground. This means that the internal audit department should report directly to the board or audit committee and auditors have complete independence from the senior and/or operational management, whose functions and systems they are to audit.

(c) MIS *provides accurate branch/field level data both from the perspective of the credit bureau (CB) and also in terms of portraying ground level reality, so that multiple and ghost lending can be tracked and dealt with*—This is a critical aspect. It also means that MFIs know their end-user clients and have a proper verifiable record of all transactions backed by prenumbered and properly dated receipts/vouchers with all necessary details.

(d) *Field-level frontline and all other staff are* **NOT** *incentivized on irresponsible disbursements, reckless burgeoning growth, and coercive repayments*—In fact, they must be trained and sensitized to believe in and work toward responsible microfinance lending, where multiple and reckless lending through the agent-led decentralized model is viewed as a bane rather than a boon for the organization. It goes without saying that the reward system and human resources function (in general) must be compatible and foster responsible microfinance lending on the ground.

(e) *A related issue here is that MFIs must wholeheartedly decide to adopt green field client acquisition processes where they form new joint liability groups (from scratch) by themselves*—Thus, they must

---

251 See article: What is said at conferences is very different from what is implemented in practice— http://www.moneylife.in/article/what-is-said-at-conferences-is-very-different-from-what-is-implemented-in-practice/22124.html

commit to not indulge in other types of (not-so-desirable and fast tracked) client acquisition methods (such as acquisition of JLGs through breaking of SHGs, etc.) in their field operations. Most importantly, they must walk the talk with regard to these commitments. Of course, robust implementation of client-level controls and periodic verification/action by the internal auditor would go a long way in helping MFIs to sustain their commitment to the green-field process of client acquisition.

(f) *Bankers exercise appropriate due diligence with regard to multiple, over, and ghost lending, as part of their (notional) supervisory role in discharging their priority sector obligations*—This calls for appropriate planning of field visits by bankers with a view to spending sufficient time at the grassroots and engaging in effective on-site monitoring of actual clients, physical/virtual records, their comparison, and so on.

(g) *The RBI ensures appropriate supervision on the ground, with regard to practices of its (NBFC) MFIs*—on aspects such as multiple, over, and ghost lending, as part of its on-site and off-site supervision obligations stemming from its non-bank supervision duties.

(h) This and much more—all with a view to put clients and their situations/needs first—would have to be done to ensure stoppage of multiple, over, and ghost lending (that caused the 2010 AP microfinance crisis in the first place) and usher in an era of responsible microfinance lending.

Therefore, the idea that a credit bureau alone[252] could eliminate multiple, over, and ghost lending and usher in responsible microfinance lending seems very naïve—let us not forget our past experiences with the voluntary codes of conduct (which were not implemented on the ground). In fact, this naiveté could result in the credit bureau becoming a red herring rather than an actual solution because it seems to be distracting the microfinance industry and its stakeholders from the real systemic problems (sharing of clients and JLGs and the prevalence of the agent-led decentralized microfinance model, etc.) at hand that need to be comprehensively tackled. And unless these systemic issues are addressed, the utility of a credit bureau and responsible microfinance lending will remain a distant dream and merely a paper concept as the MIS at MFIs will continue to be unreliable and lack integrity with regard to ground-level data.

---

252 The credit bureau is certainly a positive development. However, it also needs to be understood that a credit bureau is a necessary but not a sufficient condition for responsible microfinance lending!

# Chapter 17:
# Establishing Minimum Standards for Effective Management Information Systems (MISs) in MFIs

A good MIS is absolutely necessary for MFIs to manage the interface with clients and conduct activities/processes in a manner that is efficient, effective, and transparent. Therefore, understanding the state of management information systems (MISs) in Indian MFIs is very important for all stakeholders—in fact, many of the issues that came up in the 2010 AP crisis concerned data, or the lack of it.[253] Therefore, it is especially critical for the regulatory architecture being developed[254] to ensure that MFIs meet certain minimum MIS standards in order to get accredited as MFIs.

So what then are the various aspects that need to be emphasized as part of the minimum MIS requirements in the proposed regulatory architecture? Let us first understand why MIS is important in microfinance. At the MFI level, building an efficient/effective MIS helps manage data, information processes, and activities. This is especially crucial given that microfinance involves a large number of clients with small loans having miniscule and highly repetitive repayments. An appropriate MIS also helps the institution better understand client needs, and thereby enables it to serve them with appropriate products, tailored to their cash flows. A good MIS is, therefore, absolutely necessary for the MFI to manage its interface with clients and conduct its activities/processes in a manner that is efficient, effective, and transparent.

While many MFIs claim that they have an appropriate MIS in tune with global best practices, there are examples[255] to the contrary, and I quote Anna Somos Krishnan, a seasoned microfinance professional, who wrote in a candid article (August 21, 2010), soon after the first Indian microfinance IPO:

---

253  In 2005, just a few minutes after Dr Thorat and I had presented our paper on "Failures in Microfinance," at the NABARD high-level policy conference on microfinance at New Delhi, a prominent industry insider and well-known banker came up to us and said, *"Congratulations, that was an interesting presentation and we are indeed planning to deal with the kind of problems you have mentioned by getting MFIs to become technology users, all the way through."*

254  That is, the proposed microfinance institution development and regulation bill (2012) along with the RBI's detailed guidelines based on the Malegam report, financial inclusion policy drive and so on.

255  The example of SKS is being used for illustrative purposes and I would like to state that from my own knowledge of MIS in the Indian microfinance industry, the SKS MIS was perhaps one of the better systems in the operation in the Indian microfinance industry (during 2005–2006).

> *"Interestingly, the authorities, this time, have given the green signal for an entity that can't prove its operational strength beyond, perhaps, its head office and a couple of system generated reports. Let's face it. SKS, till date, manually reconciles the majority of its 2,000-odd branches data and its seven million clients at the end of each month, despite the unprecedented IT investment that it made four years ago. These are the three-four years when we see the largest scale of growth in an entity. What is thought-provoking, though, is the virtually non-existent digital and automated management information systems (MIS) for trustworthy record-keeping (this means that, with one or two exceptions, MFIs have no IT systems to reliably track customer transaction data)."*[256]

If what Anna Somos Krishnan had written was indeed true, then the situation is very serious. It certainly merits the attention of various stakeholders, including those developing the regulatory architecture for microfinance. Also, without question, the regulators/supervisors would need to analyze and understand the actual state of MIS in Indian MFIs—as they are intermediating increased sums of money and dealing with a larger number of clients—in order to prevent crisis situations in the future. The key questions that need to be asked in this regard are as follows:

1. Given that microfinance involves large numbers of small, repetitive transactions, how are Indian MFIs currently managing data and information on their clients, products, processes and activities?

2. Do they have a fully automated MIS, or are they still completely manual, or are they using hybrid systems? Are there differences between larger and smaller institutions, for profit and not-for-profit institutions, and so on? Are there challenges that Indian MFIs face with regard to implementation of robust MISs? What are these and how can these be addressed?

3. Is the MIS (in Indian MFIs) integrated[257] in real time across products, processes, client segments, branches, and functions (such as accounting and portfolio data)? If 'yes,' how do these systems perform in real time in terms of reliability and validity of data used/generated as well as time taken for analysis and production of reports? If 'no,' how are the MFIs, and especially those with a large number of clients and rapid growth rate, managing the crucial integration and the reliability/validity of their integrated data?

4. Are all features/aspects of all products, for all clients in all locations available in the MIS (manual or computerized or hybrid)? What is the reliability and validity of this primary data and/or analyzed information in terms of reflecting the ground reality (accuracy mainly)? For example, there were news reports in November/December 2010 that the Andhra Pradesh government claimed that one

---

256 http://business.outlookindia.com/article.aspx?266741

257 From the perspective of users of information and enabling them to make meaningful evaluations/decisions, information from MIS should be comprehensive in terms of aggregation and consolidation and assessment of information across products, processes, client segments, geographies, and activities.

of the MFIs was supposedly charging an (effective) interest rate of 60.5% and the MFI replied saying this could have been due to an error in the conversion of data. This concerns the reliability and validity of the MIS.[258]

5. Is the data provided (or information/reports generated) by the MIS sufficient (for various stakeholders) in terms of content, frequency and timeliness, so as to give a meaningful picture of the MFIs' true financial position/condition and prospects? Is it suitable for decision making and risk management from an institutional perspective?

6. Are the data/information/reports in the MIS comparable[259] to that in other institutions and as per good practices (as well as regulator/supervisor) norms?

7. Is data from the MIS consistent with financial and other statements that the MFI generates and uses internally to measure, manage, and monitor its portfolio and other risks?

8. Is the data from the MIS consistent with the financial and other statements that the MFI generates and files with concerned regulators on a periodic basis?

9. Do the MISs of Indian MFIs have transparent business rules in line with good practices, as well as regulator/supervisor norms in critical areas such as (but not limited to) the following?

    - *Asset classification and provisioning*: Including methods for determining quality of (loan and other) assets and related indicators (i.e., portfolio at risk and provisioning ratios). Some relevant aspects here are as follows:

        ✓ Transparency and verification must be possible with regard to the sequence of appropriation of client repayments, which needs to be as per good practices standards and regulator norms. The sequence in which client repayments must be appropriated should always be as follows: *fines first (if applicable), then penal interest (if applicable), interest overdue, then interest due (if due on the date on which repayment comes in), then principal overdue, and, lastly, principal.* If principal is appropriated first, then while portfolio quality would appear better, the yield on portfolio would reduce and so would the profitability/sustainability of the MFI.

---

258 See the following links http://www.thehindubusinessline.com/todays-paper/aps-microfinance-institutions-admit-to-charging-up-to-605/article1008032.ece and http://www.moneycontrol.com/news/economy/do-not-have-any-product60-interest-rate-basix_495663.html

259 Data/information needs to be compared across institutions and over time. Hence, standardized procedures must be used to develop the MIS and standard definitions of indicators, and standard methods for calculating the same must be rigorously followed. This does not imply loss of flexibility, but rather suggests standard use of best-practices-oriented indicators and methods for portfolio quality measurement. This is often reflected in the methodology of developing the business rules.

- ✓ The method of calculating age of a past due loan should be through recommended best practice procedures.[260]

- ✓ Grace periods (in terms of days or number of installments) and the specific process[261] used by the MIS for calculating various portfolio quality indicators (such as "portfolio at risk" or PAR) must be clearly discernable and/or transparently stated, if hard-coded in the MIS. For example, client repayment could be over 46 weekly installments across a 52-week loan term—this means that at any time, a client could have skipped six weekly installments and still not be classified as a past due account. This has serious implications for asset classification and provisioning and it needs to be recognized. Therefore, unusually long grace periods, or repayment moratoriums, must be stated upfront in a transparent manner.

- ✓ There must be standard good practices procedures for regular monitoring and management of past due or impaired assets/credit relationships, evaluating the adequacy of credit (loan) loss provisions[262] and credit (loan) loss allowances, and so on.

- *Accounting policies and practices:* The accounting policies and practices followed in the MIS must be as per good practices standards prescribed by the regulator. The integration[263] of the accounting, portfolio, and other modules must also be done through a transparent process and as per regulator norms.

- *Total cost to client:* The total cost for various products (interest rates, fees, all forced conditions, including credit insurance, etc.) must be transparently available in the MIS and capable of being compared with actual portfolio yield and/or earnings of the MFI. This will help highlight any hidden interest charges and costs that clients often claim to pay to MFIs—an issue that came up regularly during the 2010 AP microfinance crisis.

---

260 Where age of past due loan = date of calculating age−earliest unpaid overdue (in days). Using the installment method of aging requires adjustments to be made as this method understates age of past due loan, after the loan term and overstates age of past due loan within the loan term.

261 While selecting past due loans for calculating portfolio at risk (PAR) of any age, the reference point is to choose every loan that has either fines, or interest, or principal overdue. Technically, it is possible to have past due loans with "zero" principal overdue and some interest/fines overdue, and, therefore, using only principal overdue to determine aggregate loan outstanding of the past due loans could actually understate the risk in the portfolio.

262 In case of aging with weekly/daily installments, define age categories based on number of installments skipped rather than in days. This is to ensure appropriate provisioning. For example, in a weekly payment model, < 30 days past due could actually be 4/5 installments skipped. For example, the traditional 10% provisioning would not be appropriate here and a much higher provisioning may be required, depending on the context and actual ground situation.

263 Ensure automatic integration of portfolio and accounting modules, in that data entered in one, for example, loan disbursement through the portfolio module, automatically gets reflected in the other, as loan outstanding under assets in the balance sheet. This is very critical.

## Chapter 17: Establishing Minimum Standards for Effective Management Information Systems (MISs) in MFIs

- *Other aspects:* There must be clarity and transparency in the MIS with regard to risk-management aspects, including controls, ALM[264] issues, exposure norms across products/regions /sectors/ clients, and so on.

10. Given all these aspects, what are the minimum MIS standards that have to be set for enabling accreditation of MFIs as per the proposed regulatory architecture[265] being developed?

Without question, there is a critical need to establish minimum standards for certain non-negotiables such as MIS, in Indian MFIs. The stakeholders who are developing a robust regulatory framework for microfinance should utilize this opportunity to enable the microfinance industry to "arrive" in terms of having a transparent, integrated, and comprehensive MIS that really works on the ground. This is a crucial first step, even before we talk about the establishment of a National Credit Bureau, as only then would the proposed credit bureau be able to have reliable and valid (MIS) data, so vital and necessary for reducing the occurrence of multiple, ghost lending, and over-lending by Indian MFIs.

---

264  Asset and liability management.
265  That is, the proposed microfinance institution development and regulation bill (2012) along with the RBI's detailed guidelines based on the Malegam report, financial inclusion policy drive and so on.

# Chapter 18:
# Can the Governance of Risk Management Be Managed in Microfinance?

SKS Microfinance Limited, India's only listed micro-lender, and other NBFC MFIs have been in the news especially (in 2010–2011) for several reasons; one of the main reasons is for cash embezzlements and frauds over the years, as the examples given suggest.

As *Microfinance Focus* notes:

> "According to auditors, SKS Microfinance recorded 408 cases of cash embezzlements and frauds in the financial year 2011....Company's annual report shows 156 cases of cash embezzlements by the employees, aggregating Rs. 16,018,106 during 2011. ...There were 205 cases of loans given out to nonexistent borrowers on the basis of fictitious documentation created by the employees of the company, aggregating Rs. 45,177,531. Further, 47 cases of loans taken by borrowers under fake identity, aggregating Rs. 13,786,130, were reported during the year. The Company is pursuing the borrowers to repay the money. The outstanding loan balance (net of recovery) aggregating Rs. 6,386,267 has been written off."[266]

Here are some more examples from MFI financial statements and many more can be found at my blog:[267]

> "(xxi) Based upon the audit procedures performed for the purpose of reporting the true and fair view of the financial statements and as per the information and explanations given by the management, we report that no material frauds on or by the Company were noticed/reported during the year although there were some instances of frauds on the Company by its employees as given below:
>
> *(a) Thirty-three cases of cash embezzlements by the employees of the Company aggregating to Rs.7,079,683 were reported during the year.* The services of all such employees involved have been terminated and the

---

266 Source: Quoted from SKS Microfinance faced 408 cases of cash frauds in FY 2011, by *Microfinance Focus*, July 6, 2011.
267 http://microfinance-in-india.blogspot.com/2010/11/has-burgeoning-growth-caused-increasing.html

# Chapter 18: Can the Governance of Risk Management Be Managed in Microfinance?

Company is in the process of taking legal action. We have been informed that nine of these employees are absconding. The outstanding loan balance (net of recovery) aggregating to Rs. 5, 377,428 has been written off;

*(b) Eighteen cases of loans given to non-existent borrowers on the basis of fictitious documentation created by the employees of the Company aggregating to Rs. 5,645,657 were reported during the year.* The services of all such employees involved have been terminated and the Company is in the process of taking legal actions. The outstanding loan balance (net of recovery) aggregating to Rs. 4,253,379 has been written off; and

*(c) One case of fraud by an employee of the Company in collusion with vendors has been reported during the year. The aggregate value of transactions is Rs. 9,610,755 (including Rs. 3,051,510 in respect of the previous year).* The services of the said employee and the arrangements with the said vendors have been terminated. The Company has initiated legal action and criminal proceedings against such employees. *The financial effect of the loss incurred by the Company is not currently quantifiable."*[268]

*The icing on the cake is, of course, Sahayata Microfinance and it was again a case of a high-profile NBFC caught in a massive fraud-like situation. See the given description, which is reproduced from my blog:*[269]

"Sahayata Microfinance Pvt Ltd has suspended the top brass, including its chief executive, on charges of mismanagement. The Rajasthan-based microfinance company has also stopped fresh lending temporarily, to set its house in order. Following the suspension of management and poor performance, rating agency CARE downgraded its nonconvertible debentures of Rs. 19.5 crore from CARE BB+ to CARE B-. In September, some board members pointed out prima facie evidence of the management's misrepresentation of company performance. The board has ordered a detailed portfolio audit. The investors have placed an interim management to control operations, to ensure the business continues uninterrupted. The company will resume loan disbursement from December. The board questioned chief executive, chief financial officer and other senior managers on charges of serious misreporting and mismanagement.... While the chief executive was suspended with immediate effect, the CFO and head of operations were stripped of their duties immediately. They were subsequently suspended."[270]

"Sahayata commenced operations as a society in September 2006 in Udaipur (Rajasthan); the promoters came together with their own investments to test the viability of the business in Rajasthan. In August 2007, the promoters acquired a nonbanking finance company named Shree Hari Fintrade Pvt Ltd. In

---

268 SKS financial statement 2009.
269 http://microfinance-in-india.blogspot.in/2011/11/award-winning-sahayata-microfinance-is.html
270 Source: Sahayata Microfin sacks top mgmt for irregularities, by Abhijit Lele *Business Standard*, November 18, 2011.

August 2009, the company got its present name. Sahayata's assets under management amounted to Rs. 800 million during mid-October 2011 compared to Rs. 1260 million as on March 31, 2011."[271]

The Mix Market website lists the growth of Sahayata's gross loan portfolio and clients as follows:

| Table 18.1 Sahayata Microfinance Outreach | | | | | |
|---|---|---|---|---|---|
| Indicators | End March 2007 | End March 2008 | End March 2009 | End March 2010 | End March 2011 |
| Number of active borrowers | 194 | — | 29,171 | 139,179 | 250,631 |
| Gross loan portfolio (in US $) | 19,429 | — | 3,616,162 | 20,215,139 | 31,399,596 |
| Gross loan portfolio (in INR) | 846,900 | — | 183,918,020 | 909,074,811 | 1,394,142,054 |

Source: http://www.mixmarket.org/mfi/sahayata/report

Also, the 'Udaipur-based Sahayata Microfinance... raised Rs. 19.5 crore through the issuance of non-convertible debentures (NCDs),... purchased by DWM (Cyprus) Ltd, a member of the Developing World Markets group of companies.... IFMR Capital was the sole financial advisor to the issue."[272,273]

What is really interesting is that Sahayata had also won several awards and recognitions (national and international) for its good governance, innovative practices, and the like.

- 'First, it must also be mentioned that Sahayata Microfinance Pvt Ltd has won the prestigious award for *Commitment to Improved Implementation of Good Governance*. This international award has been conferred by Hanson Wade, an organization providing invaluable insights to businesses globally, in association with Symbiotics Research & Advisory, Gradatim IT Ventures, IBM and International Finance Corporation (IFC).'[274]

- Second, Sahayata Microfinance Pvt. Ltd,[275] also 'received the The Srijan 2009 Emerging MFI Award. The award presented today at Srijan 2009 Microfinance Forum[276] hosted by Intellecap & Standard Chartered Bank at Hyatt Regency in Mumbai....'[277]

---

271 Source: Sahayata Microfinance to face comprehensive independent audit of its operations: CRISIL, Posts by Abhay, India Microfinance.com, November 9, 2011.
272 Source: Sahayata Microfinance raises INR 195 MN through NCDs, *Microfinance Focus*, April 23, 2011.
273 http://microfinance-in-india.blogspot.in/2011/11/award-winning-sahayata-microfinance-is.html
274 http://www.sahayata.co.in/pages/news/display/8
275 http://www.microfinancefocus.com/news/tag/sahayata-microfinance-pvt-ltd/
276 http://www.microfinancefocus.com/news/tag/srijan-2009-microfinance-forum/
277 http://www.microfinancefocus.com/news/2009/12/08/sahayata-microfinance-pvt-ltd-recives-emerging-mfis-award

# Chapter 18: Can the Governance of Risk Management Be Managed in Microfinance?

- Third, apart from these prestigious awards, Sahayata's website stated that it is also a member of 'The Smart Campaign.' 'The Smart Campaign, a global initiative to incorporate strong client protection principles across the microfinance industry, today recognized Sahayata Microfinance Private Limited (Sahayata) for its outstanding efforts to train both staff and clients on institutional standards of ethical behavior. Sahayata's training document, 'Illustrations and Activities for Training Loan Officers on Customers' Rights and Responsibilities,' is now available as a 'good practice' example on the Smart Campaign website. ... 'Sahayata was selected as a winner because their practical tool is easy to create, use, and understand,' said Smart Campaign Tool Development Specialist Leah Wardle. The Smart Campaign's Client Protection Principles state that MFIs must maintain high ethical standards in their interactions with microfinance clients and ensure that adequate safeguards are in place to detect and correct corruption or mistreatment of clients. Sahayata's 'Illustrations and Activities for Training Loan Officers on Customers' Rights and Responsibilities' can help MFIs design their own tools to help them achieve this. Available in both English and Spanish, this tool is one of many available on the Smart Campaign's website, www.smartcampaign.org (Washington, DC, June 2, 2011[278]).'[279]

As I have been saying for long—for as long as from May 2005 when the NABARD high-level policy conference[280] took place at New Delhi—we surely need to determine whether the malaise in Indian microfinance is deeper than assumed and/or portrayed. Without question, we need to urgently understand whether—just as it happened at the Ramalinga Raju–led Satyam Computers—senior management and/or others at some MFIs are perhaps the cause of the burgeoning frauds and misrepresentations of performance in Indian microfinance.

*Note that these cases are not that of ordinary NBFC MFIs—SKSML is one of India's largest NBFC MFIs and only listed micro-lender and Sahayata is a high profile NBFC, whose suspended MD, Mr Ajay Verma, was on the board of MFIN and had also preached at various conferences (such as Microfinance India Summit, 2010) what he did not unfortunately practice[281] on the ground.*

*It is sad that NBFC* MFIs, which are among the largest MFIs in India both in terms of number of clients serviced as well as gross loan portfolio outstanding, have become a prey to frauds and control failures. The ramifications are significant because NBFCs account for a huge proportion of the Indian microfinance industry and it is indeed very unfortunate that these NBFCs, which are supposedly regulated by the RBI, have received very little supervisory attention. Readers would recall that the six large AP-headquartered

---

278 http://www.smartcampaign.org/news-a-highlights/press-releases/36-2011/505-sahayatas-training-staff-for-ethical-behavior-wins-honors-in-smart-campaign-call-for-tools
279 http://microfinance-in-india.blogspot.in/2011/11/award-winning-sahayata-microfinance-is.html
280 http://www.thehindubusinessline.com/todays-paper/tp-money-banking/article2191016.ece
281 Refer to the following article (What is said at conferences is very different from what is implemented in practice http://www.moneylife.in/article/what-is-said-at-conferences-is-very-different-from-what-is-implemented-in-practice/22124.html).

MFIs, which added about US$ 1.911[282] billion as GLP and 9.76 million clients during April 2008–March 2010, did not attract the *supervisory attention of the department of nonbank supervision, RBI,* which was supposed to look closely, scan, and supervise (systemically important) NBFCs with loan assets greater than Rs. 100 crore. Note that in numerical terms, the growth figures for these six AP-headquartered NBFCs for 2008–2010 are equivalent to each of these six MFIs adding about Rs. 72[283] crore every month for 24 months.

This apart, we are all aware that the RBI is supposedly preparing detailed guidelines for MFIs based on the Malegam Committee Report (MCR) and the bill for regulation of MFIs has been referred to the Parliamentary Standing Committee Finance. The Microfinance Institution Development and Regulation Bill (MFIDR Bill, 2012) is especially noteworthy because it brings greater focus on savings/thrift and perhaps in the long term it could also facilitate MFIs to offer savings services to the poor. While the need to ensure that the poor have access to savings is welcome, enabling MFIs to offer thrift is fundamentally unsound because of the several reasons, including weak internal controls, demonstrated earlier.

Therefore, I would like to use this opportunity to make a humble submission on what I think are some of the key internal control issues that caused the 2010 microfinance crisis in Andhra Pradesh, India. I sincerely hope that these are taken into account and addressed appropriately by various stakeholders developing the regulatory architecture for microfinance.

As given earlier, "nonexistent clients" and "borrowers with fake identities" are two common types of operational frauds that have been (increasingly) occurring because of the turbocharged growth in the Indian microfinance industry[284] and the commensurate lack of quality internal controls. It must also be noted that there are several other kinds of frauds[285] ("misappropriation of client repayments" and the like) prevalent in Indian microfinance and these are highlighted here.

*The loan-disbursement-related frauds typically include:* (a) loan officer[286] issues loans to "ghost" or nonexistent clients; (b) loan officer issues second or third loan to delinquent clients to facilitate repayment (top-up or greening of loans and this is evident from cases of clients with multiple loans); (c) loan officer provides bulk money to agents for onward disbursement and has no serious means to check their actual

---

282 This should have been higher at US$ 2.076 billion had the Mix Market retained the original GLP figures that it had put out in 2010/2011 for BASIX and SHARE. For some reason, Mix Market changed its original figures for BASIX and SHARE respectively from US$ 223,229,799 and US$ 490,923,201 to US$ 172,484,946 and US$ 376,593,362 (as on date). I have the original print screen data and other pieces of evidence with regard to the original data put out by Mix Market. There are several other issues with the Mix Market database and I can provide the details if required.

283 This should have been higher at Rs 78 crores had the Mix Market retained the original GLP figures that it had put out in 2010/2011 for BASIX and SHARE. For some reason, Mix Market changed its original figures for BASIX and SHARE respectively from US$ 223,229,799 and US$ 490,923,201 to US$ 172,484,946 and US$ 376,593,362 (as on date). I have the original print screen data and other pieces of evidence with regard to the original data put out by Mix Market. There are several other issues with the Mix Market database and I can provide the details if required.

284 Refer to the following link for an overview of frauds in microfinance as evident from MFI audited financial statements: http://microfinance-in-india.blogspot.com/2010/11/has-burgeoning-growth-caused-increasing.html

285 Note that there is significant evidence for increasing level of frauds in Indian microfinance through audited financial statements, e-mails, letters, and the like available in the public and private domain.

286 This could be a loan officer or a branch manager or a branch accountant or any other staff. Sometimes, center leaders, group leaders, and other kinds of agents could also be involved in this.

## Chapter 18: Can the Governance of Risk Management Be Managed in Microfinance?

disbursement to clients—in many cases, these loans are used for non-microfinance activities; (d) staff/cashiers/accountants disburse loans to themselves and show fictitious names or clients with false identities; (e) loan officer charges clients an unofficial "fee" (bakshish) to enable them to access a loan from an MFI; (e) loan officers, staff, accountants, and cashiers issue larger loans to clients and use some portion of the loan for their own consumption—they, however, do not repay and expect the client to repay, and this is an important reason for delinquency; and (f) several other aspects.

*The loan-repayment-related frauds normally include:* (a) loan officer collects payment, issues receipt, but does not deposit the money repaid (by the client) with the MFI—this could happen with client prepayments or regular payments; (b) agents collect loan payments and do not deposit them in a timely manner with the concerned MFI—agents who have not lent money to clients, but rather used loan amounts from the MFI, do not repay the MFI at all; (c) staff/loan officer charges unofficial delinquency fees to manage delinquency; (d) loan officer/others collect payments on loans that have been officially written off and keep it themselves; and (e) several other aspects.

*Other kinds of frauds that have been witnessed are:* (a) insurance payments do not reach the client nominees, who in course of time forget to ask for them; (b) insurance premiums are not deposited at the branch; and (c) higher than required insurance payments are collected in the guise of administrative charges (recall that IRDA initiated an enquiry against a large Indian MFI).[287]

Thus, one of the most important fallouts of the 2010 AP crisis has been the apparent lack of and/or failure of risk management at many MFIs. I have several generic and specific observations regarding this for various *stakeholders who are developing a new regulatory architecture for microfinance*.

- *Internal controls for financial reporting versus risk management:* In many MFIs, the (sole) focus on internal controls was mainly for the purpose of financial reporting. This resulted in risk management deviating from strategy and its implementation. Also, in several MFIs, the basic tenets of internal control, particularly those pertaining to operating risks, were not followed.

- *Risk handled in a piecemeal manner:* In a few cases, the enterprise (or MFI) as a whole was not considered and risk was handled in a piecemeal manner—so much so that even the boards were completely out of touch with the (risk management) systems in place. Thus, a holistic and comprehensive perspective on risk was lacking.

- *Risk management mistaken for risk elimination:* In one MFI, effective risk management was seen as eliminating risk taking and that is perhaps an inappropriate view of things. MFIs and other stakeholders must understand that risk is a fundamental driving force in any activity, including microfinance. Therefore, risk elimination is perhaps strictly not possible. The aim must be to ensure that risks are understood,

---

[287] IRDA finds 'massive problems' in SKS Micro's insurance operations (http://www.thehindubusinessline.com/industry-and-economy/banking/irda-finds-massive-problems-in-sks-micros-insurance-operations/article3446545.ece), by G. Naga Sridhar, May 22, 2012.

managed, and, where appropriate, communicated throughout the organization, so that the MFI as a whole can be ready for it, as and when it becomes significant.

- *Inability to seriously anticipate and properly manage political risk[288]:* In several MFIs, the political risk (as in AP) was neither (seriously) anticipated nor managed on an institution-wide basis. Those (initially) looking at this risk were perhaps either far too junior or lacked the requisite contextual experience; often, there seemed to be no serious guidance from senior management/board. Importantly, boards were, in a number of cases, ignorant of the key (political and important) risks facing their MFIs, and most came into the picture later than required.

- *Lack of board involvement in establishing/overseeing risk management structure:* Without question, the effective implementation of risk management requires involving the board in both establishing and overseeing the risk management structure. This did not happen and in many MFIs, the board neither reviewed nor provided guidance about the alignment of overall microfinance strategy with risk appetite and the internal risk management structure.

- *Lack of independence of risk management and control functions:* To assist the board in its work, risk management and control functions need to be independent, reporting directly to the board. However, this was seldom the case, and, as a result, risk perceptions often got altered (or even misreported) by the line management and other staff. In reality, such risk perceptions were perhaps not fair representations of the true risk confronting the MFI (*a situation akin to not wanting any bad news, often without realizing that timely news about things going wrong affords a great chance to undertake appropriate on-course corrections*). Thus, a true picture of the risks perhaps never reached the board, which was left high and dry when the same affected the MFI.

That said, how then can the governance of risk management be improved in MFIs? But before getting into the recommendations, let us ask a relevant question here: *why have these (increasing) frauds occurred and what are the lessons for regulation and supervision?*

*The answer is simple.* MFIs that have faced burgeoning growth in the past few years have not had commensurate capacity—including internal control and other systems—required for managing their turbocharged growth. Further, as a result of the strong decentralized (agent) model that many of these MFIs have used and some are continuing to use, they are increasingly vulnerable to frauds (especially, when their growth is rapid). It is one thing to acknowledge the frauds and isolate reasons for their existence, but given the fact that they have been increasing in Indian microfinance since 2005,[289] we cannot

---

[288] This is in spite of dress rehearsals such as the Krishna (2005–2006) microfinance crisis and Kolar 2009 microfinance crisis having occurred.

[289] Regulation and Areas of Potential Market Failure in Microfinance, by Thorat, Y. S. P. and Ramesh S. Arunachalam (2005), paper presented at the NABARD high-level policy conference in New Delhi in May 2005.

afford to let this go on. We need to learn from these internal control lapses and surely these lessons must be dovetailed into the regulatory architecture for microfinance that is being developed. The same is attempted here.

*Issue 1: Lack of sound corporate governance led to poor risk management at the MFIs.* Sound corporate governance is critical as it can enhance the quality of risk management, including the processes adopted for the same at an MFI. As governance involves many stakeholders, each with specific assigned responsibilities, they need to ensure that the system as a whole is geared to support the overall strategy of the MFI and ensure the effectiveness of various internal control mechanisms. Further, while the board is certainly not expected to understand every nuance of the microfinance business and/or to oversee every microfinance activity/transaction, they surely need to ensure that senior management does that using an organized hierarchy of responsibilities with clear authority. The board, however, has the responsibility to set the tone regarding their own MFIs' risk taking (preferences) and to oversee the internal control strategy so as to ensure that their directives are actually followed on the ground, during implementation. They also have the responsibility to hire staff, who, in their opinion, have the integrity, judgment, and competence to help achieve the same. This, unfortunately, did not happen with the AP-headquartered MFIs at the heart of the 2010 crisis.

*Issue 2: Disregard for internal controls by many line managers.* Internal controls are the responsibility of line management at MFIs. Line managers must determine the level of risks they need to accept to run their businesses and to assure themselves that the combination of earnings, capital, and internal controls is sufficient to compensate for the risk exposures. *It is clear from the 2010 AP microfinance crisis that basic tenets of internal control, particularly those pertaining to operating and related risks, were not followed*—in fact, as the analysis of many (fraud) cases demonstrate, it is apparent that the line managers in several fast growing MFIs had utter disregard for even the most basic controls, such as the segregation of duties, and so on.

*Issue 3: Enhanced people risks also causing failure of internal controls.* Internal controls and sound governance become more important when the MFIs' operations move into higher risk areas—such as the kind of growth that many of the NBFC MFIs experienced during 2008–2010. Indeed, when changes are happening, as they had been during this high growth period in AP, there is no doubt that control failures will increase significantly as has been reported in India. Thus, rapid growth, introduction of new products, and changes in delivery channels (such as the use of the decentralized agent model) are examples of situations that stress the MFI control environment. When these types of changes occur, "people risks"—risks that are related to training employees in new products and processes—escalate. Employees who join will undoubtedly need to learn about the culture and control environment at the MFI. Likewise, employees unfamiliar with their new responsibilities, including the systems they use, their changing client profile, the services they provide customers, the degree of attention expected by their own supervisors (and members of the internal control department), are more likely to create control breaks. As a result, MFIs need to be wary of and manage people risks appropriately and in a timely manner, through a good human resources function. This again has been and continues to be very weak at most MFIs in India.

*I have met a number of stakeholders at the grassroots who state that all and sundry, including some with local criminal records, had been brought in as MFI staff, to meet the burgeoning growth requirements.* Let me tell you that I felt personally intimidated by the kind of staff and agents that I met during a field visit to a few areas in 2010. They appeared to be local toughies often used by local political masters and had no idea of the microfinance spirit and mission—they just knew how to quickly disburse and recover money as tough moneylenders[290] do and, most importantly, had zero tolerance (including for PAR) in performing their duties. With many staff/agents who are not necessarily attuned to the vision and spirit of microfinance, I am not at all sure that the ongoing efforts to integrate social performance, client protection, and the like will get translated at the ground, unless some real fundamental changes are made to the MFI delivery model. And it is the duty of regulation/supervision to ensure that in real time.

*Issue 4: Drive for efficiency causing omission of key controls.* Rapid growth and change also modify the relative risks to an MFI. For example, the pressure to beat a competitor in the market with new/same products (as was the case in AP during the years preceding the 2010 crisis) may cut short the design review process and omit an important aspect of control. This has happened consistently and the drive for efficiency and use of more standardized process in microfinance led to very little time being invested in building the client-level relationships, which incidentally was the key and hallmark feature in the early success of microfinance. *The proliferation of agents and the shortest lead time to disburse loans as an incentive criterion are due to this efficiency drive and these again have resulted in omission of key controls in many MFIs.* In fact, significant controls that existed in the original Grameen (or even India-adapted Grameen model) have perhaps been forgotten and that is why we heard of unsound lending and coercive recovery practices by Indian MFIs during the 2010 AP crisis.

*Issue 5: Entrepreneurial drive and nontransparent governance results in lack of control infrastructure.* In fact, many of the MFIs that had been at the centre of the 2010 AP crisis came under the microscope for their governance failures and they demonstrated similar characteristics. They were led by hard-charging entrepreneurs whose ability to think outside the box (in all fairness) pioneered growth, advances and innovation in microfinance. *But the personalities of these individuals, in many cases, led to a single-minded focus on unmanageable growth, higher profits, increased equity investments, share valuations at a premium, higher returns and larger wealth creation for shareholders. This perhaps resulted in very little*

---

290   Why the dream of microfinance is turning sour (http://www.independent.co.uk/news/world/asia/why-the-dream-of-microfinance-is-turning-sour-2280814.html), by Leo Hornak, *Sunday, May 8, 2011.*

*time being spent on building the control infrastructure so vital for microfinance.* In fact, as a result of this, inadequate time was spent on building the control infrastructure, unequal to the amount required in such an environment. The consequences are there for all to see. Therefore, it is time that MFIs revisited their original model and brought back features that facilitated borrower preparation and participation (so significant in the original Grameen and other models), client protection, and client dignity. That would be a useful strategy to minimize and counter political risks.

*Issue 6: Irrational expectations and internal frauds.* Another form of risk is internal fraud. When the expectations of the market, supervisors, and colleagues, or pressures of professional/personal life become overwhelming, key MFI staff may overstep the ethical and legal boundaries and cover up errors or deliberately commit a fraud. *This is what has happened in many MFIs that jumped on to the equity bandwagon and were also turbocharged to grow by the misplaced enthusiasm of DFIs (such as SIDBI) and commercial banks that sought to satisfy their priority sector lending targets.* There is enough reason to believe that this may have been the case with several of the staff at these MFIs who were found to be involved in frauds in the Indian microfinance sector (before and during the 2010 crisis). Again, the human resources function must take the driver's seat and reduce (or, if possible, eliminate) unrealistic expectations and ease work time pressures—so that the MFI staff are not forced to cross the line, with regard to ethical behavior on the job. An important aspect is to ensure that there should be no disconnect between strategy and risk management, on the one hand, and incentives on the other. Incentives do not mean just remuneration but also other aspects such as promotion, stock options, and so on. That would help in reducing "people risks."

*Issue 7: Weakened internal audit function in many MFIs.* Boards of directors at MFIs are responsible for ensuring that their MFIs have an effective audit process and that internal controls are adequate for the nature and scope of their businesses. The reporting lines of the internal audit function should be such that the information that directors receive is impartial and not unduly influenced by management. Internal audit is a key element of the overall responsibility to validate the strength of internal controls. This is not to be underestimated. *This sadly did not happen in many MFIs and, especially, at the large AP-headquartered MFIs. The same weakness can be found in many large and fast growing MFIs located in other parts of India.*

*Issue 8: Greater focus on quantitative versus qualitative risks.* Thus, although risk management has become more quantitative, considerable management judgment must be applied to the process, and this is what MFIs need to get their boards to facilitate. Frequent and small losses can generally be absorbed in the operating margin of the product or service and MFIs have tended to focus more on such risks and problems. It is the low-probability, large losses that provide the greatest challenge. And, it is just such risks—the ones that can severely damage, if not kill, an organization—that too many MFIs have not formally taken into consideration. And that, in many ways, had resulted in many problems on the ground in the 2010 AP microfinance crisis. *Most, if not all, MFIs did not expect the AP government to act against them and they surely did not factor in the political risk despite the serious problems that they had faced in the past few years.*

Sometimes I wonder whether MFIs took the risk of political action (because the industry was, after all, widely regarded as the holy cow of financial inclusion) lightly, and this gross underestimation may have been one of the main reasons why they were taken aback when this risk became a reality in AP in October 2010. Further, I would like to mention that as the industry moves forward, risk assessment and risk-based auditing[291] at systemically important and large MFIs become necessary. I do hope that all MFIs—including growing and large NBFCs—adopt this and the regulatory framework makes it necessary for them to do so. This alone can help prevent the kind of institutional lapses that led to the 2010 AP crises.

To summarize, the burgeoning growth of Indian microfinance led by a flawed business model (as stated by Dr Rangarajan) has meant that frauds and control failures have become more common in Indian MFIs. These have serious implications for the regulation and supervision of microfinance in India. First, under no circumstance should MFIs be allowed to collect savings from poor people as their control infrastructure is very weak and their business model is seriously flawed. Second, *hands-off regulation* will not work. Therefore, neither detailed regulatory guidelines from the RBI (based on the Malegam Committee) nor the passing of a microfinance bill will help, until appropriate and local level supervisory arrangements are in place. With all due respect, among other things, it certainly calls for a greater role for the State governments, as much of this supervision will have to occur at the local level—something that neither the RBI nor the Union Ministry of Finance can hope to ensure from Mumbai or New Delhi. If poor people are indeed to be protected, their vulnerability not exploited and valuable money safeguarded, there is no doubt that a constructive role for the state government must be envisaged and provided for in any regulatory architecture. Make no mistake about this! On their part, the state governments must be fair and permit the MFI model to operate normally, as long as legally tenable and sound business models (as Dr Rangarajan has argued for) are used by them.

I do sincerely hope that the relevant authorities look at these and other issues related to internal controls in the crisis-affected Indian microfinance industry. That is one area, among many others, where rebuilding can and must start as soon as possible. Only this can put the Indian microfinance sector back on the rails and get it to implement—through a sound independent internal audit function[292]—the great sounding ideas that MFIs have always wanted to implement. And this is certainly another good place for regulatory reform to start.

---

291 In simple terms, risk assessment is a process by which an auditor identifies and evaluates the quantity of the MFI's risks and the quality of its controls over those risks. Through risk-based auditing, the board and auditors will use the results of the risk assessments to focus on the areas of greatest risk and to set priorities for audit work. That, however, does not mean that the audit department can lose sight of or ignore areas that are rated low risk. An effective risk-based auditing program will ensure adequate audit coverage for all of an MFI's auditable activities. The frequency and depth of each area's audit should vary according to the auditor's risk assessment.

292 Independent internal audits, which are equally important, are dealt with in the next chapter.

# Chapter 19:
# Do Independent Internal Audits Have Real Value?

The microfinance institution (MFI) model in India has been through a (serious) crisis over the past few years (since 2005 and especially in 2010) and a lot of this has to do with the inability of the boards of MFIs to actually implement (in real time) some of the very (high sounding) concepts and prescriptions for responsible finance that came from various quarters.

While it cannot be denied that some MFIs were not interested in responsible microfinance, some others perhaps could not ensure the implementation of these well-meaning concepts on a consistent basis in real time. A classic example is the well-intentioned (Sa-Dhan) code of conduct in 2006, which was often waved at meetings with the AP government but rarely visible, in terms of practice, on the ground. Slowly, perverse incentives (as Vijay Mahajan had famously noted in 2010) set in and eventually led to what is now referred to as the 2010 Andhra Pradesh microfinance crisis.

In retrospect, what essentially happened was a failure of commercial microfinance—primarily because the checks and balances required for commercial microfinance (to actually work on the ground) were almost absent. By checks and balances, I mean two things, including lack of (i) supervisory oversight, and that contributed in huge measure to the crisis, and (ii) a strong, independent, and objective internal audit function within these MFIs. While even a single letter from the supervisor (or regulator) could have mitigated the scale of the problems that happened in AP in the years preceding 2010, the absence of an independent and objective internal audit system certainly hurt the MFIs even more.

Why is an independent and objective internal audit system critical for the well-being of MFIs, especially those desiring to practice responsible commercial microfinance? From a larger perspective, internal audits are perhaps the first means for well-meaning MFI boards to get regular feedback on whether the concept of responsible microfinance is being implemented on the ground. In other words, an independent and objective internal audit system can provide useful feedback on how processes and procedures (to promote responsible microfinance) are supposedly being implemented on the ground. Therefore, even before credit/social ratings and/or the newly established code of compliance assessments point out any discrepancies, it is the internal audit system that can provide useful early warning signals for the MFIs and their boards. Without question, just as charity begins at home, the first step in responsible microfinance is to ensure that MFIs have such an independent and objective internal audit system in the first place.

So, what do I mean by an independent and objective internal audit system? Let me first set out the strategic context of internal audits from which it will be apparent that their independence and objectivity are critical and necessary. This strategic context clearly determines the extent to which internal audits can become a powerful and independent tool that boards of MFIs can use to ensure responsible microfinance on the ground and in real time.

Essentially, according to The Institute of Internal Auditors (www.theiia.org), internal auditing is defined as:

> *"An independent, objective assurance... activity designed to add value and improve an organization's operations. It helps an organization accomplish its objectives by bringing a systematic, disciplined approach to evaluate and improve the effectiveness of risk management, control, and governance processes."*

This definition is critical because it sets forth the parameters on which an internal audit system can be designed at the MFIs.

First and foremost, *an internal audit system must be independent of the MFI activities being audited.* This implies that internal auditors at MFIs do not report to line management and/or senior management. Often, at some MFIs, which had an elaborate internal audit function, the independence of this function was hugely compromised because the internal audit department came under senior management whose very activities were also to be assessed.

Tell me, how can an internal audit department that reports to the CEO or CFO (or anyone else who is part of the line/operational management) accurately assess and provide objective feedback on the working of processes and procedures? *Therefore, MFI boards must ensure that there is an internal audit department that reports directly (and independent of senior management) to the board or its audit subcommittee.* This is mandatory and this independence in functioning will facilitate greater objectivity in the working of the internal audit department. It will also position the internal audit department appropriately within the MFI, in terms of its strategic context.

Second, an additional caveat is in order here. Many organizations including MFIs may find it tempting to get internal auditors to design their risk management, control, and governance systems. While it is true that internal auditors have intimate knowledge of what systems work on the ground and why, if they are asked to design these MFI systems, then, it is unlikely that they would be able to assess the functioning of these systems dispassionately and objectively. *This means that at no time should MFIs use their internal auditors to design the risk management, control, and governance systems and processes.* At best, feedback—through discussions with the internal auditors and/or studying of their internal audit reports—could be taken with regard to these systems so that appropriate on-course corrections are made. This again will ensure that the internal auditors are truly independent of the activities that they are auditing.

A third issue is relevant here. That is the scope of internal audits and this again is critical to understanding the reality from across the organization (MFI). Very often, the activities of the senior management are excluded from internal audits for various reasons. That should not be the case. If only this had perhaps been done at Sahayata Microfinance,[293] much of the damage could have been avoided.

Fourth, senior management in MFIs preach extensively about internal audits but they forget one important aspect—ensuring its independence. Take a look at what Mr Ajay Verma, MD of Sahayata Microfinance (in 2011), said in a promotional video for a global microfinance consulting company:

> "The Internal Audit (IA) function is designed to check, whether the internal controls in the MFI are functioning as intended? Internal controls are designed to provide reasonable assurance regarding the efficiency and effectiveness of operations, the reliability and completeness of financial and operational information, and the compliance with applicable laws and regulations.
>
> *Ajay Verma, CEO, and Sahayata:* In terms of internal audit and controls, you need to very clearly define what is auditable and what is not auditable. Like what we have done, we have three types of audit. One is the process audit which happens in the field, then second is the branch audit. We audit all the branch documentation, which the loan officers have to do and the branch manager has to do; and third one is the cash and the finance audit which happens on the branch and the head office levels."[294]

All of these sound good to hear but the Sahayata Microfinance case[295] demonstrates that senior management do *not* necessarily practice what they preach. And if only the internal audit function had been independent, the Sahayata board would perhaps have got some early warning signals of the impending crisis. Sadly, this independence is never permitted by senior management, and then, internal audits become useless.

In short, internal audits must (independently) cover each and every activity at the MFI with the objective of evaluating (but not limited to) the following:

---

293 Award winning Sahayata Microfinance is the latest to go astray (http://moneylife.in/article/award-winning-sahayata-microfinance-is-the-latest-to-go-astray/21549.html), by Ramesh S Arunachalam, November 18, 2011 and What is said at conferences is very different from what is implemented in practice (http://www.moneylife.in/article/what-is-said-at-conferences-is-very-different-from-what-is-implemented-in-practice/22124.html), by Ramesh S Arunachalam, December 12, 2011.

294 Source: http://www.youtube.com/watch?v=ChKgQrDQUk8

295 Award winning Sahayata Microfinance is the latest to go astray (http://moneylife.in/article/award-winning-sahayata-microfinance-is-the-latest-to-go-astray/21549.html), by Ramesh S Arunachalam, November 18, 2011 and What is said at conferences is very different from what is implemented in practice (http://www.moneylife.in/article/what-is-said-at-conferences-is-very-different-from-what-is-implemented-in-practice/22124.html), by Ramesh S Arunachalam, December 12, 2011.

- Integrity, reliability, and effectiveness (including the relevance, accuracy, and comprehensiveness) of risk management, control, and governance processes and related systems;

- Monitoring of legal compliances—with extant laws and regulations—including any changing requirements from regulator/supervisors; and

- Safeguarding of all assets of the MFI.

Without question, the need for strong, independent, and objective internal audits has never been more important in the Indian microfinance sector. I certainly hope that the boards (in MFIs) recognize this and facilitate the adoption of well-functioning independent internal audit systems that can go a long way in protecting their MFIs and enhancing their reputation as *real* practitioners of responsible microfinance in India. *And this again is something that the regulatory architecture can seek to promote as part of the minimum standards required for accreditation as an MFI.*

# Chapter 20:
# How Reliable and Valid are Code of Conduct Assessments?

In 2011, The Microfinance India Summit[296] was trying to revive the Indian microfinance sector that had been blasted off its feet by the 2010 AP crisis. It even had a special session titled, *'Client protection and code of conduct: From principles to practice and compliance'* and the session introducer stated as follows:

> "One of the key factors that precipitated the AP (Andhra Pradesh) crisis was the accusation that microfinance institutions (MFIs) were employing coercive measures with clients, were not transparent in their pricing and largely profiteering from the poor. While for several years, there has been a growing concern on the issues of client protection, the AP crisis significantly helped in exacerbating the issue. Since the AP ordinance in October 2010, the efforts in the sector towards ensuring client protection have gained primacy. Industry associations Sa-dhan and MFIN have developed their own Codes of Conduct (CoCs), but their compliance has been a major issue. In recent months, through an IFC effort, a Responsible Finance Forum has been instituted which has been working on harmonizing the two COCs. The Codes go beyond client protection and incorporate standards for governance, staff and recruitment policies, data sharing etc. **SIDBI has been conducting Code of Conduct assessments of MFIs as a pre-requisite for lending, thereby emphasizing the importance of adherence to code by the institutions**. The panel will discuss the next steps towards supporting translation of the codes and principles into practice including building awareness and capacities of MFIs to enforce CoC, raising awareness of clients of their rights and responsibilities, uniformity in compliance assessment, consequences of non-compliance, role of investors and other stakeholders etc., drawing from good examples in India and globally both within the microfinance industry and in the mainstream."[297]

---

296 The Microfinance India Summit is organized by Access Development Services and Access Assist, New Delhi.
297 http://www.microfinanceindia.org/content/35/63/blog.php

Almost always after a crisis, key microfinance stakeholders (especially in India) react and voluntarily offer to subscribe to all kinds of codes of conduct (Sa-Dhan, MFIN), client protection principles, social performance, and other self-regulating initiatives. To set the record straight, had all the stakeholders really subscribed to these in the first place, there would have not been such a crisis in Indian microfinance. What happened is that there was a strong disconnect between intention and practice at MFIs and many stakeholders including bankers, investors, regulators, supervisors, and others (perhaps) did nothing to clean up the stables! They simply turned a blind eye and pretended that all was well, and so it seemed until the crisis blew up in 2010 in Andhra Pradesh. How else could their silence be interpreted? And in the urge to grow, make profits, and get investments at a premium and/or tap primary markets, MFIs did not practice what they had supposedly subscribed to in terms of ethical practices and good governance. And the MFIs associations and the regulators/supervisors just watched as the situation deteriorated as did the commercial bankers (especially, HDFC Bank, AXIS Bank, and ICICI Bank) and DFIs such as SIDBI (which undoubtedly played a predominant role in the AP microfinance crisis of 2010).

So what happened in 2011 was nothing new. The industry and its various stakeholders have always attempted, post crisis, to salvage the situation through code of conduct assessments. In fact, an advisory company (M2i[298]) even launched the Code of Conduct Assessment (COCA) Tool in India. According to industry sources, this was a pioneering initiative—a global first in the microfinance domain. It must also be mentioned that SIDBI had commissioned eight such assessments perhaps as part of the SIDBI–World Bank Responsible Microfinance Project and also made them public.[299]

The COCA Tool of M2i was positioned as a *"comprehensive review of MFIs' policies and systems and whether these translate into ethical microfinance practice.' It utilizes the ADDO framework developed by M2i."*[300]

When this happened in 2011, I wrote in my blog and *Moneylife magazine*[301] *as follows:*

> "At the outset, the World Bank, IFC, SIDBI and M2i must be congratulated for their desire to bring such a tool. However, given the strategic importance of these code of conduct (CoC) assessments, it also seems

---

298 What is written in this chapter is based on the situation that existed in December 2011, but note that changes to the framework and/or reports could have been made subsequent to the author's comments on the Code of Conduct Assessments in a series of articles in *Moneylife* personal finance magazine in December 2011. The originally cited documents are mentioned at the following link: http://www.moneylife.in/article/have-sophisticated-thermometers-ever-reduced-the-temperature/22144.html. I also have copies of these documents and would be happy to share them, subject to certain terms and conditions.

299 http://www.sidbi.com/micro/WorldBankInitiative.htm—these are however not available at this link after I had written articles about them in *Moneylife*.

300 http://www.m2iconsulting.com/m2i_coca.htm (as per the definitions that existed in December 2011).

301 (a) Have sophisticated thermometers ever reduced the temperature? (http://www.moneylife.in/article/have-sophisticated-thermometers-ever-reduced-the-temperature/22144.html) by Ramesh S Arunachalam, December 12, 2011; (b) The award of free points in microfinance code of conduct assessments (http://www.moneylife.in/article/the-award-of-free-points-in-microfinance-code-of-conduct-assessments/22207.html) by Ramesh S Arunachalam, December 15, 2011; (c) Subjectivity and inconsistencies in microfinance code of conduct assessments (http://moneylife.in/article/subjectivity-and-inconsistencies-in-microfinance-code-of-conduct-assessments/22221.html) by Ramesh S Arunachalam, December 15, 2011; and (d) Lessons from the Indian microfinance crisis, an open letter to Andrew Mitchell (http://www.moneylife.in/article/lessons-from-the-indian-microfinance-crisis-an-open-letter-to-andrew-mitchell/22234.html) by Ramesh S Arunachalam, December 16, 2011

## Chapter 20: How Reliable and Valid are Code of Conduct Assessments?

imperative to analyze them and examine their objectivity and effectiveness. This is done in a series of articles and should certainly help to focus Tuesday's session at the Microfinance India Summit with greater precision.

Let us get the context of the COCA tool first as all COCA reports are based on the tool. The COCA tool measures the adherence to the Code of Conduct on four basic parameters:
1. <u>A</u>pproval at the policy level from the board (of the MFI or institution) (A)
2. <u>Do</u>cumentation of the guidelines and procedures that emerge from the policy (D)
3. <u>Dis</u>semination of the guidelines and procedures across the organization (D)
4. <u>O</u>bservance in practice of these guidelines and procedures. (O)

Table 20.1 Example Matrix of Score Obtained

| Indicators | A (Approval at the policy level from the board) | | Do (Documentation of the guidelines and procedures that emerge from the policy) | | Ds (Dissemination of the guidelines and procedures across the organization) | | O (Observance in practice of these guidelines and procedures) | | Total | |
|---|---|---|---|---|---|---|---|---|---|---|
| | Maximum score | Obtained score | Maximum score | Obtained score | Maximum score | Obtained score | Maximum score | Obtained score | Maximum score | Obtained score |
| Client origination and targeting | 5 | 3 | 5 | 2 | 5 | 2 | 9 | 9 | 24 | 16 |
| Loan pricing | 3 | 2 | 1 | — | 2 | — | 9 | 7 | 15 | 8 |
| Loan appraisal | 4 | 4 | 4 | 3 | 3 | 3 | 5 | 2 | 16 | 11 |
| Client data security | 1 | 1 | 3 | 2 | 2 | 2 | 2 | 2 | 8 | 7 |
| Staff conduct | 7 | 6 | 7 | 5 | 10 | 9 | 11 | 9 | 35 | 29 |
| Client relationship and feedback | 2 | 2 | 8 | 7 | 6 | 4 | 10 | 6 | 26 | 19 |
| Total | 22 | 17 | 28 | 19 | 28 | 20 | 46 | 35 | 124 | 90 |

*Source: http://www.sidbi.com/micro/COCA%20SKDRDP.pdf*

The results of the eight SIDBI-sponsored COCA assessments are interesting to say the least and without question the findings are rather surprising. Table 20.2 presents the COCA scores for the eight MFIs from SIDBI's sponsored assessments, along with portfolio outstanding data.

| Rank | Name of the MFI | COCA score | Level of adherence | Portfolio outstanding (Rs. in million) | | | Growth March 2009 to September 2010 (in %) |
|---|---|---|---|---|---|---|---|
| | | | | March 2009 | March 2010 | September 2010* | |
| 1 | Equitas | 88% | Very high level of adherence | 2880 | 6053 | 8684 | 201.53 |
| 2 | Ujjivan | 87% | Very high level of adherence | 1690 | 3708 | NA | 119.41 |
| 2 | ASA International India Microfinance | 87% | Very high level of adherence | 329 | 869 | 1520 | 362.01 |
| 3 | Bharatiya Samruddhi Finance Ltd (Basix) | 84% | Very high level of adherence | 4621 | 10038 | 18081 | 291.28 |
| 3 | Bandhan | 84% | Very high level of adherence | 7035 | 14951 | 19837 | 181.98 |
| 4 | Arohan | 81% | High level of adherence | 419 | 978 | NA | 133.41 |
| 5 | Cashpor | 75% | Reasonable high level of adherence | 1810 | 2674 | 3020 | 66.85 |
| 6 | SKDRDP | 73% | Reasonable high level of adherence | 4893 | 6149 | 7906 | 61.58 |

*All portfolio outstanding data is up to September 2010, unless otherwise noted. There are two exceptions: a) For SKDRDP, the portfolio outstanding data is up to December 2010 and has therefore been included; and b) The portfolio outstanding data for September 2010 for Arohan and Ujjivan are not provided in the report and such data for December 2010 is also not provided. Hence, the corresponding data point is listed as NA.

Source: http://www.sidbi.in/Micro/COCA%20Equitas.pdf, http://www.sidbi.com/micro/COCAUjjivan.pdf, http://www.sidbi.com/micro/COCA%20ASA.pdf, http://www.sidbi.com/micro/COCA%20Samruddhi.pdf, http://www.sidbi.com/micro/Bandhan.pdf, http://www.sidbi.in/micro/COCA%20Arohan.pdf, http://www.sidbi.in/Micro/CASHPOR.pdf and http://www.sidbi.com/micro/COCA%20SKDRDP.pdf

- An immediate observation is that the for-profit fast growing NBFC-MFIs receive the highest COCA scores. (*A higher COCA score signifies a high degree of organizational adherence with regard to the Voluntary Code of Conduct*).

- The two not-for-profits (a Section 25 company and a charitable trust) and low-growth MFIs receive the lowest COCA scores. (*A lower COCA score means that organizational adherence to the Voluntary Code of Conduct is low*).

- The COCA results—which show that the fastest growing for-profit MFIs have the highest COCA scores—seem to be contradictory to the well-accepted idea that the fast growth of the microfinance sector contributed to the 2010 AP microfinance crisis. Surely, something counterintuitive is happening here as the relationship between fast growth and the AP 2010 microfinance crisis is now well recognized, established, and documented. In fact, by November/December 2010, many MFIs had begun to admit that growth caused by over-lending was responsible for the crisis and this is evident from the quote of the then CEO of BASIX, one of the pioneering Indian NBFC MFIs:

# Chapter 20: How Reliable and Valid are Code of Conduct Assessments?

'That (following sound lending practices) is where we failed, says Sajeev Viswanathan, CEO of Basix. MFIs lent liberally to individuals who didn't have a corresponding ability to repay. The mismatch had to hurt sometime, and that's what is happening now.... Mr Viswanathan says MFI lending in Andhra rose from Rs. 5,000–Rs.6,000 crore in 2009 to Rs. 9,000 crore this year.'[302]

Likewise, Prof. M. S, Sriram in his article has noted:

'In about a decade, microfinance has moved from helping the poor to access finance to an interesting business at the bottom of the pyramid. This paradigm shift happened with the entry of funding, initially from Silicon Valley and then from the people who funded and fuelled the growth of Silicon Valley. Somebody from Silicon Valley would typically be an entrepreneur who started small, scaled up fast, used the asymmetries in the market and logically and legally became rich. Many were first-generation entrepreneurs and did not forget their roots. It was logical for them to invest their surpluses into the business of doing good. However, their own success and growth experience dictated that while they do good, they should also do well. Doing well translated into good business plans, targets, and also growing at a scorching pace. All was well for us, within the industry, when the base was small. There were several 100 percents in the microfinance sector. The growth rate was in excess of 100%, recovery was 100% and the sustainability indices quickly crossed 100%. Voila, we had found a magic mantra where the poor could be served, we could look good and put 'eradication of poverty' as our mission statement and of course, lead a comfortable life. The alternative sources that were funding the poor made us look like messiahs.

The problem was that we were dealing with people and not processes and systems. This involved group formation and dealing with behavioural patterns of people. But we got addicted to the heady growth target. And when we chase targets without logic, we cut corners. We became cut-throat in competition and we lost a sense of balance.... The question is whether the lender knows the absorption and repayment capacity of the borrower. It is impossible to know this if we are doing a group meeting in 20 minutes and moving on. It is impossible to address this when we have standardised products and offer a higher loan each cycle. Our credit officers are trained to be robots following a process mechanically and are prohibited to think. Therefore multiple lending is a problem of the MFIs. We clearly do not know our customers enough, and do not have the time to know them.'[303]

A third comment on the relationship between growth and the 2010 AP microfinance crisis uses a great metaphor—in the words of Alok Prasad, CEO of MFIN, who spoke at the Responsible Finance Forum at the Hague in January 2011, the AP crisis occurred mainly because MFI growth was burgeoning. His analogy was brilliant when he said that **'it was like driving a Ferrari at more than**

---

[302] Source: Microfinance: What's wrong with it (http://articles.economictimes.indiatimes.com/2010-11-11/news/27577103_1_sks-microfinance-mfis-shgs) by M. Rajshekhar, *The Economic Times*, November 11, 2010.
[303] What is Wrong With Indian Microfinance (http://business.in.com/article/special/what-is-wrong-with-indian-microfinance/12962/1) by M. S. Sriram, *Forbes*, 2010.

**200km/h on Indian roads which is asking for trouble.**[304] And there are many more such quotes and I could go on but the larger point is that, given the above relationship between burgeoning growth and the AP crisis, I find it rather strange that the COCA scores[305] are highest[306] for the NBFC-MFIs that grew at a scorching pace and they are the lowest for the non-for-profit MFIs that grew a snail's pace. *The results seem weird, are they not?* This peculiar finding has prompted me to take a closer look at the SIDBI-World Bank sponsored COCA tool (and the results therein) in a series of articles in December 2011."[307]

I further wrote in the same article in *Moneylife*[308]:

"I do hope that tomorrow's session and panel discussion (at the Microfinance India Summit 2011) focus on the aspect of how the fastest growing MFIs managed a much better (higher) COCA score than their low growth and not-for-profit MFI counterparts? All in all, this session, undoubtedly promises to be an exciting one given the peculiar results from the SIDBI-World Bank sponsored COCA assessments and I hope that the regulators and key industry stakeholders are watching this controversial session closely…"[309]

I followed up my first article with a second article titled *'The award of free points in microfinance code of conduct assessments'*[310] and in this article, I came to the conclusion that

"It is meaningless that the COCA tool rewards mere existence of policy and/or management statements of policy implementation when it should be really looking at solid evidence in support of implementation of the voluntary codes of conduct on the ground."

---

304 From comments by Jan Postmus at http://www.microfinancefocus.com/content/global-investors-meet-promote-new-principles-inclusive-finance. This link is now not available. You can however get a sense of this by looking at http://www.cgap.org/blog/driving-fast-indian-country-roads-learning-crisis

305 Source: http://www.sidbi.in/Micro/COCA%20Equitas.pdf, http://www.sidbi.com/micro/COCAUjjivan.pdf, http://www.sidbi.com/micro/COCA%20ASA.pdf, http://www.sidbi.com/micro/COCA%20Samruddhi.pdf, http://www.sidbi.com/micro/Bandhan.pdf, http://www.sidbi.in/micro/COCA%20Arohan.pdf, http://www.sidbi.in/Micro/CASHPOR.pdf and http://www.sidbi.com/micro/COCA%20SKDRDP.pdf. These articles appear to have been taken off but the interested reader can get back to me for copies of the reports as they existed then, and I can provide them subject to certain terms and conditions.

306 A higher COCA score implies greater adherence to the voluntary code of conduct.

307 Have sophisticated thermometers ever reduced the temperature? (http://www.moneylife.in/article/have-sophisticated-thermometers-ever-reduced-the-temperature/22144.html), by Ramesh S. Arunachalam, December 12, 2011, and other articles referred to earlier.

308 Have sophisticated thermometers ever reduced the temperature? (http://www.moneylife.in/article/have-sophisticated-thermometers-ever-reduced-the-temperature/22144.html) by Ramesh S. Arunachalam, December 12, 2011.

309 Have sophisticated thermometers ever reduced the temperature? (http://www.moneylife.in/article/have-sophisticated-thermometers-ever-reduced-the-temperature/22144.html) by Ramesh S. Arunachalam, December 12, 2011.

310 The award of free points in microfinance code of conduct assessments (http://www.moneylife.in/article/the-award-of-free-points-in-microfinance-code-of-conduct-assessments/22207.html) by Ramesh S Arunachalam, December 15, 2011.

## Chapter 20: How Reliable and Valid are Code of Conduct Assessments?

Specifically, I wrote in the article that:

> "An earlier *Moneylife* article[311] raised the issue of how the fastest growing NBFC-MFIs received higher (better) code of conduct assessments (COCA) scores in relation to the lower growth and not-for-profit counterparts. This peculiar finding has necessitated a close analysis of the eight SIDBI-World Bank sponsored code of conduct assessments found in the public domain.[312] And my analysis suggests three main conclusions:
>
> a. There are too many 'free' points (liberally given) in the COCA tool.[313]
> b. There's a great deal of subjectivity and/or inconsistency in the application of the tool.
> c. There are serious findings resulting from the assessments that have implications for Indian and global microfinance.
>
> Each of these aspects is dealt with in detail hereafter. We first look at the aspect of *too many free points* being given. The COCA tool looks at four parameters. The first parameter is *Approval at the policy level from the board*, which is shown as A. Here, the COCA tool looks at the intention of the microfinance institution (MFI) only and I provide three examples that should easily help illustrate the fact that free points were being given away in these CoC assessments:
>
> 1. *Equitas:* For example, Equitas receives 4.5 out of 5 on A (Approval at the policy level from the board) for client origination and targeting (COT).

**Table 20.3 Matrix of Score Obtained**

| Indicators | A (Approval) | | Do (Documentation) | | Ds (Dissemination) | | O (Observance) | | Total | |
|---|---|---|---|---|---|---|---|---|---|---|
| | Maximum | Obtained score | Maximum | Obtained score | Maximum | Obtained score | Maximum | Obtained score | Maximum | Obtained score |
| **Client origination and targeting** | 5 | **4.5** | 5 | 4.5 | 5 | 5.0 | 9 | 7.6 | 24 | 21.6 |
| Loan pricing | 3 | 3.0 | 1 | 1.0 | 2 | 2.0 | 9 | 7.6 | 15 | 13.6 |
| Loan appraisal | 4 | 3.5 | 4 | 2.0 | 3 | 3.0 | 5 | 3.9 | 16 | 12.4 |
| Client data security | 1 | 1.0 | 3 | 3.0 | 2 | 2.0 | 2 | 2.0 | 8 | 8.0 |
| Staff conduct | 7 | 7.0 | 7 | 7.0 | 10 | 10.0 | 11 | 11.0 | 35 | 35.0 |
| Client relationship and feedback | 2 | 2.0 | 8 | 4.0 | 6 | 5.0 | 10 | 8.0 | 26 | 19.0 |
| **Total** | 22 | 21.0 | 28 | 21.5 | 28 | 27.0 | 46 | 40.2 | 124 | 109.7 |

*Source:* http://www.sidbi.in/Micro/COCA%20Equitas.pdf, Page 18.

---

311 Have sophisticated thermometers ever reduced the temperature? (http://www.moneylife.in/article/have-sophisticated-thermometers-ever-reduced-the-temperature/22144.html) by Ramesh S Arunachalam, December 12, 2011.
312 http://www.sidbi.com/micro/codeofconduct.html
313 A description of the COCA tool can be found here http://www.m2iconsulting.com/coca-reports.html (at least until December 2011).

The assessment report[314] justifies this high score as follows: 'Equitas score on Client Origination and Targeting (COT) is high on account of its strong systems to ensure identity of clients, commitments towards not involving unauthorized agents in the client origination process and its focus on avoiding clients who have taken loan from three or more MFIs.'[315] The key point to be noted here is that as long as the Equitas board has approved this policy, the MFI will receive a high score. Whether the policy is implemented in practice does not seem to matter for assessment and this is where the tool is weak in terms of award of free points (mentioned earlier and demonstrated later).

Two aspects stand out here:

1. A reading of the Equitas COCA report makes it clear that there is lack of comprehensive evidence with regard to ground level implementation of the above policy and that is why the assessment report itself argues that—*'In M2i's opinion, despite all sincere efforts, some of these agents may still be in existence (though their influence may now be low) as shown in Caselet 1.'*

> **'Caselet 1, Dhanalxmi Nagar, Chennai**
> This case pertains to the Dhanalxmi-1, 2 and 3 centers of Arumbakkam branch in Chennai district of Tamil Nadu. Regular center meetings of this group is held at the place of a person (male) who operates a milk distribution agency apparently on behalf of some of the centers of Equitas who have got together as an informal Self-Help Group. At this place, meetings of one of the groups of L&T Microfinance also takes place and the center leader of one of Dhanalxmi-1 group is also the leader of L&T's groups. The operator of the milk distribution agency and the center leader have been instrumental in organising some of the groups of Equitas and L&T. Although they insist that they received no monetary compensation for doing this, they may influence the behaviour of the clients in the future.'

2. It must also be noted that Tamil Nadu is one of the [316] major operational areas for Equitas and in Tamil Nadu, MFIs themselves have admitted to the existence of agents. See *Moneylife* article[317] that provides tangible evidence regarding the same. The *Moneylife* article has published the relevant e-mails, which are reproduced here:

*First e-mail:* This is from a former DGM (Deputy General Manager) of a large private sector bank and the same person is now the CEO of an important MFI that operates in Tamil Nadu

---

314 http://www.sidbi.in/Micro/COCA%20Equitas.pdf
315 http://www.sidbi.in/Micro/COCA%20Equitas.pdf, Page 6.
316 http://www.sidbi.in/Micro/COCA%20Equitas.pdf, Page 7.
317 MFIN-NCAER study: Here's the proof that microfinance agents are thriving in Tamil Nadu (http://moneylife.in/article/mfin-ncaer-study-heres-the-proof-that-microfinance-agents-are-thriving-in-tamil-nadu/20717.html), by Ramesh S. Arunachalam, October 19, 2011.

also. The mail is a forward of a mail (from the Vice President, Business) that talks of several loans taken by one Ms Eshwari, a center leader, from seven or eight MFIs and also of several *benami* loans taken by her, using names of other members. The forwarded mail also mentions that Ms Eshwari paid a commission of between Rs. 500–Rs. 1,000 to each of the members who cooperated with her in the matter of the *benami* loans. It also clearly states that a money-lending operation was being run by Ms Eshwari for almost three years. It further mentions that Ms Eshwari had been making the repayments on behalf of the members for the other *benami* loans. It also clearly states that because MFIs have faced difficulty in raising money in the last three months (i.e., three months before 12 January 2011), Ms Eshwari's cash flow and rotation of money (from 'ever-greening' of loans, or top-up of loans), have been seriously affected (presumably because she could not access fresh loans from any of the MFIs, which were already cash strapped for lending funds). Therefore, she just absconded one day and when the concerned MFIs went for collection, other (*benami*) members said that they have not taken any loans.

This e-mail thus clearly shows what a center leader can do as an agent—in terms of taking multiple loans from multiple MFIs and also using the BENAMI route to take more *benami* (ghost) loans and use the money for further money lending, at the local level. I am not sure that this is financial inclusion or inclusive finance. As I have been saying for a long, long time now (since 2005), the outreach of Indian microfinance is very suspect and perhaps it has more of multiple, *benami* and ghost loans than estimated. That is why I have been requesting the RBI (Reserve Bank of India) to get an army of people to the grass-roots and get a real handle on the happenings. My repeated pleas have gone in vain ...

# An Idea Which Went Wrong

> **Box 20.1 MAIL # 1: Presence of Agents # 1** [318]
>
> From: Brahmanand Hegde [mailto:brahmanand.hegde@vistaarlfi.com]
> Sent: Wednesday, January 12, 2011 5:31 PM
> To: vasudevanpn@equitas.in
> Subject: FW: Kulithalai Incident
>
> Dear Vasudevan,
>
> Wish you Happy New Year and Pongal (Sankranti) !
>
> While you may be aware of this incident, I thought of sharing the same with you. The mail below is sent by our business head to president of TN-MFI forum.
>
> With regards,
>
> Brahmanand
> _____
>
> Dear Sir,
>
> We wanted to update TN-MFI forum on recent press coverage about MFIs operating in Kulithalai. We feel this issue need to betaken up by MFI- TN chapter with District Administration to sensitise the government machinery.
>
> Brief details of the same is as under:
>
> 1. At Kulithalai (Karur dist) one customer namely Eshwari has taken loans from 7-8 MFIs and had also arranged another 7-8 members to pose as customers. These benami customers were given Rs.500-1000 commission by Eshwari and remaining loans amount was used by her.
> 2. Members have informed that she has been running this (money lending) business for last 3 years and paying instalments of self as well as other 7-8 customers also.
> 3. As last 3 months have been difficult for MFIs to raise funds, few MFIs have stopped giving new loans and this affected Eshwari's cash flow and rotation of money and she absconded from her home.
> 4. After she left her home, these benami customers came out in open and informed that they have not taken any loan and they were only used by Eshwari.
>
> Now, we understand that Eshwari has gone to collector and given a complaint against all the MFIs informing MFIs are harassing her and other members. There is also article in local magazine about the incident and it has projected MFIs as doing everything wrong (scan copy of article is attached).
> Requesting you to look into the matter and initiate steps to educate concerned authorities on entire incident and also to minimise negative press coverage.
>
> Regards,
>
> Sankar Sastri
> Vice President, Business

---

[318] **All the e-mails have been reproduced** verbatim, **and have not been corrected for grammar.**

## Chapter 20: How Reliable and Valid are Code of Conduct Assessments?

*Second e-mail:* This one is an update on collection issues in two specific areas where MFI collections had been impacted and one of them relates to the Ms Eshwari case stated above. It again talks about Ms Eshwari, a center leader, borrowing by using names of other members (*benami* loans) in the center, defaulting on repayments thereafter, absconding and finally, ganging up with another woman (Roopa Gandhi) and telling all center members not to repay MFI loans! This mail is also from the former DGM of a large private sector bank, who is now the CEO of an MFI. It is addressed to some of the top NBFC MFIs in Tamil Nadu. This mail was written on January 25, 2011.

---

**Box 20.2 MAIL # 2**

**From:** Brahmanand Hegde [mailto:brahmanand.hegde@vistaarlfi.com]
**Sent:** Tuesday, January 25, 2011 4:53 PM
**To:** Tamilarason; BWDA; vasudevanpn@equitas.in; perumal.k@gvmfl.com; Krishna Chandran V; venkateshkp@equitas.in; arjun.m@gvmfl.com; praveen.vecha@fullertonindia.com
**Cc:** Ramakrishna Nishtala; Sankar Sastri

**Subject:** Update on collection issues at Kulithalai (Karur dist) and Musuri (Trichy dist)

Dear All,
This is to update you all on few recent happenings at above two locations during last few days, impacting collection of all the MFIs operating in the area. It all started with one centre leader namely Eshwari borrowing on behalf of few members of the centre and defaulting on repayment. I understand, she is now absconding from the village and joined hands with another lady by name Mrs Roopa Gandhi. I get to hear that, both these ladies are instigating other members of the centre and location not to repay the loans to MFIs. I also understand that they have gone and met Karur collector and complained about harassment by MFIs. Default by few members of the one weeks back, now has spread to few centres in Kulithalai.

Further, local newspaper and a posters by local CPI further fuelled this and few centres in Musari also impacted and customers are refusing to repay. Also, I understand one local lawyer is attending centre meetings and telling MFI credit officers not to force the customer to repay at Musari.

Therefore I suggest that those MFIs impacted by these issues at Kulithalai and Musuri, proactively go and meet local revenue officer (Tahashildar), police and also Dist collector and appraise them about our activities and about recovery issues. I also feel, we could have joint communication with centre members at these places, which might help us to convince good customers to keep their credit record good.

I feel we should take up this issue ASAP, may be on 27th or 28th itself. Sankar is our business head and he will be travelling to Kulithalai and Musari on 27th and 28th. It would be good, if you all depute your representatives to meet, discuss and take next steps on the above lines.

Please let me know if any one of you have any alternative thoughts.

With best regards,
**Brahmanand Hegde,** *Managing Director & CEO*

## An Idea Which Went Wrong

*Third e-mail:* This is a response to the second mail and it clearly suggests that there are agents all over Tamil Nadu who are causing huge problems and the MFIs are sort of helpless—indeed, these agents are now like Frankenstein's monsters. Some of the top NBFC MFIs[319] are copied in the third mail, which is addressed to their senior/operational management.

---

**Box 20.3 MAIL # 3**

---------- Forwarded message ----------
From: **Krishna Chandran V** <Krishna.Chandran@sksindia.com>
Date: Tue, Jan 25, 2011 at 5:34 PM
Subject: RE: Update on collection issues at Kulithalai(Karur dist) and Musuri (Trichy dist)
To: Brahmanand Hegde <brahmanand.hegde@vistaarlfi.com>, Tamilarason <meenat_123@yahoo.com>, BWDA <bwdavpm@yahoo.com>, "vasudevanpn@equitas.in" <vasudevanpn@equitas.in>, "perumal.k@gvmfl.com" <perumal.k@gvmfl.com>, "venkateshkp@equitas.in" <venkateshkp@equitas.in>, "arjun.m@gvmfl.com" <arjun.m@gvmfl.com>, "praveen.vecha@fullertonindia.com" <praveen.vecha@fullertonindia.com>, Ramakrishna Nishtala <ramakrishna.nishtala@vistaarlfi.com>, Sankar Sastri <sankar.sastri@vistaarlfi.com>

Cc: Pushparaj M <Pushparaj.M@sksindia.com>, Gopikrishna A <Gopikrishna@sksindia.com>, K V Rao <Kv.Rao@sksindia.com>, Sateesh Kumar A V <avsateeshkumar@sksindia.com>, Rashmi Singh <rashmi@sksindia.com>

Dear Sir,

We faced similar problems in two of our centers so far and had discussed the same.

We heard from the field that few members have gone to meet the District Collector again today. It would be better if all the concerned MFIs could meet and discuss POA before meeting the government representatives.

We welcome the idea of jointly addressing the concerns of the members. **Also lot of problems are being caused throughout TN by commission agents. Please give a thought on whether we can issue legal notice to such people jointly through Sa-Dhan. Such people are indulging in cheating the members and the MFIs, but if a singly MFI takes legal action against them they can easily ask the members not to repay to the particular MFI and also give promise that they will arrange funds from other MFIs.**

Warm regards,
Krishna"[320]

---

[319] NBFCs are generally MFIN members but some of them are also Sa-Dhan members.

[320] The award of free points in microfinance code of conduct assessments (http://www.moneylife.in/article/the-award-of-free-points-in-microfinance-code-of-conduct-assessments/22207.html). The e-mail exhibits cited in the above article were originally from the article: MFIN-NCAER study: Here's the proof that microfinance agents are thriving in Tamil Nadu (http://www.moneylife.in/article/mfin-ncaer-study-heres-the-proof-that-microfinance-agents-are-thriving-in-tamil-nadu/20717.html).

## Chapter 20: How Reliable and Valid are Code of Conduct Assessments?

The e-mail exhibits given in the *Moneylife* article(s) are dated January 2011, whereas the M2i CoC assessments are said to have taken place in December 2010. And when these e-mails literally cry foul about the huge problems created by agents, how does the COCA report justify a high score on client origination and targeting for (Equitas), merely because of the existence of a board-level policy of not using agents henceforth. This is especially a concern given that agents had been used by Equitas (even according to the M2i report itself) and as stated in the M2i report, they could still have been in existence at the time of writing the COCA report—that needs strong emphasis here. Further, let us remember that a policy is helpful *only* if it is implemented—otherwise, it is of no use at all. It is no point having great intentions, what we need is solid action and COC assessments must reward action rather than mere intentions. Let us be absolutely clear about that.

2. *"Basix:* A second instance of 'free points' being given pertains to Basix, which receives the full score (4 of 4) on A (Approval at the policy level from the board) for loan appraisal.

Table 20.4 Matrix of Score Obtained

| Indicators | A (Approval) | | Do (Documentation) | | Ds (Dissemination) | | O (Observance) | | Total | |
|---|---|---|---|---|---|---|---|---|---|---|
| | Maximum | Obtained score | Maximum | Obtained score | Maximum | Obtained score | Maximum | Obtained score | Maximum | Obtained score |
| Client origination and targeting | 5 | 4 | 5 | 3 | 5 | 4 | 9 | 7 | **24** | 18 |
| Loan Pricing | 3 | 2 | 1 | 0.5 | 2 | 2 | 9 | 7 | **15** | 12 |
| **Loan Appraisal** | 4 | 4 | 4 | 3.5 | 3 | 3 | 5 | 4 | **16** | 15 |
| Client Data Security | 1 | 1 | 3 | 3 | 2 | 2 | 2 | 2 | **8** | 8 |
| Staff Conduct | 7 | 7 | 7 | 7 | 10 | 10 | 11 | 11 | **35** | 35 |
| Client Relationship and Feedback | 2 | 2 | 8 | 8 | 6 | 0.5 | 10 | 6 | **26** | 17 |
| Total | 22 | 20 | 28 | 25 | 28 | 21.5 | 46 | 38 | **124** | 104 |

Source: http://www.sidbi.com/micro/COCA%20Samruddhi.pdf, Page 18.

The COCA report justifies this 4 on 4 by stating that 'Samruddhi's policy requires a careful appraisal of the repayment capacity of the borrowers.'[321] Again, this does not have to be reflected in practice, but as long as the required policies are approved by the board then the MFI will receive a high score.

---
321 http://www.sidbi.com/micro/COCA%20Samruddhi.pdf, Page 13.

Let us now step back and juxtapose this with what Sajeev Viswanathan, the CEO of BASIX, said in November 2010 and I quote, 'That (following sound lending practices) is where we failed... MFIs lent liberally to individuals who didn't have a corresponding ability to repay. The mismatch had to hurt sometime, and that's what is happening now.... MFI lending in Andhra Pradesh rose from Rs.5,000–Rs.6,000 crore in 2009 to Rs.9,000 crore this year.'[322]

In fact, the M2i report[323] makes statements that are contradictory to what the then CEO of BASIX himself said (as given). The M2i statements (based on its visits to BASIX from 20th to 27th of December 2010) are also internally inconsistent as shown here:

*Statement 1:* 'Samruddhi receives a high composite score on account of a high focus on maintaining high standards of staff conduct and sound loan appraisal systems.'[324]

*Statement 2:* 'Samruddhi should have higher focus on ensuring that informal agents do not influence client origination, and a few clients do not exert undue influence on a larger number of clients.'[325]

*Statement 3:* 'However, it was observed that the practice of recording the existing loans of clients is not uniformly practiced across all the units. We found during client interviews that some of the clients had borrowed from other MFIs but this had not been recorded in their loan forms. In one of the units—Kamareddy in Andhra Pradesh—a random inspection of 15 loan appraisal forms revealed that none of them had a mention of any other lender. It is improbable that none of the clients would have borrowed from any other MFI in the region given the prevalence of MFIs. Also, interviews with the LSPs revealed that nearly 70% of his clients had borrowings from other MFIs. (Also see caselet 2 of Dumka unit in Jharkhand.)'[326]

---

322 Source: Microfinance: What's wrong with it (http://articles.economictimes.indiatimes.com/2010-11-11/news/27577103_1_sks-microfinance-mfis-shgs) by M. Rajshekhar, *The Economic Times*, November 11, 2010.
323 http://www.sidbi.com/micro/COCA%20Samruddhi.pdf
324 http://www.sidbi.com/micro/COCA%20Samruddhi.pdf, Page 1.
325 http://www.sidbi.com/micro/COCA%20Samruddhi.pdf, Page 1.
326 http://www.sidbi.com/micro/COCA%20Samruddhi.pdf, Page 12.

## Chapter 20: How Reliable and Valid are Code of Conduct Assessments?

> **Caselet 2:** Kamarpara village of Dumka district has four MFIs operating. BSFL entered this village in December 2009 and was the fourth MFI in the village to start operations. Saima is part of a five member JLG which has taken a loan of Rs. 12,000 from BSFL. She and other members of their JLG have been taking loans from another MFI for the past three years. Total monthly instalment for both the loans taken together comes to about Rs. 2,500. Saima has taken the loan to invest in the cloth trading business being carried out by her son and she is not directly involved in the business. Details of loans from other MFIs are not mentioned in the loan application form or the loan appraisal form.'[327]

Given these statements, it is clear that lender names were not recorded in all cases based on the random inspection of 15 loan appraisal forms at the Kamareddy unit of Basix. The same also appears to have happened in Dumka unit of Jharkhand.

At this juncture, I would like to quote some data from an APMAS study on effective interest rates[328] done in Kamareddy and other mandals. The study shows cases of multiple borrowing among clients of BASIX as given in Table 20.5:[329]

| Table 20.5 List of Borrowers with Loans From Several MFIs, As per APMAS Sheet | | | | |
|---|---|---|---|---|
| Name of the institution | Loan amount | No. installments | Period of installments | Equated installment amounts |
| Hameeda, (Durga Bhavani SHG of Sarampalli Village), Kamareddy Cluster, Kamareddy Mandal | | | | |
| BASIX | 10,000 | 11 | Monthly | 1000 |
| Sharemola | 10,000 | 50 | Weekly | 225 |
| SKS | 10,000 | 50 | Weekly | 225 |
| Spandana | 10,000 | 50 | Weekly | 225 |
| Vanajamma, ODC Cluster, Nallacheruvu Mandal | | | | |
| BASIX | 12,000 | 15 | Monthly | 1200 |
| Sharemola | 20,000 | 50 | Weekly | 450 |
| Spandana | 20,000 | 50 | Weekly | 450 |

Therefore, it clear that details of loans from other MFIs were not recorded in loan appraisal forms (as found at the Kamareddy unit of Basix). Without question, the lack of this data (about other MFI

---
327 http://www.sidbi.com/micro/COCA%20Samruddhi.pdf, Page 12.
328 http://microfinance-in-india.blogspot.com/2010/11/analysis-of-apmas-april-2010-study-on.html
329 The award of free points in microfinance code of conduct assessments (http://www.moneylife.in/article/the-award-of-free-points-in-microfinance-code-of-conduct-assessments/22207.html) by Ramesh S Arunachalam, December 15, 2011

loans) makes it almost impossible to have a good judgment of the debt servicing capacity of the borrowers. And when this information is missing, there is no way the loan appraisal systems can be called as 'sound.' In fact, this is where free points were given away (to BASIX) by the COCA report and let us be clear about that!

3. "*Bandhan:* Let us look at the *third instance of free points where Bandhan* receives the full score (4 of 4) on A (Approval at the policy level from the board) for loan appraisal, whereas the observance score is somewhat low.

**Table 20.6 Matrix of Score Obtained**

| Indicators | A (Approval) | | Do (Documentation) | | Ds (Dissemination) | | O (Observance) | | Total | |
|---|---|---|---|---|---|---|---|---|---|---|
| | Maximum | Obtained score | Maximum | Obtained score | Maximum | Obtained score | Maximum | Obtained score | Maximum | Obtained score |
| Client origination and targeting | 5 | 4 | 5 | 4 | 5 | 4 | 9 | 9 | 24 | 21 |
| Loan pricing | 3 | 1.5 | 1 | 0.5 | 2 | 1 | 9 | 7 | 15 | 10 |
| **Loan appraisal** | **4** | **4** | 4 | 3 | 3 | 3 | 5 | 2 | **16** | **12** |
| Client data security | 1 | 1 | 3 | 2 | 2 | 2 | 2 | 2 | 8 | 7 |
| Staff conduct | 7 | 7 | 7 | 7 | 10 | 9 | 11 | 11 | 35 | 34 |
| Client relationship and feedback | 2 | 2 | 8 | 5 | 6 | 6 | 10 | 8 | 26 | 21 |
| Total | 22 | 19.5 | 28 | 21.5 | 28 | 25 | 46 | 39 | 124 | 105 |

*Source*: http://www.sidbi.com/micro/Bandhan.pdf, Page 15.

That is all right but what needs to be noted is that despite low observance and the lack of a policy until recently (as indicated by quotes from the M2i report given subsequently), Bandhan still has a good total score on the loan appraisal—12 out of a maximum of 16. In fact, in the report, M2i notes that:

'Given that many of the old forms are currently in use, we did not come across a cash flow analysis in 90% of the loan forms reviewed. Bandhan maintains that the system of informal appraisal has been effective in helping it maintain a sound portfolio quality. Still, it has initiated the process to standardize and formalize loan appraisal with the introduction of the new forms. Bandhan has recently incorporated details pertaining to income, expenses, cash flows and indebtedness in the loan applications for the micro-loans. Earlier loan application forms of micro loans did not contain these details. On an average, each branch manager has to undertake about 10–15 loan appraisals every day. While the branch managers interviewed revealed that they perform informal assessment of loan supplications which includes an assessment of incomes and expenses of potential clients, the loan appraisal for the microloans has till now been not incorporated with formal analysis of the cash flows of the households, as most of the loan forms being used are old ones which did not include this analysis.'[330]

> Without question, these points are best considered as free points, since practice does differ from policy. I am sure that we all agree on the fact that no points should be awarded on the basis of intention alone; the key is implementation of the policy in practice."[331]

Therefore, the starting point should not have been the intention, as approved by the board of each MFI. The starting point of the COCA tool should have been the COCA framework itself. The COCA framework has been distilled from different accepted self-regulation tools and the MFIs should have been judged on the basis of how they implemented these instead of awarding them free points for nicely written intentions in the form of great sounding policies (that were *not* seen in practice). As Jack Welch,[332] talking of the new breed of strategic planners, once said, 'We had these great sounding plans but somehow we put these plans in the shelf and kept doing what we had always been doing.'

Without any doubt, the purpose of the CoC assessments is to distinguish between having mere (policy) intentions with regard to the voluntary code of conduct as opposed to real ground level implementation of the same. Therefore, it is meaningless that the COCA tool rewards mere existence of policy and/or management statements of policy implementation when it should be really looking at solid evidence in support of implementation of the voluntary codes of conduct on the ground.

While my second article looked at the award of free points in the code of conduct assessments (COCA) reports and the peculiar findings arising therein, a third article[333] looked at issues of subjectivity and inconsistency in CoC assessments with tangible examples.

1. "It has been observed that Bandhan has only recently incorporated a cash flow analysis of clients' households in its loan forms. Rightfully Bandhan did not receive a high score on O (Observance).

---

330 http://www.sidbi.com/micro/Bandhan.pdf, Page 9.
331 The award of free points in microfinance code of conduct assessments (http://www.moneylife.in/article/the-award-of-free-points-in-microfinance-code-of-conduct-assessments/22207.html) by Ramesh S Arunachalam, December 15, 2011
332 Paraphrased from *Business Week*, The New Breed of Strategic Planner.
333 Subjectivity and inconsistencies in microfinance code of conduct assessments (http://moneylife.in/article/subjectivity-and-inconsistencies-in-microfinance-code-of-conduct-assessments/22221.html), by Ramesh S. Arunachalam, December 15, 2011.

## An Idea Which Went Wrong

**Table 20.7 Matrix of Score Obtained**

| Indicators | A (Approval) | | Do (Documentation) | | Ds (Dissemination) | | O (Observance) | | Total | |
|---|---|---|---|---|---|---|---|---|---|---|
| | Maximum | Obtained score | Maximum | Obtained score | Maximum | Obtained score | Maximum | Obtained score | Maximum | Obtained score |
| Client origination and targeting | 5 | 4 | 5 | 4 | 5 | 4 | 9 | 9 | 24 | 21 |
| Loan pricing | 3 | 1.5 | 1 | 0.5 | 2 | 1 | 9 | 7 | 15 | 10 |
| **Loan appraisal** | 4 | 4 | 4 | 3 | 3 | 3 | 5 | 2 | 16 | 12 |
| Client data security | 1 | 1 | 3 | 2 | 2 | 2 | 2 | 2 | 8 | 7 |
| Staff conduct | 7 | 7 | 7 | 7 | 10 | 9 | 11 | 11 | 35 | 34 |
| Client relationship and feedback | 2 | 2 | 8 | 5 | 6 | 6 | 10 | 8 | 26 | 21 |
| Total | 22 | 19.5 | 28 | 21.5 | 28 | 25 | 46 | 39 | 124 | 105 |

Source: http://www.sidbi.com/micro/Bandhan.pdf, Page 15.

The case of Equitas is contrary to this. One month before the COC assessment took place (i.e., one month after the AP crisis had started), Equitas is said to have rigorously changed its policies.

**Table 20.8 Matrix of Score Obtained**

| Indicators | A (Approval) | | Do (Documentation) | | Ds (Dissemination) | | O (Observance) | | Total | |
|---|---|---|---|---|---|---|---|---|---|---|
| | Maximum | Obtained score | Maximum | Obtained score | Maximum | Obtained score | Maximum | Obtained score | Maximum | Obtained score |
| Client origination and targeting | 5 | 4.5 | 5 | 4.5 | 5 | 5.0 | 9 | 7.6 | 24 | 21.6 |
| Loan pricing | 3 | 3.0 | 1 | 1.0 | 2 | 2.0 | 9 | 7.6 | 15 | 13.6 |
| Loan appraisal | 4 | 3.5 | 4 | 2.0 | 3 | 3.0 | 5 | 3.9 | 16 | 12.4 |
| Client data security | 1 | 1.0 | 3 | 3.0 | 2 | 2.0 | 2 | 2.0 | 8 | 8.0 |
| Staff conduct | 7 | 7.0 | 7 | 7.0 | 10 | 10.0 | 11 | 11.0 | 35 | 35.0 |
| Client relationship and feedback | 2 | 2.0 | 8 | 4.0 | 6 | 5.0 | 10 | 8.0 | 26 | 19.0 |
| Total | 22 | 21.0 | 28 | 21.5 | 28 | 27.0 | 46 | 40.2 | 124 | 109.7 |

Source: http://www.sidbi.in/Micro/COCA%20Equitas.pdf, Page 18.

The M2i COCA report concludes that 'the management now feels that due to these measures it (Equitas) has been able to overcome the problems related to unauthorised agents even in

## Chapter 20: How Reliable and Valid are Code of Conduct Assessments?

the areas where the problem was quite acute. In M2i's opinion, despite all sincere efforts, some of these agents may still be in existence.'[334]

This COCA judgment appears to be based on soft factors: the assessment is relying on the interpretation of the management and the management 'feels' that it (Equitas) has been able to overcome the problems. Even though agents continued to exist in areas where Equitas operated (as per self-admittance e mails in circulation among the NBFC MFIs including Equitas as at January 2011)[335] and problems due to agents had not been ruled out by the M2i COCA report (on Equitas) itself, Equitas still received a high score (7.6 out of 9) on O (observance) as shown in Table 20.8.

Thus, we have the diametrically opposite cases of Bandhan and Equitas, both of which had changed their policies (Bandhan on Loan Appriasal and Equitas on CoT) after the crisis and stated that they were implementing the new policies. On one hand, Bandhan was rightfully given a low score, whereas Equitas surprisingly got a high score—even though (as per the COCA reports) both the MFIs had not fully overcome the observed problems. This proves that there is a great deal of subjectivity and inconsistency with regard to the COCA tool and its application.

2. With regard to pricing, transparency in pricing is the major concern in COCA tool. Given so, I found it very strange that SKDRDP, which charges by far the lowest interest rates, got the lowest score on pricing—because SKDRDP *'accounts for and communicates interest on a flat rate basis.'*[336] This is the main reason for providing the exceptionally low grading on pricing to SKDRDP, whereas the same SKDRDP COCA report states that SKDRDP's 'Annualized Percentage Rate is among the lowest for the MFIs in India.'[337] This needs to be noted carefully.

The implication of this is that MFIs that mention their interest rates on a declining balance but charge higher (APR) rates of interest are rewarded with higher (and better) scores. And MFIs that state their interest rates on a flat basis but charge lower (APR) rates are penalized with lower scores. I am not sure that this is fair at all!

That transparency on pricing is not always understood by the clients becomes evident from the Equitas COCA report. Equitas is known for its transparency in pricing and it communicates these on a declining balance basis. The Equitas COCA report, however, states that 'the

---

334 http://www.sidbi.in/Micro/COCA%20Equitas.pdf
335 MFIN-NCAER study: Here's the proof that microfinance agents are thriving in Tamil Nadu (http://www.moneylife.in/article/mfin-ncaer-study-heres-the-proof-that-microfinance-agents-are-thriving-in-tamil-nadu/20717.html), by Ramesh S. Arunachalam, October19, 2011.
336 http://www.sidbi.com/micro/COCA%20SKDRDP.pdf
337 http://www.sidbi.com/micro/COCA%20SKDRDP.pdf

level of awareness of the clients about the effective interest rates and method of application was found to be low.'[338] This being the case, what then is the great benefit from communicating interest rates to clients on a declining basis?

Without question, clients are surely better off with lower (annualized percentage) interest rates (stated on a flat basis) as compared to higher rates of interest presented to them on a declining balance. There should be no ambiguity with regard to that!

3. Let us look at another example. Bandhan received a high score on Staff Conduct (97%).[339]

   The COCA report says: 'None of the clients reported any misconduct by the staff. However, the internal audits were not found covering staff conduct issues adequately and explicitly.'[340]

   The key question here is how did M2i come to award an overall score of 97% on staff conduct when internal audits do not cover staff conduct? Moreover, M2i allotted the maximum score of 11 points out of 11 points on Observance[341] even though a serious concern (internal audits were not found covering staff conduct issues adequately and explicitly) had been observed at Bandhan. When staff conduct is not under the purview of the internal audit team, what is the guarantee that staff conduct is indeed good and as per policy? And given such a situation, how can Bandhan be given such a high score for observance?

4. Let us take yet another example. Also related to staff conduct is the case of Equitas. Equitas received a 100% score (35 points) on staff conduct.[342] It may be good to realize that staff conduct is the indicator that accounts for about 28% of the total COCA score[343] and it is an important indicator.

   The Equitas COCA report says that in the past,

   'Equitas has faced problems pertaining to involvement of unauthorised agents in the client origination process, particularly in some of the branches of Chennai, primarily on account of high sales targets of the SOs (sales officers) and weaker controls.'[344] Thus

---

338 http://www.sidbi.in/Micro/COCA%20Equitas.pdf
339 See Section 1: Scores and facts in the report page 2 given at http://www.sidbi.com/micro/Bandhan.pdf
340 http://www.sidbi.com/micro/Bandhan.pdf, Page 13.
341 See Annex 1, page no 15 in the Bandhan COCA report.
342 See Section 1: Scores and facts in the report page 2 given at http://www.sidbi.in/Micro/COCA%20Equitas.pdf.
343 See the Equitas COCA report, Page 22.
344 http://www.sidbi.in/Micro/COCA%20Equitas.pdf, Page 7.

the SOs were dealing with the clients through the unauthorized agents. So while the relationship of the SOs with the agents may have been good, given that the ultimate clients dealt with the agents and nothing was stated on how good that relationship was, it seems rather erroneous to give 100% for staff conduct (at Equitas).

Further, the report says that Equitas has done away with targets and related incentives for enrolment of new clients from 'November 2010 onwards in order to reduce the likelihood of the SOs getting involved with the unauthorized agents. In M2i's opinion, despite all sincere efforts, some of these agents may still be in existence.'[345]

Given that, in M2i's own assessment, agents may still be (and perhaps are) in existence, surely, it cannot be expected that they (these agents) will follow any laid down policies on staff conduct. So how can M2i justify a 100% score for Equitas on this aspect? It seems that not-so-good practices here are rewarded with the maximum score!

5. Let us look further at another instance. Ujjivan experienced problems with unauthorized agents and the COCA report says that:

'There are instances of presence of unauthorized agents and influential group leaders as has been pointed out in many Internal Audit reports of Ujjivan. The assessment team also observed many instances where the same center leader has been the leader for many years and that the same person is leader of more than one MFI center/group.'[346]

How is it possible that Ujjivan receives a 92% score on client origination,[347] while these serious concerns are found to be in existence? The M2i Ujjivan COCA report is also inconsistent in that these serious problems (mentioned) have not been addressed as an area of improvement. While M2i considers enhancing client awareness of the declining balance interest rates and improving the dissemination of grievance redressal mechanisms to be more important for Ujjivan, it has *not* listed client origination at Ujjivan as worthy of improvement.

6. Last but not the least, SKDRDP received a low score on client origination among others because the organization does not have a policy on avoidance of unauthorized agents.[348]

---

345 http://www.sidbi.in/Micro/COCA%20Equitas.pdf, Page 7.
346 http://www.sidbi.com/micro/COCAUjjivan.pdf, Page 8.
347 See Section 1: Scores and facts in the report page 2 given at http://www.sidbi.com/micro/COCAUjjivan.pdf
348 http://www.sidbi.com/micro/COCA%20SKDRDP.pdf.

The same report also says that 'at present, SKDRDP mostly operates in areas where other MFIs are not operating. In the current assessment, no evidence could be found to suggest that unauthorized agents are affecting the operations of the organization in any significant manner.'[349]

In other assessments like those of Basix, Equitas, and Ujjivan, the scores for client origination were high because the MFIs have a policy not to deal with unauthorized agents. However, in practice, these three NBFC-MFIs had been actively using agents. The COCA reports also do not rule out the use of agents by some of these three NBFC MFIs (even at the time of the COCA assessments). That being the case, why is their score for Client Origination and Targeting (COT) higher than SKDRDP, where no serious evidence with regard to use of agents was found by the M2i team.

7. And I could go on but it is time to stop.

From the analysis given above, it becomes very clear that there are many contradictions, inconsistencies, and subjective interpretations in the CoC assessments and these seem to draw the attention away from the real issues. I hope that the sponsors and developers of the SIDBI–World Bank COCA tool recognize the fact that it is far from being a reliable and valid psychometric measure of code of conduct assessments..."[350]

*This then made me write the final piece in this series of articles,*[351] which was an open letter to the Right Honorable Andrew Mitchell, UK International Development Secretary, on lessons from the Indian microfinance crisis. The letter is reproduced in Appendix 13 and it is self-explanatory.

It is altogether a different point that I did not hear back from the Right Hon. Andrew Mitchell. In fact, I did not expect to hear from him but I expected some action from SIDBI or the India DFID office involved in the implementation of the PSIG.[352] That sadly did not happen either and I was not surprised at this because the person at the helm of the affairs of PSIG had a shocking point of view about microfinance and I reproduce what happened at a high-level meeting at the DFID office in New Delhi where officials of DFID, SIDBI, and the PSIG design team were present. I am sure you will find the same interesting[353]:

---

349 http://www.sidbi.com/micro/COCA%20SKDRDP.pdf, Page 7.
350 Subjectivity and inconsistencies in microfinance code of conduct assessments
http://www.moneylife.in/article/subjectivity-and-inconsistencies-in-microfinance-code-of-conduct-assessments/22221.html, by Ramesh S. Arunachalam, December 15, 2011.
351 Lessons from the Indian microfinance crisis, an open letter to Andrew Mitchell
http://www.moneylife.in/article/lessons-from-the-indian-microfinance-crisis-an-open-letter-to-andrew-mitchell/22234.html, by Ramesh S. Arunachalam, December 16, 2011.
352 Poorest States Inclusive Growth Program of the DFID being implemented by the SIDBI-led consortium.
353 http://microfinance-in-india.blogspot.in/2011/03/do-we-need-new-cgap-consultative-group.html

## Chapter 20: How Reliable and Valid are Code of Conduct Assessments?

"I want to share a recent incident **(not to blame anyone and with no Malice what-so-ever),** without identifying a large project, for which I led the proposal writing team and unexpectedly *(I must be honest),* our consortium won the bid. At the inception meeting in Delhi, in January 2010, even as the microfinance crisis was quietly simmering in India, I repeatedly made the point that, their (DFID's) emphasis on enhancing quantity *(= large numbers)* of financial services through the traditional MFI consumption route is perhaps not appropriate and also that the quality of financial services *(= wide range of need based vulnerability reducing financial services including post harvest agriculture and post production financing)* and access to other issues like markets/infrastructure are very crucial and will have to go hand in hand. I was really shocked when one of the donor team members dismissed this flatly and said that:

'the delivery of financial services to low income people in India through MFIs is a no brainer and we just need to push that agenda to scale in the specified underserved PSIG states.'"

This was in January 2010 when the AP crisis was already burgeoning and about to reach flashpoint over the next few months. I do hope that these people have kept abreast of the 2010 AP microfinance crisis that unfolded thereafter and understood the real impact of the mindless growth of traditional consumption (and/or small production) loans on the low-income clients.

That said, the larger point that I want to make here is about the role that donors and various international agencies can play in shaping the future of low-income people. They often get caught in rhetoric and forget grassroots realities; besides, they like hearing what they want to hear. It is about time that they change and encourage honest feedback and support strategies that are consistent with peoples' real aspirations.

Back to CoC assessments, the key point that I want to make here is that the Indian microfinance sector's response after a crisis has always been to distract, talk rhetoric, and finally propose a self-regulatory mechanism that will not work on the ground—as demonstrated in the next chapter. Further, just as much of the Indian establishment is currently in denial about the present day (2013) economic crisis, all key stakeholders (including CGAP and DFID) in microfinance have always been in denial about any crisis caused by the NBFC MFIs in Andhra Pradesh. And when caught off guard, they have sought an easy way out and proposed some mechanism—*in 2005–2006 it was the Sa-Dhan code of conduct (CoC); in 2009, it was the MFIN CoC and credit bureau; in 2010, it was the unified CoC with assessments, social performance, and credit bureau* —all of which are best regarded as red herrings.

I seriously hope that the stakeholders developing the regulatory architecture for microfinance take into account all these aspects and build in appropriate safeguards. Otherwise, like the 2005–2006 Sa-Dhan code of conduct, the 2009 MFIN code of conduct, 2010–2011 credit bureau, and so on, we will continue to have many wonderful proposals for self-regulation that will not be implemented in real time. And crisis situations will again reappear and we will all continue to echo the phrase—history repeats itself after all.

# Chapter 21:
# MFIs and SROs: Critical Issues and Lessons

On November 26, 2013, the RBI issued a circular[354] with regard to self regulatory organizations (SRO) for NBFC-MFIs. The circular noted that:

> "To give effect to the recommendation of the Sub-Committee on formation of industry associations, to ensure effective monitoring of the functioning of NBFC-MFIs, their compliance with the regulations and code of conduct and in the best interest of the customers of the NBFC-MFIs, the Reserve Bank has decided to accord recognition to industry associations as SRO of NBFC-MFIs. The membership of NBFC-MFIs in the industry association/SRO will be seen by the trade, borrowers and lenders as a mark of confidence and removal from membership will be seen as having an adverse impact on the reputation of such removed NBFC-MFIs. While membership to the SRO is not mandatory, NBFC-MFIs are encouraged to voluntarily become members of at least one SRO.
>
> The SRO holding recognition from the Reserve Bank will have to adhere to a set of functions and responsibilities, such as formulating and administering a Code of Conduct recognized by the Bank, having a grievance and dispute redressal mechanism for the clients of NBFC-MFIs, responsibility of ensuring borrower protection and education, monitoring compliance by NBFC-MFIs with the regulatory framework put in place by the Reserve Bank, surveillance of the microfinance sector, training and awareness programmes for the members, Self Help Groups, etc and submission of its financials, including Annual Report, to the Reserve Bank. The minimum responsibilities of the SRO towards the microfinance sector and the Reserve Bank is given in Annex I. The same may be modified by the Reserve Bank from time to time to improve the efficiency of the sector.
>
> Interested parties are required to apply to the Reserve Bank, seeking recognition as SRO and furnish all details as per Annex[355], to the Principal Chief General Manager, Department of Non-Banking Supervision, Central Office, World Trade Centre, Cuffe Parade, Mumbai–400 005.

---
354 http://www.rbi.org.in/scripts/BS_PressReleaseDisplay.aspx?prid=30052
355 See http://www.rbi.org.in/scripts/BS_PressReleaseDisplay.aspx?prid=30052

## Chapter 21: MFIs and SROs: Critical Issues and Lessons

The recognition of the SRO by the Bank will be communicated by letter giving the detailed terms and conditions and other obligations associated with the recognition."

Just about 2 weeks after the circular, I came across an interesting article[356] in Livemint which noted:

"For giving effect to the recommendations of the Malegam committee on industry SROs, RBI issued the necessary guidelines on 26 November 2013. The guidelines represent a major step forward in the creation of a layered regulatory architecture for the microfinance industry. This emerging architecture has far-reaching ramifications for the healthy development of the industry and its ability to get fully embedded into the national financial system. The industry SROs acting practically as the designated delegatees of the apex financial services regulator, namely RBI, will carry a large burden. This burden will also be a burden of faith; the faith which both RBI and the industry would have reposed on them."

Enthused by the article, I continued reading and here is what made it more engrossing for me:

"Established in December 2009, constitutionally, structurally, and functionally, Micro Finance Institutions Network (MFIN) has been acting as a de facto SRO for its members. Its 43 members, all NBFC-MFIs, have a client outreach of over 25 million low-income borrowers with a loan outstanding of approximately Rs.23,000 crore. The MFIN Code of Conduct, almost a precursor to RBI guidelines and regulations for the industry, was released in April 2010. It covered a range of areas such as governance, client protection, staff behaviour, resolution of complaints, promoting transparency and whistle blowing. It also provided for setting up an ombudsman for member-MFIs for fair and transparent adjudication of disputes and client protection. For ensuring adherence to the code, a self-certification process and an enforcement committee were put in place. The measures taken, while far from perfect, have led to a distinct improvement in industry practices and creation of an ethos of responsible lending.

Another large initiative taken by MFIN has been the development of a credit bureau ecosystem for the microfinance sector. Over the past two years, MFIN's efforts have resulted in 100% adoption of the use of Credit Bureau checks by member-MFIs. In this context, it is noteworthy that an industry which did not have any credit bureau till 2009, had, as of 30 September, contributed over 100 million loan records to the credit bureaus. And every month, about 2 million credit queries are made.

Self-regulation will boost the overall franchise value of the microfinance sector and reduce costs associated with limited trust and asymmetric information. The grant of formal SRO status to MFIN will improve the governance process and redressal mechanism in the sector. The SRO guidelines provide the much-needed impetus to the goal of inclusive growth for the vast unserved and underserved segments

---

356 The microfinance sentinels (http://www.livemint.com/Opinion/dR8Z95eP6woqMlFCEmaRiJ/The-microfinance-sentinels.html), Alok Prasad and Vipin Sharma, Tuesday, Dec 10, 2013.

of the population by facilitating access to inclusive financial services in a responsible and transparent manner.

With its members representing over 80% of the industry and the experience gained over the past three years, MFIN is arguably the most appropriate organization for grant of SRO status by RBI. In many ways this will merely represent a shift from a de facto to a de jure position."

Puzzled at these statements, I looked for the authors and I found them to be (a) Alok Prasad; and (b) Vipin Sharma-both of whom are interested parties and closely related to MFIN.

It was déjà vu for me as 'conflict of interest' had again raised its ugly head in microfinance regulation.

Given this context, let us now ask the question as to whether MFIN—one of the so-called unofficial self-regulatory bodies in Indian microfinance—has been accountable for its actions and statements? I provide two concrete examples here, while undertaking this analysis.

First, the MFIN enquiry initiated in February 2011 (on governance and transparency) is still not in the public domain. Second, the MFIN-sponsored NCAER study, which suffers several serious shortcomings, makes one wonder whether MFIN can function as an objective association—without conflicts of interest—and as an effective self-regulatory body for Indian microfinance. While these two instances are sufficient to come to a conclusion about MFIN's objectivity and its ability to carry out the tasks as an SRO, let us nonetheless look at MFIN-related issues in greater detail.

MFIN was formed in 2009 after the Kolar (Karnataka) crisis. Since then, a lot of water has flowed under the microfinance bridge in India. It is in this context that the *Hindustan Times* (October 20, 2011) news item quoting MFIN's CEO, Alok Prasad, assumes tremendous significance. The article noted that,[357] "MFI Network (MFIN), an umbrella body of non-banking finance company (NBFC) microfinance institutions (MFIs) that also seeks to serve as a self-regulatory body, admitted that the sector erred in chasing a high growth trajectory at the expense of corporate best practices as it went for coercive methods in loan recovery while keeping interest rates two or three times that of banks."

According to this news article, "Where the MFIs went wrong was in growing too rapidly, lured by the business opportunity, without paying much thought to execution or hiring the right kind of people. And there was a disconnect between the headquarters and the field agents," MFIN CEO Alok Prasad told HT.

Indeed, while MFIN needs to be appreciated for its candid (although late) admittance of what went wrong in Indian microfinance, it also seems appropriate to look at what MFIN has really done to defuse the microfinance crisis in India and the extent to which it has been accountable for its statements and promised actions.

First, recall that after the 2010 microfinance crisis in Andhra Pradesh (AP), MFIN announced that it would enquire into the suicides in AP, using independent researchers/stakeholders. It is over 3 years to date and we have heard nothing about this report. *What has happened to MFIN's study on*

---

357 http://www.hindustantimes.com/business-news/CorporateNews/Microfinance-body-admits-goof-ups/Article1-759651.aspx

## Chapter 21: MFIs and SROs: Critical Issues and Lessons

*suicides is a question that certainly begs an answer?* As Prof. Sriram noted in an article in *Mint*,[358] "It is also a bit intriguing that MFIN has gone to town with this (NCAER Small Borrowing Study) report claiming that all is well with microfinance, while it is shying away from releasing another important study that it had commissioned in AP. This report on the suicides of microfinance clients was done by a credible researcher. Possibly, the findings are not convenient for MFIN to make the report public?"

Second, MFIN ordered an enquiry into the governance and transparency deficit of select MFIs after an *Economic Times* (ET) investigation in early 2011. As noted in ET (February 4, 2011):[359]

> "Four days after an ET investigation outlined the deficit in governance and transparency in a shareholding vehicle typical to microfinance institutions, the Microfinance Institutions Network (MFIN) has set up a committee to look into those charges. A statement on Thursday by MFIN, an association of for-profit micro-lenders, said that based on the study's findings, disciplinary action could be taken. According to Vijay Mahajan, president of MFIN, the inquiry is against three MFIs—Share Microfin, Spandana Sphoorty Financial and SKS Microfinance. The ET investigation centred around the governance of the shareholding vehicle, called mutual benefit trusts (MBTs), in these three companies. MFIs used MBTs, in which poor women were shareholders, to transform themselves from NGOs to for-profit entities. The MFIN statement said: 'The inquiry will address concerns raised by the media and other stakeholders, vis-à-vis the appropriateness of processes followed during the course of these transformations and the evolution of the shareholding pattern of these entities.' And MFIN board member Samit Ghosh (who is also the current chairman), the founder of Ujjivan, said there is a possibility that any of the three can be expelled if found guilty. The committee is also expected to draft guidelines for good governance of MBTs. The members of the inquiry committee will be announced on Friday. It is expected to have a banker, an auditor and a retired bureaucrat. The committee will have 30 days to submit its report. Alok Prasad, CEO of MFIN, says the association had been discussing the move for the past three days."

*What happened to this enquiry (and draft guidelines for good governance) is YET another question that begs an answer?*

Third, the MFIN-sponsored NCAER small borrowing study was released on October 10, 2011. The NCAER study suffers from several limitations as outlined by Prof. Sriram, who noted in an article[360] that "the report falls short of its objectives because of three aspects:

1) The study was funded by the Microfinance Institutions Network (MFIN), an industry body representing only commercial MFIs. MFIN is an interested party and has been defending the 'deeds' and 'misdeeds' of the members through the crisis, and would be interested in whitewashing MFIs;

---

358 http://www.livemint.com/2011/10/21004414/An-incomplete-story-from-the-m.html?h=B
359 http://articles.economictimes.indiatimes.com/2011-02-04/news/28433279_1_mfin-microfinance-institutions-network-shareholding-pattern
360 http://www.livemint.com/2011/10/21004414/An-incomplete-story-from-the-m.html?h=B

2) The study was conducted in the urban centers of Jaipur, Lucknow, Chennai, Kolkata and Hyderabad. While the report claims that 70% of the respondents were 'rural', the sampling plan indicates that the 'rural' areas were at a maximum distance of 14 km from the urban settlement. This is not an inclusive study—it is a study on small borrowing in urban India. While the report refers to 'a raging controversy over the role and anti-poor activities of MFIs in India, especially those operating in Andhra Pradesh (AP)' and the three contentious issues namely 'usurious interest rates, strong-arm collection tactics, multiple lending and compensation received by top management' as a background for the study, the sample selection is not representative of the problem geographies—Telangana and coastal districts of AP from where reports of borrower suicides were reported. Thus, the findings of the study that there were few instances of multiple borrowing—and where found, it was associated with informal finance and not MFIs—and indicating that there were no strong-arm tactics do not cut much ice. The findings do not come from the same area where the problems existed. Moreover, Jaipur and Lucknow are not great centres of microfinance. The choice of these centres could be justified for an exploratory study and not an evaluative one. These two locations distort the numbers and the conclusions significantly in justifying the role and behaviour of MFIs; and

3) The vehemence with which the report defends MFIs is problematic, as the objective of the study was to assess the effectiveness of small borrowing. While there are the usual disclaimers that conclusions are drawn on the basis of data from the five clusters, this disclaimer is weak because each time a conclusion is drawn, it is placed along with the problems identified in AP."

A more detailed critique of the NCAER study can be found elsewhere.[361]

Let us go back even further in time and recall statements made by MFIN's (then) Chairman (Vijay Mahajan); MFIN's CEO (Alok Prasad) and the Chairman of one of MFIN's largest members (Dr Vikram Akula), SKS, at the height of the crisis—they talked of 'Rogue MFIs' or 'Fly by Night Operators' as the ones responsible for the 2010 Andhra Crisis.[362] *This seems directly out of tune with the recent candid admittance of (MFI) guilt by MFIN's CEO, Alok Prasad.* Also, the hard data available and provided in this book[363] (based on data available in the public domain and the Mix Market database) suggests that it is the 13 MFIN members (all NBFC MFIs)—and especially, the six large AP-headquartered NBFC

---

361 (a) Microfinance institutions not the answer for poverty alleviation, says Jairam Ramesh http://www.moneylife.in/article/microfinance-institutions-not-the-answer-for-poverty-alleviation-says-jairam-ramesh/20513.html; (b) The RBI and the Ministry of Finance should view the MFIN-sponsored NCAER study on small borrowings with a great deal of caution http://www.moneylife.in/article/the-rbi-and-the-ministry-of-finance-should-view-the-mfin-sponsored-ncaer-study-on-small-borrowings-with-a-great-deal-of-caution/20566.html; (c) MFIN-NCAER study: Here's the proof that microfinance agents are thriving in Tamil Nadu http://www.moneylife.in/article/mfin-ncaer-study-heres-the-proof-that-microfinance-agents-are-thriving-in-tamil-nadu/20717.html; and (d) MFIN-NCAER study unearths agents' role in microfinance, but does not find these middlemen in Chennai http://www.moneylife.in/article/mfin-ncaer-study-unearths-agents-role-in-microfinance-but-does-not-find-these-middlemen-in-chennai/20674.html.

362 http://microfinance-in-india.blogspot.com/2010/11/who-are-rogue-mfis-that-have-supposedly.html

363 See Chapter 6.

## Chapter 21: MFIs and SROs: Critical Issues and Lessons

MFIs-who grew at a burgeoning pace during the years (April 2008–March 2010) preceding the 2010 AP crisis.[364] And last but not the least, recall that the MD of Sahayata Microfinance,[365] was a member of the board of MFIN. We all know what happened at Sahayata Microfinance and who was responsible for the collateral damage done!

These are just a few instances and there are many more such happenings, statements, and actions where MFIN has not been accountable but the idea is not to find fault with MFIN! However, the issues that arises now are: (a) how to make MFIN more accountable for the statements that it makes and the actions that it promises to undertake?, and (b) how to ensure that MFIN and other unofficial self-regulatory organizations (SROs) function as responsible and reliable pillars in the overall microfinance regulatory framework, especially if and when they are given official SRO status?

Apart from the study on suicides, which is yet to be made public, the findings of the MFIN enquiry initiated in February 2011 with regard to governance and transparency are not available in the public domain, despite a promise by MFIN to do so within 30 days. These coupled with the 'not-so-objective' MFIN-sponsored NCAER study (that suffers several serious shortcomings) and burgeoning growth of many MFIN members during the years preceding the crisis, makes one wonder whether at all MFIN can function as an objective association (without conflicts of interest) and an effective self-regulatory body for Indian microfinance. This question is especially crucial given that the Malegam Committee Report (MCR) lists SROs as one of the major pillars in its regulatory framework and the RBI has issued a circular[366] following up on this recommendation of the MCR.

As usual, I leave it to you to make your own judgment(s) and sincerely hope that the regulators and concerned authorities developing a robust regulatory architecture for Indian microfinance take notice of what has been happening among so-called SROs such as MFIN as they are likely to have an important official role in the regulatory architecture being developed.

In fact, the MCR has provided for a significant level of self-regulation in Indian microfinance. However, given the dismal track record of self-regulation over the years, I am somewhat skeptical on how well it will work this time around. That said, given that irrespective of whether we like it or not, SROs are here to stay, the more practical strategy would be to ensure that the proposed self-regulation is effective and works well on the ground. Without question, for self-regulation to be effective and offer benefits to the microfinance industry and its consumers, it must be consistent with the overall regulatory framework and its accountability must be strong. In fact, accountability is most critical in this context

---

364 The RBI and the Ministry of Finance should view the MFIN-sponsored NCAER study on small borrowings with a great deal of caution (http://www.moneylife.in/article/the-rbi-and-the-ministry-of-finance-should-view-the-mfin-sponsored-ncaer-study-on-small-borrowings-with-a-great-deal-of-caution/20566.html), by Ramesh S Arunachalam, October 13, 2011.

365 Award winning Sahayata Microfinance is the latest to go astray (http://moneylife.in/article/award-winning-sahayata-microfinance-is-the-latest-to-go-astray/21549.html), by Ramesh S Arunachalam, November 18, 2011 and What is said at conferences is very different from what is implemented in practice (http://www.moneylife.in/article/what-is-said-at-conferences-is-very-different-from-what-is-implemented-in-practice/22124.html), by Ramesh S Arunachalam, December 12, 2011.

366 See http://www.rbi.org.in/scripts/BS_PressReleaseDisplay.aspx?prid=30052

for having good regulatory outcomes. Unless this accountability is built into the system, no amount of self-regulation will help the beleaguered Indian microfinance industry. Let us be clear on that aspect!

Whenever one considers introducing a new self-regulatory system (or for that matter, reforming an existing system as is the case in India), a number of important issues need to be addressed. Some of these are highlighted here and one hopes that stakeholders developing the regulatory architecture look into both the substantive policy issues (which concern the design of the self-regulatory system) as well as process aspects (that arise in implementing the self-regulatory reform). These are dealt with sequentially in this chapter.

In terms of substantive policy issues, several issues need attention and these are highlighted here:

*National (country) strategy for development of microfinance:* Here, one needs to look closely at the government's (and prime regulators') strategy for developing the microfinance industry. And any such strategy should, in turn, consider the structure and competitive position of the microfinance industry and briefly attempt to answer these questions: (i) how to ensure that the microfinance industry best supports economic development; (ii) how to enable the industry to foster market development, competition, and innovation to better meet the needs of clients in microfinance; (iii) how to alter/raise/revise standards of regulation and conduct to ensure that clients and other stakeholders (including investors and other participants) are treated fairly; (iv) how to improve integrity of the microfinance market in general; (v) how to achieve an appropriate cost level for regulation of the microfinance industry; and (vi) how to ensure that the MFIs, financial institutions, and various stakeholders have the business focus, competitive positioning, systems, and governance standards required to succeed in their missions. That we, as a country, even today, lack a clear national policy regarding microfinance requires emphasis here. In fact, because of this, there is confusion regarding what microfinance is expected to achieve on the ground, who the key players are, and the like. All these need clarification and such a policy will have to clarify the role of self-regulation within the larger policy framework. In fact, that should be the starting input for any regulatory architecture (for microfinance) being developed.

*Commitment to self-regulation:* The microfinance industry's commitment to self-regulation needs to be understood especially in the context of the 2010 AP crisis and its aftermath. There are several key questions here: (i) Do clients, investors, lenders, MFIs, and other stakeholders have a sufficient degree of confidence in self-regulation to make the system viable, both today and going forward?; (ii) Are the members of the SROs/industry associations committed to the concept of self-regulation, and are they prepared to invest the requisite time and resources?; and (iii) Do the regulatory authorities believe that the use of self-regulation in the microfinance industry is indeed appropriate, given all that has happened in the past few years? This is especially critical given the fact that self-regulation has hardly worked in India and, also given the 2010 AP microfinance crisis and its resultant impact, this aspect needs to be ascertained unequivocally.

*Size and complexity of the microfinance industry:* The microfinance industry is complex, with a range of players including not-for-profits, mutual benefits, and for-profits. It has also experienced burgeoning growth in the past few years and its scale and size raise critical questions: (i) whether the industry needs multiple layers of regulation including self-regulation; (ii) can the industry afford and support such multiple layers of regulation, including self-regulation; (iii) what approaches, according to the authorities and industry stakeholders (including clients), are likely to deliver the most efficient and effective regulation of the industry; (iv) do the benefits of self-regulation outweigh the potential extra costs and disadvantages; (v) what about the issue of regulatory efficiency and costs—is it likely to be significant; and (vi) can the conflicts of interest that arise in self-regulation be managed appropriately?

*Regulatory priorities and key risks:* The regulators/supervisors, MFIs, and other stakeholders should determine and agree on what regulatory issues and risks need to be prioritized. The three issues that are of relevance here are: (i) Does the existing system adequately address those issues and manage those risks?; (ii) If not, how should the system be reformed to respond more effectively to the issues and what role should SROs/industry associations play?; and (iii) Does the use of SROs enhance the likelihood of occurrence of some of the risks and, if so, how? I think this deserves close attention and concerned stakeholders should particularly look to address, in a *practical* and *feasible* manner, some of the key issues (and associated risks) that have caused the 2010 AP crisis.

*Fairness and consistency:* In choosing a particular SRO/industry association structure, the fairness and consistency of regulation for different segments of the microfinance and larger financial services industry need to be ascertained and maintained. The key questions here are: (i) Are players in different segments of the industry that offer similar services treated equally; and (ii) Do different legal forms of MFIs have a level playing field? These questions are especially valid with regard to the MCR that seems to lay greater emphasis on for-profit MFIs and thereby on related SROs/associations.

*Funding:* This is an important issue and the critical aspects are: (i) Who should bear the cost of self-regulation; (ii) While industry players may fund governments and regulators to a significant degree in many countries, can MFIs and other stakeholders do that in the present Indian context; and (iii) If so, on what basis should MFIs/stakeholders fund a self-regulatory system, and how should the costs be allocated across categories of MFIs or even members within a category? These issues are invariably contentious, but certainly need to be addressed as well.

*Legal framework:* Lastly, the legal framework needs to be looked at and would entail answering questions such as the following: (i) Does or will an SRO/industry association have sufficient powers to perform the responsibilities allocated to it; and (ii) if not, is changing the applicable/related laws possible in practice and feasible from an implementation sense?

Two specific comments are in order here. First, in many contexts, most SROs/industry associations have the statutory authority to perform their regulatory responsibilities but they can also obtain or reinforce jurisdiction by specific contracts with its members. Second, because SROs/industry associations are private bodies, India's larger civil/legal code and systems will also need to be examined for any limits that they may place on SRO's (industry association's) rule-making authority or regarding the extent to which the regulator can delegate activities to an SRO/industry association. However, some obstacles may, however, be addressed rather easily: (i) by relying on SROs/industry associations mainly to supervise compliance with regulations (*this is a critical aspect of regulation versus supervision*), (ii) by designing effective working agreements, and/or (iii) through MOUs to clarify the role and working relationships of SROs/industry associations with the regulator. This would need to be kept in mind by the stakeholders developing the regulatory architecture for microfinance. In this context, it must be mentioned that any adhoc attempt to arbitrarily bring in the use of SROs could be counterproductive.

*Supervision of an SRO/industry association:* This is an aspect that should not be underestimated and would entail answering questions such as the following: (i) Does the regulator have the powers and, more importantly, the *capacity* to effectively oversee an SRO's/industry association's operations; (ii) What are the relative cost benefits of supervising SROs and who would bear the cost; and (iii) Given the cost–benefit analysis, is a limited or extensive role for self-regulation[367] more appropriate?

While this discussion looked at the substantive policy issues with regard to regulatory reform of SROs in Indian microfinance, significant design and process issues must also be considered as outlined here.

*Design risks:* The concerned stakeholders should articulate the key drivers for changing the current approach to regulation (say, for example, officially introducing or strengthening self-regulation as has been done in the MCR (by the RBI), which uses the SRO/industry approach as one of its pillars) and should critically assess the importance and practical feasibility of achieving the objectives related to reforming the system. Every change and objective carries associated risks and the broader the scope of the planned changes, the greater the risk of implementation problems and/or even failure.

Some of the major risks are: (i) increased conflict of interest in self-regulation, as has been demonstrated in Indian microfinance; (ii) inability of the SRO/industry association to operate effectively and in an independent manner, again as demonstrated during and after the 2010 AP crisis; (iii) the potential for "regulatory control and/or capture" of the SRO/industry association system by regulated MFIs or by one powerful segment of the industry (say, for example, NBFC MFIs or large MFIs etc.); (iv) disruption of standards of regulation and supervision during the transition period because of organizational conflict and uncertainty as has been the case in microfinance; (v) reduced standards of regulation and supervision under the new system, especially post MCR, because the microfinance institution development

---

367 For example, an SRO/industry association may mainly be made responsible for supervision of compliance with the regulations set by the regulator. As an example, MFIN or Sa-Dhan could be used to supervise the RBI circulars emanating from the MCR.

and regulation bill (MFIDR Bill, 2012) has been on the horizon for some time now; (vi) overloading the SRO/industry association system with new responsibilities, when it has neither the ability/resources/willingness to address these nor the time to build the requisite capacity to address the various responsibilities—this has to be seen in the light of the past track record of the SRO/industry association and is an important issue in Indian microfinance, especially after the 2010 AP microfinance crisis; (vii) the aspect of micromanagement and excessive interference by the statutory regulator in the governance and management of SROs/industry associations; and (viii) failure to design the new system appropriately, leading to excessive duplication of roles, functions, and activities with cost implications.

*Transitional risks:* Transitional risks are temporary risks that arise from the process of implementing changes in the case of regulatory systems, among a group of organizations. There are important transitional issues that must be addressed whenever structural changes are to be made to a regulatory system (as has been proposed in the MCR and is being implemented by the RBI). These include ensuring that: (i) regulatory processes continue uninterrupted, especially supervision of the industry players and intermediaries—*I am not sure of what is happening presently in India, especially in respect to MBTs and not-for-profits MFIs*; (ii) regulated entities/persons remain within the legal jurisdiction of a regulator at all times; (iii) the transition to the new arrangement is as seamless as possible; and (iv) dispute resolution mechanisms are agreed on to address any unforeseen issues that may arise during the transition period. Further, if the changes contemplated are major and radical, then the industry and authorities may want to consider taking an evolutionary or phased approach to implementation so that the transitional risks involved are minimized, if not eliminated. Again, I am not sure if these are being addressed in Indian microfinance, given the changes being carried out, post the 2010 AP crisis.

*Stakeholders' views:* In considering any changes to the present system of regulation in microfinance, including legitimizing self-regulation, it is important to understand and consider the views of various stakeholders such as: (i) intermediaries (banks, different kinds of MFIs, and others); (ii) clients of the above-mentioned institutions; (iii) retail and institutional investors; (iv) government and statutory authorities; (v) existing SROs and industry associations; and (vi) other related regulators and stakeholders. This is a critical issue and I am not sure of what the degree of support is for the changes proposed compared with the resistance to change. Building consensus among the various stakeholders on a "common vision" for the regulatory structure with regard to microfinance is highly desirable. I truly hope that those developing a new regulatory architecture take this process forward quickly and earnestly.

*Legal and regulatory risk*: If institutions' regulatory responsibilities are changed in the new structure, plans to minimize legal and regulatory risk would be needed. Transfer of responsibilities will likely require transfer of: (i) rules from one body's rulebook to another, (ii) responsibility for supervision programs, (iii) experienced officers and staff, and (iv) infrastructure including information. These are aspects that would especially require attention if a new regulatory/supervisory body is to be created for microfinance.

Another aspect here is that if a prominent role is being accorded to self-regulation (as is presently the case), then the primary regulator (whoever it is) must have an appropriate *oversight* program for the SRO/industry association. Among other things, they should ensure the following:

- The SRO has appropriate corporate governance policies and procedures and that it follows them in practice. This is critical as many institutions have great governance policies and procedures on paper but rarely implement them. In this case, the lack of appropriate governance at the industry associations is a major factor for the lack of effectiveness of these bodies, as the experiences of the past few years have shown. When you have people like Mr. Ajay Verma[368] and such others on the board of MFIN (as was the case in 2011), the SRO can hardly act as a self-regulating body.

- The SRO's functions and rules cover its regulation/supervision responsibilities. They are fair and balanced, treating all categories of members equally.

- Its regulation, supervision, and risk management responsibilities are being met and systems and processes meet the appropriate standards required. In addition, the primary regulator must ensure that the SRO has effective compliance, supervision, and enforcement programs, within its structure. This needs to be done actively by the primary regulator.

- Any identified conflicts of interest, within the SRO, are squarely and appropriately addressed. This is a critical aspect as there have been huge conflicts of interest in the Indian microfinance sector and this is one of the main reasons why the Sa-Dhan and MFIN CoCs were not implemented on the ground.

- Shortcomings or needs that require a response from the SRO are identified and adequately addressed in a timely manner and also periodically.

In addition, the regulator, through appropriate supervision, must ensure that the SRO continues to meet all the conditions of its license[369] and other obligations imposed on it by law and/or regulation. Some of the main processes that regulators could use in the oversight of SROs/industry associations are given here.

*Process 1: Review and ensure highest corporate governance standards in SROs.* The primary regulator will have to ensure the following:

---

368 The MD of Sahayata Microfinance who was suspended in 2011. He was also a board member of MFIN in 2011.
369 The operationalization of the MCR requires the provision of a license (or official sanction) to industry associations for acting as SROs. The RBI circular of November 26, 2013 is an implementation of the MCR recommendation.

- The SRO meets high standards of corporate governance required for being a part of the overall regulatory system. Among other things, this would include consideration of all aspects including functioning of the board of directors (or equivalent), their independence, and the like.

- It is responsive to all stakeholders including clients and also meets its public interest/civil society mandate in terms of transparency and disclosure.

- It is fully compliant with the laws as well as the conditions of its license.

- Its internal functioning, management, and various systems are consistent with its regulatory mandate, objectives, and overall regulation.

- The rules and processes of the SRO are fair and balanced and treat all members equally. In addition, they must ensure that the interests of all stakeholders, including low-income clients, are met.

*Process 2: Periodically monitor the SRO and its reports.* The primary regulator will have to perform the following:

- Periodic review of the status of SRO's monitoring and other programs, activities, roles, and functions as well as its financial condition.

- Provide ongoing supervision and practical advice to ensure that the SRO is able to discharge its functions in an effective, fair, and transparent manner. This is especially critical because the industry associations in India have neither had any such regulatory/supervisory experience nor serious guidance from the primary regulators.

- Help in coordination activities of an SRO with others in the regulatory system as well as the larger microfinance industry, as may be required.

*Process 3: Enable self-assessment of its own performance, activities, and operations by the SRO.* The primary regulator will have to facilitate the following:

- Independent review of SRO performance in line with its supervisory and related duties.

- Establish an objective process of self-evaluation and related measures for assessing its performance. In this regard, it seems critical to provide inputs to the SRO to enable it to develop its (own) self-monitoring system so that its performance with regard to supervisory and other duties can be gauged consistently and periodically, without any conflicts of interest.

- Identify areas of risk in SRO's operations and suggest mitigants and strategies for addressing these risks.

- Ensure that the SRO has a CoC that is followed on a day-to-day basis by both the management and the staff. This is critical and it has been a major reason for (industry associations) not being able to enforce their CoCs with their respective member MFIs.

All these design, process, and monitoring issues will have to be considered and dealt with by the key stakeholders, before full-fledged implementation of self-regulation, as part of the overall regulatory architecture for microfinance in India.

# Chapter 22:
# Zero PAR, Legal Notices, and Insolvency Petitions: Delinquency Management from the Field

The issue of delinquency has long dominated the microfinance debate and it has been said that microfinance boasted among the best repayment rates till some years back in the financial sector. This has usually reflected itself as "zero" or "near-zero" PAR. However, as I traveled through the field areas during the 2010 AP microfinance crisis, I realized that zero "PAR" was a conscious strategy pursued by MFIs and that the real repayment situation may *not* be quite as good as portrayed. I will attempt to highlight lessons/issues relating to zero PAR and delinquency in this chapter for the benefit of various stakeholders, including those developing a regulatory architecture for microfinance in India. I shall first introduce the concept of PAR and identify its strengths/weaknesses before moving on to zero PAR phenomenon.

*Relevance of PAR:* The loan portfolio outstanding is the largest income-generating asset for an MFI[370] and the quality of this asset is therefore critical to its survival. Thus, it is imperative that judgments about the quality of an MFI's portfolio are made in a (reliable) manner, so as to accurately portray the level of default or credit risk. While the extant literature suggests that one of the best measures of asset quality is called PAR, practical situations reveal that this measure also suffers from several limitations, which, if unaddressed, could result in an inaccurate portrayal of the default/credit risk.

*PAR defined:* PAR is a percentage measure[371] and it denotes the "proportion of an MFI's total gross outstanding loan portfolio that is at default/credit risk. The formula[372] for PAR is as follows:

> "Sum of unpaid principal balance of all loans with payments past due (1 to 365 days and more)" divided by "Total gross outstanding loan portfolio (sum of principal outstanding of all loans)"

---

370 This is the case with most MFIs that tend to have a larger portfolio in loans as compared other financial products.
371 This is the standardized CGAP definition and is called the normal PAR.
372 As CGAP introduced it to me in a ToT at Manila, way back in 1998.

Three aspects about PAR deserve mention: (i) it is a stock measure and reflects the default/credit risk as at a given date; (ii) it attempts to measure the default/credit risk by extrapolating past client behavior into the future; and (iii) specifically, its estimation of the default/credit risk is based on one critical question—*as on a given date, if every delinquent borrower were to completely default, then how much (money) is the MFI likely to lose?* PAR therefore provides a very pessimistic[373] estimate of the default/credit risk as it assumes that today's (delinquent) behavior by clients would be prevalent in the future[374] as well.

*Methodological deficiencies that impact PAR:* Several methodological aspects also affect PAR and could result in an inaccurate portrayal of the default/credit risk prevalent in an MFI's loan portfolio. These include (i) improper rules for classifying a loan as past due—sometimes, a loan may not be classified as past due even if (all) the concerned installments have not been paid by the due dates. In some cases, due dates may themselves be variable. In still others, an official grace period[375] may prevent a risky (several installment skipped) loan from being classified as past due. Finally, classification of loans as past due may be based on "principal amounts" that are past due rather than all amounts (including interest) that need to be considered. (ii) Incorrect sequence for appropriating client repayments—whereby repayments are first appropriated[376] toward principal and later toward interest. (iii) Incorrect method of aging of past due loans—whereby the installment method is used for aging of past due loans. As has been shown,[377] the installment method of aging understates age of a past due loan (if the loan is beyond its term) and overstates the age of a past due loan (if it is within its loan term). These deficiencies have an impact on PAR as they reduce the numerator.

Having set the context, let us now look at the zero PAR policy followed in some[378] MFIs. We have heard of various strategies to keep PAR low or zero. The most obvious, something that has come through the 2010 AP (Indian) microfinance crisis, is of loan officers/field workers/microfinance agents sitting outside a client's house till the money is paid. If the concerned officer (or field worker or agent) does not get back in an hour, another staff/agent joins him. I have heard of cases where two or more officers/agents and at times even a branch manager sat outside a first-time delinquent client's house or place of work till 6.30 p.m. to recover the money. The pressure increases exponentially if multiple loans are taken, with the client facing MFI 1 on Monday, MFI 2 on Tuesday, MFI 3 on Wednesday, and so on, day after day, week after week. In my opinion, this strategy perhaps played a major role in pushing clients to desperation in AP in 2010 and before.

---

373 Arrears rate is an optimistic default/credit risk measure as it uses the delinquent amount rather than the entire loan outstanding in the numerator.

374 That is why the entire loan outstanding of delinquent clients is represented in the numerator of the given formula.

375 An MFI had a product where clients had to repay in 46 weekly instalments spread over 52 weeks. So, while MFI reported 0% PAR, as high as 23% of the clients with outstanding loans had skipped 4/5/6 weekly payments. In reality, PAR > 1 day exceeded 38% when all past due loans (even those with one skipped installment) were considered.

376 Such a sequence of appropriation may reduce the principal amounts overdue, and hence PAR, but more importantly result in lower income for the MFI because of lost/delayed interest payments and thereby affect its sustainability and survival.

377 Refer to Microfinance Capacity Builder, Volume 1, Issue 1, (2002) for a complete discussion of the best practices method of aging and limitations in using the installment method of aging.

378 This note pertains to some Indian MFIs that the author has had experience with, but does not imply that these aspects are prominent in all Indian MFIs.

# Chapter 22: Zero PAR, Legal Notices, and Insolvency Petitions: Delinquency Management from the Field

In one of the earliest CGAP ToT[379] courses on delinquency that Ms. Brigitte Helms (with Janet and Joyita) conducted way back in 1998 at AIM Manila, the biggest take away for me was/is—*there are no bad borrowers, only bad loans*. This means that the institution is primarily responsible if any loan goes delinquent because it may have granted a bad loan. So, from that perspective, putting such pressure on the clients is unfortunate. Interestingly, some MFIs describe the above-mentioned method of collection (where field workers/loan officers/agents sit outside the house/work place of the client) as one of satyagraha and equated it to the *modus operandi* of the late Mahatma Gandhiji[380]-something the Mahatma would never have approved of, as Satyagraha and Civil Disobedience, as espoused by him, were for public and not selfish causes. This apart, in the past, I have also observed the zero PAR policy manifesting itself as staff taking loans from the MFI to pay back client overdues and then collecting the overdue amounts from the clients.

Some MFIs have also used the following strategies to keep PAR low or near zero:

- *Rescheduling:* Reduces the whole PAR ratio while default risk still exists. If all overdue loans are rescheduled, then PAR will become zero.

- *Refinancing* (overdue amounts are rescheduled and fresh amounts including through successive and perhaps multiple loans are given to the same borrower): Reduces the whole PAR ratio while default risk still exists. If all overdue loans are rescheduled, then PAR will become zero.

- *Write-offs:* Reduce the whole PAR ratio while default risk still exists. If all overdue loans are written off, then PAR will become zero.

- *Fresh loan disbursements for which repayments are yet to begin* (including those with a grace/moratorium period): Reduce the whole PAR ratio while default risk still exists. If the fresh disbursements (including through multiple, ghost and successive loans) are sudden and huge, they may result in PAR approaching insignificant percentages or even zero

- *Sequence of client repayments, principal first and interest next:* Reduces the whole PAR ratio while default risk still exists. Distorts the age of past dues (overdues) and affects provisioning, reserve, and sustainability and through reduction of interest payments (yield). Technically, if this is done, PAR will be zero if it is defined as unpaid principal balance of all loans with payments past due/total outstanding portfolio.

However, the most interesting case that I came across was where the MIS was used to underreport PAR. The following example should serve to elaborate the same.

---
379 Training of Trainers.
380 Widely accepted as The Father of the Nation in India.

Client A had taken a loan of Rs. 1000 and this was payable in 10 installments of Rs. 100, each with 18% interest. The repayment was due at the end of every month and at the end of the first month, the client paid Rs. 215—of this, Rs. 100 went toward the first month principal, Rs. 15 toward interest due at end of the first month and Rs. 100 was taken as prepayment of the second month principal.

When the second installment became due, the client did *not* make any repayment (because she may have assumed she had prepaid the amount); the MIS also showed there was no principal overdue. While this is true in a sense, the fact is that the client *still* had to pay interest on the Rs. 800 that was outstanding (Rs. 1000–200) for a whole month and, therefore, the loan did have an interest overdue.

The PAR measure, as per the traditional good practices PAR definition (unpaid principal balance of all loans with payments past due/total outstanding portfolio), would not capture this as a risky loan as there was no principal overdue, although, in reality, this loan did have an interest overdue (which may not even be collected later).

Thus, the MIS had strategically used the technical definition of PAR (provided by global microfinance good practices) to (incorrectly) define the MIS process for calculating PAR, which then selected risky loans *only* based on principal overdue. It omitted loans that had an interest overdue from the pool of risky loans. There were several such loans in the MIS, and a query for calculating PAR based on interest OD as well resulted in the PAR figure changing significantly. And, in conjunction with this, when the sequence of client repayment appropriation was towards principal first and interest last, then the level of understatement of PAR proved to be even higher. Thus, when the MIS is accurate in terms of the sequence rules for client repayment appropriation, this may not be such a huge issue but if the sequence of client repayment appropriation is not as per the correct (good practices) sequence, then things such as mentioned here will undoubtedly play a huge role in contributing to near-zero PAR, even when the default risk is high.

*Implications for credit risk management:* Thus, several events such as rescheduling; refinancing; loan write-offs and fresh loan disbursements; and methodological aspects including improper rules for classifying a loan as past due, inappropriate sequence for appropriating client repayments, incorrect method of aging of past due loans, and multiple/ghost lending could result in a lower and close to zero PAR ratio, while the default/credit risk may still be quite high. These situations have several implications for effective management of credit/default risk in an MFI's portfolio, the most important being that credit/default risk should be promptly recognized (so that it can be dealt with).

This means accurate, reliable, and timely information should be available about the loan portfolio from the MIS. This mandates the use of a standard best practices methodology in estimating PAR. It would entail incorporation of several standard best practices features into the manual or automated MIS used by the MFI: (i) fixed and *a priori* terms for loans including repayment frequency, installment amounts, due dates, loan tenure, and so on with provision for changes under special circumstances[381] along with prompt disclosures; (ii) timely recognition of a loan as past due even if a fraction of the

---

381 In case of natural calamities such as tsunami, earthquake, and so on.

# Chapter 22: Zero PAR, Legal Notices, and Insolvency Petitions: Delinquency Management from the Field

interest and principal amounts due/past due are not paid by the due date; (iii) disclosure of unduly long grace periods and making appropriate adjustments to PAR for the same; (iv) use of a correct sequence for appropriating client repayments whereby interest amounts are credited first and principal portions thereafter; (v) use of the best practices method for aging past due loans whereby the age of a past due loan is equal to the difference in the number of days between the date at which PAR is being calculated and the date of the earliest unpaid past due amount;[382] and (vi) disclosures of any loan rescheduling, refinancing (including multiple lending), write-offs, and fresh loan disbursements to delinquent clients (greening) as well as those for which repayments are yet to begin and making appropriate adjustments to PAR for all of these situations.

Only if these standardized best practices are implemented and reliable/accurate/timely information from the MIS is available, can MFIs clearly understand the credit/default risks in their loan portfolio, set acceptable limits on these risks, and, most importantly, take necessary steps to monitor and control these risks. Senior management must therefore accept the responsibility of implementing these best practices with regard to PAR/MIS and ensure their consistent use in the operational situation. Otherwise, they run the risk of delinquency, "the hidden beast," manifesting itself suddenly and exploding to the detriment of their institution as it happened during the 2010 AP crisis and years before when zero PAR was the predominant approach used to tackle delinquency.

In fact, interaction with over 200 microfinance clients in the field, during 2010–2011 provides an idea of coercive repayment tactics and strategies used by MFIs and their staff/agents to achieve zero PAR. The statements represent a compilation of what several clients (especially those with multiple loans) and/or their families said during my travels to various places in AP, Tamil Nadu, Karnataka, Orissa, West Bengal, Rajasthan, Madhya Pradesh, and Delhi.

*Client A:* "The fact that fieldworkers/agents came day after day (week after week) and pressured me to pay back is itself a sort of harassment and coercion. As I (and family) do not have serious livelihood means, we have to either borrow from another MFI (this would help consumption and also repayment for some time) or borrow from moneylenders (at even 10% per month) to pay them and get them off our backs. The idea is *we have to somehow pay them* or they will not leave. When all options of borrowing run out, we either have to migrate or die. This is what is happening to other women and may happen to me someday soon."

*Client B's husband:* "My wife who committed suicide had taken eight loans and had to pay back two loans on Monday, one on Tuesday, one on Wednesday, one on Thursday, one on Friday, one on Saturday (every fortnight one), and one once a month. There was no respite during the week, but on Saturday she would feel happy since the following day was Sunday. But the peace was short lived, as we had to make

---

[382] Additional conditions would include consideration of all amounts due (principal, interest, etc.) as well as use of the correct method of client repayment appropriation.

payments again from Monday and the cycle continued. When one has to pay loan repayments six days a week and people will not leave without collecting payments, it is downright harassment."

*Client C:* "The collection agents/staff came and stayed put until we paid the installments and this built up pressure as they would be watching us, often passing snide remarks and insulting us. They would even ridicule our children and basically try to embarrass us—so much so that we would not even hesitate to go to a moneylender and get the installment amount as a loan at 5–10% rates of interest (per month) and send them off."

*Client D:* "One MFI had the practice whereby if the first staff did *not* return within a stipulated time of 2 hours, other staff would successively join him. Soon, by 10/11 AM, there could be 4/5 people sitting near our house and making all sorts of insulting remarks. They also publicly shamed us in the village. I remember once running around here and there and finally rustling up the money to repay them by 4.30 PM that evening and I was traumatized at the end of it all. Now, I dread their coming every time."

*Client E's husband:* "Some collection agents were really rude after my wife committed suicide." They came and said, "If you cannot find means to repay, then you should send out your two beautiful daughters, and get them to earn money by other means (prostitution...) and then repay us." One of them even said, "If you cannot do that, send them to me and I will use them and pay off your installments. They are very beautiful and would be able to earn a lot. I wept as I heard this."

*Client F:* This client says that she is unable to bear the harsh language of MFI staff and, as a result, was pressured to take loans from local money lenders at 4% interest per month. She claimed to have sold her jewels to repay MFI loans as the staff abused her when they came to the village for collections.

*Client G's husband:* The staff said, "We do not care if your wife died. You better pay when we come back tomorrow." He further said, "I had to borrow at 12% to pay them the next day as otherwise, they threatened to chain me to the Big Tree outside the village, and make me a laughing stock."

*Client H:* "The earlier support groups have now become pressure groups that insult. So there is no respite, and harassment is 24 × 7 as group leaders and other members live in the village itself and they obstruct participation in village activities if the loan installments have not been paid. You just cannot get away without paying as they have a lot of local influence and can do anything."

*Client I:* This client said that in case defaulting members did not repay overdues, the group leaders and MFI center leader took over the defaulter's assets and repaid the loan by liquidating it.

# Chapter 22: Zero PAR, Legal Notices, and Insolvency Petitions: Delinquency Management from the Field

*Client J:* "Once at the time of weekly repayment, there was a death in the house of a neighbor, who was also a member, and the collection agents told the bereaved family that unless the last two overdue installments were paid up, they would not allow the body to be removed or the rites performed." The client claimed she went to a moneylender in a nearby bigger village and got an emergency loan at 7% per month and helped her neighbor pay back the installment."

While this is by no means a scientific study, it nonetheless provides an indication of the coercive mechanisms (not exhaustive) being used at the field level by some MFIs and converges with the findings of previous research into coercive repayment (APMAS and others). These have been compiled into key coercive recovery strategies that are being used by **some** MFIs to achieve zero PAR, and they are summarized here.

*Strategy 1: Life/work obstruction.* Field workers, agents, center leaders and/or group leaders/members obstruct normal life and work of clients and/or their families, thereby forcing them to repay by using means (borrowing from moneylenders, taking over assets, etc.) that may not necessarily be in the clients' interest and one that could cause them undue hardship.

*Strategy 2: Threats.* Collection agents/field workers threaten that they would resort to violence and/or physical abuse if money is not repaid; they sometimes may also carry out the threat.

*Strategy 3: Verbal abuse.* Field workers/agents may insult, abuse and/or intimidate the borrowers and their family members and get the repayment.

*Strategy 4: Pestering the client.* Field workers/agents continually follow the borrowers and family members and pester them for payment and embarrass them until the money is paid.

*Strategy 5: Repossession and sale of property.* Sometimes, the center leaders and/or group leaders/other members take over property owned or used by clients and sell that to take the repayment.

*Strategy 6: Satyagraha outside client's house/place of work.* Field workers/collection agents sit outside the house or places of work (such as fields/shops) for hours together and harass the family for payment and leave only after they get it.

*Strategy 7: Embarrassment strategy.* Field workers/collection agents sometimes talk to business customers and/or guests of the clients and embarrass them, thereby getting them to repay.

*Strategy 8: Taking over assets/documents as collateral.* The center leaders, group leaders, and/or other members may sometimes forcibly remove assets/documents of the borrower (such as ration card) and not return them until the repayment is made.

*Strategy 9: Physical intimidation.* Field workers/collection agents physically intimidate the clients and get local toughs to rough them up once or twice, so that repayment is forthcoming thereafter.

Several questions arise from this discussion and the stakeholders developing the regulatory architecture for microfinance would have to look into the (range of) mechanisms that have been and are perhaps being used by (some) MFIs to collect loans at the grassroots. *A rigorous scientific study will have to be commissioned and undertaken by a neutral set of people*; only such a study can reveal the extent to which such coercive tactics and strategies are used by (some) MFIs to achieve zero PAR. Only then can the regulatory architecture really protect low-income clients in microfinance, from such abusive collection practices.

# Chapter 23:
# What is the Real Secret Behind the Burgeoning Growth of Indian Microfinance?

Sometime during December 2010, at the peak of the 2010 AP crisis, I had an interesting telephone conversation with a colleague from the Netherlands. We were discussing multiple lending and shared JLGs/clients when he asked me a question, *"Have you ever thought of how the fast growing (NBFC) MFIs acquired their clients?"* Spontaneously, I said, *"they perhaps form new JLGs,"* before I realized that I had made a mistake by jumping to conclusions. My mind went back to the shared JLG/clients model that I had been seeing very often—where a particular JLG and its member clients are serviced by different MFIs on successive days of the week and the same happens to other JLGs in the same village/cluster. Table 23.1 illustrates the concept of shared JLG/clients—let us assume that a cluster of three hamlets has seven JLGs, each JLG has five members and there are 35 members in all—the typical size of a center in the traditional Grameen model.

| Table 23.1 How the Concept of Shared JLGs/Clients Works on the Ground | | | | | | | |
|---|---|---|---|---|---|---|---|
| JLG number / Day | JLG 1 | JLG 2 | JLG 3 | JLG 4 | JLG 5 | JLG 6 | JLG 7 |
| Monday | **Meeting for MFI 1** | Meeting for MFI 7 | Meeting for MFI 6 | Meeting for MFI 5 | Meeting for MFI 4 | *Meeting for MFI 3* | Meeting for MFI 2 |
| Tuesday | Meeting for MFI 2 | **Meeting for MFI 1** | Meeting for MFI 7 | Meeting for MFI 6 | Meeting for MFI 5 | Meeting for MFI 4 | *Meeting for MFI 3* |
| Wednesday | *Meeting for MFI 3* | Meeting for MFI 2 | **Meeting for MFI 1** | Meeting for MFI 7 | Meeting for MFI 6 | Meeting for MFI 5 | Meeting for MFI 4 |
| Thursday | Meeting for MFI 4 | *Meeting for MFI 3* | Meeting for MFI 2 | **Meeting for MFI 1** | Meeting for MFI 7 | Meeting for MFI 6 | Meeting for MFI 5 |
| Friday | Meeting for MFI 5 | Meeting for MFI 4 | *Meeting for MFI 3* | Meeting for MFI 2 | **Meeting for MFI 1** | Meeting for MFI 7 | Meeting for MFI 6 |
| Saturday | Meeting for MFI 6 | Meeting for MFI 5 | Meeting for MFI 4 | *Meeting for MFI 3* | Meeting for MFI 2 | **Meeting for MFI 1** | Meeting for MFI 7 |
| Sunday | Meeting for MFI 7 | Meeting for MFI 6 | Meeting for MFI 5 | Meeting for MFI 4 | *Meeting for MFI 3* | Meeting for MFI 2 | **Meeting for MFI 1** |

This is an illustrative case and it highlights how JLGs and clients are (could be) shared in practice. However, I have personally seen several cases where there are four to seven JLGs in a cluster of villages and at least three or five JLGs are shared between MFIs—mostly with weekly repayment and one or two cases with monthly repayments. Therefore, while multiple lending and overindebtedness are cited as a major reason for the 2010 AP microfinance crisis, *there is reasonable evidence that the "phenomenon of shared JLGs and clients" is the most important antecedent factor in the entire scheme of things*. Several questions still seem relevant here.

- How widespread was (is) this phenomenon of shared clients and JLGs? To what extent did (do) MFIs actually share JLG and clients, across districts in AP and in other states? How much multiple lending actually existed on the ground, from state to state, across these shared JLGs and clients? How much multiple lending exists currently across shared clients and JLGs? How then can this multiple lending phenomenon be resolved across shared JLGs and clients? What range of strategies exist—in terms of apportioning of JLGs/clients and their loans across MFIs, rescheduling, refinancing, waivers, debt swaps, and so on—and how are these to be used and in what situations and for whom? What *credible* safeguards can be built to prevent recurrence of the shared JLGs/clients and the resultant multiple lending problems in the future?[383]

In my opinion, given the fact that JLGs/clients are shared through use on successive days by different MFIs, as illustrated in Table 23.1 and also given that this model is somewhat widespread, unless this problem is sorted out, there is a very high likelihood of the problems caused by multiple lending problem recurring. So, another key question here is "How to allocate JLG and clients across MFIs—in a fair and transparent manner—so that the above model of same JLG/clients being used on successive days by different MFIs goes out of vogue in Indian microfinance?" While shared JLGs are a problem and deserve a close look, it is also important to focus on something more fundamental—the manner in which MFIs acquire clients and also understand their reasons for doing so.

*Client acquisition process in MFIs:* There are several ways in which this is done: (i) green field strategy, (ii) acquisition, (iii) joint venture, (iv) simple reciprocal arrangement, and (v) conversion/cannibalization of SHGs and several other strategies. Some of these are explained below.

---

383 I still see significant multiple lending in over saturated microfinance areas.

# Chapter 23: What is the Real Secret Behind the Burgeoning Growth of Indian Microfinance?

| | Table 23.2 Typical Client Acquisition Process in MFIs (not exhaustive) | |
|---|---|---|
| S. No | Client acquisition strategy | Description and examples are available |
| 1 | Green field | MFI forms JLGs from scratch and develops them. This is an intensive and costly process. A strategy used in areas where there is very little previous microfinance activity. As this strategy entails significant cost, interest rates would have to be higher than the MCR suggested cap and margins. The pressure to reduce interest rates may have led the MFIs to move away from this original strategy |
| 2 | Acquisition | MFI takes over the portfolio of another smaller MFI or its JLGs. Sometimes, SHGs could also be taken over and split into several JLGs (depending on size of the SHG). This happens when several smaller NGOs/MFIs want to acquire scale quickly. Have witnessed this in a couple of cases but it is not very common. This strategy is also used to break a competitor's hold on the market—the examples of Krishna and Guntur districts in 2005–2006 are cases in point here, where this happened between two MFIs. Again, the pressure to reduce interest rates probably led the MFIs to move toward this strategy. Likewise, the desire for turbocharged growth may have also caused this strategy to be used |
| 3 | Joint venture | Two or more MFIs decide to pool resources and form a joint venture and, in the process, their existing groups are pooled and used. Alternatively, two or more MFIs could contribute resources to create JLGs or even develop JLGs and then share them with joint venture partners. Have observed this in a couple of cases but again not very common |
| 4 | Simple reciprocal arrangement | Two or more MFIs decide to use each other's JLGs on the basis of a simple reciprocal arrangement, which is often informal. This is an oft-used arrangement and perhaps the most common today. Again, the pressure to reduce interest rates probably led the MFIs to move toward this strategy. This essentially represents cartelization in a sense. Likewise, the desire for turbocharged growth may have also caused this strategy to be used |
| 5 | Conversion/cannibalization of SHGs | An MFI could forcibly break an existing SHG affiliated to another MFI, cooperative, village organization or government scheme into several JLGs. This has been observed by APMAS, and I too have personally seen this—especially in areas where a lot of SHGs were available and well developed. Again, the pressure to reduce interest rates probably led the MFIs to move toward this strategy. Likewise, the desire for turbocharged growth may have also caused this strategy to be used |
| 6 | Several other strategies | Taking of individual clients from other MFIs and forming them into a JLG, etc. This strategy is also used to break a competitor's hold on the market. The events that occurred in Krishna and Guntur districts in 2005–2006 and the Tamil Nadu/AP happenings in 2010 are cases in point here |
| 7 | Using agents in a decentralized model to acquire clients<br><br>See chapter 27 on agent-led microfinance and the resultant implications | If the agent is a center leader, then a large proportion of clients may exist. But if the agent is a local political honcho, then the end-user clients may not be known at all. Overall, if the MFI uses an agent-led microfinance strategy, then not much confidence can be had with regard to the MFI having real clients on the ground. The desire for turbocharged growth may have caused this strategy to be used |

Thus, the various stakeholders developing a new regulatory architecture for Indian microfinance may want to ascertain how the MFIs have grown in the past few years and how they intend to grow in the next few years. Have they formed green field (own) JLGs? Have they acquired JLGs from other MFIs? Have they had joint venture and/or simple reciprocal arrangements to share JLGs? Have they split SHGs[384] to create several JLGs? What other strategies have they used to gather clients at such a fast pace and why?

---

384 As Mr. C.S Reddy of APMAS often argues and as stated by him in the CGAP blog.

These and similar questions certainly deserve an answer, and I believe that the client acquisition process is a crucial aspect that should not be ignored. Without question, we need to ascertain and understand how MFIs have grown during their period of fastest growth and how they intend to do so in the future. In my opinion, unless suitable safeguards are built into the client acquisition process adopted by MFIs and unless the omnipresent sharing of JLGs/clients is resolved, the problems related to multiple lending will resurface again and perhaps on a higher scale and at a national level—just as the lessons from the localized Krishna (2005–2006) and Kolar (2009) crises led to the Andhra Pradesh (state-wide) 2010 microfinance crisis. Therefore, it is imperative for the concerned stakeholders developing the regulatory architecture for microfinance, to look at the above issues and come out with practical suggestions on: (i) how the ever-present shared JLGs/clients and the associated multiple lending can be resolved; and (ii) how the client acquisition process of MFIs can be reengineered to avoid sharing of JLG/clients. Unless these operational issues are sorted out, we can be certain that multiple lending in Indian microfinance would exist, much to our discomfort. This would also immediately call for complete deregulation in interest rates by the regulators with regard to microfinance, in its entirety and I am very glad that the RBI has taken some initial steps toward the same.[385]

---

385 See RBI circular at http://www.rbi.org.in/scripts/BS_ViewMasCirculardetails.aspx?id=8195

# Chapter 24:
# Is Lending to the Poor Costly?

Much has been written about interest rates charged by Indian MFIs but it is time that the RBI (through a neutral set of stakeholders) conducted a nationwide study on EIRs and related practices in microfinance. The issue of interest rates has always been hotly debated and I, for one, am not for capping interest rates of MFIs as servicing the last mile in microfinance is costly. I am glad that the RBI has tried to deregulate interest rates vide its circular dated July 1, 2013.[386]

That said, we, however, need to be absolutely transparent about interest rates in microfinance. While I appreciate the work of MFT,[387] as I travel through the field, my sense is that there is, however, a difference between intended and realized interest rates (both for nominal and EIRs). Part of the issue has been the use of the agent-led model, but, even otherwise, I believe there are differences between the intended and realized interest rates (as the staff often take advantage of the hapless low-income clients). Recall that the media (in AP) had reported huge EIRs for some MFIs after they had submitted data to the AP government, which were later explained away using the classic data error/data conversion concept.[388]

Thus, the time is ripe for a nationwide study on interest rates prevalent in microfinance. In fact, I do recall having seen an informative study by the RBI's RPCD[389] division on the MFI model in Orissa in 2006, and it contained transparent information on interest rates. Therefore, I would like the RBI to do a national study on interest rates, agent models, shared JLGs/clients, extent of multiple lending and the like—unless it is done by the RBI (through a neutral team of stakeholders), establishing their prevalence would be impossible, and without that, corrective action cannot be taken.

So much for a study and let me now turn my attention to the capping of interest rates and margins—something that the RBI had resorted to after the MCR. I am against such capping and I outline the rationale by raising some fundamental cost issues. I do hope the stakeholders involved in developing the regulatory architecture for microfinance in India take cognizance of the various issues mentioned here and address the interest rate issue once for all.

---

386 http://www.rbi.org.in/scripts/BS_ViewMasCirculardetails.aspx?id=8195
387 An international organization working toward ensuring transparent pricing in microfinance across the world.
388 See news clipping at http://www.thehindubusinessline.in/bline/2010/10/31/stories/2010103151310500.htm
389 Rural Planning and Credit Department.

Let us start with the different costs that are incurred in delivering financial services to low-income people. I see four major costs and they are as follows:

- Transaction/financial costs[390]$_{\text{Institutions}}$ = $\text{TFC}_{\text{Institution}}$
- Transaction/financial costs[391]$_{\text{Intermediary}}$ = $\text{TFC}_{\text{Intermediary}}$
- Transaction/financial costs $_{\text{Clients}}$ = $\text{TFC}_{\text{Clients}}$
- Transaction/financial costs $_{\text{Total}}$ = $\text{TFC}_{\text{Total}}$

$\text{TFC}_{\text{Institutions}} + \text{TFC}_{\text{Intermediaries}} + \text{TFC}_{\text{Clients}} = \text{TFC}_{\text{Total}}$ (This is the basic equation.)

*Premise 1:* Total costs ($\text{TFC}_{\text{Total}}$) and apportioned costs ($\text{TFC}_{\text{Institutions}} + \text{TFC}_{\text{Intermediaries}} + \text{TFC}_{\text{Clients}}$) of delivery will vary across models, contexts, and related parameters. First, the total and apportioned costs will vary by

- *the model used*—group versus individual, bank/MFI-branch-based versus center-meeting-based versus agent-based.

- *the number of years in operation and life cycle stage of the different channel partners*—the experience/learning curve aspect should reflect here.

- *the economies of scale and scope available including aspects of fixed/variable costs*—enhancing major product outreach to larger number of clients as well as offering them a range of other products.

- *the trade-off between risk, efficiency, and controls in delivery*—efficiency can be gained by reducing controls but then a high level of risk will have to be tolerated.

- *the product strategy*—in terms of savings alone, credit alone, savings + credit + others including risk management products.

- *the number of channel partners (or intermediaries)*—this decision is critical to the cost and more intermediaries should just result in increased costs.

- *the strategic context*—including clients, geography, and so on.

- *the basis for the competitive strategy*—in terms of differentiation versus quality versus cost leadership (this can also be thought of as the overall strategy of managing total costs) and other such factors.

---

390 Includes financial costs plus operational costs, loan loss provisions plus inflation adjustment, and so on.
391 Same as above.

Thus, we have the following:

Total and apportioned costs of financial services delivery to low-income people = function of model chosen; life cycle stage and age of channel partners; economies of scale and scope available; trade-off between risk, efficiency and controls; product strategy; length of channel; strategic context; and competitive strategy.

We need to recognize that all these are strategic choices exercised by organizations, depending on various factors. Therefore, we must understand that it would not be appropriate to expect all institutions to be able to deliver financial services to low-income people at the same interest rate/level of fees. That said, I am not arguing for any (high) level of interest/fees to be charged from low-income people—all I am saying is that we need to be sensitive to the fact that it may not be possible for all different models to levy a uniform, specified rate.

The most appropriate strategy here would be to get answers to the following question for a typology of contexts, models, and related parameters:

1. *"Given a typology of contexts, models, and related parameters, what constitutes the optimal range of interest/fees that need to be charged from low-income clients to fully cover total costs?"*

This critical aspect is best understood through the following example: for a grameen MFI, 36% could be the full cost as it is operating in a hilly and difficult terrain and providing doorstep services; for an SHG MFI, 22% could be the full cost as it lends directly to SHGs and thereby is almost a semi-wholesaler; for SHG federations or cooperatives, 18% could be the full cost as they accept deposits that are the cheapest source of nonsubsidized capital and so on. (These numbers are illustrative and can vary from context to context and model to model. They are not indicative of live rates.)

This strategy would also be a fair approach in my opinion. The RBI must try and recognize this, study this aspect,[392] and make recommendations accordingly. *Please note that my first emphasis is on understanding what the full (total and apportioned) costs are and this could be very different from full (total and apportioned) cost recovery (taken up thereafter).*

Now, with the total and apportioned costs—for different contexts, models, and related parameters—that need to be charged for a full cost recovery out of the way, let us get to the next aspect of how to recover these full costs.

*Premise 2:* Full costs are always recovered as a combination of interest/fees and different kinds of subsidies. This is again a strategic choice aspect and different models do it differently. There are two major ways in which this cost recovery can be handled: (i) apportion the same across the institution, intermediaries, and clients—this is a creative strategy as it transfers the costs from one stakeholder to another and (ii) decide on the extent to which costs will be actually recovered and balance will be subsidized. We will look at each of these issues separately (Table 24.1).

---

392 I will try and outline the methodology for undertaking such a study, to determine full costs for different models, in a separate post.

Table 24.1 Full Cost Recovery as a Combination of Partial Cost Recovery and Subsidies[a]

| $TFC_{Institutions}$ | $+ TFC_{Intermediaries}$ | $+ TFC_{Clients}$ | $= TFC_{Total}$ | This is the basic equation |
|---|---|---|---|---|
| $TFC_{Institutions}$ | $+ TFC_{Intermediaries}$ | $+ TFC_{Clients}$ | $= TFC_{Total}$ | = recovered cost (as interest plus fees, etc.) + unrecovered cost |
| $TFC_{Institutions}$ | $+ TFC_{Intermediaries}$ | $+ TFC_{Clients}$ | $= TFC_{Total}$ | = recovered cost (as interest plus fees etc.) + unrecovered cost (direct subsidies + cross subsidies + indirect subsidies + hidden subsidies) |

[a] *I make no value judgment on subsidies here except to say that subsidies represent an opportunity cost to society and need to be used appropriately and carefully.*

As you can see, the full (total and apportioned) costs comprise two portions—recovered and unrecovered costs. And the unrecovered cost contains different types of subsidies—direct, cross-indirect, and hidden subsidies.

*Therefore, in some sense, there is always full cost recovery through interest plus fees and a range of subsidies provided. This is a critical aspect and much of the arguments over interest rates can be better understood if this crucial aspect is noted.*

The second strategic choice entails decision making within the organization on (i) the extent to which full (total and apportioned) costs are to be actually recovered; and (ii) the different kinds of subsidies that (need to be and) are provided to cover the balance portion of total costs minus recovered costs (i.e., interest plus fees etc.).

The most appropriate strategy here would be to get answers to the following question for a typology of contexts, models, and related parameters:

2. *"Given a typology of models, contexts, and related parameters, what is the proportion of costs that are actually recovered (from clients etc.) and how are the remaining (unrecovered) costs met through various subsidies?"*

This critical aspect is best understood through the following example: MFIs perhaps charge 24–36% or more, recover all/most costs and sometimes even have a surplus. Banks charge 12% and cross-subsidize costs; SHG federations or cooperatives charge 24% and recover full costs, and government programs perhaps lend at 3–6%, with the major costs being subsidized.[393]

So, from the discussion it is clear that in some organizations, the whole cost could be recovered, whereas in others there is only partial recovery and the rest is subsidized. MFIs perhaps charge what they do because they have less subsidies and practice doorstep banking; cooperatives and community models charge what they do because of using local and low-cost staff and community for various aspects

---

393 The numbers given are merely illustrative and they can vary from one organization to another—so kindly do not join issue with me on this.

and also have access to savings (which is the cheapest source of nonsubsidized capital); banks charge what they do because of norms set by regulators and supervisors and manage actual (unrecovered) costs differently through cross-subsidies, outsourcing, and so on; and governments directly subsidize clients and charge as low as they do for various reasons.

To summarize, the aspect of transactions and financial costs primarily centers around strategic decision making by organizations on the following basic aspects. What brings diversity in terms of the costs is the strategic choice that organizations exercise with regard to these decisions:

- *Whom to serve?* Clientele, especially, with decision making on whether to serve the poor, not-so-poor, excluded, included, men, women, and so on.

- *How many clients to cater to, where to operate, and how to expand?* Outreach, geographic dispersion and/or growth strategy (incremental, quantum, etc.).

- *What specific services to offer to the clients?* Products (financial intermediation encompasses a large number of products and combinations thereof).

- *What methods of service delivery to employ?* How to organize these channels such as groups, individuals, and so on, and their tasks/roles and outsourcing, if any, and the implications thereof?

- *What organizational mechanisms to use?* Legal/institutional forms?

- *How to communicate the availability of various services?* Promotion?

- *What are the medium-/long-term objectives?* Single versus double versus triple bottom lines?

As noted earlier, while full costs are always recovered from various sources, the strategic choices exercised regarding the above-mentioned points result in some models choosing to recover costs fully from clients and others recovering these partially from clients and covering the balance through different kinds of subsidies.

Therefore, it is humbly submitted to those developing the regulatory architecture for microfinance that interest rates should *not* be viewed in rigid terms, but understood in terms of the broader context as well as implications in terms of full cost recovery from clients versus partial cost recovery from clients plus use of different kinds of subsidies. At the end of the day, there must be sufficient justification for pursuing either of the strategies and that must be ascertained and understood.

It goes without saying that condemning the seemingly normal interest rates (*I am sure we can discern exorbitant interest rates straightaway*) charged by institutions without understanding the above issues would be unfair and perhaps even unjustified. It is also sincerely hoped that decisions on (regulating) interest rates should be made only after the RBI undertakes a rigorous national study[394] encompassing alternative models in various contexts and benchmarks a range of interest rates for different contexts and models. That alone will bring the interest rate controversy to its logical conclusion.

---

394 Existing studies of interest rates have several limitations and have been critiqued. See http://www.microfinance-in-india.blogspot.in/search/label/Interest%20Rates, http://microfinance-in-india.blogspot.in/2011/01/cmf-study-on-access-to-finance-in.html, and several others such as the MFIN NCAER study that has already been mentioned in the chapter on agents.

# Chapter 25:
# How Safe is the Securitized Microfinance Portfolio?

Recall that I have been talking about how fast MFIs have grown especially during April 2008–March 2010. Now you may ask where they got their resources to grow this fast. While equity investments and bank lending into Indian microfinance had certainly burgeoned during the same time, there appear to be more sources for this phenomenal growth. This is best summarized by Mr N. Srinivasan, in The State of the Sector Report (2010), where he argues that:

> "MFIs ramped up their loan portfolio in India from US$ 252 million to US$ 3.8 billion between 2005 and 2010. The funding for this expansion came from several sources apart from equity funding. Bulk loans from banks are the most important source of funds. In recent years, quasi-equity, mezzanine funding, non-convertible debentures, debt assignments and sale of securitized debt have all emerged as other means of raising resources."[395]

When I read this paragraph in the report and especially saw the word securitization, alarm bells started ringing in my mind. I saw the connection to Dr Y V Reddy's statement in *The Economic Times* in 2010. According to Dr. Reddy, "microfinance is India's subprime." "Ultimately, it is something like subprime lending," he told *The Economic Times* in an interview ahead of his book release. "The same incentives are operating here… it was securitization and derivatives that operated in the US. Here it is the priority sector lending by banks."[396]

While a lot has been written about securitization in microfinance, The State of the Sector (2010) report provides a good overview:

> "Micro-loan securitization provides banks a profitable way to increase their investment in the microfinance sector through rated and tradable securities.

---

395 *Source*: Microfinance in India: The State of the Sector Report 2010, by N. Srinivasan, Sage Publication.
396 *Source*: http://economictimes.indiatimes.com/news/economy/indicators/Microfinance-in-India-is-like-subprime-lending-Y-V-Reddy/articleshow/6972903.cms

| Table 25.1 Major Securitization Deals in 2009–2010 ||
| Originator | Amount (in Rs. crores) |
| --- | --- |
| SKS Microfinance | 100.00 |
| Bandhan | 75.00 |
| Grameen Koota | 31.10 |
| Equitas Microfinance | 48.20 |
| Sahayata Microfinance, Asirvada, Sonata, Satin Credit Care | 30.90 |
| Spandana | 25.00 |
| Grameen Financial Services | 29.40 |
| Janalakshmi Financial Services | 24.80 |
| Share | 70.00 |
| Grameen Koota | 24.80 |
| SKS | 137.40 |
| Sahayata Microfinance, Asirvada, Sonata, Satin Credit Care | 27.30 |
| SKS | 107.60 |
| Share | 49.30 |
| Equitas Microfinance | 42.20 |
| Equitas Microfinance | 15.70 |

The securitization process, which allows MFIs to pool the receivables from loans and sell the same to third parties such as banks, mutual funds, and insurance companies, could perhaps be another big opportunity for MFIs to increase their funding sources. IFMR Capital, a Chennai-based NBFC expects more than Rs. 1000 crore worth of securitization transactions to take place in the Indian micro finance sector for the financial year 2010–2011.[397] Securitization enables lower costs to originating MFIs, quality assets to buyers, and a means of participation for insurance companies, mutual funds and potentially even pension funds."[398]

However, not all analysts were euphoric about securitization and perhaps rightly so. As Kothari and Rozas (2010)[399] noted in an excellent article, "It is necessary to rectify and discipline present practices in securitization, but even when that is accomplished, the strong tie between an MFI and its portfolio remains a serious conundrum for securitizations, which after all depend on breaking that very tie through *true sale.*"

While Kothari and Rozas talk about the aspect of what Prof. Oliver Williamson and/or Prof. Ronald Coase would call an idiosyncratic relationship with significant asset specificity, a related issue is brought up by Chanana[400] (2009) who noted that "Securitization creates a moral hazard that adversely affects the

---
397 *Source*: http://indiamicrofinance.com/ifmr-capital-targets-rs-1000-cr-securitisation-deals-current-financial-year.html
398 *Source*: Microfinance in India: The State of The Sector Report 2010, by N Srinivasan, Sage Publication.
399 http://www.microfinancefocus.com/news/2010/07/06/the-hidden-risks-behind-microfinance-securitization/
400 http://www.planetd.org/2009/03/18/securitizing-microfinance-bad-idea/

screening incentives of lenders. In the MFI world, this means that if MFIs do not own the risk of a loan, they are less likely to screen potential creditors properly. The result is likely to be an increase in default rates. This is not all, though. If the subprime crisis was caused partly by moral hazard, the impact of that hazard was magnified by the availability of cheap and plentiful credit. Banks vastly increased credit availability to subprime creditors simply because money was cheap and easy to be had. This reduced any remaining incentive on the part of lenders to conduct proper due diligence."

A close look at the previous paragraph suggests that a similar situation perhaps existed in the Indian microfinance industry (and in AP specifically) before the AP government passed its ordinance.[401]

Equity investments[402] were available in plenty, until then.

| Table 25.2 Equity Investments in Indian MFIs Across Equity Leaders and Followers (million dollars) | | | |
|---|---|---|---|
| Years | Equity leader MFIs (6) | Equity followers (22) | Total |
| Before March 2007 | 32.51 | 0 | 32.51 |
| April 2007–March 2008 | 118.34 | 0 | 118.34 |
| April 2008–July 2010 | 398.40 | 130.23 | 528.63 |
| Total | **549.25** | **130.23** | **679.48** |

Clearly, it is more than mere coincidence that equity investments into Indian microfinance almost burgeoned at almost the same time (or a little after) when MFIs grew at their fastest pace. That said, the buoyancy of equity investors is perhaps best matched by bank credit. This is exemplified by the following quote:

"Bank loans to MFIs did not exhibit any overt signs of increased risk perceptions towards the microfinance sector. The total loans extended to MFIs and outstanding at the end of March 2010 is estimated at Rs. 15085 crore.[403] Public sector banks have taken to MFI financing in a big way. Public sector banks (not including SIDBI) had an exposure of Rs. 4737 crore to MFIs in comparison to private sector banks' exposure of Rs. 4133 crore. Foreign banks had outstanding loans of Rs.1994 crore and FWWB had increased its exposure from Rs. 295 crore last year to Rs. 360 crore. SIDBI almost doubled its exposure to Rs. 3808 crores during the year. At this level SIDBI had a share of more than 25 per cent of the market."[404]

Thus, looking at the above-mentioned situation, it clearly seemed a case of déjà vu at least as far as support to Indian microfinance was concerned. Equity investors and bankers (as noted) were vying with each other to provide financial resources (through innovative deals and instruments) to the MFIs.

---

401 I personally feel that regulating microfinance is the job of the financial regulator—that is, the RBI or a specialized microfinance regulator. From that perspective, I am of the opinion that the AP ordinance and bill are not at all appropriate although I feel that states have an important constitutional duty and space to protect their citizens from excesses of any kind.

402 Subject to caveats mentioned in an earlier chapter on equity investment (Chapter 4).

403 Based on provisional data made available by NABARD and further information collected by N. Srinivasan individually from some banks.

404 *Source*: Quoted from Microfinance in India: The State of the Sector Report 2010, by N. Srinivasan, Sage Publication.

And these MFIs, in turn, grew at a scorching pace—using funds from banks through priority sector, equity investments, and other innovative mechanisms such as securitization—through multiple lending and not-so-ethical recovery practices, both of which enhanced the indebtedness of the low-income people. And these surely made the parallels with the subprime situation rather strong.

Accordingly, as a measure of caution, I attempt to provide some discussion on the impact of client acquisition strategies and other factors on microfinance securitization for the benefit of stakeholders who are seemingly involved in this in an increasing manner. A few other very important issues unique to microfinance appear to have an impact on securitizing microfinance assets and those involved in such deals may want to watch out for these. In other words, there are several peculiarities with regard to microfinance loan assets that need to be carefully considered while engaging in aspects such as securitization:

a. Microfinance loan assets tend to be predominantly small in amounts but large in number.

b. While the transactions are small, they are however numerous (repetitive) and most often, predominantly cash oriented—this makes it difficult to trace the source as well as end use.

c. The geographic diversity is huge in a country like India and these assets tend to be spread over remote rural areas and/or urban slums, which makes it rather difficult to physically locate them. Therefore, establishing the identity of the microfinance borrower and, hence, the loan asset becomes rather difficult. This is a critical issue for securitization.

d. While many of the lenders ask for KYC documentation, it must be noted that what is provided is far from accurate. Therefore, it is very easy for an MFI to show the same assets for different lenders and redeploy the (surplus) funds in other activities such as real estate and the like. Much of this was highlighted, as far back as May 2005, in the paper[405] by Thorat and Arunachalam (2005).

Thus, as noted, these peculiarities can cause serious problems for securitization of microfinance assets, and those who buy these securitized assets must be very careful as there is a good chance that there may be no real persons at all with the associated assets or the assets themselves may have been hypothecated or pledged to other lenders. Also, there are other issues that impact securitization and need to be considered by the RBI and other stakeholders involved in developing the regulatory architecture for microfinance—while these issues are drawn from the microfinance crisis in the Indian context, they can be adapted and used in other countries/contexts also by other central banks/regulators.

(a) *Client Acquisition Approaches Used by MFI:* First and foremost, this is a crucial issue and there are several ways in which this can be done. The various methods and their implications for microfinance securitization are given here.

---

[405] Thorat, Y. S. P. and Ramesh S. Arunachalam, (May, 2005), "Regulation and Areas of Potential Market Failure in Microfinance", paper presented at the NABARD high-level policy conference in New Delhi.

## Chapter 25: How Safe is the Securitized Microfinance Portfolio?

| Table 25.3 Client Acquisition Process in MFIs and Implications for Securitization | |
|---|---|
| **Client acquisition strategy** | **Implications for securitization** |
| **Green field strategy**<br>• Here the MFI forms joint liability groups (JLGs) using first principles.<br>• This is a very intensive and costly process and this would have to be factored in while doing the securitization deal<br>• A strategy used in areas where there is very little microfinance activity<br>• The culture of the MFI could have been imposed on the clients | • Relatively safest from a securitization perspective<br>• The very close relationship of the MFI with its clients could become a handicap, for securitization, as Kothari and Rozas[*] note, under some special circumstances<br>• It would be good to get an estimate of the percentage of clients who have been sourced through the green field strategy<br>• It would also be good to understand the exact process by which the clients are sourced through the green field process |
| **Acquisition**<br>• MFI takes over the portfolio of another smaller MFI or its JLGs<br>• Sometimes, SHGs could also be taken over and split into several JLGs (depending on size of SHG)<br>• This happens when several smaller NGOs/MFIs want to acquire scale quickly | • Not so safe from a securitization perspective as credit discipline cannot be guaranteed<br>• The mismatch of organizational cultures could affect MFI–client relationship unless the acquiring MFI has an absolutely similar model and approach<br>• There could be some Akerloff's lemons in the portfolio being securitized |
| **Joint venture**<br>• Two or more MFIs decide to pool resources and form a joint venture and in the process, their existing groups are pooled and used<br>• Alternatively, two or more MFIs could contribute resources to create JLGs or even develop JLGs and then share them as joint venture partners<br>• Have seen this in a couple of cases but not very common | • Not so safe from a securitization perspective as credit discipline cannot be guaranteed<br>• The mismatch of organizational cultures could affect MFI–client relationship unless the joint venture partners have almost identical/similar approaches<br>• There could be some Akerloff's lemons in the portfolio being securitized |
| **Simple reciprocal arrangement**<br>• Two or more MFIs decide to use each others' JLGs on the basis of a simple reciprocal arrangement, which could be formal/informal<br>• This is an often used arrangement | • **Most unsafe from a securitization perspective**<br>• Here, several MFIS could share the same clients and JLGs and lend to them (and have weekly collection meetings) on successive days—as has happened during (year preceding) in the 2010 Indian (Andhra Pradesh) microfinance crisis<br>• Multiple, over and ghost lending could be prevalent and may have resulted in huge indebtedness (already)<br>• Perhaps most unsafe from a securitization perspective as political risk could also be rather high—as has been borne out by the 2010 AP crisis in India<br>• There could be a lot of Akerloff's lemons in the portfolio being securitized |
| **Conversion/cannibalization of SHGs**<br>• An MFI could forcibly break an existing SHG affiliated to another MFI, cooperative, village organization or government scheme into several JLGs<br>• This has been mentioned by organizations such as APMAS. I have also personally witnessed this, especially in areas where a lot of SHGs were available and well developed | • Rather unsafe from a securitization perspective as credit discipline cannot be guaranteed and political risk could be rather high<br>• The mismatch of organizational cultures could affect MFI–client relationship<br>• Clients acquired through such a process are usually prone to similar attack by competitor MFIs—the former Krishna crisis was a witness to this aspect<br>• There could be a high proportion of Akerloff's lemons in the portfolio being securitized |

[*] http://www.danielrozas.com/2010/07/06/the-hidden-risks-behind-microfinance-securitization/

## An Idea Which Went Wrong

*This apart, several other strategies are used.* Poaching of individual clients from other MFIs and forming them into JLGs is one such strategy. This strategy is also used to break a competitor's hold on the market and it is rather unsafe from a securitization perspective as credit discipline cannot be guaranteed and competitor/political risk could be rather high. Also, the mismatch of organizational cultures could affect MFI–client relationship unless the aggressor MFI has an absolutely similar approach. Further, the risk of reciprocal aggression by competitor MFI is also high and there could be a high proportion of Akerloff's lemons in the portfolio being securitized.

*Similarly, using agents[406] in a decentralized model to acquire clients is one another strategy.* This is most unsafe from a securitization perspective. If the agent is a center leader, then a large proportion of clients may exist but if the agent is a local political honcho, then the end user clients may not be known at all. Overall, the use of the agent strategy represents a huge risk for securitization. In my view, a significant proportion of the Indian microfinance portfolio is still agent controlled.

So, I would ask the following key questions here (not exhaustive): (i) How did the MFI, whose portfolio is being securitized, acquire its clients?; and (ii) Do the client acquisition strategies adopted by the MFI pose any problems for securitization? If 'yes,' what safeguards need to be built into the deal to mitigate the risks?

(b) *Frauds and internal control failures in portfolio:* A second issue is the aspect of growth pattern of the MFI whose assets are being securitized and whether there could be frauds and internal control failures because of this. MFIs that have grown very, very fast could have a significant proportion of (Akerloff's) lemons in their portfolio because of the rapid pace of their growth, which may have undermined, stressed, and/or sheared existing systems. Examples of the kind of frauds and control failures that could exist are given elsewhere.[407] The implications of such kinds of frauds and control failures for securitization are given here.

- *Loan-disbursement-related frauds:* The most common ones are *ghost or nonexistent clients and staff giving loans to themselves (through nonexistent clients)*—the securitized portfolio in such cases could have a significant proportion of Akerloff lemons. It goes without saying that such a portfolio would constitute a very serious credit risk. Further, sometimes, the staff indulge the clients and get them higher than required loans and take the remaining (excess) loan amount from clients—here too, there would be a serious credit risk as most often, such staff either migrate or leave and the clients are thereafter unwilling to pay back the portion of loans not used by themselves (rather taken by the staff). Sometimes, staff have collected some extra fees upfront and, again, there could be a credit risk as clients may not be able to or want to pay back, given that some "corruption" charge has been paid already by them. In a few MFIs in India, I have found

---

406 See chapter on agents as well as other resources on different agent-led microfinance models and the resultant implications.
407 See chapter on Governance of Risk Management and http://www.moneylife.in/article/indian-microfinance-credit-bureau-why-is-it-not-fully-operational-yet/20091.html

that while incentive systems based on loan disbursement do not exist on paper, they actually operate on the ground. That needs to be ascertained during any securitization deal.

- *Loan-repayment-related frauds:* A very common occurrence here is that staff retain regular and/or pre-payments by clients and do not pay back to the institution. This has implications for securitization. Further, in a few MFIs in India, I have found that while incentive systems based on loan repayment do not exist formally on paper, they actually operate on the ground through different means including the Zero Par Policy of MFI and related mechanisms whereby field staff cannot come back without collecting client repayment. In a few cases, I have seen staff even being given loans and/or having to pay large delinquent amounts from their personal resources. When this is the case, after some time, it is only natural that the staff try and minimize their personal losses and hence, they talk and act very tough on the ground with clients resulting in what is often called coercive repayment recovery. This problem gets even more exacerbated when loan disbursement is supply led and this again would have implications for securitization.

Thus, these aspects also need to be ascertained during any securitization deal and here too, I would ask the following critical questions (not exhaustive):

1. What can be said with regard to the growth pattern of the MFI whose portfolio is being securitized?

2. Are systems, practices, and procedures at the MFI strong enough to withstand this rapid growth?

3. Are there any differences between various (MIS, internal audit, etc.) intended systems, procedures and practices (as they exist on paper), and the implementation on the ground (realized systems in operation)? Is it likely to have caused loan disbursement and/or loan repayment frauds and control failures? If 'yes,' what are the implications for future repayments?

4. Does the growth pattern of the MFI, whose portfolio is to be securitized, suggest that growth has come from offering supply-led (multiple) loans to shared JLGs and clients? Could this growth have caused high levels of indebtedness in the clients whose portfolio is being securitized?

Thus, these and related questions (on all the aspects given here) certainly need to be asked during a securitization deal as they have implications concerning the nature of the obligor(s) on whom cash flows are dependent and the ability to estimate the cash flows from the assets being securitized as well as payment frequency and the propensity to prepay or make delayed payment. Three possible strategies could help in alleviating these problems and ensure a higher degree of safety in securitization of microfinance assets. First, stakeholders need to be aware of the critical issues such as those mentioned and constantly keep asking questions as part of a securitization deal. Second, it seems like an appropriate strategy and well worth the cost for securitizers to commission small sample studies by unrelated third parties (with no conflict of interest)—especially for first the time as well as large quantum securitization deals. Third, it also seems necessary to bring in a fair trade kind of certification (or equivalent) and permit securitization only if the relevant MFI associations (and/or regulators) certify that the concerned MFI is indeed practicing ethical lending practices (defined appropriately). I hope that the stakeholders developing the regulatory architecture for microfinance consider these issues and deal with them in an appropriate manner to make securitization 'safe' as an instrument. That will go a long way toward eliminating the above-mentioned problems in securitization and getting the incentives right for microfinance securitization.

A final caveat is in order. Despite the widespread use of agents in Indian microfinance, securitization still seems to be popular and I am amazed at what has been happening over the past couple of years. Table 25.4 lists some of the major securitization deals that have occurred after the 2010 AP crisis.

| Table 25.4 Some Major Securitization Deals Since 2010 AP Crisis ||
| --- | --- |
| Originator (partner, year) | Amount (in Rs. crores) |
| SKS Microfinance | 600.00 |
| Ujjivan (Yes Bank) | 17.30 |
| Satin Credit Care (Yes Bank) | 30.00 |
| Grama Vidiyal (IFMR) | 10.8 |
| Grama Vidiyal (IFMR) | 44.87 |
| Satin Credit Care (IFMR) | 7.92 |
| Bandhan (Axis Bank Ltd and Development Credit Bank Ltd) | 50 |

As the chapter on agents[408] highlights, the agent-led microfinance model in India is still in vogue, and I sincerely hope that those who securitize microfinance assets as well as the stakeholders involved in developing the regulatory architecture for microfinance ensure that there are necessary safeguards with regard to securitization in the future, especially given the increasing use of these instruments and agents in Indian microfinance.

---

408 See Chapter 27.

# Chapter 26:
# Developing a Robust Regulatory Architecture for Microfinance: What Past Experience Tells Us?

A bill to regulate microfinance was introduced in Parliament in May 2012 and it is currently with the *Parliamentary Standing Committee* on *Finance* (PSCF). This bill is likely to form the core of the future regulatory architecture for microfinance in India.

The stakeholders[409] involved in this exercise, will need to use critical lessons from past crises situations as they plan the course ahead for the Indian microfinance sector. The past crisis situations that I am referring to are: (i) the NBFC scam of the 1990s; and (ii) the Satyam saga of 2009. Both these are relevant to the MFIDRB (2012) as they are somewhat similar to the 2010 AP microfinance crisis, at least from the manner in which they unfolded and the widespread impact they had on the ground. I am sure that these stakeholders will find this comparative analysis (given in Tables 26.1 to Tables 26.5) interesting.

---

409 The MoF, RBI, PSCF, and several others involved in the developing the regulatory architecture for microfinance.

| | Table 26.1 Comparative Analysis of Crisis Situations in India | | |
|---|---|---|---|
| | **Crisis situation 1:** *NBFC scam of the 1990s* | **Crisis situation 2:** *The Satyam episode of 2009* | **Crisis situation 3:** *The Andhra Pradesh and Indian microfinance crisis of 2010* |
| Legal form and regulation and supervision: | The legal entities were different kinds of (for profit) non-bank finance companies (NBFCs) who promised the world to their depositors in terms of returns.<br><br>Regulation and supervision, although mainly under the ambit of the Reserve Bank of India (RBI), was passive by most standards, as the NBFCs pretty much had a free run in terms of offering abnormal returns to depositors—precisely because they knew upfront that they were not going to refund the deposits to the people concerned. | The legal entities were mainly for-profit companies (Satyam and its related entities) engaged in providing a range of services, in the information technology sector, although the group companies were involved in unrelated businesses such as real estate (Maytas).<br><br>While regulation and supervision were the responsibility of the Registrar of Companies, in real terms it was minimal and perhaps limited to the verification of statutory filings and the like. For those companies in the group that were listed (such as Satyam), the Securities and Exchange Board of India (SEBI) came in as the market regulator and again, the emphasis was on checklist compliance rather than real supervision. | In terms of legal form, microfinance institutions (MFIs) were mainly for-profit companies registered as NBFCs with the RBI.<br><br>While there were other forms of MFIs including nonprofits (societies, trusts, and Section 25 companies) and mutual benefit organizations (such as different types of cooperatives), the large MFIs that dominated the Indian microfinance market, were predominantly for-profit NBFCs, most of whom were headquartered in AP.<br><br>RBI is the regulator/supervisor for the largest group of MFIs—i.e., NBFCs. In addition, SEBI is the market regulator when such NBFC MFIs get listed. In terms of regulation/supervision, it has basically been statutory filings (and perhaps compliance-checklist-type regulation) for the NBFC MFIs.<br><br>There was no serious on-site or, for that matter, even off-site supervision. The other legal forms were supposedly regulated and supervised by the registrar of societies, trusts, and cooperatives under various acts of the central and state governments—in reality, regulation/supervision translated to statutory filings (at most) |

# Chapter 26: Developing a Robust Regulatory Architecture for Microfinance: What Past Experience Tells Us?

| Table 26.2 Comparative Analysis of Crisis Situations in India | | | |
|---|---|---|---|
| | **Crisis situation 1:**<br>*NBFC scam of the 1990s* | **Crisis situation 2:**<br>*The Satyam episode of 2009* | **Crisis situation 3:**<br>*The Andhra Pradesh and Indian microfinance crisis of 2010* |
| ***Growth and competition:*** | The growth was indeed explosive as more and more gullible people deposited money, lured by higher than normal returns.<br><br>Competition made things worse, as the fight for market share to loot innocent people off their savings led to these NBFCs (especially, plantation companies) announcing outrageous schemes, offering whimsical returns to woo customers—some advertisements (e.g., Anubhav Plantations and some others) carried the caption, *"Can you spot Rs.36 lakhs in this advertisement?"*<br><br>Without question, growth and competition brought their own problems and in many local settings, 'crisis flash points' were evident, not to the regulator, who was far away (both physically as well as operationally) | Indeed, competition for Satyam and its businesses were all along burgeoning and margins were perhaps being forced down. Satyam was also often getting caught in its own cycle of trying to catch up and keep pace with its three major IT competitors—in terms of quality, cost leadership, scale, and service differentiation.<br><br>This perhaps also made the Satyam group look seriously at other unrelated activities such as real estate, infrastructure, ambulance services, etc. through related companies such as Maytas and others. The strong desire to diversify into various other businesses suggested that all was not well inside. Yet, the subtle signals were not picked up by the regulators, who were busy looking at awards and paper compliances and least concerned about the real operations | The NBFC MFIs experienced burgeoning growth, through the years, and especially from April 2008 onward until the crisis in October 2010. During April 2008 to March 2010, six of the top 14 MFIs were headquartered in Andhra Pradesh and these NBFC MFIs increased their gross loan portfolio outstanding by a little over $1.912* billion and added almost 9.59 million clients. This is phenomenal growth by any standards.<br><br>Although a large part of India remained unsaturated as far as microfinance services were concerned, several pockets—especially urban and peri-urban areas of Andhra Pradesh, Tamil Nadu, Karnataka, West Bengal and Orissa—witnessed significant competition. And multiple/successive/ghost lending to same clients became the norm for growth. In other words, many MFIs aspired to be the fastest to disburse a loan. As a result, clients and joint liability groups (JLGs) were shared between MFIs and different MFIs serviced the same clients/JLGs on successive days. Surely, a recipe for long-term disaster. Burgeoning growth also meant that frauds (ghost lending) increased, as admitted in the financial statements of several MFIs, mainly due to failure of credit delivery and other systems. The NBFC MFIs that grew very fast also used the decentralized agent model to expand rapidly and reach significant scale |

\* This should have been higher at US$ 2.076 billion had the Mix Market retained the original GLP figures that it had put out in 2010/2011 for BASIX and SHARE. For some reason, Mix Market changed its original figures for BASIX and SHARE respectively from US$ 223,229,799 and US$ for 490,923,201 to US$ 172,484,946 and US$ 376,593,362 (as on date). I have the original print screen data and other pieces of evidence with regard to the original data put out by Mix Market. There are several other issues with the Mix Market database and I can provide the details if required.

| | Table 26.3 Comparative Analysis of Crisis Situations in India | | |
|---|---|---|---|
| | **Crisis situation 1:** *NBFC scam of the 1990s* | **Crisis situation 2:** *The Satyam episode of 2009* | **Crisis situation 3:** *The Andhra Pradesh and Indian microfinance crisis of 2010* |
| ***Group entities and non-transparent transactions:*** | Interestingly, this was among the first instances where group companies with complex institutional arrangements could be seen. Transfer of funds through non-transparent transactions was also evident. And much of this was controlled by the promoter and his/her confidants, with significant support from the auditors | The Satyam saga took the related companies concept to a new height, where several group entities with complex relationships were seen transferring funds through non-transparent transactions on a regular basis. While there had been widespread speculation about the diversion of funds, ironically, the cat was out of the bag only when the promoter made a proposal to facilitate the funds transfer under the garb of diversification into other (unrelated) businesses.<br><br>In fact, this incident led to the famous 2009 crisis caused by shareholder activism. As in the first situation, much of the happenings were directly controlled by the promoter, Ramalinga Raju, and one/two of his henchmen. Of course, the auditors and other stakeholders also appeared to have been involved | The MFIs made the related entities concept even more complex with the introduction of not-so-legal entities such as Mutual Benefit Trusts (MBTs) a part of the overall group structure. MBTs were strange animals because they had no real law of legislature backing their existence, let alone their regulation and supervision—I am still puzzled as to how they can be called body corporates. There is also strong evidence of non-transparent relationships between these group companies as espoused by dilution and/or liquidation of MBT shares and the like.<br><br>There are also clear cases of significant related-party transactions between group entities and promoters—such as loans given by a large MFI to the promoter to buy shares in the same MFI (as per Prof. Sriram's article in the *Economic and Political Weekly*, June 2010). And further, there are so many legal entities involved in similar and related activities under the same group—an NBFC, a society, a Section 25 company, several MBTs, and even cooperatives. All this makes the various institutional relationships within the group very complex and, as a result, the microfinance operations are like a black box. And as with the other two crises, the promoter and his chosen colleagues (stage) "managed" the various situations. What, however, needs to be ascertained is whether the auditors were involved in some of these non-transparent transactions |

# Chapter 26: Developing a Robust Regulatory Architecture for Microfinance: What Past Experience Tells Us?

## Table 26.4 Comparative Analysis of Crisis Situations in India

| | **Crisis situation 1:** *NBFC scam of the 1990s* | **Crisis situation 2:** *The Satyam episode of 2009* | **Crisis situation 3:** *The Andhra Pradesh and Indian microfinance crisis of 2010* |
|---|---|---|---|
| ***Financing, governance, systems and operations:*** | 'Cheap* and unlimited public deposits and other forms of capital were the primary source of funds for these NBFCs, which had weak governance, poor MIS and very little internal controls. Risk management did not appear to be a part of their institutional systems. Ghost plantations and fraudulent transactions were the major phenomenon that caused institutional failure. In fact, the same plantations were sold to many investors—for example, I have personally seen what happened at places such as Bodinayakanur (Tamil Nadu), where teak farms (in terms of the same land titles and survey numbers) were sold to different clients in Mumbai, Delhi, and elsewhere. Unscrupulous agents convinced people to deposit money and then they simply disappeared | Shareholder investment and other liabilities were the major resources for Satyam, although operational surpluses were claimed to be significant. Despite the various corporate governance awards, the company and its group, in reality, had very poor governance and systems—as it became clear when the scam broke out.

This was the first large Indian company in recent times to illustrate the fact that neither corporate governance awards (such as the Golden Peacock award) nor the presence of a high-profile board symbolize (and/or ensure) good corporate governance in implementation. It is clear that MIS (including invoices and records) were fabricated, as proved later by the existence of fraudulent financial transactions undertaken by the company.

Controls also seemed to have been manipulated and a self-confession is what let the "cat" out of the bag. Without question, ghost (sometimes, duplicate) invoices to boost operating results and a whole range of fraudulent and very complex transactions led to the collapse of the financial system in the Satyam group and this resulted in institutional failure eventually | By and large, most MFIs had access to priority sector lending funds from commercial banks and soft loans from DFIs (such as SIDBI) and donors—these were typically large, collateral-free, soft interest loans with no personal guarantees. They were generally available on virtually unlimited scale during the years preceding the crisis. Many MFIs also had access to significant equity investments—both from secondary and primary markets. IPOs had indeed become the buzzword just before the crisis in October 2010. Last but not the least, some MFIs received grants from donors, which were subsequently capitalized, and often in the names of the promoters!

Further, despite corporate governance and transparency awards (from CGAP** /others), many MFIs had weak governance as espoused by the happenings in (2010 and before). The tampering of board minutes, loans to founder promoters, irrational compensation to MFI promoters in many instances, and the unceremonious sacking of a CEO who led the concerned MFI through a spectacular IPO are all aspects that raise serious questions about corporate governance.

In addition, MIS at these MFIs suffered from several weaknesses too—including lack of aggregation across geographies, clients, and products. Internal controls and audits were also weak and risk management was almost absent and all of these made the microfinance industry a perfect setting for institutional failure.

It is now clear from several sources (including e-mails in circulation between MFIs) that center leaders and local political leaders functioned as MFI agents and pushed loans to poor people, and used coercive methods and greening techniques to recover loans from them. In fact, the audit statements of some MFIs themselves pointed to the presence of ghost and nonexistent clients, misappropriation of client repayment collections and several other kinds of frauds, primarily caused by the decentralized MFI model that used different kinds of broker agents. The financial statements reconfirmed the trends of ghost clients and the like.

It is now also apparent that some MFIs (perhaps even many) engaged in not-so-desirable practices such as multiple lending, top-up loans, over-lending to the same clients and even creation of non-existent borrowers (sometimes to manage delinquency) and so on. In my opinion, the above illustrations of not-so-good governance, poor systems, and non-transparent operations, along with client suicides, acted as one of the major triggers for the 2010 AP microfinance crisis. Everything else, more or less, followed from these |

\* Cheap is low cost essentially as public deposits are the cheapest source of nonsubsidized capital.
\*\* A multidonor body which functions from The World Bank – CGAP Stands for The Consultative Group to Assist the Poor. I wish it were the Consultative Group to Alleviate Poverty.

| | Table 26.5 Comparative Analysis of Crisis Situations in India | | |
|---|---|---|---|
| | **Crisis situation 1:** *NBFC scam of the 1990s* | **Crisis situation 2:** *The Satyam episode of 2009* | **Crisis situation 3:** *The Andhra Pradesh and Indian microfinance crisis of 2010* |
| **Target clients and impact of the crisis:** | A majority of the target clients were from middle-income and economically well-off classes. The loss of deposits wreaked havoc on clients who lost their valuable savings, which is a safety net for the rainy day. Many farmers who had sold their land to the concerned companies were affected in terms of not having received their entire sale consideration and of course, their land was already sold. In institutional terms, the NBFCs became bankrupt and there was significant loss of faith in the NBFC (financial) system in civil society and much of that distrust continues today among the middle-income group | Again, the majority of target clients were middle income to economically well-off classes and they were affected in two ways: (i) the loss of work wreaked havoc on hired (regular as well as surplus) employees who could not even meet their regular housing EMIs and (ii) shareholders were badly affected as the stock price of Satyam and related companies plummeted and significant wealth was lost. Most importantly, the Satyam fiasco dented corporate India like no other event in terms of the financial and image loss suffered. | Most of the target clients were low-income and financially excluded people. The vulnerability of the clients and lack of sufficient livelihood opportunities for them were major factors in their getting exploited by the system. The multiple loans wreaked havoc in the lives of clients and the enhanced and ever increasing indebtedness was certainly a very important factor for the suicides.<br><br>The rural and urban low-income (credit) economy was in shambles. Many of the low-income clients lost access to finance in the long term as financial institutions became reluctant to lend to them (anymore), especially in the wake of the various problems identified during the 2010 AP microfinance crisis.<br><br>Shareholders of the only listed MFI took a beating as the stock price plummeted hugely and still continues to be volatile, causing significant erosion of investor wealth. Further, the private equity investors were left without an exit strategy and many of them, have actually suffered huge losses as they had bought the MFI shares at abnormally high valuations. And last but not the least, the reputation of microfinance, as a pro-poor industry was in tatters and its image took a severe beating. MFIs are no longer considered the torchbearers of development and poverty reduction |

*Lessons from the three crises situations:* We can take some key lessons from the above comparative analysis.

- First, every potential crisis situation had early warning signals, which, when ignored, resulted in the crisis snowballing into a major one. I am sure that all of us recognize the "early flash points" in the various crisis situations (including the incidents in 2008–2010 with regard to the AP microfinance crisis). That these early warning signals did not catch the attention of the regulators/supervisors is something that needs to strong emphasis here.

- Second, in almost all the three situations, the companies that were involved were once much-feted and had received (corporate governance) awards and significant (positive) media attention. Their fall from grace was however swift, post crisis. Clearly all that glitters is not gold and it is better to avoid face value interpretations of corporate governance based on the mere presence of a high-profile board. Five-star boards do not guarantee good corporate governance and let us be clear about that!

# Chapter 26: Developing a Robust Regulatory Architecture for Microfinance: What Past Experience Tells Us?

- Third, in almost all three crisis situations, the companies/entities involved were purported to be doing something exceptionally innovative for the times and context that they existed in. They were therefore given the long rope but because their innovation was legally untenable, the long rope eventually turned out to be their (own) nemesis.

- Fourth, in all three cases, there was no (one) serious regulator, and the lack of coordination among multiple regulators resulted in regulatory arbitrage, thereby causing institutional failure. Alternatively, it can be argued that "hands-off" regulation is a common factor that aided the crisis and, from this, it is clear that any well-meaning regulation must be coupled with commensurate and effective supervision on the ground. Otherwise, the "subjects" of regulation (companies, NBFCs, MFIs, etc.) will claim to be complying, even while actually engaging in not-so-good practices. Thus, a hands-off regulatory approach could lead an industry to a serious crisis and well-intentioned regulation is of no real use if not backed by strong and local level supervision, which clearly indicates an appropriate role for state governments. This is a serious aspect that needs to be appreciated and taken cognizance of by the various stakeholders developing the regulatory architecture for Indian microfinance.

- Fifth, in each of these cases, it was extraneous events that led to the crisis erupting and getting large-scale public attention and only after that did the regulators come in! Thus, all these three crises situations clearly symbolize regulatory failure to a large extent and the fact of the matter is that the concerned regulators/supervisors were perhaps caught totally unawares (when the crisis first erupted). Further, interestingly, the regulatory responses, in two cases,[410] were stringent to the point of crippling the operations post crisis, indicating an extreme and complete swing of the regulatory pendulum. Balance in regulation is therefore critical, as otherwise regulation may strangulate the very industry that it is trying to serve. Therefore, regulation must also seek to enable and incentivize behaviors rather than merely prescribe rules and rely on compliance checklists, which suit most companies/entities. Put differently, as Dr Raghuram Rajan, the present RBI governor has often argued, *'the cure should not become worse than the disease itself'*[411] and that is why balance in regulation is required.

- Sixth, self-regulation does not and will not work on the ground and this is a clear message from all the crisis situations. In fact, 'self-regulation' could lead to the crisis deepening further, as the concerned stakeholders (or subjects of regulation) rarely have right incentives to comply.

- Seventh, multiple regulators can only lead to chaos on the ground and whenever you have several regulators, there is confusion and important aspects are not properly enforced—like corporate governance for private limited companies and/or NBFCs, where circulars exist but are not fully

---

[410] This is true of the RBI and State Government directions (in Tamil Nadu) in the 1990s. The Andhra Pradesh Microfinance Institutions (Regulation of Money Lending) Ordinance, 2010 is another case in point, as also its subsequent enactment as a Bill.

[411] Taken from statements made to the media by Dr Raghuram Rajan.

implemented, thereby enabling the subjects of regulation to engage in not-so-good practices. The issue of related-party transactions for NBFCs is a case in point. See the RBI circular on corporate governance (of May 2007 on the RBI website), parts of which—including loans to directors—were kept in abeyance, even in 2010, at the peak of the AP microfinance crisis.

- Eighth, regulation must first and foremost provide legitimacy to the industry and this legitimacy must be backed by certain non-negotiables and safeguards, including minimum standards for governance, client protection, various systems (finance and accounting, internal controls, internal audit, human resources management, management information systems, etc.), operations (lending and recovery aspects included) and the like.

One other special aspect deserves mention here. Laws will have to follow policies and the key point to note here is that we have no serious national microfinance policy in India, as on date, despite the acknowledged importance of the subject. Therefore, while finalizing the regulatory architecture, the concerned stakeholders could also facilitate the drafting of a suitable microfinance policy that outlines aspects such as the following:

1. What is the proper scope of microfinance, given the Indian context? What specific problems and issues should it address, especially based on the lessons from the 2010/past microfinance crisis situations, especially in Andhra Pradesh? This is critical as the essence of any regulation is to prevent market/institutional failures.

2. Which institutions (stakeholders) are providing such microfinance services, through what delivery channels and to whom? What key lessons with regard to these different models are discernible and especially, in the light of the 2010 AP microfinance crisis? *The aspect to be noted here is that while past policy pronouncements have been well-intentioned and talked of a range of financial services, in reality, microfinance has been somewhat limited to the delivery of large scale consumption credit (and perhaps some small production credit) to low-income people. Therefore, it cannot be assumed that a wide range of financial services will indeed be delivered. This difference between intended and realized strategies on the ground is an aspect that needs to be factored in thoroughly and this leads to the next question.*

3. What is expected of microfinance over the next 3 years? 5 years? 10 years? 20 years and so on?

4. Given these, what should the scope of regulation/supervision be? Who should be the regulator(s), supervisor(s) etc.?

In other words, the need of the hour is a proper national microfinance policy that can drive the laws and not vice versa. In fact, policy sums up aspirations and laws become enabling mechanisms to achieve

## Chapter 26: Developing a Robust Regulatory Architecture for Microfinance: What Past Experience Tells Us?

that. So, it would be great if the stakeholders developing the regulatory architecture for microfinance can make an effort towards that (as well).

*Thus, a key challenge for policy making is, therefore, one of developing appropriate and sound policy, sensitive to the existing practices and methods as also the compliance costs involved for MFIs, which are organizations with somewhat limited resources.* This balance undoubtedly has to be struck, and, toward meeting this objective, a number of practical criteria can be used and these are given here.

- *Criterion 1:* Policy and associated regulation must have broad stakeholder and public support. Without this, compliance is likely to be low and cannot be enforced in reality.

- *Criterion 2:* The regulation must be *enforceable on the ground*. It must not conflict (too much) with existing ways of doing business and ongoing methods of operating. An additional practical rule here is not to regulate anything that *cannot* be supervised.

- *Criterion 3:* All relevant stakeholders must easily understand the policy and associated regulations. Complexity in policy/regulation undermines their effectiveness and often leads to difficulty in compliance. Therefore, simplicity and clarity are critical and necessary attributes of good policy/regulation.

- *Criterion 4:* Regulation must be *balanced and sensitive to the needs of those being regulated* and there should be an awareness of the possible costs of compliance, while framing the broad policy and associated regulations. *Oppressive regulations may, in fact, encourage institutions (MFIs etc.) to move out or even drive them to their ultimate death.* This is a crucial aspect that needs to be focused on while developing policy and associated regulation.

- *Criterion 5:* Policy (and regulation) should *not be overly paternalistic*. In other words, it should not remove all decision making from institutions (or individuals) who can decide for themselves.

- *Criterion 6:* Regulation should attempt to resolve *potentially conflicting policy objectives*—for example, they could encourage the growth of employment in MFIs, but, at the same time, protect the rights and working conditions of employees, which is rather inadequate in most MFI contexts. A similar quandary exists in the case of growth and preventing overindebtedness.

- *Criterion 7:* Policy (and associated regulation) must provide *clear and identifiable accountability* when things go wrong. The buck must stop somewhere clearly and the blame should not simply be passed around.

- *Criterion 8:* Regulation should be designed in a way that competitive disadvantages are reduced in favor of those (institutions) being regulated without creating new disadvantages.

- *Criterion 9:* MFI policy (and associated regulation) must seek to promote access to a wide range of (financial and nonfinancial) services required by their clients for inclusive growth and development.

- *Criterion 10:* Regulation must enable end-user clients to take advantage of opportunities for economic growth in the environment in an equitable and sustainable manner. It must also strengthen the various systems to attract capital flows and manage increased levels of investment. Further, it should facilitate the creation of an environment to promote viable and competitive MFIs that can contribute to employment, income generation, and poverty reduction.

- *Criterion 11:* Overall, the policy and associated regulation must ensure that all aspects to be regulated and supervised (such as governance, systems, and other operational aspects in MFIs) are regulated and properly supervised. They should not leave the onus for this regulation/supervision of mandatory aspects (non-negotiables) on the very institutions that need to be regulated and supervised. The incentives for self-regulation to work are rather low in many contexts (including microfinance) and this must be clearly recognized and addressed by policy/regulation.

- *Criterion 12:* The policy and associated regulation must be reviewed (perhaps not too frequently) and adapted to suit changing circumstances, using the outcomes of an embedded monitoring and evaluation system in the policy framework.

I hope that the concerned stakeholders learn from these past crisis situations and use the lessons and practical criteria given earlier, while developing the regulatory architecture for Indian microfinance.

Last but not the last, while on the topic of the regulatory architecture being developed, I would also like to bring up the aspect of incentives, which are critical for implementation. Indeed, incentives are necessary in a nascent industry such as microfinance and their impact is likely to be phenomenal, provided they are well structured. Accordingly, I suggest some incentives for the regulatory framework and hope that the concerned stakeholders will also factor these into the framework being established for MFIs.

a. *Dividend and bonus share issue cap[412] for MFIs:* The regulatory architecture would have to specify a permanent specified cap on dividends[413] and issue of bonus shares for any MFI that wants to be officially accredited by the regulator.

---

412 Return on assets and return on equity caps are possible but there will be workarounds to that by bundling products along with the loan. Thus, the MFIs will be able to show that their revenues are now coming from other income streams. If these caps are in place, then the existing caps on interest rates and margins can be done away with.

413 It could be 10–15% on shareholder equity and decided through consensus among industry stakeholders.

Accreditation, in turn, will provide such MFIs with access to priority sector loan funds from banks, the complete freedom to act as banking correspondents,[414] and immunity from state-level usury laws. In addition, the MFI will be required to meet certain minimum standards with regard to governance, systems (human resources, portfolio management, MIS, finance and accounting, internal audits, internal controls, and so on), client protection/literacy and other aspects.

It also goes without saying that the regulatory architecture will need to utilize various means (on-site and off-site supervision, etc.) to ensure that these non-negotiable minimum standards are indeed met in a dynamically changing microfinance environment, quarter-on-quarter, year-on-year.

b. *Compensation caps for MFIs:* All stakeholders (from senior management, right up to field level staff and directors/board members, if appropriate) at accredited MFIs, would have to adhere to compensation caps as per those recommended by the proposed regulatory architecture. At any cost, the compensation should not exceed that of similar positions in public/private sector banks, whichever is higher. Further, for salaries/compensation above a certain limit (to be fixed in the proposed regulatory architecture) and for certain key positions (such as managing director, CEO, CFO, etc.), the accredited MFI would have to take necessary approvals under the regulatory framework.

c. *Disclosure by promoters/directors/senior management of their personal assets and shareholding in the MFI*: Promoters, directors and senior management at all accredited MFIs would have to provide yearly statements of their assets and liabilities, as also transparently list their and their family/friends' investment in the MFIs. This would be mandatory as part of the proposed regulatory architecture. If any MFI does not want to accept the dividend cap, bonus share issue cap, compensation cap and disclosure norms, then it would be free to raise funds from banks and/or other sources at commercial rates to carry on business. In such a case, the loan will not be from a bank's priority sector quota. So, a bank can lend to an MFI at a higher interest rate after factoring in the appropriate risks for the sector. Thus, such MFIs that are not eligible to be accredited under the legal framework offered by the proposed MFIDRB (2012), will *not:* (i) gain access to priority sector funds; (ii) be able to act as banking correspondents; and (iii) enjoy the benefits and/or immunity provided by this framework against state level usury laws.

d. *Focus on all kinds of MFIs by banks:* Encourage banks to lend to large and small MFIs (with different models) so that the overall risk for the banking sector is minimized. Also, under such circumstances,

---

[414] Dividend-capped NBFC MFIs, with their primary social orientation, should be allowed to become banking correspondents as there is minimized conflict of interest. Further, they should be encouraged to open savings bank accounts with banks and eventually the loan size to the borrower by the MFI should be linked to the savings of the borrower with the bank (perhaps the supervisory authority can come out with prudential guidelines for ratio of loan to savings). This, in essence, will: (i) encourage savings for clients; (ii) simplify regulation: one will be able to allow savings to clients without creating deposit taking MFIs in the short and medium term; and (iii) reduce chances of over indebtedness by linking loan size to savings amount.

no MFI becomes too big to fail (from a bank's perspective). This will also minimize the material impact on a bank's balance sheet in case a large MFI fails. This is a very important lesson from the 2010 AP microfinance crisis.

e. *Priority sector loans:* Loans made to MFIs that have a dividend, bonus share issue, and compensation cap in place that have agreed to certain minimum standards with regard to governance, systems, and client protection and provide the mandatory disclosures as per the proposed MFIDRB (2012), will have to come under priority sector targets. That these loans have to be reasonably priced follows naturally. As noted earlier, banks would be free to set a true risk-based price for loans made to MFIs that do not have a dividend, bonus share issue, and compensation cap in place, reflecting the level of operational and other risks (including political risks).

And if we get these incentives right, here is what I foresee for each of the players.

f. *For banks:* Their systemic risk would be considerably reduced as their lending would be spread across a much bigger portfolio of MFIs—different types, sizes, scale, and so on. The political risk would also be reduced somewhat—especially it banks service MFIs operating as part of the proposed MFIDRB (2012).

g. *For MFIs:* Some large MFIs may borrow from banks under priority sector lending, while others may not. But that is a choice that each MFI will have to make, based on its vision and mission and the perceived benefit of operating under the proposed regulatory architecture. Large MFIs that do not accept dividends, bonus share issues, and compensation caps are likely to become pure play financial institutions. They will be able to give reasonable returns to their investors but they may be more prone to operational and political risks. However, that is something that they may choose to live with.

Likewise, large MFIs who have accepted a dividend, bonus share issue, and compensation cap, and who remain pure financial institutions, will start getting surpluses. This can then be ploughed back for the development of the microfinance industry at large. Thus, they will be able to build their reserves and, over a course of time, will be able to offer cross-subsidization across different kinds of products to clients. For example, an income generating loan at 24% or less, education loan at 8%, and so on.

Socially focused MFIs will now get adequate funding and will become true livelihood finance and support institutions, where credit would be just one of the products on offer. They may also offer additional support such as health advisory services. Thus, these organizations will be able to work on poverty reduction as well as financial inclusion and, thereby, contribute meaningfully to the inclusive growth agenda in India.

# Chapter 26: Developing a Robust Regulatory Architecture for Microfinance: What Past Experience Tells Us?

h. *For clients:* Their interests will be protected. They will have true choice. If they want only credit, they will perhaps get it from a large registered MFI at a relatively lower rate. If they want livelihood support with credit, they will get it from a socially focused MFI. And if they want to increase their loan size slowly, they can approach a socially focused/small MFI. On the other hand, if they want to increase loan size faster, they can go to the larger MFIs.

i. *For investors:* They will now have wider choices. They can either invest in truly commercial for-profit MFIs or they can invest in and/or support MFIs that have capped dividends, bonus share issue and compensation, and those that avail priority sector funding, and can act as banking correspondents. It would entirely depend on their social and commercial goals. Investors who believe that all problems can be solved only commercially, can invest in non-dividend-capped MFIs while those who believe in the double bottom line can invest in dividend-capped MFIs. And, of course, donors can support small and nascent NGO MFIs, cooperatives, and the like.

I hope that I have been sufficiently clear in outlining my incentive proposals. I strongly believe that a crisis should never be wasted, but rather converted into a learning opportunity instead. Before I sign off in this chapter, it is my eternal optimism that makes me seek a proper regulatory/supervisory architecture for microfinance—one that can enable MFIs to grow and flower, one that can protect clients, and one that can safeguard public and people's money (loans that are public deposits). All three aspects are important and there can be no compromise on that. I hope that the concerned stakeholders developing the regulatory architecture understand this and attempt to help the microfinance industry with such a clear enabling regulatory/supervisory architecture. It is not too late even now.

In summary, I hope that these stakeholders recognize that "regulatory" and "supervisory" failure was an important cause of the 2010 AP microfinance crisis and attempt to redress the situation of regulatory failure and regulatory arbitrage by designing and implementing a sound enabling regulatory framework for microfinance. This will hopefully help in the creation of a vibrant and healthy microfinance sector, which can then truly benefit large numbers of excluded and low-income people in the country, who continue to struggle for their daily survival.

# Chapter 27:
# Safeguards against Notorious Broker Agents: A Consumer Protection and Regulatory Imperative

Even as policymakers are trying to solve the Indian microfinance regulatory puzzle, let us look at a specific field-level problem that led to the 2010 AP microfinance crisis and ask the question as to how the regulatory architecture being developed will prevent the use of the notorious agents in the future.

In fact, many people have brought up the aspect of broker agents driving Indian microfinance but their (loud) voices seem to have fallen on deaf years. Several stakeholders including regulators have not even acknowledged this (serious) agent phenomenon. And those who accepted the fact that agents did exist, described it more as an aberration. However, to the best of my knowledge, agents appeared to be more of the norm in Indian microfinance—at least in the years preceding and succeeding the 2010 AP crisis.

The e-mails in circulation among MFIs—given earlier in this book[415]—clearly demonstrated that the use of agents in Indian microfinance was significant in the years before and after the 2010 AP crisis. Some stakeholders have concurred with my view and also argued that it is the widespread use of agents—to turbocharge growth, create efficiencies, increase profits and the like—that led to the 2010 AP crisis in the first place. In fact, experts like N. Srinivasan (author of *State of the Sector Report*) and knowledge portals such as *Microfinance Focus* (MF) have made a strong mention of these (broker) agents. Mr Srinivasan noted in the *State of the Sector*[416] *Report* (2010),

> "As in the example from Karnataka, MFIs in other states too have tended to concentrate around the same towns and peripheries, serving the same set of households. The deluge of availability of loans from several institutions has led to multiple borrowing and, in some cases, excessive debt. The pressure to

---

415 See Chapter 20 on Code of Conduct Assessments.
416 Source: Quoted from Microfinance in India: State of the Sector Report, 2010, by N. Srinivasan, Sage Publications.

# Chapter 27: Safeguards against Notorious Broker Agents: A Consumer Protection and Regulatory Imperative

achieve performance targets and breakeven within a short period of time has pushed the relatively new staff of MFIs to look to centre leaders who are in the know of MFI operations. These centre leaders have become a critical rallying point and are today termed as 'ring leaders': In state after state (Madhya Pradesh, Rajasthan, Orissa, West Bengal, Andhra Pradesh, Karnataka and Tamil Nadu), stories abound of how ring leaders informally register new customers promising loans for a fee. Most new MFIs setting up operations in such areas approach these centre leaders as an easy and natural entry point. This provides the necessary influence to the ring leaders to deliver on the promise made to several registrants for loans. The centre leaders are also in a position to obtain loans in the name of others, advantageously using the relative unfamiliarity of new field staff and new MFIs. The resultant ghost loans have a tendency towards default. The clients that pay the registration fee in order to get a loan feel justified in holding up repayments. This behaviour has an adverse effect on repayment rates and necessitates stronger recovery efforts. Some MFIs (including those in the list of top 10) had to wind down operations in some pockets of states such as West Bengal, Chhattisgarh, Rajasthan and Maharashtra without making an attempt to consolidate."

Likewise, *Microfinance Focus* wrote (Dec 22, 2010):

"Moulding business models to meet their growth targets, some of the largest microfinance institutions are using group leaders as interface agents between borrowers and loan officers. Popularly called as 'Ring Leaders', these agents are responsible for conducting meetings in their premises and collecting weekly repayments from the borrowers... Borrowers of microfinance institutions in townships of Mehndipatnam, Begumpet and Dilkhushnagar of Hyderabad (capital of Andhra Pradesh) told the microfinance focus team that now these ring leaders have become a major cause of distress for them. The principle of 'Know Your Customer' is one of the keystones around which microfinance practices have been evolved. However, with the introduction of the 'ring leaders' into the process, it seems that this essential requirement of lending is being compromised. The end borrowers interact with the ring leaders who maintain their passbooks and repayments. The loan officers, in turn, collect these from the ring leaders, reducing the amount of their interaction with the borrowers to almost negligible levels. Another disturbing practice which came to light was the charging of 'membership fees' by the ring leaders from the borrowers to join an MFI group. Ranging in the amounts of Rs. 300–Rs. 500, these membership fees are over and above the interest paid to service the loan. This fee was pocketed entirely by the ring leaders and is their 'commission' for allowing a prospective borrower to be part of the group. "Ring leaders have become a major cause of distress for us but as we need money and don't have any better sources, we give in to their demands," one of the borrowers said."[417]

---

[417] Source: Quoted from http://www.microfinancefocus.com/content/big-league-microfinance-institutions-using-group-leaders-agents

Why is the agent phenomenon so important to tackle? In my opinion, there are several aspects that make it mandatory for the regulatory architecture being developed for Indian microfinance to have safeguards against broker agents: (i) these broker agents very dangerous and extremely powerful in that they not only can get new clients for the MFIs, they can also make these clients disappear (quickly) from an MFI's horizon; (ii) they can shift clients from one MFI to another seamlessly and thereby cause irreparable damage to the MFI's overall portfolio, growth strategy and reputation; (iii) they are capable of (suddenly) stopping client repayments, just at the flick of a finger; and (iv) they can physically intimidate clients as they often have the backing of thugs and criminals (locally). Once created by the MFIs in search of fast growth and greater efficiency, these agents have proved to be the bane of Indian microfinance. Therefore, it is imperative that the concerned stakeholders (involved in developing the regulatory architecture) ensure that there are necessary mechanisms to deal effectively with broker agents and their operations, as, otherwise, crisis situations (similar to the 2010 AP microfinance crisis) could easily recur. And for this, these stakeholders first need to understand what types of agents are there and how these agents have operated in Indian microfinance. Accordingly, I provide a brief overview here.

Basically, there are two types of agents that I have seen: center leaders and local political honchos. Each of them has distinct backgrounds and characteristics and they perform differing roles as microfinance agents. However, because the center agent model was more prevalent in the years before and after the 2010 AP crisis, I describe "the center leader microfinance agent model" in detail. A brief description of the other agent model is also given later.

*Profile of the center leader*: Center leader agents are typically women who have risen through the ranks in the MFI (microfinance institution)—that is, from being group members/leaders to center leaders. Sometimes, they could have been appointed as a center leader directly. Either way, the key point to note is that center leaders generally have tremendous local knowledge. By virtue of this, the center leaders, usually, have significant local support in their village. In fact, they are local opinion leaders, who are involved in key activities in the concerned villages/areas. Irrespective of the path of progress, such agents possess extreme familiarity with the microfinance concept, processes, and procedures and this gives them crucial domain knowledge. These agents are also familiar with staff and clients of MFIs. Thus, good domain knowledge, superior information with regard to microfinance, good contacts in the local community, and the associated social acceptability provide this type of agent tremendous clout.

Chapter 27: Safeguards against Notorious Broker Agents: A Consumer Protection and Regulatory Imperative

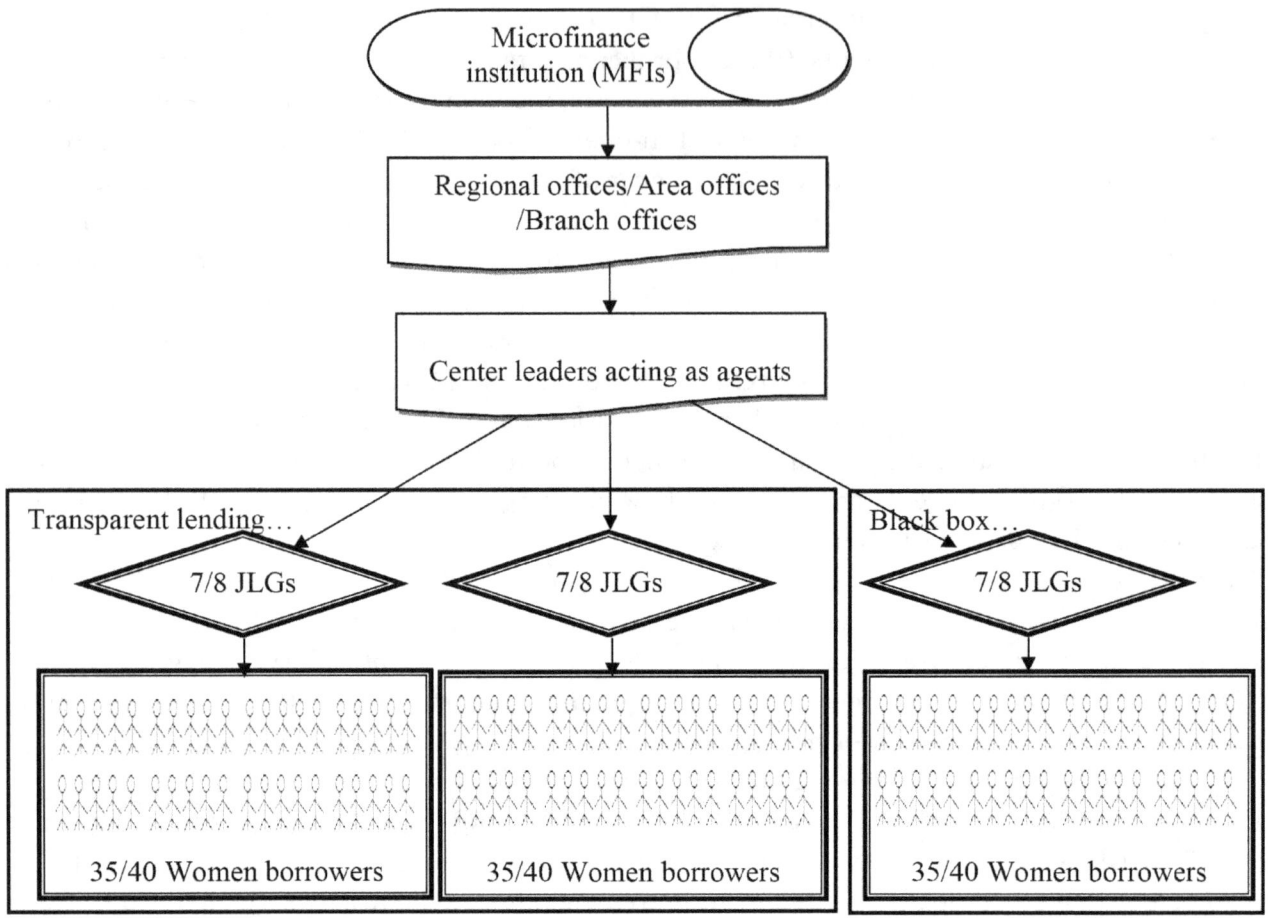

Figure 27.1 Center Leader as the Microfinance Agent

*Operational Issues:* The operational scope of center leader agents typically encompasses seven to eight groups (at least initially). Center leader agents, as they gain experience, generally start to handle as many as 35/40 joint liability groups (JLGs). Very senior center leader agents look after even 75 to 100 JLGs—at which point their case load is much greater than the normal case load of a typical Grameen MFI loan officer. In fact, if you see the data for the fastest growing and largest MFIs in India during the period April 2008–March 2010, then a lot of this will become clear.

Of course, a center leader's ability to grow depends on her experience, age, clout, and also her capacity to position key support staff (agent associates) in the neighboring villages in the same/adjacent cluster. Often, group leaders working under her graduate to become agent associates, each one supervising the microfinance operations in the villages where they live. The center leader, as the main agent, covers the entire cluster of villages. This is the decentralized agent model in its complete sense where authority for disbursement and collection of loans as also money management is fully localized.

Sometimes, the center leader agents tend to have a local support group comprising their husbands or younger brothers or sons or other male relatives—basically, a male brigade, in the 20–55 year age bracket, who can talk tough with any stakeholder, including clients and/or MFI staff, as and when required. As noted by an industry commentator, "The centre leader, usually a more affluent woman, uses her position to hold on to some of the borrowers' loans. If she oversees, say, 8–10 groups (about 40–50 women), she retains and uses a part of the overall loan portfolio—for consumption, or to put into her own business. While the loans continue to be in the names of the members, the centre leader makes the repayments. For this to happen, the field executive and the branch manager have to outsource the responsibility for disbursing and collecting the money to the centre leader. She then decides whom to lend to." This aspect has been shown in Figure 27.1.

*Roles and functions:* Among other things, the center leaders, as agents, perform several key functions:

- They act as primary catalysts in the acquisition of new groups (JLGs). This calls for significant manoeuvring at the local level and this is where their clout becomes immensely handy.

- Sometimes, they assist loan officers in new JLG formation by pulling out clients from SHGs or JLGs belonging to competitor MFIs/agents. Much of the Krishna/Guntur (AP) problem in 2005–2006 happened because two large MFIs were involved in breaking each other's JLGs and taking over each other's clients. Center leaders, as (quasi) agents, played no small role in this.

- They also assist in the formation of green field JLGs—although this is rare as these center leader agents work more toward building scale rather than do the hard work of green field JLG formation.

- Many of them supervise the working of the JLGs and maintain tight control over these JLGs and their members through loyal group leaders (who function as associates)—often guarding them from takeover by other center leaders and types of agents. Therefore, constantly servicing clients with loans becomes an absolute imperative and there is no escape route whatsoever.

- They organize (informal) meetings for disbursement and recovery of loans and meet with their clients on a weekly basis (at least).

- In several cases, senior center leaders with a large territory may be involved with several MFIs and they certainly play the most important role in negotiating and scheduling meetings with the various MFIs. So, when new MFIs try to enter a (new) area, these center leaders help schedule their weekly group meetings through mutual discussion and negotiation with other MFIs/agents.

- Many of them maintain records and facilitate documentation with regard to KYC norms, to the best extent possible. However, this is where serious frauds and shortcomings occur.

# Chapter 27: Safeguards against Notorious Broker Agents: A Consumer Protection and Regulatory Imperative

- They disburse and collect on behalf of the MFIs whose field level contacts are limited to the agent and her associates. Hence, MFIs often do not know the last mile end-user clients as the e-mails, given earlier in the book,[418] clearly indicate.

*Compensation:* Initially, the center leader (agent) gets the incentive of a higher or additional loan—with passage of time, the center leader slowly begins to understand the importance of the crucial role she plays and is slowly able to extract more monetary payment, which also includes larger loans for some of her colleagues, out of which she takes a straight cut. As she gets more clients and disburses more loans, she begins to talk a new language—payment per loan (irrespective of size). Over time, this gets converted to a commission per loan (which makes her payment proportionate to the loan size). Therefore, perverse incentives can be found at even the grassroots in Indian microfinance.

When agents reach this level of seniority, they do everything—from KYC (Know Your Customer) documentation to recovery and remittance at the MFI branch. Such agents also take a cut/fee (from clients) on loans disbursed. Therefore, in reality, they get monetary payments from MFIs as well as clients. As they service both MFIs/clients, they are often called broker agents in the decentralized microfinance contract. When center leaders take an agent's cut from the loan to the client, the effective interest rate to the client shoots up. Sometimes, they also mark up the interest rate and this is one of the major reasons as to why there could be a difference in the nominal and effective interest rates stated by MFIs on paper and those observed in practice on the ground—a remark that many industry stakeholders have made in the past.

*Credit risk and problems:* While the credit risk may not seem huge, it nonetheless remains—there is very little that the MFI can do to tackle the agents, in case they renege on their implicit /informal contracts. This aspect gets exacerbated by the fact that the MFI rarely knows the end-user clients. It is the lure of greater wealth (through larger portfolio growth) and promise of future incentives that perhaps keep these kinds of agents under check. This apart, I have seen several other problems in the center leader agent model:

- Ghost/*benami* clients with money taken entirely by the center leader and used for various purposes including (local level) money lending. The MFI money is thus re-lent through a separate money-lending operation.

- I have also seen the case of real clients who part with some amount of their loan (a proportion), which is then used by the center leaders for various purposes ranging from money lending to own

---

[418] Refer to Chapter 20 on Code of Conduct Assessments.

consumption as well as working capital for other businesses (liquor, etc.) that the center leaders could be running locally. The extra money could also be got by enhancing the loan amount and giving the correct loan amount to the clients with the balance being pocketed by the center leaders (again observed a lot in the field among MFIs that took margin money from clients in order to pay the deposit of 10% to SIDBI and other lenders).[419]

- A third possibility is to provide larger loans to clients, using names of several small clients. This is something that happens despite regulations recommending a loan ceiling size of Rs. 50,000 (as was the case before the MCR). In fact, this is exactly what happened with much of the multiple lending as well. The credit risks in this are huge because several clients are (falsely) assessed for smaller loan amounts each, when in reality all the money is going as one large loan to a single client (on several fictitious client names) who may not have the capacity to service such a large debt.

- I have seen cases where the center leaders and staff collude and take a much higher loan and disburse the required amount to the clients and then divide the balance amount among themselves.

Let me reiterate here that center leaders, as agents, are engaged in activities similar to what they were originally doing along with branch staff and that has been the real secret behind the burgeoning growth of (much of) Indian microfinance prior to the 2010 AP crisis. However, there appears to be one major difference—when pushed to doing it independently (as agents), there have been no checks and balances on these center leaders and that is where the seeds of the 2010 AP crisis were initially sown.

If the center leader acting as the (independent) agent caused significant havoc in the field, the negative impact of the second agent model—where a "local political member" acts as the agent—has been even greater. The key relationships in the "local political member as an agent model" are shown in Figure 27.2.

---

[419] When SIDBI and/or lenders had the practice of asking MFIs to deposit 10% of the loan taken by MFIs in a special account.

# Chapter 27: Safeguards against Notorious Broker Agents: A Consumer Protection and Regulatory Imperative

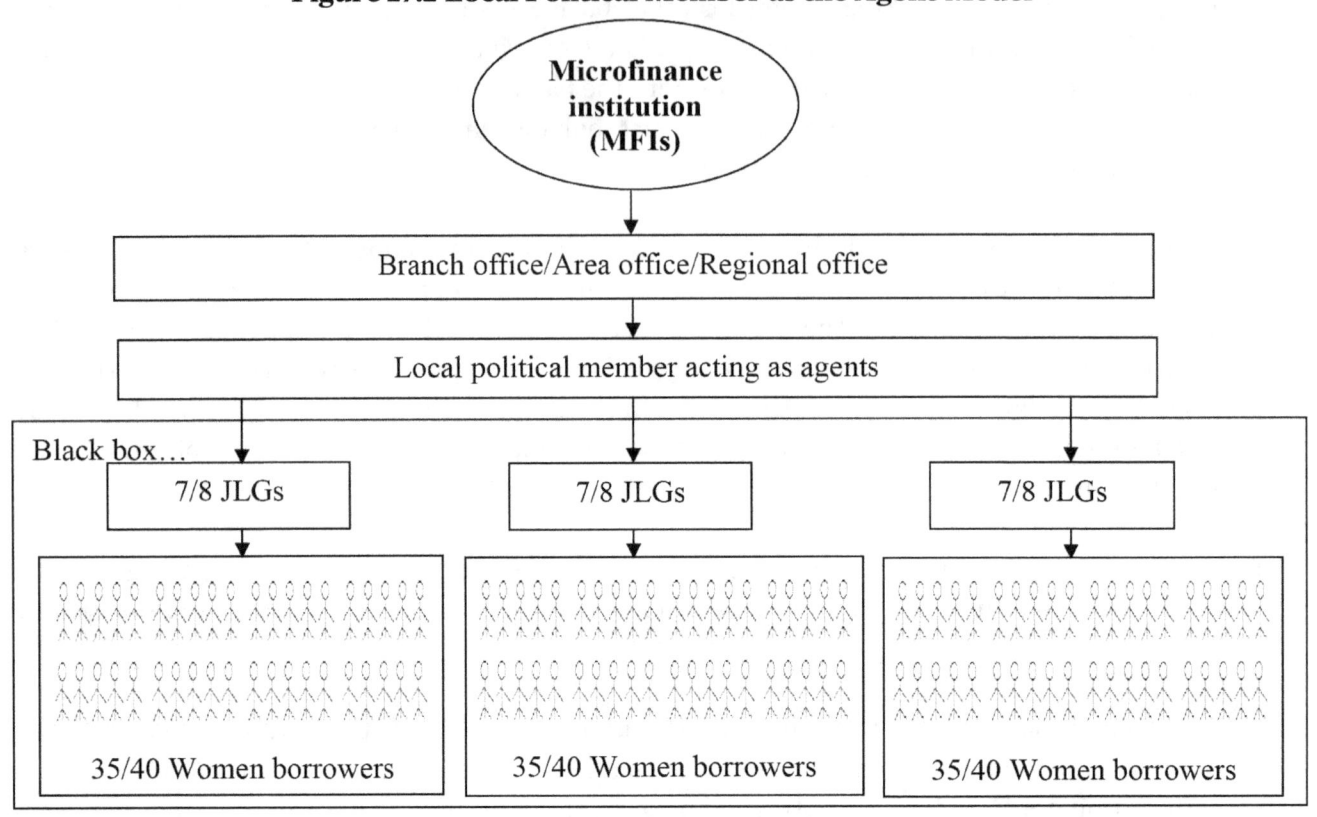

Figure 27.2 Local Political Member as the Agent Model

*Agent's background:* Typically, such agents are members of a political party. Alternatively, they could be organizers for local politicians.

*Clout:* These agents derive their clout mainly from local organizing of people for political and related work. They have extreme familiarity with the local political/social milieu and also possess tremendous contacts with the local politicians and officials. They have an excellent and well-entrenched local network comprising the village administrative officers, tehsildars, and/or other revenue officials. Thus, their muscle power and contacts with local politicians (and village administrators) give them strong clout in their respective areas.

*Type and structure of agent model:* Not much is known about the detailed structure of this agent model as much of it is a black box as shown in Figure 27.2. This agent model is totally decentralized and the MFI only knows the agent as the last mile. End-user clients are rarely known and records may not even exist, let alone be inspected. A lot of KYC violations would occur here and the agent assumes responsibility for completing KYC documentation, using local educated people, often youth including own children or relatives. There is very little control that the MFI has over this kind of agent. Under this model, a lump sum amount is given to the agent to disburse as microfinance loans, and, in return, names, identity proof, and other required documentation are collected by the MFI.

*Roles:* Loan disbursement and collections are done mainly by the agent's own staff/helpers (who are toughies). Such agents initially started to work with MFIs. Later, they graduated to working with the SHGBLP and other government programs (became of their vast political/administrative contacts). This agent is also a good conduit for channeling local (illegal) money into microfinance.

*Agent compensation:* This agent marks up on interest as well as charges a flat fee to quicken the loan disbursement process. In addition, the agents have as their return the money gained by deploying/rotating (microfinance) funds in their own business, which also includes emergency money lending (at exorbitant rates of interest).

*Credit risk:* The credit risk is huge as the agents carry enormous power and there is very little that the MFIs can do to tackle such agents in case they renege on their implicit/informal contractual obligations. Getting into a relationship with such agents is a recipe for medium-/long-term disaster, as many MFIs found out during the 2010 AP crisis.

*Other issues:* Several issues are critical here and must be noted from a regulatory/supervisory perspective:

- The balance of power here is almost always in the agent's favor and he/she controls the local activity.

- Often, the agent claims to disburse at a very fast pace and this burgeoning portfolio growth could result in failures of established systems at higher levels of the MFI.

- Also, the complete decentralization in this model often causes deviation from prescribed credit policy and results in fraud, error, or manipulation—and much of it is unknown to the MFI.

- Weak integration of information systems at the MFI level may not even permit MFIs to recognize problems associated with this agent model.

- There is great difficulty in maintaining portfolio information when the agent is of this kind and has complete control. Much of the data is what is provided by the agents, who have helpers/assistants (including former group/center leaders) aiding them to fabricate data.

- The mandate of efficiency and the desire (for lesser controls, procedures, information and supervision) to reduce costs—both of which can help lower interest rates—seem to have prompted MFIs to go in for this model initially, which later proved to be a bane for many of them.

# Chapter 27: Safeguards against Notorious Broker Agents: A Consumer Protection and Regulatory Imperative

- The last mile is the agent and the MFI will not know who the actual clients are, and any attempt to do so will be taken as a serious loss of face for the local political agent—the end result being loss of money for the MFI and an effective ban on its working in the area(s)/villages(s).

- If the agent were to abscond, the MFI will not know who its final clients were. Nor would the clients know who the MFI is—because, as noted earlier, if the MFI tries to promote itself in the villages/localities, it will alienate its agent.

- Also, if other MFIs come in, the agent will usually play one against the other and/or even start representing the other MFIs as well. The branch staff of the first MFI will rarely be in a position to object and they may not even know of it.

- If the agent is not able to keep the repayments coming, the branch staff advance her a fresh loan to avoid default (which could expose the distortions at the grassroots). Thus, restructuring (rescheduling and refinancing) of delinquent amounts is an often-used strategy to camouflage portfolio quality and keep this model going.

- Finally, this agent plays a huge role in transferring money during electioneering—something that the Election Commission had woken up to in recent times. It may be worth noting that huge consignments of cash were confiscated from two major MFIs in Tamil Nadu during the last assembly elections in 2011—while some of this was genuine microfinance money, much of it was (supposedly) money meant for distribution to candidates of some political parties.

Thus, without any doubt, agents caused problems on the ground. However, there is no escaping the fact that these problems were exacerbated by a weak[420] internal audit department in many MFIs. Such departments often reported to senior and/or line management, who had very little incentive to hear about systemic flaws in operations that they managed and oversaw—this is the classic conflict of interest problem. Rarely have I seen internal audit departments report to the board (as they should) and this conflict of interest in reporting to the CEO or COO has often prevented their effective functioning. I know of an internal auditor who quit a growing MFI (it is one of the largest MFIs in India currently) when he came to know that the very mistakes that he had uncovered in the field had (in fact) been sanctioned by his seniors. This is a real incident that happened in 2005–2006 in Andhra Pradesh during the Krishna crisis.

Therefore, with very little internal audits (in real time), many of the MFIs took a more withdrawn approach to grassroots functioning in their quest for growth and greater efficiencies—this can be seen from the fact that case loads for MFI loan officers increased very significantly from the 200/300 clients range per loan officer to sometimes as high as 600/900 clients. In other words, the center leader and

---

420 See Chapter 19.

other types of agents took the decentralized model to its extreme, and this led to several problems such as multiple, over and ghost lending, coercive repayments, diversion of funds, and the like.

In fact, on the basis of my interaction with various types of agents and especially the center-leader-turned agents, I think I have understood the evolutionary process that (first) led to the use of agents in Indian microfinance. I attempt to describe these here for the wider benefit of various stakeholders, including those who are developing the regulatory architecture for microfinance in India.

*Desire of many MFIs to rapidly build scale:* First, at least initially, the desire to use center leaders as agents seems to have emanated from the desire of MFIs to build scale quickly in the delivery of microfinance services to low-income people. And many MFIs got carried away and did not give a second thought to the kind of impact that these agents could have in the long run. As one MFI staff put it, *"We wanted to disburse several crores[421] of rupees on a daily basis and there was a lot of pressure from the senior management and also bankers/equity investors. We were told that if we show exponentially increasing disbursements, we would be able to attract more equity capital (at higher valuations) and also go in for a large-scale IPO. Of course, stock options had by then become the standard way of compensating staff and this skewed the incentives all the more...."*

*Consistent pressure on MFIs to reduce interest rates:* A second reason seems to be related to the (consistent) pressure to reduce interest rates from several quarters.[422] As I have always been saying, *servicing the last mile is costly in microfinance and any attempts to force interest rate reductions will cut out important controls and may even incentivize MFIs to adopt short cuts.* And that is exactly what seems to have happened. The drive for artificial interest rate reductions and the constant pressure on MFIs to achieve this appears to have resulted in several things: (i) omission of important client-level and other controls at the last mile; (ii) the proliferation and use of the decentralized model in its ultimate form—the agent-led model of microfinance; (iii) further reduction in engagement with client (which was a significant one even in the original Grameen model adapted for its use in India); and (iv) several other aspects that favored complete decentralization of microfinance operations.

*Adoption of the profit/value maximization syndrome by many MFIs:* A third reason appears to be the preoccupation of many (NBFC) MFIs with the efficiency and value maximization syndrome—as part of the commercial microfinance movement over the past several years—where cost leadership (at scale), profit maximization, and shareholder value enhancement became the order of the day, courtesy equity investors and others including bankers. According to a senior manager at an MFI, *"We started to look at ways to increase case load of staff significantly and this meant that we reduced the duration of center meetings (through process mapping and other such techniques), where we conducted these meetings directly. Then, we realized that we could do better by outsourcing center meetings with some quality checks and that is how*

---

421 1 US $ = 46 rupees in 2010 and 10 million rupees = 1 crore.
422 Led by policy makers and administrators.

# Chapter 27: Safeguards against Notorious Broker Agents: A Consumer Protection and Regulatory Imperative

*the center leader agent model came into being. As these efforts expanded, in some cases we faced serious delinquency problems and to counter that in an effective manner, we used local opinion leaders and these strong women later became agents themselves. And then, there was no real exit for us. Loan after loan had to be made and as long as the problems did not show up, we were just not bothered. The use of agents was soon picked up by many MFIs and, in fact, that used to be the strongest and fastest route to build scale and have the rapid burgeoning growth that the global microfinance industry desired of Indian microfinance. Multiple lending and high indebtedness became natural phenomena in the agent-led commercial model of Indian microfinance."*

Thus, while there could be other reasons for use of agents, these aspects of "building scale quickly," the "pressure to reduce interest rates," and the "desire to be a cost leader and maximize profits and share values" look like the major ones that seem to have pushed the Indian microfinance industry to *using agents (through a decentralized model) in a big way.*

To summarize, without question, there has been increasing (widespread) evidence[423] with regard to the use of agents in Indian microfinance. However, the industry and key stakeholders have continued to be in *denial* mode, often *pretending* that there was nothing wrong—until, of course, the 2010 AP microfinance crisis erupted and the cat was finally out of the bag.

I hope that the stakeholders developing the regulatory architecture take these ground realities into consideration while finalizing the same. Specifically, safeguards would be needed in the regulatory architecture to ensure that use of agents by MFIs is completely prohibited under the new regulatory framework being developed.

Therefore, it would be useful if the regulatory architecture being developed comes up with a concrete proposal for banning the use of agents (in totality) under a proper legal framework. Allowing agents to operate under an *ad hoc,* unclear (regulatory) framework (or even no framework at all) is bound to be disastrous, as can be seen from the 2010 AP microfinance crisis. This is one of the most pressing issues in customer protection (in microfinance) that needs to be addressed with utmost urgency.[424]

---

423 Rozas and Krishnaswamy 2011; Microfinance Focus 2011; Srinivasan 2010; Thorat and Arunachalam 2005b, and several others.

424 I am not confident that the RBI can address the agent issue effectively because it is often far removed from the real microfinance action on the ground.

# Chapter 28:
# Does the RBI have the Capacity to Regulate and Supervise Microfinance in India?

As noted earlier, without any doubt, it is clear that regulatory failure has played an important role in the disorderly growth of MFIs, which, in turn, resulted in the 2010 AP microfinance crisis. This is looked at in detail in this chapter, as MFIDRB[425] (2012) is part of the regulatory architecture being developed and also because MFIDRB (2012) has proposed the RBI as the sole regulator/supervisor for all of microfinance in India!

*First, let us look at the substantive aspects related to the MFIDRB (2012). There are five major reasons for (having) a bill like the MFIDRB (2012), which was under the consideration of the PSCF (Parliamentary Standing Committee on Finance):*

1. To provide legitimacy and a proper regulatory framework to MFIs *and others involved in delivery of financial services to low-income people* (*legitimacy for microfinance institutions and players*);

2. To ensure that MFIs indeed satisfy the broader objectives for which they have come into being (in the first place) and also that they operate and function in a sound and legal manner, in accordance with norms and standards required of such (pro-poor financial) institutions. This would also involve ensuring that MFIs don't operate like moneylenders (*regulation and supervision of microfinance institutions and players*);

3. To protect clients from MFI bad practices like coercive repayment, abusive interest rates, fraudulent products and the like (*protection of microfinance clients*);

4. To protect MFIs that operate legally and correctly from usury laws (*protection of microfinance institutions*);

5. To prevent crisis situations like what happened in AP in 2010 (*systemic impact and influence on socio-economic milieu and credit culture*).

---

425 The MFIDRB was introduced in the Lok Sabha in May 2012 and has been referred to the PSCF.

## Chapter 28: Does the RBI have the Capacity to Regulate and Supervise Microfinance in India?

*What will the MFIDRB (2012) be able to achieve in its current form?*

1. The MFIDRB (2012) certainly will address the aspect of providing legitimacy to MFIs.

2. It will also protect MFIs from State Usury Laws!

3. However, it will not be able to ensure that MFIs operate in a sound and legal manner.

4. It will also not be able to protect the MFI clients from abusive practices.

5. In short, it will not be able to prevent crisis situations like the 2010 AP crisis—where banks and MFIs lost significant (public) money including deposits *(all priority sector loans come from public deposits)*, the credit culture was destroyed and clients (who had once been financially included) were excluded from the larger financial system as no one would lend to defaulters marked as such in the credit bureau.

That said, should the MFIDRB (2012) protect *all MFIs* from "state-level" usury laws? Clearly, as all of you would agree, only those MFIs that operate within the ambit of the law must be (so) protected:

- MFIs that engage in multiple, successive, and/or ghost lending and/or use coercive recovery practices must (surely) not be legitimized; and

- Likewise, those institutions that have improper governance and fraudulent systems must not be protected.

What is worrying here is that the MFIDRB (2012) does not appear to have the ability to distinguish MFIs that operate legally from those MFIs that: (i) engage in multiple, over- and ghost lending; (ii) have bad governance; (iii) use coercive recovery methods; (iv) adopt abusive practices; (v) engage in frauds; (vi) use the decentralized agent model which has many weaknesses; and (vii) lack proper systems including MIS, internal control, internal audits, and so on.

Further, the aspects of regulation and supervision of MFIs (in terms of the real and specific provisions) are not known, as much of it is to be outlined at a later date. This is a very dangerous aspect and a bill like MFIDRB (2012) cannot be loosely structured (as is presently the case).

Also, the mechanisms for client protection and grievance redressal (including self-regulation) are not adequate. Self regulation has never worked in microfinance as the past experiences have *repeatedly* shown—be it the Krishna 2006 AP crisis, 2009 Kolar Crisis, 2010 AP crisis and thereafter. In fact, previous chapters[426] talk clearly about the lack of accountability of SROs like MFIN and Sa-Dhan. And the track record—of Sa-Dhan and MFIN—amply demonstrates their ineffectiveness as SROs as they did not take any action against many of their own member MFIs involved in abusive client practices. And given that representatives of these

---
426 See Chapters 20 and 21 of this book.

member MFIs who committed frauds (like Sahayata Microfinance's former MD, Mr Ajay Verma) themselves sat on the board of SROs like MFIN, expecting the (unofficial) SRO to act against other errant member MFIs (or the black sheep) seems an unrealistic and impractical one. Thus, as the experience of many countries has shown, self regulation in microfinance cannot and will not work. This needs strong emphasis again!

Also, permitting thrift by the MFIs would be a recipe for disaster. Rather than that, if MFIs want to offer savings, they would need to enhance their systems and governance and then apply to RBI to become full-fledged banks.[427] Given the burgeoning frauds and also the increasing use of the decentralized agent model (that caused the 2010 AP crisis in the first place), under no circumstances should thrift be permitted. If MFIs are allowed to offer savings, I am sure that frauds and failures will become even more frequent and the hard earned money of the poor would be lost. Therefore, savings or thrift should not be permitted by the MFIDRB (2012) as MFIs neither have the internal control nor internal audit systems required to safely manage peoples' savings. And, the lessons from the 2010 AP crisis clearly articulate that. So, in the light of these and also given the lack of a clear national microfinance policy guiding its overall strategy and implementation, the MFIDRB (2012) is indeed hugely incomplete. I hope that the PSCF takes note of these aspects and ensures that these are redressed, before the bill is passed.

*Second, specifically, the MFIDRB (2012) proposes under Section 24 (1)[428] the several functions and powers of the RBI.* Further, on the aspect of RBI as the sole regulator/supervisor of Indian microfinance, there are serious concerns, as the following discussion will illustrate. Specifically, the MFIDRB (2012) proposes under Section 24 (1)[429] the following as functions and powers of the RBI.

> "24. (1) The Reserve Bank shall regulate, promote and ensure orderly growth of the micro finance institutions and take measures as it deems fit, for the purpose of promoting financial inclusion through such institutions.
>
> (2) Without prejudice to the generality of the foregoing provisions contained in sub-section (1), the powers and functions shall include—
>
> (*a*) grant of certificate of registration to the applicant micro finance institution under section 15 or cancellation of such certificate under section 16;
>
> (*b*) making of schemes for the orderly growth of the micro finance services provided by micro finance institutions so as to ensure greater transparency, effective management and good governance in an efficient manner;
>
> (*c*) specifying the maximum limit of the margin and the annual percentage rate to be charged by the micro finance institution for providing micro credit facilities to its clients;

---

427 Bandhan and Janalakshmi have applied for a banking license in 2013.
428 *Source*: The Microfinance Institutions (Development and Regulation) Bill, 2012.
429 *Source*: The Microfinance Institutions (Development and Regulation) Bill, 2012.

(d) specifying the sector related benchmarks and performance standards pertaining to methods of operation, fair and reasonable methods of recovery, management and governance including model codes for conduct of activities of micro finance institutions;

(e) facilitating the development of credit rating norms or rating norms for other purposes for micro finance institutions;

(f) specifying the form and manner of books of account to be maintained by micro finance institutions;

(g) specifying the form and manner of accounting of business operations of micro finance institutions and auditing standards relating thereto;

(h) calling for information and data from micro finance institutions for maintaining an appropriate database in the public domain relating to micro finance services and disseminating the same through a national dissemination network;

(i) constituting a Micro Finance Development Fund and to apply it for the purposes as provided in section 32;

(j) promoting development of micro finance institutions, engaged in micro finance services through training and capacity building measures;

(k) promoting customer education of all institutions engaged in micro finance services for greater awareness and for economic empowerment of micro finance clients;

(l) supporting research, field research, documentation and dissemination thereof relating to micro finance sector;

(m) coordinating with other agencies for orderly growth and development of institutions engaged in the micro finance services;

(n) documenting and disseminating information relating to best practices with a view to ensuring provision of micro finance services at an affordable cost to eligible clients; and

(o) perform such other functions as may be prescribed."

These are huge tasks and certainly merit a close analysis of the RBI's capacity, especially in the light of what happened in AP in 2010. Admittedly, while the MFIDRB (2012) says that the Reserve Bank can either do it directly and/or delegate these to other institutions, several key questions arise: (i) how are these tasks to be structured at the RBI (assuming that they would be done by RBI in the first place); (ii) does the RBI have sufficient capacity to effectively and efficiently manage the various tasks including supervision, which requires a significant local presence; and (iii) in case the RBI delegates these tasks, what about the alternative institution and its capabilities with regard to these tasks including supervision?

The rationale behind asking these questions is that a regulatory/supervisory system is more efficient if the responsibilities are assigned to the institutions/bodies that have the *powers, resources, skills, and knowledge to perform their roles most effectively*. If one uses such a framework of analysis (as given in Box 28.1), the assets of various institutions that are candidates for regulation/supervision of microfinance in India should be compared as they pertain to the required regulatory and supervisory activities. This is a critical exercise and must be done objectively by the various stakeholders (including the PSCF), even as they evaluate RBI's capacity to act as the sole regulator and supervisor for Indian microfinance. A related key question here is whether the said institutions/bodies can obtain sufficient skills, resources, and capacity to undertake the regulatory/supervisory responsibilities effectively. And if sufficient capacity neither exists nor can be developed, then building a regulatory structure that relies on such institutions will not yield the desired result. Maybe a new institution will have to be created. These are aspects that the various stakeholders involved in developing the regulatory architecture—for microfinance—will have to consider as they make recommendations on the MFIDRB, 2012.

---

**Box 28.1 Evaluating RBI's Capacity to be Sole Regulator and Supervisor of Microfinance in India**

The following factors should be considered, while evaluating RBI's capacity:
- *Legal jurisdictions:* Which institution has the legal jurisdiction to make rules and to supervise the microfinance industry players involved—especially, given their diverse and varied legal forms?
- *Power, authority, and local presence:* Which body has the power and authority to investigate, discipline, and impose effective sanctions on the microfinance industry players involved?
- *Conflicts of interest:* Do significant conflicts of interest arise/exist? Conflicts of interest always exist in regulatory systems, but vary depending on the type of regulation and institution involved. There are obvious trade-offs and these need to be evaluated objectively.
- *Existing regulatory mechanism as a platform:* Is there an existing regulatory institution that can serve as a foundation for the proposed microfinance regulatory system? Has it been effective in the past and can it be used as a platform for the future? If not, should a new institution be established to regulate/supervise microfinance?
- *Industry specific knowledge, skills, experience, and data:* Who possesses the knowledge, expertise, and skills required to regulate and supervise microfinance? Which institution has access to the information and data needed for the task of regulation and supervision? Which body has the necessary tools (including information technology tools) for the complex task of microfinance regulation/supervision?
- *Resources including finance:* Last, but not the least, which institution has the funding and resources to do an effective job in terms of regulating and supervising Indian microfinance in an enabling manner?

# Chapter 28: Does the RBI have the Capacity to Regulate and Supervise Microfinance in India?

Having set the context, let us now look at regulatory/supervisory issues from the 2010 AP microfinance crisis using the specific examples of NBFC MFIs and banks [with regard to their priority sector lending (PSL) microfinance portfolio]. While doing so we raise the important question of *whether the RBI and its concerned departments indeed have the wherewithal to ensure the effective implementation of the various provisions of the MFIDRB (2012).*

But before that, let us understand some basic issues with regard to Indian microfinance.

The dominant MFI model in India is the commercial model, where the MFI is registered as an NBFC with the RBI and taps commercial funding (debt and equity) through different means. This model is based on fast-tracked growth and generally carries a standard loan product—delivered to clients through joint liability groups and/or agents—based on weekly repayments and having (mandatory) loan-related insurance. The emphasis is on efficiency, standardized processes, large outreach, and enhanced profitability—all elements of hardcore commercialization, strongly supported by international agencies such as the CGAP.

While there could be some modifications to this model to suit different contexts, the description is true, by and large, of most NBFC MFIs. The dominant NBFC MFI model is also based on the notion that to reach and include a vast number of unreached and excluded people (including the poor), MFIs must tap commercial funding in a big way from lenders and investors—Mr Vijay Mahajan's[430] statement to this effect, when SKS was to tap the capital markets, resounds in memory. To do this successfully, the model also believes that commensurate (market) returns must be provided to the commercial investors. It is important to note that much of the basic tenets of this (commercial) model have evolved from the global development of new wave microfinance—which was spearheaded by several stakeholders including the CGAP, since 1997.[431]

A critical point to be noted is that the fastest growing MFIs, which contributed to the 2010 AP microfinance crisis situation, were primarily NBFCs that came under the *purview of the Department of Non-Bank Supervision (DNBS), RBI*. These NBFC MFIs grew at a phenomenal rate, adding several million clients and dollars to their gross loan portfolio over the period April 2008 to March 2010. The following basic facts are discernible from the data given in the earlier part of the book[432]:

- *Thirteen of the top 14 MFIs (ranked on the basis of active clients and gross loan portfolio added from April 2008 to March 2010) are NBFCs.*

- *All the 13 NBFC MFIs (including the six large AP-headquartered NBFC MFIs) are supposed to file quarterly papers with the Department of Non-Bank Supervision (RBI), as part of the NBFC regulations vide circulars issued by the RBI.*

---

430 Mr Vijay Mahajan is Chairman, BASIX. He was Chairman at MFIN previously. He has also served as Chair, Executive Committee, CGAP.
431 This is a description of the commercial model as I understand it.
432 Chapters 4, 5, 6 and 7.

- Six of them are AP-headquartered NBFC MFIs and they constitute the largest chunk within this group of 13 NBFC MFIs. A total of *9.76 million clients were added by these six large AP-headquartered NBFC MFIs from April 2008 to March 2010*, whereas the eight other state MFIs (seven NBFCs + one Trust) added just 4.52 million clients (this is less than 50% of the outreach of AP-headquartered NBFC MFIs).

- *Likewise, these six large AP-headquartered NBFC MFIs increased their gross loan portfolio by US$ 1.912[433] billion* during the period (April 2008–March 2010), whereas the eight other state NBFC (seven NBFCs + one Trust) recorded a growth of just US$ 701 million (which is about a little more than one-third of the gross loan portfolio added by the six large AP-headquartered NBFCs).

*Among the top six large AP-headquartered MFIs, the phenomenal growth spurt was specifically <u>led</u> by five large AP-headquartered NBFC MFIs (SKS, Spandana, Share, Basix, and Asmitha), who between themselves added US$ 1.884[434] billion and 9.59 million clients between April 2008 and March 2010—which is very significant.*

In rupee terms, this is equivalent to each of these five large AP-headquartered NBFC MFIs adding a gross loan portfolio of Rs. 72.22 crore[435] per month, *month on month, quarter after quarter, year on year for the 24 months in question*. Likewise, in numerical terms, this is equivalent to each of these five large AP-headquartered NBFC MFIs adding almost 79,916 clients every month, *quarter on quarter, year on year for the 2 years in question—April 2008 to March 2010*. This translates to adding about 2664 (fresh) active clients every day, *month after month, quarter on quarter, year after year for the 2 years in question*. This is indeed a huge task by any standards!

And as shown in Box 28.2, the Department of Non-Bank Supervision (RBI) is supposed to closely supervise every NBFC that has a loan portfolio of over Rs. 100 crore. In fact, in the past, it has taken many MFIs several years to reach the figure of 50,000 clients and/or portfolio size of Rs. 50 crore, which is why the RBI probably specified that NBFCs with an asset size greater than Rs. 100 crore as important and had implied that they need to be closely supervised.

---

433 This should have been higher at US$ 2.076 billion had the Mix Market retained the original GLP figures that it had put out in 2010/2011 for BASIX and SHARE. For some reason, Mix Market changed its original figures for BASIX and SHARE respectively from US$ 223,229,799 and US$ 490,923,201 to US$ 172,484,946 and US$ 376,593,362 (as on date). I have the original print screen data and other pieces of evidence with regard to the original data put out by Mix Market. There are several other issues with the Mix Market database and I can provide the details if required.

434 This should have been higher at US$ 2.049 billion had the Mix Market retained the original GLP figures that it had put out in 2010/2011 for BASIX and SHARE. For some reason, Mix Market changed its original figures for BASIX and SHARE respectively from US$ 223,229,799 and US$ 490,923,201 to US$ 172,484,946 and US$ 376,593,362 (as on date). I have the original print screen data and other pieces of evidence with regard to the original data put out by Mix Market. There are several other issues with the Mix Market database and I can provide the details if required.

435 Rs. 1 crore = Rs. 10 million and exchange rate assumed is Rs. 46 per dollar. This should have been higher at Rs. 78 crores had the Mix Market retained the original GLP figures that it had put out in 2010/2011 for BASIX and SHARE. For some reason, Mix Market changed its original figures for BASIX and SHARE respectively from US$ 223,229,799 and US$ 490,923,201 to US$ 172,484,946 and US$ 376,593,362 (as on date). I have the original print screen data and other pieces of evidence with regard to the original data put out by Mix Market. There are several other issues with the Mix Market database and I can provide the details if required.

# Chapter 28: Does the RBI have the Capacity to Regulate and Supervise Microfinance in India?

---

**Box 28.2 Off-site Monitoring and Surveillance System and On-site Inspection for Non-Banking Financial Companies**

"Off-site surveillance of NBFCs involves scrutiny of various statutory returns (quarterly/half yearly/annual), balance sheets, profit and loss accounts, auditors' reports, etc. A format for conducting the off-site surveillance of the companies with asset size of Rs.100 crore and above has also been devised.

The system of on-site examination is structured on the basis of CAMELS approach and the same is akin to the supervisory model adopted for the banking system. A comprehensive Inspection Manual has been brought out for the use of Inspecting Officers. Appropriate supervisory framework, wherever necessary with the assistance of external chartered accountant firms, has been evolved for on-site inspection of all NBFCs...."

Source: http://www.rbi.org.in/scripts/PublicationsView.aspx?id=2545

---

Now let us refocus on the portfolio growth in the years preceding the 2010 AP crisis. It can be clearly seen from the data given earlier that each of the five AP-headquartered NBFCs MFIs[436] were adding the equivalent of almost 72% of the threshold portfolio value of Rs. 100 crore-specified by the RBI for special monitoring—every month, *quarter on quarter, year after year for the 2 years in question (April 2008 to March 2010). And it should also be noted that bulk of the loans for this turbocharged growth (by the NBFCs) came through the priority sector lending (PSL) route of commercial banks and term loans from DFIs such as SIDBI.*

This being the case, the above-mentioned trends should have grabbed the attention of everyone, let alone the concerned departments at RBI. However, for some strange reason, it perhaps did not grab their attention. This aspect needs to be carefully noted by the various stakeholders[437] (involved in developing the regulatory architecture for microfinance) as it indicates a serious flaw in the existing NBFC and Commercial Bank/DFI supervision activity by the concerned departments at the RBI. There are several issues here and each of these is highlighted sequentially.

*The key question here is whether this huge and unnatural growth of the NBFC MFIs (especially the five large AP-headquartered MFIs)—quarter on quarter during the period April 2008–March 2010—raised any alarms within the Department of Non-Bank Supervision, RBI, especially with regard to the following:*

- What was the motivation of these NBFC MFIs to grow at this never before seen pace?

---

436 SKS, SPANDANA, SHARE, ASMITHA and BASIX.
437 Including PSCF.

- How were they growing[438] in terms of market development strategies (client acquisition, etc.)?

- What was their business model and was it in accordance with the RBI NBFC regulations and the RBI code of conduct?

- Where and how were they getting the resources (debt, equity, etc.) for this burgeoning growth? Where exactly were these resources coming in from (India, abroad, etc.)? See *India Today*[439] (June 6, 2011, issue) which states that terrorist Dawood Ibrahim was involved in both secondary and primary equity markets under the guise of foreign institutional investors. Under these circumstances, I am sure it is important for the regulator/supervisor to know about the antecedents of the various foreign institutional investors. *Again, I am not sure whether the Department of Non-Bank Supervision was even aware of the burgeoning equity investments (including their antecedents) in Indian microfinance, especially during the years 2008–2010.*

- What was the likely impact of this burgeoning growth of consumption-oriented micro-credit on the low-income clients?

- Were the RBI NBFC and other codes of conduct being followed in letter and spirit? Did the NBFCs have the required governance and systems to manage this turbocharged growth without violating the laws of the land, both in letter and spirit?

- Was the required KYC documentation available?

At this juncture, it seems pertinent to look at what Dr Rangarajan and others have said about the business model of the NBFC MFIs and also apply the same to this analysis.

> "The business model of microfinance institutions is faulty. They must revisit the model to support the income earning ability of the borrower," Prime Minister's Economic Advisory Council Chairman Dr C. Rangarajan said at an event organized here by Skoch Consultancy. Rangarajan said multiple lending done by MFIs is inconsistent with the very repayment capacity of borrower. He said MFIs have been indulging in multiple lending and large parts of the loans are given for consumption purposes and this model of business has landed them in trouble. "Income earning capacity must be criteria for granting

---

438  Green field client acquisition versus other strategies (including sharing of clients, takeover of SHGs/other MFI JLGs, etc.), market skimming (first-time loans to new clients), financial deepening/multiple lending to older clients and several other strategies.
439  The House of Dawood, by *India Today*, June 6, 2011.

## Chapter 28: Does the RBI have the Capacity to Regulate and Supervise Microfinance in India?

loans... The provision of credit for consumption must be a small part of the total loan," Rangarajan said.[440]

Others have tended to argue for the same and I reproduce a quote from Dr Al Fernandez's post on the CGAP blog. As Mr. Fernandez argued:

"The State of the Sector report 2010 (N. Srinivasan) indicates that out of 60 MFIs which reported on profitability, six had ROAs over 7%; thirty five had ROAs over 2%. In contrast the public sector banks in 2009 had average ROAs of 0.6% with the best being 1.6%, while the best private bank had ROAs of 2%. The yield on portfolio confirms this picture; in the case of 23 MFIs it was above 30% (the highest being 41.29%). The report also says that economies of scale have not led to lower interest rates or lower yields. This implies that MFIs maximized their profits and competition did not decrease rates as it was expected to. The largest MFI recorded a 116% jump in net profit at Rupees 81 crores ($18 million) in the second quarter ending September 2010 as against the corresponding period last year."

The cornerstone of these arguments is essentially this and it must be noted carefully.

Many NBFC MFIs engaged in excessive and multiple lending for consumption purposes and often granted loans without assessing the loan absorption capacity of the clients. Implied in this statement is the fact that these NBFC MFIs pushed loans indiscriminately to low-income clients for consumption purposes without any sensitivity to their debt servicing ability and tried to grow (very fast) in this manner and make unnatural profits. And, it seems rather clear that these NBCF MFIs grew fast to attract capital at high valuations and, thereafter, had to justify these high valuations by providing better returns to investors. And investors likewise, as they had paid huge premiums, wanted to recover their investment fast and hence were also pushing the MFIs to grow faster. Hence, as shown in Figure 28.1, there appears to have been a mutually reinforcing cycle of multiple/over/ghost lending, fast growth, high profits, very high share valuations, equity investments along with granting of significant sweat equity to promoters, faster growth, greater profits, more returns, turbocharged growth, and so on.

---

440  Source: Quoted from http://economictimes.indiatimes.com/news/news-by-industry/banking/finance/finance/mfis-business-model-faulty-pm-panel/articleshow/7225090.cms

**Figure 28.1 Mutually Reinforcing Cycle of Growth Followed by Some MFIs**

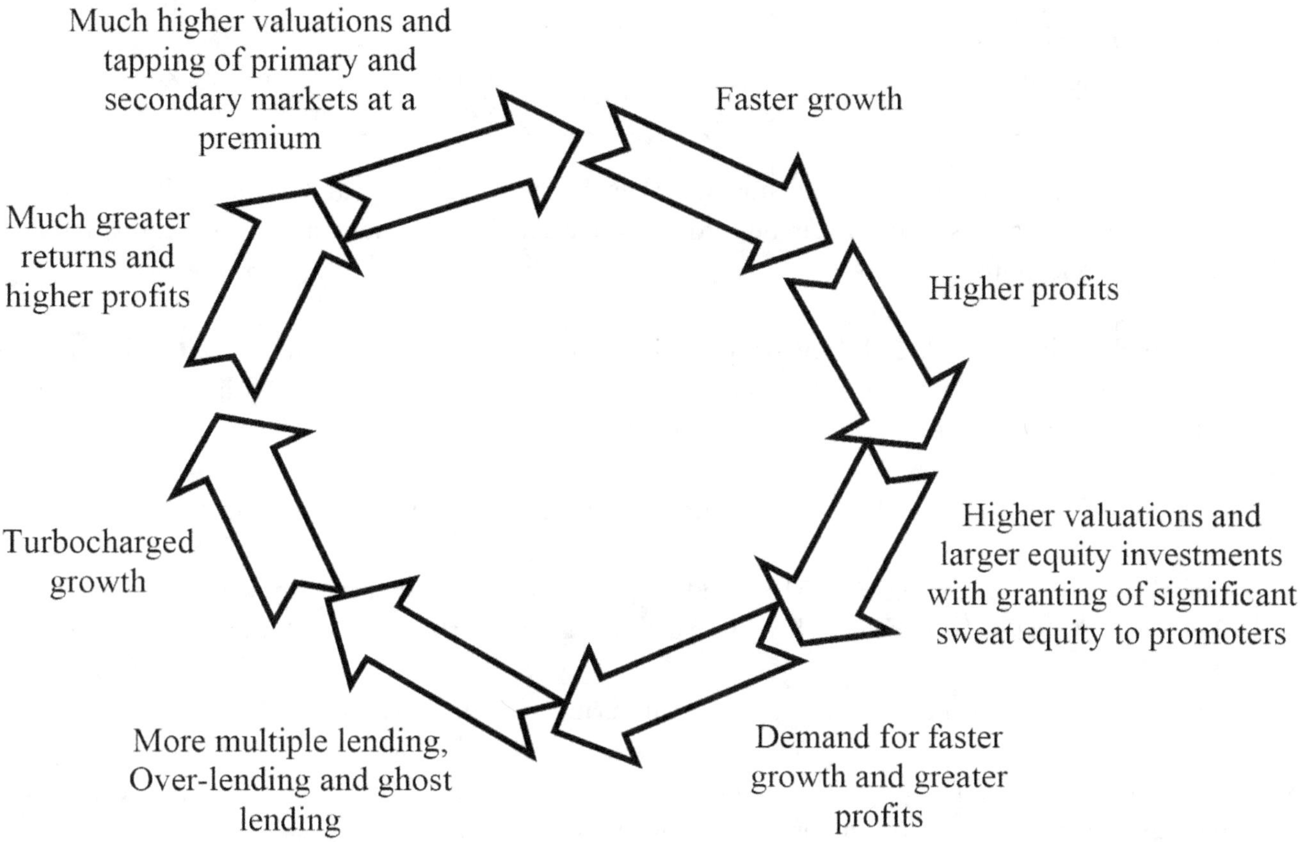

- Faster growth
- Higher profits
- Higher valuations and larger equity investments with granting of significant sweat equity to promoters
- Demand for faster growth and greater profits
- More multiple lending, Over-lending and ghost lending
- Turbocharged growth
- Much greater returns and higher profits
- Much higher valuations and tapping of primary and secondary markets at a premium

*Now, another key question here is whether the Department of Non-Bank Supervision at the RBI had spotted any of this?*

An important aspect deserves mention here. It is during this period (April 2008–March 2010) that the NBFC MFIs received equity worth several million dollars (Table 28.1) and this again should have been disclosed as per their filings with the RBI.

## Chapter 28: Does the RBI have the Capacity to Regulate and Supervise Microfinance in India?

| Table 28.1 Equity Investments in Indian MFIs Across Equity Leaders and Followers (US$ million) | | | |
|---|---|---|---|
| Years | Equity leader MFIs (6) | Equity followers (22) | Total |
| Before March 2007 | 32.51 | 0 | 32.51 |
| April 2007–March 2008 | 118.34 | 0 | 118.34 |
| April 2008–July 2010 | 398.40 | 130.23 | 528.63 |
| **Total** | **549.25** | **130.23** | **679.48** |

Given this data, it would be useful to know whether this unprecedented and sudden inflow of equity, into select NBFC MFIs, raised any alarm bells for the concerned department at RBI, especially in terms of the following questions.

- Why has there been a sudden inflow of equity into microfinance[441] and, that too, at a scale not seen before at all? What has made microfinance so attractive (as an asset class) to equity investors, especially during a period of serious global economic crisis?

- What kind of NBFC MFIs received this equity inflow, at what valuations, and why?

- Who was investing in these NBFC MFIs and what were their expectations in terms of returns, and so on? What returns, if any, did the investors actually get from these NBFC MFIs?

- Where was this equity money coming in from, in terms of countries and types of institutions?

- Was there anything abnormal with the operations of these NBFC MFIs in terms of growth, profits, earnings per share, and/or promoter and management compensation?

In fact, there is some very interesting data—on the last point with regard to these five AP-headquartered MFIs—in Intellecap's Inverting the Pyramid[442] report. As the Intellecap report[443] noted:

> "Indian MFIs are receiving the highest valuations in the world. A recent report by the Consultative Group to Assist the Poor (CGAP) and JP Morgan[444] shows that the median price to book value (P/BV) multiple is 5.9 in India, thrice that of global multiples. Some have been quick to call this "irrational exuberance" on the part of investors.

---

441 As Ms Naina Lal Kidwai is said to have argued at the Sa-Dhan March 2010 National Microfinance Conference and similarly, as Mr N. Srinivasan wrote in the State of the Sector Report (2010), we surely need to understand this phenomenon.
442 Inverting the Pyramid (Third Edition), Indian Microfinance Coming of Age, published by Intellecap (2010).
443 Inverting the Pyramid (Third Edition), Indian Microfinance Coming of Age, published by Intellecap (2010).
444 CGAP, JP Morgan, occasional paper: Microfinance Global Valuation Survey 2010, March 2010.

Analysis shows that while the leading large MFIs have been able to command very high premiums, valuations vary across the sector based on investor type, MFI class and stage of investment. The vast market potential, demonstrated growth of the sector and positive macro-economic outlook contribute to relatively higher valuations in India.

In addition, the number of investors (see below) chasing deals with the few large, high growth MFIs has driven up their valuations considerably. These MFIs are able to command valuations upwards of 10 times their projected profit after tax (PAT). Early stage MFIs are, on the other hand, typically valued lower, at between one and three times the book value[445]. Across the sector, the drivers of value are primarily growth and returns, both demonstrated and potential. Thus, to put Indian MFI valuations in perspective, it is instructive to compare the return on equity (RoE) and PAT growth of the leading MFIs with other financial service business, banks and NBFCs. As shown in Table 28.2,[446] leading MFIs outperformed Banks and NBFCs on both counts. On average, MFI RoE is 32.1%, a full 12 percentage points higher than that of Banks and NBFCs. MFI profits grew over three times that of the sample banks', and five times that of the sample NBFCs' between 2006 and 2009. The closest comparable, in this sample, to MFIs in terms of business model is Mannapuram General Finance,[447] as their clientele is similar to that of MFIs and loan sizes are relatively low (INR 20,000), although their loans are backed with collateral. Despite the company's RoE and PAT growth being lower than those of MFIs, its P/BV is at 8.4, higher than average for leading MFIs. Thus, given the enormous market potential; the ambition of leading Indian MFIs; and their demonstrated high growth, prudent cost management, and thus the high returns, the current valuation levels are not surprising."[448]

---

[445] Analysis by Intellecap in the report Inverting the Pyramid (Third Edition), Indian Microfinance Coming of Age, Published by Intellecap (2010).

[446] This table was numbered differently in the original Intellecap report. I just wanted to state that the table number has been changed in accordance with norms followed in this book. The data remain the same, as originally quoted in the Intellecap report referred to.

[447] A listed NBFC that provides gold and vehicle loans, amongst other services.

[448] Inverting the Pyramid (Third Edition), Indian Microfinance Coming of Age, published by Intellecap (2010).

## Chapter 28: Does the RBI have the Capacity to Regulate and Supervise Microfinance in India?

| Table 28.2 ROE, PAT Growth and P/BV of Leading MFIs, Banks and NBFCs | | | | |
|---|---|---|---|---|
| Type of institution | ROE (%) (2009) | PAT CAGR (%) 2006–2009 | PAT growth (%) 2008–2009 | P/BV (2009) |
| **MFI** | | | | |
| SKS | 18.30 | 466 | 382 | |
| Spandana | 44.60 | 102 | 234 | |
| Share | 37.60 | 99 | 795 | 5–7 |
| Basix | 17.80 | 79 | 118 | |
| Asmitha | 37.10 | 111 | 408 | |
| Average | 31.08 | 171 | 387 | |
| **Select listed banks** | | | | |
| Axis Bank | 19.10 | 55.30 | 69.50 | 3.9 |
| Yes Bank | 20.60 | 76.60 | 51.50 | 5.3 |
| HDFC Bank | 17.20 | 37.10 | 41.10 | 5.3 |
| Average | 19.00 | 56 | 54 | 4.8 |
| **Select listed NBFCs** | | | | |
| Mahindra Finance | 15.40 | 25.70 | 21.20 | 2.4 |
| Shriram City Union Finance | 20.20 | 14.00 | 33.60 | 3.1 |
| Sundaram Finance | 13.70 | −4.00 | −29.10 | 1.7 |
| Mannapuram General Finance and Leasing | 23.20 | 97.20 | 44.40 | 8.4 |
| **Average** | **18.20** | **33.20** | **17.50** | **3.9** |
| Source: Intellecap | | | | |

This makes it very clear that one of the major reasons for the NBFC MFIs (especially, the five large AP NBFC MFIs) to grow, in the manner that they did, was to show abnormal profitability in a short span of time, thereby attract huge amounts of capital at higher valuations, and finally move toward tapping the primary market. With increasing sweat equity and abundant availability of stock options to senior management, board, and staff members, it is also clear that the real motive (for this turbocharged growth) was not financial inclusion but rather the building of greater wealth for investors, senior management, staff, board members, shareholders and all others, except clients.[449] The fact that many of these (NBFC) MFIs used the MBT route to first capitalize their NBFCs and then simply got rid of (or reduced) the client ownership is clear proof of the fact that everyone's interest—other than that of clients—was put first. This is a classic case of the NBFC MFIs putting the clients last. Even in the case of SKSML, the clients were not allowed to 'cash in' prior to the IPO, whereas most others including the founder, senior management, board members, and staff did so.

*Again, the key question here is whether the Department of Non-Bank Supervision (DNBS) at the RBI spotted (any) of this?*

---

[449] Refer to: (i) Commercialization of Microfinance in India: A Discussion of the Emperor's Apparel by Prof. M. S. Sriram, *Economic and Political Weekly* (EPW), June 12, 2010—Vol: XLV No: 24; (ii) Commercialization of Microfinance in India: A Discussion on the Emperor's Apparel by Prof. M. S. Sriram, W.P. No. 2010-03-04, March 2010; (iii) Share Microfin MD takes home Rs. 7.4 crore, more than double HDFC Bank MD's salary by John Samuel Raja D. & M. Rajshekhar, *The Economic Times*, February 1, 2011; (iv) Microfinance at a Crossroads—The Need for Social Equity by Jan Postmus, unpublished paper (2010); (v) More to SKS script than meets the eye, by M. Rajshekhar and M. Anand, *The Economic Times*, October 8, 2010; and (vi) SKS Microfinance: Promoters got the better of poor women borrowers, by John Samuel Raja D. and M. Rajshekhar, *The Economic Times*, January 31, 2011.

- Did returns by NBFC MFIs show unusual trends with regard to microfinance asset growth? Was there any cause to believe that growth in microfinance assets had occurred through multiple lending, over-lending and/or ghost lending? Had any of the institutions provided interest-free loans from their PSL funds to their promoters, senior management, and/or board members? If so, for what purposes?

In fact, questions such as these should have been raised by the RBI. Even an iota of interest from the concerned departments at the RBI (and/or any of their local offices) in cautioning the (NBFC) MFIs could have, perhaps, prevented the 2010 AP crisis (or at least mitigated the damage, to a large measure). That it did not happen is something that should be carefully noted.

Therefore, it is imperative that the stakeholders looking into the MFIDRB (2012) take proper note of the regulatory and supervisory failures highlighted thus far. And much as the microfinance industry is a sunrise sector, as claimed by several industry experts, it is also a very sensitive area that requires careful handling from a client perspective. And this is especially true given the fact that MFIs are trying to sell what is perhaps the most attractive product on the face of this planet to a very vulnerable set of people.

It would also be interesting for the stakeholders involved in developing the regulatory architecture for microfinance, to look at whether the Department of Non-Bank Supervision and the RBI department that deals with supervising priority sector lending to banks (the DBOD plus Department of Banking Supervision) were in fact even talking to each other on something very unusual happening in the microfinance industry. In fact, these stakeholders should summon the heads of these departments at the RBI and also the highest supervisory authority in the country—the Central Board of Financial Supervision at the RBI—and ascertain the facts behind these serious lapses. All of these will certainly provide very valuable lessons for the design of future regulatory and supervisory arrangements, as part of MFIDRB (2012). Overall, I would like to sign off on this chapter with the following key questions:

1. Did the DNBS miss these (significant) trends? If so, why? What lessons can be learnt from this with regard to structuring of regulatory/supervisory arrangements for microfinance in the future, especially in the context of the MFIDRB 2012?

2. Alternatively, having spotted these happenings in the first place, why did not the DNBS take necessary corrective action? Again, what lessons can be learnt from this with regard to structuring regulatory/supervisory arrangements for the future, especially given the MFIDRB 2012?

3. If the concerned RBI departments could not even monitor five large AP-headquartered NBFC MFIs that were supposedly systemically very important, then how can they be expected to set up

## Chapter 28: Does the RBI have the Capacity to Regulate and Supervise Microfinance in India?

a regulatory/supervisory mechanism that would need to oversee several hundred MFIs as per the MFIDRB 2012? Without sufficient supervision, the MFIDRB (2012) will *not* work as a regulatory mechanism on the ground!

4. Further, the MFIDRB (2012) clubs all of the MFIs together and this means that some several hundred (or even thousand) organizations (including cooperatives) may have to be regulated/supervised. Without any doubt, no single regulator/supervisor would be able to do this task effectively, especially without constructive support from the concerned state governments as effective supervision of microfinance definitely requires local clout and presence. This is a very important lesson from the 2010 AP crisis.

All these need to be considered by the relevant stakeholders providing recommendations with regard to the MFIDRB (2012).

To summarize, India is a great country for enacting many legislations but the implementation record of the same is rather poor in most cases. I hope that the same does not happen with the MFIDRB (2012). We certainly need the MFIDRB (2012) to provide legitimacy to the microfinance sector. However, we cannot stop with that. Rather than being a paper tiger, the MFIDRB (2012) should have the teeth and mechanisms to ensure orderly growth of the microfinance sector. For this, the most critical aspect would be to objectively analyze the regulatory/supervisory capacity of the RBI and evaluate it to see what needs to be done to ensure ground-level supervisory effectiveness. I do hope that sufficient attention is given to these critical issues by the stakeholders developing the regulatory architecture for microfinance. One further point—I have flagged critical issues and the objective here is not to undermine the capacity of the RBI or the good work being planned. *The objective, solely, is to assist in the development of enabling and effective regulatory and supervisory mechanisms that can work on the ground toward the benefit of large numbers of low-income people, who continue to lack access to* quality *financial services at the grassroots.*

Last but not the least, in my humble opinion, *neither the Reserve Bank of India nor, for that matter, any central institution can on its own undertake this task of effectively regulating and supervising MFIs as they do not have the necessary resources or the local presence.* And having seen the 2010 AP and other crisis situations in microfinance in India from very close quarters, I strongly believe that the following regulatory/supervisory arrangement would perhaps be most appropriate in the Indian context:

a. Prudential regulation/supervision for all types of MFIs should be under the RBI (or a specialized microfinance regulatory and supervisory authority), which can also confer on them the legitimacy to operate in the larger financial sector. Such regulation must ensure minimum standards on various parameters, including governance, risk management, compensation, internal controls, internal audits, MIS, and the like;

b. Capital market regulation/supervision of listed microfinance institutions (MFIs) should be under the oversight of the Securities and Exchange Board of India (SEBI); and

c. Consumer protection and grievance redressal mechanisms must be led by the respective state governments,[452] which are locally present and have the wherewithal to supervise microfinance operations on the ground.

Only such a multipronged approach to regulation/supervision of MFIs would be most effective from an implementation perspective.

---

[452] Not at the level of the district administration independently as has been currently proposed in the MFIDRB (2012) but rather at the level of the state government and using a proper coordination mechanism.

# Chapter 29:
# Should Not Microfinance Investment Vehicles Be Judged by the Same Standards Set for Retail MFIs?

It was the early 1980s and I happened to have a fascinating meeting with a fine gentleman (a noted British academic and practitioner) in the development sector and he said a lot of things that have stayed in my memory and I relate one such statement here—"it is ironic that we sit from where we do and preach to others on what they should do at the grassroots. And it becomes even more ironic when we do not practice what we preach."

Viewed in this context, governance, reporting, and transparency are three key words that I have heard a lot in the microfinance sector (from bilateral and multilateral donors, global funds, banks, investors, and others) over the past two decades and especially, in the past few years. At many conferences, I have heard these (high and mighty) stakeholders literally ram these ideas into the heads of MFI practitioners. While much of this has been mentioned globally with reference to retail microfinance institutions (MFIs), I think that the time has now come to apply the same yardstick to microfinance investment vehicles (MIVs) and all other stakeholders who invest in microfinance (be it multilateral agencies, bilateral donors, or others).

Without question, MIVs and other investors must subject themselves to the same scrutiny and standards that they expect of retail MFIs that they invest in. And you will appreciate this fact more when you read Hugh Sinclair's book, "Confessions of a Microfinance Heretic: How Microlending Lost Its Way and Betrayed the Poor."[453]

Sinclair essentially talks about the case of a few MIVs and other stakeholders who invested in LAPO despite knowing LAPO's serious limitations.[454] Indeed, MIVs and global banks had a lot of explaining to do with regard to why they invested in LAPO (in the first place) despite public domain material that pointed to serious weaknesses in the investee: (i) illegal collection of savings; (ii) inordinately high interest rates; (iii) an illegal loan product (perhaps) because illegal savings collection was a part of it; (iv) conflict of interest in terms of the auditor being related to the CEO and other such issues; (v) high levels of client desertion; (vi) lack of transparency with regard to data (which led to MicroRate's subsequent withdrawal of its rat-

---

453 *Confessions of a Microfinance Heretic: How Microlending Lost Its Way And Betrayed the Poor"* by Hugh Sinclair, (2012) published by Berrett-Koehler Publishers, Inc. (http://www.microfinancetransparency.com/).

454 See *Moneylife* article Why blame the MFIs alone? (http://www.moneylife.in/article/why-blame-the-mfis-alone/26994.html) by Ramesh S. Arunachalam, July 16, 2012.

ing); and (vii) poor governance among other things. Without any doubt, the sanctity of these MIVs having invested in LAPO can be questioned on the basis of evidence available in the public domain. And, sloppy due diligence (including inadequate scanning/reading of publicly available material) and/or short cuts adopted (cut paste presentation of credit proposals to different investors) may have resulted in this failure caused primarily by lack of appropriate systems, governance, and management at MIVs.

What is interesting is that some of the MIVs (like responsAbility) that invested in LAPO were LuxFLAG labeled but that hardly provides any comfort because when I tried to get to LuxFLAG[455] and look at whether any documents of responsAbility were available, I found none[456] for the specific period (when the investment in LAPO was made). So much for the labeling and associated comfort that it is said to provide with regard to MIV operations. And if you look at the Luminis database[457]—which is a good start to having publicly available information on MIVs, the pressure to invest may have been huge for responsAbility as shown in Exhibit 29.1.[458]

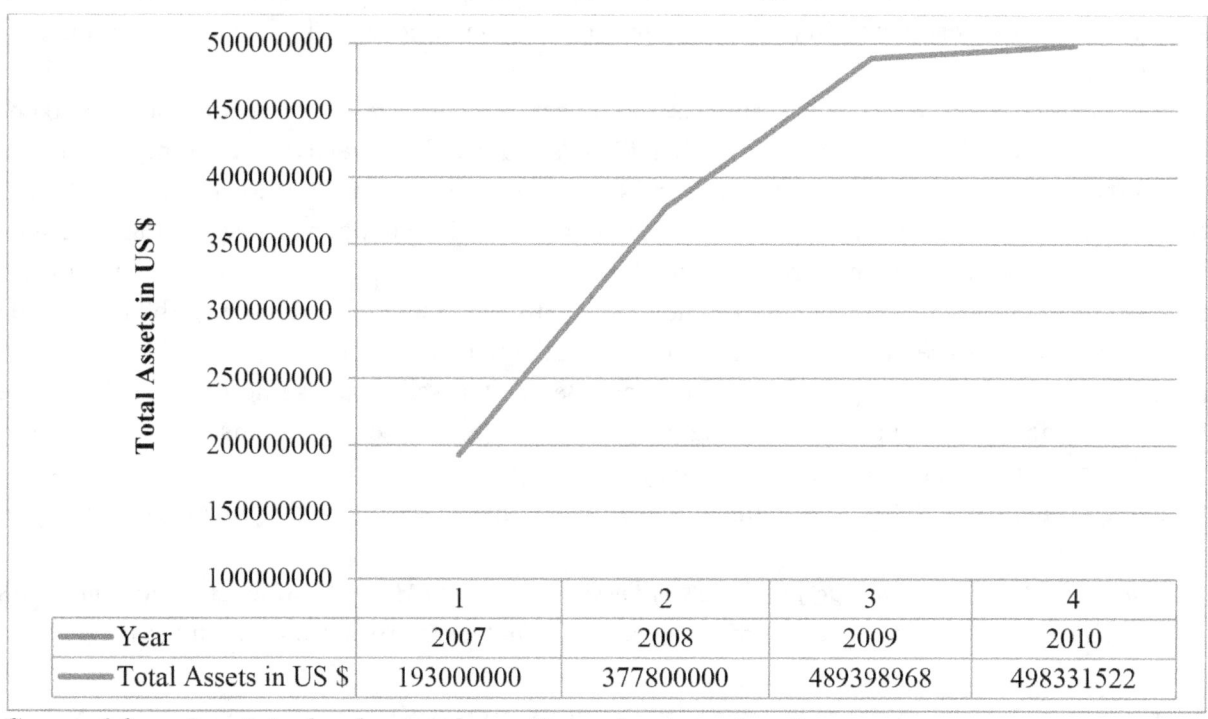

Exhibit 29.1 Asset Growth for Responsibility, 2007 to 2010

| | 1 | 2 | 3 | 4 |
|---|---|---|---|---|
| Year | 2007 | 2008 | 2009 | 2010 |
| Total Assets in US $ | 193000000 | 377800000 | 489398968 | 498331522 |

*Sourced from Luminis database at* https://www.luminismicrofinance.com

---

455  http://www.luxflag.org/

456  I can provide tangible evidence in this regard and I have print screens with regard to the non availability of all these specified reports that were shown as not found.

457  https://www.luminismicrofinance.com

458  Sourced from Luminis database at https://www.luminismicrofinance.com

# Chapter 29: Should Not Microfinance Investment Vehicles Be Judged by the Same Standards Set for Retail MFIs?

Much of the same argument goes for the Dexia Micro-Credit Fund (Blue Orchard Finance), which is another large LuxFlag-labeled MIV. Apart from LAPO, Blue Orchard invested in MFIs such as Sahayata Microfinance in India, whose operations did come under a cloud, especially after the 2010 Indian microfinance crisis.[459]

| Table 29.1 Dexia Micro-Credit Fund (Blue Orchard Finance) | | | | | |
|---|---|---|---|---|---|
| Investor | Investee | Region | Amount (USD) | Type | Date |
| Dexia Micro-Credit Fund (BlueOrchard Finance) | Sahayata | SA | 1,000,000 | Debt | August 2009 |

*Source: CGAP Microfinance Dealbook Quarterly Review—Third Quarter 2009, Page3, www.microcapital.org/downloads/Dealbook/Dealbook_3Q2009.pdf*

Blue Orchard's other investments in India are also of questionable nature, because they were made in MFI(s) that were directly linked to the *irresponsible and phenomenally high portfolio growth* that caused the 2010 AP microfinance crisis in the first place. Therefore, it appears that investments decisions of MIVs (such as responsAbility and Blue Orchard) need not necessarily be called responsible and accountable investing.

That is a critical point that needs emphasis and it certainly deserves the attention of key stakeholders in the global microfinance value chain—so that MIVs acquire the governance, systems, and management necessary to protect their primary investors. Some may argue that LuxFlag's attempt to certify MIVs is a step in that direction. Probably, yes, but a lot more needs to happen on the ground. And indeed, if the LuxFlag label is to be taken more seriously, we also need transparent and accountable information with regard to the entire process of certification—so that we can judge for ourselves the quality of *due diligence* applied prior to certification, information so collected, and so on.

Let us look at another example—that of Deutsche Bank. Deutsche Bank's microfinance investments certainly need good explaining by their management. This is because of the claims that the bank makes with regard to microfinance and microfinance investments.

In fact, commenting on Deutsche Bank's microfinance investments, Hugh Sinclair noted[460]:

> "Deutsche Bank has recently <u>acquired</u> 9.15% of the shares of Indian MFI SKS, which is a bank I question substantially in the book. It would be hard to defend any claim that Deutsche Bank were unaware of the claims

---

[459] See chapter on the Governance of Risk Management. Also refer to the following articles: (i) Award winning Sahayata Microfinance is the latest to go astray (http://moneylife.in/article/award-winning-sahayata-microfinance-is-the-latest-to-go-astray/21549.html), by Ramesh S. Arunachalam, November 18, 2011; and (ii) What is said at conferences is very different from what is implemented in practice (http://www.moneylife.in/article/what-is-said-at-conferences-is-very-different-from-what-is-implemented-in-practice/22124.html), by Ramesh S. Arunachalam, December 12, 2011.

[460] Does Sinclair's Open Challenge (to the Global Microfinance Industry) Make His Claims True? (http://microfinance-in-india.blogspot.in/2012/07/does-sinclairs-open-challenge-to-global.html); and Hugh Sinclair's Response to My Earlier Post – "Does Sinclair's Open Challenge (to the Global MicroFinance Industry) Make His Claims True?" (http://microfinance-in-india.blogspot.in/2012/08/hugh-sinclairs-response-to-my-earlier.html).

*about SKS given the adverse publicity the institution has received. Criticism involves the IPO process and personal enrichment of a few individuals and private investors; abusive debt-collection practices, leading to explicit mention in the SERP report regarding client suicides; and most recently, "massive problems" with their life insurance practices, amongst other criticisms. Deutsche presumably found such factors compatible with their ethical practices.*

*Therefore, I believe that there are genuine concerns about the role of Deutsche Bank in the battle to reduce poverty. I believe there are valid reasons to support the case that their due diligence is not as thorough as it could be. I believe there are fundamental contradictions between the claims made in the SMART Campaign (which Deutsche Bank endorse and support financially) and Deutsche Bank's subsequent actions. I believe that the MIVs are largely (not entirely) responsible for a significant part of the adverse activities of some of the less scrupulous MFIs globally, not simply in India, by providing fuel for the fire and turning convenient blind eyes when it suits them.*

*I also await a formal response from Deutsche Bank in this regard, and I would like to hear Asad Mahmood's defence of the claims made in this book, and his explanation of the recent SKS investment. I assumed they may be shaken into acting more ethically in response to the book, but in my personal opinion, the fact that they now invest in an institution such as SKS, and did so via a tax-efficient investing vehicle based in Mauritius, leads me to a personal conclusion:*

*There is little evidence of concern for the welfare of the poor; profit is the driving force (acquiring equity in SKS following a 90% fall in share price); and their actions are inconsistent either with the best wishes of the investors in their fund (assuming these wishes to be social impact rather than profit) or those of the poor. This is my personal opinion, others are free to disagree."*

What convinced me—that indeed what Hugh Sinclair has been saying may be a "correct" representation of the reality as far as investors like *Deutsche Bank* are concerned—was the investment by Deutsche Securities Mauritius in SKS Microfinance, India's only listed micro-lender. The investment that I am referring to was the purchase of shares worth Rs. 77.9 crore (US[461] $13.90 million) by Deutsche Securities Mauritius in SKS Microfinance. As the Bombay Stock Exchange (BSE) listed under "*Disclosures under SEBI (Substantial Acquisition of Shares and Takeovers) Regulations, 2011,*"[462] it is indeed true that Deutsche Securities Mauritius acquired (on 25 July 2012) through a QIP allotment, 9.5 million shares in SKS Microfinance. The original table from the BSE site is reproduced.

---

461  The exchange rate on 25 July, 2012 was Rs. 56.0465 = 1 US$. This would mean that the total investment was of the order of over US$ 13.90 million Source: http://www.oanda.com/currency/converter/). The RBI reference rate as on that day was Rs. 56.37.
462  http://beta.bseindia.com/corporates/Sast.aspx?scripcd=533228

# Chapter 29: Should Not Microfinance Investment Vehicles Be Judged by the Same Standards Set for Retail MFIs?

**Exhibit 29.2 Bombay Stock Exchange (BSE) and SKS Microfinance Private Limited**

| Scrip code | Scrip name | Name of acquirer/ seller | Promoter/ promoter group | Transaction period | Acq/ sale | Mode of buy/sale | No. of shares/ voting rights/ warrants transacted | | Holding after transaction | |
|---|---|---|---|---|---|---|---|---|---|---|
| | | | | | | | Quantity | Percentage | Quantity | Percentage (w.r.t total capital) |
| 533228 | SKS MICROFINANCE LTD | Deutsche Securities Mauritius Ltd | No | 25/07/2012 | ACQ | QIP allotment | 9500000 | 9.15 | 9500000 | 9.15 |

*This data was last updated on 8/3/2012 12:19:15 PM*

Source: BSE, *http://beta.bseindia.com/corporates/Sast.aspx?scripcd=533228*).

And a *Times of India* article[463] commenting on this transaction, observed:

> "Interestingly, Deutsche Securities Mauritius held 3.82% stake (27,61,174 shares) up to March 2012 but had exited the company during the April-June 2012 quarter as per shareholding data available on BSE. Deutsche Securities re-entered India's only listed MFI player through the QIP that was offered at a price of Rs 75.4 per share, a discount to the then prevailing stock price. CLSA (Mauritius) too has picked up 9.15% in SKS through the QIP and was allotted the stake last week. The QIP issue had opened on 12th July and closed on 17th July, with SKS mopping up a total of Rs 230 crore through the Rs 165 crore QIP issue.... SKS, which was once India's largest MFI player, has strapped for cash after it was plunged into losses by the AP MFI crisis that was triggered in mid October 2010... after a string of borrower suicides rocked the state due to the alleged strong arm tactics of MFI agents."

Now, what do we know about Deutsche Securities Mauritius? According to available secondary data in the Internet,[464] Deutsche Securities Mauritius is incorporated in Mauritius with Registration No. INMUFD175508 valid up to 06-JAN-2014. According to other information available across the Internet,[465] *Deutsche Securities Mauritius is said to operate as a subsidiary of a Singapore-based company called Deutsche Asia Pacific Holdings Pte Ltd.*

Deutsche Asia Pacific Holdings Pte Ltd, as a company, is said to engage in financial futures, options broking, stock broking, foreign exchange trading, and provision of related financial advisory services. Deutsche Asia Pacific Holdings Pte Ltd is said to have been formerly known by the name—"Deutsche Morgan Grenfell Asia Pacific Holdings Pte Ltd."

---

463 http://timesofindia.indiatimes.com/business/india-business/Deutsche-Securities-mops-up-9-15-in-SKS-via-QIP/articleshow/15169644.cms
464 http://www.sebi.gov.in/FIIIndex.jsp?fiiIndxName=D
465 http://investing.businessweek.com/research/stocks/private/snapshot.asp?privcapId=36660922

And going further up the ladder, we find that Deutsche Asia Pacific Holdings Pte Ltd is said to be operating as a subsidiary of DB Valoren S.à r.l, which in turn is said to be a Luxembourg-based company. And completing the circle, we find that DB Valoren S.à r.l. is said to operate as a subsidiary of Deutsche Bank AG. Refer Exhibit 29.3 which shows this relationship to Deutsche Bank AG clearly.

It becomes clear that the purchase of shares—of SKS Microfinance—was done by one of the key subsidiaries of Deutsche Bank AG. Therefore, this investment can certainty be described as an investment made by Deutsche Bank AG or the Deutsche Bank group.

**Exhibit 29.3 Deutsche Bank—Annual Report 2011**

| Deutsche Bank—Annual Report 2011 | |
|---|---|
| Significant subsidiaries of Deutsche Bank AG | |
| Subsidiary | Place of incorporation |
| Taunus Corporation[1] | Delaware, United States |
|    Deutsche Bank Trust Company Americas[2] | New York, United States |
|    Deutsche Bank Securities Inc.[3] | Delaware, United States |
| Deutsche Bank Luxembourg S.A.[4] | Luxembourg |
| Deutsche Bank Privat-und Geschäftskunden Aktiengesellschaft[5] | Frankfurt am Main, Germany |
| DB Finanz-Holding GmbH[6] | Frankfurt am Main, Germany |
| DB Valoren S.à.r.l.[7] | Luxembourg |
|    DB Equity S.à.r.l.[8] | Luxembourg |
|    Deutsche Postbank AG[9] | Bonn, Germany |
| [1]This company is a holding company for most of the Group's subsidiaries in the United States. Effective February 1, 2012, Taunus Corporation is no longer a holding company for Deutsche Bank Trust Company Americas, and Deutsche Bank Trust Corp. has become the top-level U.S. holding company through which Deutsche Bank Trust Company Americas is held. | |
| [2]Deutsche Bank Trust Company Americas is a New York State–chartered bank that originates loans and other forms of credit, accepts deposits, arranges financings, and provides numerous other commercial banking and financial services. | |
| [3]Deutsche Bank Securities Inc. is a U.S. SEC-registered broker dealer and is a member of the New York Stock Exchange and regulated by the Financial Industry Regulatory Authority. It is also regulated by the individual state securities authorities in the states in which it operates. | |
| [4]The primary business of this company comprises treasury and markets activities, especially as a major supplier of Euro liquidity for the Deutsche Bank Group. Further business activities are the international loan business, where the bank acts as lending office for continental Europe and as risk hub for the loan exposure management group, and private banking. | |
| [5]The company serves private individuals, affluent clients, and small business clients with banking products. | |
| [6]The company holds the majority stake in Deutsche Postbank AG. | |
| [7]This company is a holding company for Deutsche Bank subgroups in Australia, New Zealand, and Singapore. It is also the holding company for DB Equity S.à.r.l. | |
| [8]The company holds a part of the stake in Deutsche Postbank AG. | |
| [9]The business activities of this company and its subsidiaries comprise retail banking, business with corporate customers, capital markets activities, as well as home savings loans. | |
| Source: *https://annualreport.deutsche-bank.com/2011/ar/servicepages/downloads/files/dbfy2011_subsidiaries_db_ag.xls* | |

# Chapter 29: Should Not Microfinance Investment Vehicles Be Judged by the Same Standards Set for Retail MFIs?

*You may wonder why all this fuss? Alternatively, you may ask what are the key issues concerning this investment made by Deutsche Bank?* Read the following news items and it will become clearer.

First, according to a news item in *The Hindu Business Line*[466] (May 22, 2012):

*"'We have found massive problems in insurance operations of SKS Microfinance', J Hari Narayan, chairman, Insurance Regulatory and Development Authority, told Business Line. IRDA teams conducted field enquires and inspections for a long time, he said. The irregularities included receiving the cheques of death claims from its insurers on its name, which is illegal. The only listed MFI in the country, based out of Hyderabad, had also 'collected' higher commissions than permitted by the insurance regulator while selling the insurance policies."*

Second, according to a news item in *Moneylife* article[467] (July 27, 2012):

*"SKS Microfinance has said that some of its employees have cheated the company to the tune of Rs15.8 crore in the last financial year, reports PTI. The services of employees involved have been terminated and the company has written off over Rs14 crore. The auditors of the company have reported that there was cash embezzlement by the employees to the tune of Rs2.5 crore and loans given to non-existent borrowers was Rs13.3 crore, the micro lender said in its annual report"*

I am not sure that anyone would invest in a company that has been directly accused (of having massive problems in their insurance operations) by no less a person than the (then) chairman of a major regulatory authority covering insurance operations in India. And for the record, J. Hari Narayan, (the then) chairman, Insurance Regulatory and Development Authority (IRDA), is a well-respected (professional) regulator. That apart, investing in a company that self-admits increasing ghost clients and frauds[468] in its operations is again a very serious matter.[469]

And coming in the backdrop of the (now) famous LAPO (Nigeria) case—where Deutsch Bank's Community Development Finance Group (CDFG) lent money to the MFI despite publicly available information with regard to illegal savings collection and intermediation by the same MFI and presence of several other serious weaknesses in the same MFI's operations—*Deutsche Bank's microfinance investments certainly need good explaining by their management.* This is because of the claims that Deutsche Bank makes with regard to microfinance and microfinance investments:

---

[466] *Source:* Quoted from http://www.thehindubusinessline.com/industry-and-economy/banking/article3446545.ece
[467] *Source:* Quoted from http://www.moneylife.in/article/sks-microfinance-employees-swindle-rs158-crore/27247.html. The *Moneylife* article was based on the SKS annual report and therefore the annual report must have been released earlier than the date of the news item.
[468] See Chapter 18 on Governance of Risk Management.
[469] See Chapters 8, 9, and 10 for other issues covering SKS.

"Deutsche Bank was the first global bank to establish a socially motivated microfinance fund more than a decade ago. Our activities in the microfinance sector are led by the Community Development Finance Group as part of the Bank's overall Corporate Social Responsibility commitment. We provide loans, investments and limited philanthropic grants to the microfinance sector towards the goal of enabling the poor throughout the developing world to access credit for self-employment as a poverty alleviation strategy. We have served over 120 microfinance institutions (MFIs) in 50 countries over the last decade, with $215.5 million in capital benefitting as many as 2.8 million poor entrepreneurs. **While India is one of the largest potential markets for microfinance, Deutsche Bank currently does not have any loans to microfinance institutions there due to the rapid commercialization of the sector and concerns with pricing of the loans to poor clients.**

Deutsche Bank is not active in the microfinance sector as a commercial activity to realize financial gains for the bank. However, Deutsche Bank recognizes that the success of microfinance depends upon its ability to utilize business discipline and financial techniques to achieve the goal of scale and sustainability in serving the financial needs of the un-banked poor. Deutsche Bank has developed social scorecards through which it judges the social intentions and the extent of social framework of MFIs in its underwriting. **Deutsche Bank's MFI clients must meet standards of good governance, transparency, and interest rates that are reasonable within the country and regional context.**"[470]

Thus, whether it is the huge investment in SKS (an MFI under fire from the regulators and having increasing ghost clients/frauds as per its own admittance[471]) to supporting the illegal operations of LAPO[472] (Nigeria) some years ago and attempting to cover up the same (Mr Asad Mahmood tried to do so as per Hugh Sinclair's book and related communication),[473] *Deutsche Bank* has an immense amount of explaining to do. And going by the same transparency principle (that *Deutsche Bank claims to have helped create for MFIs*), it is time that Deutsche Bank comes clean on its global microfinance investment story! And for the record, I must clarify that despite several e-mails to Asad Mahmood, the public face of the Community Development Finance Group (CDFG) at Deutsche Bank, there has been no reply whatsoever till date from him.[474]

---

470  https://www.db.com/usa/content/en/1077.html

471  See Chapters 8, 9, 10, and 12 for more issues concerning SKS.

472  See the following articles in this regard: Why blame the MFIs alone? (http://www.moneylife.in/article/why-blame-the-mfis-alone/26994.html) by Ramesh S Arunachalam, July 16, 2012; Should not microfinance investment vehicles be judged by the same standards set for retail MFIs? (http://www.moneylife.in/article/should-not-microfinance-investment-vehicles-be-judged-by-the-same-standards-set-for-retail-mfis/27041.html) by Ramesh S Arunachalam, July 17, 2012; and Does Sinclair's open challenge to the global microfinance industry make his claims true? (http://www.moneylife.in/article/does-sinclairs-open-challenge-to-the-global-microfinance-industry-make-his-claims-true/27106.html) by Ramesh S Arunachalam, July 20, 2012.

473  See the following articles in this regard: Does Sinclair's open challenge to the global microfinance industry make his claims true? (http://www.moneylife.in/article/does-sinclairs-open-challenge-to-the-global-microfinance-industry-make-his-claims-true/27106.html) by Ramesh S Arunachalam, July 20, 2012.

474  See the following articles in this regard: Does Sinclair's open challenge to the global microfinance industry make his claims true?) (http://www.moneylife.in/article/does-sinclairs-open-challenge-to-the-global-microfinance-industry-make-his-claims-true/27106.html)

# Chapter 29: Should Not Microfinance Investment Vehicles Be Judged by the Same Standards Set for Retail MFIs?

Some of the key questions that Deutsche Bank would need to provide answers to include (but are not limited to) the following:

a. Why did Deutsche Bank invest in SKS at a time when even the regulator (chairperson, IRDA) saw massive problems with its (insurance) operations?

b. How could Deutsche Bank invest in SKS despite admittance by the company to presence of increasing ghost clients and frauds in its microfinance operations?

c. How did Deutsche Bank invest in an Indian MFI when it (publicly claimed and) thought it unfit to even lend money to Indian MFIs? Please see statement reproduced from Deutsche Bank's website:— *"While India is one of the largest potential markets for microfinance, Deutsche Bank currently does not have any loans to microfinance institutions there due to the rapid commercialization of the sector and concerns with pricing of the loans to poor clients."*[475]

d. The Deutsche Bank website notes that, *"Deutsche Bank's MFI clients must meet standards of good governance, transparency, and interest rates that are reasonable within the country and regional context."* If that was the norm, then how did Deutsche Bank invest in LAPO (Nigeria), which, according to public domain information, suffered from several weaknesses: (i) illegal collection and intermediation of savings; (ii) inordinately high interest rates touching 144% under specific situations; (iii) an illegal loan product (perhaps) because illegal savings collection was a part of it; (iv) conflict of interest in terms of the auditor being related to the CEO and other such issues; (v) high levels of client desertion; (vi) lack of transparency with regard to data (which led to MicroRate's subsequent withdrawal of its rating); and (vii) poor governance among other things.

e. Who coordinates the various Deutsche Bank investments in microfinance? According to their *Focus* magazine, it is the Community Development Finance Group (CDFG) that coordinates this! If so, how did the CDFG recommend SKS Microfinance despite the various ongoing problems? At least, should not have Deutsche Bank waited until the enquiry by the regulator was over?

f. And last but not the least, why did the same Deutsche Securities Mauritius sell off its stake in SKS Microfinance just some months before (according to the *Economic Times*[476] as well as filings with the BSE) and then again buy back SKS Microfinance shares and sell the same to RBS and others subsequently?

---

by Ramesh S Arunachalam, July 20, 2012.
475 https://www.db.com/usa/content/en/1077.html
476 http://articles.economictimes.indiatimes.com/2012-07-26/news/32869385_1_sks-microfinance-deutsche-securities-stake

g. See Table 29.2 that shows huge profit (Rs. 41.39 crore[477] in just about 2 months) generated by Deutsche Bank from the SKS transactions. Making a profit of Rs. 41.39 crores in 2 months (on Rs. 71.3 crores of investment) translates to an annualized return of around 347%. This is certainly not banking for the poor as Table 29.2 suggests. I am not sure that all that Deutsche Bank says on its web page regarding the concern the poor alone drove it to engage in such a transaction and, especially, in an MFI that had been caught in significant controversy. I am inclined to go with the view that profit was the primary motive for Deutsche Bank rather than the mumbo jumbo of financial inclusion, access to finance, and the like. In fact, the transaction runs counter to what is said on Deutsch Bank's website—*"Deutsche Bank is not active in the microfinance sector as a commercial activity to realize financial gains for the bank."*[478]

| Table 29.2 Deutsch Bank SKS Transactions and Profit Generated Therein | | | | | | | |
|---|---|---|---|---|---|---|---|
| Seller | Buyer | Type of Transaction | Action | Date | Number of SKS shares | Price per share (in Rs.) | Total (in Rs. crores) |
| SKSML | Deutsche Bank | QIP | Bought | July 26, 2012 | 9,500,000 | 75.4 | 71.63 |
| Deutsche Bank | Royal Bank of Scotland | Open market | Sold | September 25, 2012 | 5,000,000 | 117.15 | 58.575 |
| Deutsche Bank | Morgan Stanley | Open market | Sold | September 27, 2012 | 4,500,000 | 121 | 54.45 |

In short, for me, Hugh Sinclair's book[479] was indeed a revelation about how MIVs and other institutional investors operate in the international supply chain of delivering financial services to low-income people. And after reading the book and looking at the behavior of other investors like Deutsch Bank, I am left searching for answers to questions such as (but not limited to) the following:

a. How do MIVs make investment decisions? What systems do they have to ensure that the pressure to lend/invest does *not* result in poor investment? Should not MIVs have minimum governance standards and internal audit requirements just as *retail* MFIs do?

b. How do MIVs protect the overall interest of their primary investors? What systems do they have to ensure this in real time? What else may be necessary given the experiences narrated in this chapter and also several incidents given in Hugh Sinclair's book?

c. What standards of governance, transparency, and reporting are MIVs currently subject to? Who sets these standards and who enforces them? How adequate are these?

---

477 This is indeed a huge sum of money anywhere in the world.
478 https://www.db.com/usa/content/en/1077.html. Print screens of the same are available!
479 *"Confessions of a Microfinance Heretic: How Microlending Lost Its Way And Betrayed the Poor"* by Hugh Sinclair, 2012, Berrett-Koehler Publishers, Inc. (http://www.microfinancetransparency.com/).

# Chapter 29: Should Not Microfinance Investment Vehicles Be Judged by the Same Standards Set for Retail MFIs?

d. Given the huge diversity in legal form, location (of incorporation), and products, what can be said about the regulation and supervision of MIVs in an overall sense? And specifically, who regulates these MIVs? Who supervises them? What is the role of central banks in all of this? Does this regulation/supervision afford any protection to the primary investors in these MIVs? And what about the accountability of MIVs to the low-income (poor) people of the world, for whose benefit they supposedly operate?

e. Last but not the least comes the question of whether there is any regulatory arbitrage with regard to MIV operations. That is a key issue.

I do hope that the stakeholders developing the regulatory architecture for microfinance in India and elsewhere and bodies like CGAP, a prime mover in the global microfinance industry, play a constructive role by looking at issues such as the above and facilitating the necessary changes on the ground with regard to MIV operations. And if that happens, we would have made a significant difference to the practice of responsible microfinance globally. Accordingly, the aspect of responsible and accountable investing by MIVs is dealt with in Chapters 30, 31, and 32. While Chapters 30 and 31 focus on what—external stakeholders—regulators and supervisors can do to enable this on the ground, Chapter 32 looks at how institutional stakeholders can use the internal control system to ensure that an MIV's investments are responsible and accountable from a diverse perspective.

# Chapter 30:
# Understanding the Role of MIVs in Microfinance: An Urgent Task for Central Banks and Regulators in Recipient (Host) Countries

The microfinance crisis of 2010 in AP underlines the urgent need for greater understanding (in India) of microfinance investment vehicles (MIVs) and their operations. In fact, ever since I read Hugh Sinclair's book,[480] I have been intrigued by the MIV phenomenon. And true to my nature, I started some research on MIVs using the Luminis[481] database. While the database is a good start to getting information on MIVs, however, even there, I found little information on specifics regarding regulation/supervision of these MIVs. In fact, as I searched around, I realized that there is very little credible information on how (many of these) MIVs are regulated and supervised in real time.

And this indeed becomes a matter of concern when you consider the fact that a very significant number of MIVs[482] (almost as many as 64) are incorporated in Luxemburg (45), Mauritius (8), and Cayman Islands (11). Likewise, among the developed nations, the highest number of MIVs can be found in the United States (30), the Netherlands (12), Canada (6) and Belgium (6) among others. It must also be noted with interest that there are very few MIVs incorporated in large microfinance markets like India. What needs to be appreciated here is the fact that most of the MIVs have registered domicile in countries that offer little potential for microfinance—in very broad terms, over 75% of the MIVs are registered in (home) countries that have very little microfinancing in the first place. Whether this is a case of regulatory arbitrage is a question that begs an answer.

This apart, it should be noted that MIVs have been incorporated as very diverse legal entities and this again raises the aspect of regulatory arbitrage. Therefore, without any doubt, the onus is perhaps on the regulators in the recipient countries to understand from where exactly is the (foreign) money

---

480 *"Confessions of a Microfinance Heretic: How Microlending Lost Its Way And Betrayed the Poor"* by Hugh Sinclair, 2012, Berrett-Koehler Publishers, Inc. (http://www.microfinancetransparency.com/)

481 I do believe that there are more MIVs than those listed in the Luminis database (https://www.luminismicrofinance.com).

482 Source: https://www.luminismicrofinance.com

flowing into the microfinance sector (in their respective countries) along with the motivations for such investment.

In fact, during the Indian microfinance crisis, I realized that India's central bank (Reserve Bank of India), to the best of my knowledge, did not have (in one place) all the requisite information with regard to foreign equity and debt flow into the Indian microfinance sector. And as I have previously mentioned, (and as Mix Market has so eloquently put it), it is the *unique* combination of significant equity flows (and debt funds) from abroad with local banking funds and their subsequent and continuous investment as "microfinance loan assets" that created the perfect storm for the 2010 AP microfinance crisis. It is precisely against this that regulators have to guard against globally.

So, what needs to be done in tangible terms by regulators in host (recipient) and home countries?

First, in the recipient (host) countries there must be a regulatory focal point for foreign investment (debt and equity) flows into microfinance. When this information is dispersed and scattered, it becomes rather difficult to gauge what is happening, what the key trends are in terms of MIVs who are investing, which MFIs attract significant investments and why, and so on. Therefore, it is imperative that in every recipient country, a designated authority[483] becomes fully aware of foreign debt and equity investment into their MFIs. And for this to happen in real time, the designated institutions must allocate specific staff (team or unit) to focus on this. In countries like India that have a huge untapped microfinance market, this may entail significant resources.

Second, the primary work of this team (or unit) should be to help *create a reliable and valid database with regard to foreign investments (equity and debt) in microfinance*. Such a database, apart from providing statistical information on foreign fund flows, should also help answer questions such as (but not limited to) the following:

a. Which MIVs (or investors) are putting money into the (local) microfinance sector? Why?

b. What are the MIV's antecedents in terms of ownership, governance, and management? What is their primary motivation for operating in microfinance? What is the reason for registering the MIV in a specific place (home country)? What are the implications for microfinance in the host (recipient) countries?

c. Which MFIs have received the maximum inflow and why? Is there anything unusual with regard to their model that attracts foreign investment?

d. What impact will these investments have on the microfinance in the host country—in terms of over indebtedness and related client protection issues?

---

[483] It could be the central bank or a specialized regulator for microfinance.

Third, whenever the potential for regulatory arbitrage exists, balanced coordination among regulators is necessary and this needs to be achieved across home and host countries. Together, the regulators would need to look at and understand issues such as (but not limited to) the following:

a. Who (in the home country) regulates and supervises the various MIVs that have significant investments in the various host (recipient) countries?

b. What does regulation of these MIVs mean? Is it effective in terms of ensuring safety of investor funds? Does it ensure good governance and prudent management at the MIVs?

c. Does regulation subject MIVs to minimum standards in governance, management, and systems, and are these adhered to and followed in practice? Are there key issues with regard to ownership, governance, and management at MIVs that need attention?

d. What about minimum requirements for reporting and disclosure by MIVs to their regulators?

e. What about supervision of MIVs? Are there on-site and off-site mechanisms? How effective are these?

f. Plus other questions.

The Bank for International Settlements (BIS) could perhaps be entrusted with this enormous task—of helping to create a coordination mechanism among central banks as well as facilitating the establishment of a framework for regulating/supervising MIVs globally—as they have the ability, expertise, and objectivity to create such a mechanism/framework.

To summarize, some may argue that understanding MIVs and their operations is not important but looking at what happened in India in 2010,[484] it is clear that there is an urgent need for greater knowledge with regard to MIVs and their regulation/supervision. I sincerely hope that the powers that be in home and host countries attend to the issues mentioned (here) in an expeditious manner, as part of the overall regulatory framework for microfinance. In India, this then would necessitate that the stakeholders—developing the regulatory architecture for microfinance—also look into aspects concerning MIVs, their operations, and their regulation/supervision. The increasing globalization of the microfinance industry leaves them with no other option!

---

[484] http://microfinance-in-india.blogspot.in/search/label/AP%20Micro-Finance%20Crisis; and http://microfinance-in-india.blogspot.in/2011/11/lessons-from-commercial-micro-finance.html

# Chapter 31:
# Regulation and Supervision of Microfinance Investment Vehicles: A Suggested Practical Framework

MIVs currently do not appear to undergo any meaningful regulation/supervision. However, there is a critical need to regulate/supervise the MIVs. This is because MIVs—apart from being investment companies and/or financial intermediaries—have very diverse operations in terms of innovative products, geographies, and so on. And most importantly, they are able to provide crucial capital to microfinance institutions (MFIs), which then leverage the same (from commercial banks/others)—manifold—and enhance the outreach of their services.

Readers may want to recall that much of the impetus for the devastating growth of the MFI sector in Andhra Pradesh (AP), which then led to the 2010 crisis, came from the following:

a. MIVs/other investors who (irresponsibly) pumped in huge amounts of money (in relatively shorter amounts of time) into MFIs after the 2005–2006 Krishna crisis;

b. Riding on the back of these investments, MFIs were able to leverage huge amounts of commercial bank lending and grow[485] (using multiple lending, ghost lending and overlending) at phenomenal rates.

This, in short, resulted in the 2010 AP microfinance crisis, which is still unprecedented (as on date) in terms of its sheer enormity, scale, and impact. See the kind of investment that some Indian MFIs received during the years preceding the 2010 AP microfinance crisis and the kind of growth they experienced. You will understand what I am saying.[486]

Therefore, I think that it is imperative that any kind of MIV (irrespective of its legal form, geography of incorporation, countries of investment, etc.) should be subject—under its extant laws—to some

---

[485] See Mix Market http://www.mixmarket.org/— *"MFIs, unlike before, were able to deploy funds as microfinance assets."* In my opinion, they did so using multiple lending, ghost lending and overlending and primarily consumption/loans.

[486] See Chapters 4, 5, 6, 7 and 28.

minimum regulation/supervision[487] as is required for any form of organization involved in making investments (often collected from investors) and engaging in financial intermediation.

Looking at the huge assets that MIVs control (Table 31.1) and keeping in mind the potential damage that they could cause by their irresponsible investments (as was done in India), the case for minimum regulation/supervision of MIVs becomes very strong indeed. This is something that the stakeholders involved in developing the regulatory architecture for microfinance (in India and elsewhere) should carefully note.

| Table 31.1 Total Assets of MIVs in Luxembourg, the Netherlands, and the United States ||||||
|---|---|---|---|---|---|
| Fund | No. of MIVs | Legal form as listed in the *Syminvest* and *Luminis microfinance* database | Total assets (USD million) | Microfinance (MF) portfolio (USD million) | Microfinance Portfolio (MFPF)/Total Assets (TA) |
| Luxembourg | 40 | Various legal forms include | 3454.3 | 2755.3 | 79.76% |
| The Netherlands | 14 | Various legal forms include | 2055.6 | 1222.8 | 59.49% |
| United States | 32 | Various legal forms include | 665.0 | 304.9 | 45.85% |
| *Subtotal of MIVs in Luxembourg, The Netherlands, and the United States* | 86 | *Various Legal Forms* | 6174.9 | 4283 | 69.36% |
| **Total of all MIVs (all over the world)** | **142** | **Various Legal Forms** | **6630.7** | **4564.4** | **68.84%** |
| Percentage of MIVs in Luxembourg, The Netherlands, and the United States/total MIVs | 60.56% | Various Legal Forms | 93.13% | 93.83% | — |
| *Source:* Compiled from *Syminvest* (http://www.syminvest.com/) and *Luminis microfinance* (https://www.luminismicrofinance.com) database. Usual disclaimers, with regard to the data, apply! If the original data found in these two databases are incorrect, then the above data may also be incorrect! ||||||

While there are many facets that regulators would have to consider when looking at ways to supervise MIVs, in my opinion, an important aspect is the level of analysis and the issues that are relevant at each of these various levels. Typically, three levels of analysis are usually relevant with regard to MIVs, from a regulatory/supervisory perspective, as given below:

*Level 1: Investor–Fund*

*Level 2: Fund–Fund Manager (or Fund–Subadvisor)*

*Level 3: Fund/Fund Manager–MFI*

---

487 Regulation is essentially about making rules and/or principles and influencing behavior and enforcement. Supervision concerns continuous or specific verification of the application of these principles/rules through various mechanisms.

## Chapter 31: Regulation and Supervision of Microfinance Investment Vehicles

While supervision of MIVs should concern all levels—*that is, levels 1, 2, and 3*—levels 1 and 2 would be most important from a regulatory/supervisory standpoint in the home (parent) country. Accordingly, these are focused on in this chapter. Level 3 is complex as it would involve both home and host countries and it is perhaps better explored after the Bank for International Settlements (BIS) has—studied MIV phenomenon and associated relationships and—come up with a coordinating mechanism and organizing framework for the regulation/supervision of MIVs (in a global sense).

And before we get into the levels of analysis issue, one critical point must be made—for all practical purposes, irrespective of wherever the fund or fund managers get their investment from, regulating/supervising them at the place of incorporation and/or place at which their establishment exists would be most appropriate. Sometimes, even these could be in multiple countries (as noted earlier) and that would need to be appropriately handled.

Let us now look at practical questions that regulators/supervisors would need to ask at levels 1 and 2 to ensure minimum regulation/supervision of MIVs concerned. What is provided here is only a starter's set[488] and that needs to be stated upfront and clearly.

*At level 1, the following questions appear to be relevant:*

a. *What has the (MIV) fund promised investors when collecting their money?*

b. *Has the MIV fund delivered (at the most basic level) what it has promised to its investors?*

c. *Is the MIV fund legal in its operations in terms of its investments? Is it supporting legal organizations/activities?*

The regulator also needs to be sure that the fund does not invest in activities or organizations (MFIs, etc.) that are engaged in and/or support illegal activities. And I think that the definition of legal should be based on laws in the home (parent) country as well as the host country.

d. *Is the fund tapping legal sources of money?*

Regulators must be clear that the contributions by investors are indeed from legal sources and this is especially difficult, especially when web-based and related mechanisms are used. But this is an important aspect and should not be ignored.

*At level 2,* the following questions are relevant:

e. *Is the (MIV) fund taking adequate steps to protect its investors?*

---

[488] At the outset, let me state that these are *not* exhaustive and/or comprehensive by any means. They are intended to be a starter's set only.

f.  *Does the (MIV) fund have minimum standards/systems to ensure that investments made by the fund manager are in line with what has been promised by the fund to its investors?*

g.  *Does the (MIV) fund have sufficient supervisory mechanisms to ensure that the fund manager (subadvisor) safeguards the interests of the fund and its investors?*

h.  *Does the (MIV) fund have independent access to information about the investees in which the fund manager (subadvisor) proposes to invest and/or has invested?*

And herein lie important lessons for all stakeholders including MIVs (and/or investors) who use fund managers/subadvisors:

*Lesson 1: Irrespective of any circumstances, it is the paramount duty of funds to actively supervise their fund managers/subadvisors* (so as to safeguard their own and investor funds). And *the regulator needs to ensure that such effective and timely supervision of the fund manager (subadvisor) by the fund happens on the ground in a continuous manner.*

From a regulatory standpoint, this is indeed a serious issue because when a fund makes investments through fund managers/subadvisors, it does so (for and) on behalf of its investors. And therefore the regulator must be sure that the fund has a strong mechanism/method (system) to ensure that the investments made (by the fund manager/subadvisor) have been done with required care and are in the best interests of the investor(s). The mechanism could range from mere inspection (by the fund) of a fund manager/subadvisor's due diligence records to even actual due diligence (on a random basis) of the investees covered. And, especially, the regulator also needs to be sure that funds indeed have the requisite systems and processes to do this in real time. Therefore, it would be useful for the regulator/supervisor to randomly and selectively test the strength of internal control and other such systems at the level of the fund, fund managers, and subadvisors.

Another question is relevant at this juncture.

i.  *Does the fund manager have minimum standards of governance, management, and systems to ensure that investments made are in line with what has been promised by to the investors?*

Accordingly, another important lesson for the regulator is given here.

*Lesson 2: Irrespective of the circumstances, regulators must ensure that fund managers (subadvisors) adhere to prescribed minimum standards of governance, management, and systems.*

While the tendency of the microfinance industry is to prefer voluntary codes (or self-regulation), regulators must ensure that "uniform" codes exist and that these codes are "consistently" implemented on the ground. Readers may be well versed with the problems associated with such (well-intentioned)

## Chapter 31: Regulation and Supervision of Microfinance Investment Vehicles

voluntary codes, at least in India.[489] More often than not, such codes do not get implemented as past experience has shown in the case of retail MFIs, especially in India. Therefore, even if voluntary codes are to be used for fund managers (or even for the funds themselves), it would be important to have some regulatory oversight (in real time) into the actual implementation of these voluntary codes.

One final set of questions is very relevant to the operations of the funds/fund managers and the regulators ought to be interested in aspects such as these:

j. *Does the fund/fund manager have appropriate internal control and independent internal audit systems vital for making prudent investments?*

k. *What about the extent and quality of due diligence prior to investment?*

l. *What about the extent and quality of monitoring post investment?*

The various problems mentioned by Hugh Sinclair in his book[490] and analyzed elsewhere,[491] also appear to represent serious control breakdowns that can be grouped into the categories shown here:

- Lack of adequate management oversight and accountability, and failure to develop a strong control culture within the MIV, from top to bottom;

- Inadequate recognition and assessment of the risk of certain activities, whether on- or off-balance sheet and especially in relation to the MIV's strategic objectives;

---

489  See Chapters 20 and 21.

490  *"Confessions of a Microfinance Heretic: How Microlending Lost Its Way And Betrayed the Poor"* by Hugh Sinclair (2012), Berrett-Koehler Publishers, Inc. (http://www.microfinancetransparency.com/).

491  (a) Effective control systems at MIVs: The key to accountable investing and responsible microfinance globally (http://www.moneylife.in/article/effective-control-systems-at-mivs-the-key-to-accountable-investing-and-responsible-microfinance-globally/28376.html) by Ramesh S. Arunachalam, September 10, 2012, (b) Regulation and supervision of microfinance investment vehicles: A suggested practical framework—Part I (http://www.moneylife.in/article/regulation-and-supervision-of-microfinance-investment-vehicles-a-suggested-practical-frameworkmdashpart-i/28284.html) by Ramesh S. Arunachalam, September 5, 2012, (c) Regulation and supervision of microfinance investment vehicles: A suggested practical framework— Part II (http://www.moneylife.in/article/regulation-and-supervision-of-microfinance-investment-vehicles-a-suggested-practical-frameworkmdash-part-ii/28314.html) by Ramesh S. Arunachalam, September 6, 2012, (d) Why not regulate and supervise microfinance investment vehicles in their country of incorporation? (http://www.moneylife.in/article/why-not-regulate-and-supervise-microfinance-investment-vehicles-in-their-country-of-incorporation/27871.html) by Ramesh S. Arunachalam, August 20, 2012; (e) Regulation and supervision of MIVs: An urgent task for central banks and regulators globally (http://www.moneylife.in/article/regulation-and-supervision-of-mivs-an-urgent-task-for-ral-banks-and-regulators-globally/27327.html) by Ramesh S. Arunachalam, July 28, 2012; and (f) Should not microfinance investment vehicles be judged by the same standards set for retail MFIs? (http://www.moneylife.in/article/should-not-microfinance-investment-vehicles-be-judged-by-the-same-standards-set-for-retail-mfis/27041.html) by Ramesh S. Arunachalam, July 17, 2012.

- The absence or failure of key control structures and activities—at MIVs—such as segregation of duties, due diligence, and approvals for strategic investments and other activities, verifications, reconciliations, and reviews of operating and other performance, and the like;

- Inadequate communication of information between levels of management within MIVs, causing significant opacity;

- Lack of independent and effective (internal and external) audit programs and monitoring activities at MIVs.

To summarize, while all of these aspects are important from a regulatory/supervisory standpoint with regard to MIVs (and fund managers/subadvisors), two crucial areas are important from an internal organization as well as regulatory (external) standpoint: (i) *the extent and adequacy of internal control systems at the fund/fund manager level*; and (ii) *the presence of independent and effective internal audits*. Without question, both these can provide a good basis for ensuring prudent and responsible investment by MIVs in the long run. *And many of the problems mentioned earlier could have (perhaps) been mitigated (if not completely avoided) if only the MIVs (concerned) had been required (by regulators) to institute well-functioning and appropriate internal control systems and also ensure effective independent internal audits of the same.* Anyway, while the past provides good learning, we also need to move forward and, therefore, the critical aspect of a well-functioning internal control system at MIVs is dealt with in the next chapter.

# Chapter 32:
# Effective Control Systems at MIVs: The Key to Accountable Investing and Responsible Microfinance Globally

This chapter takes a first look at such control systems and provides practical (starter) suggestions to MIVs, policy makers, regulators, and other stakeholders on how (best) to structure the systems so as to achieve the goal of accountable investing as well as responsible microfinance, in a global sense.

The formality of any control system will depend largely on an MIV's size, the scale and complexity of its operations, its risk profile, and so on. Less formal/structured internal control systems at smaller MIVs can be as effective as highly formal/structured internal control systems at larger (and complexly structured) MIVs. *But the key is that every MIV should have an internal control system; this system should be commensurate with the size, scale, and complexity of its operations; and most importantly, the system should actually work on the ground in real time.*

Many of the problems with MIVs[492] could have (perhaps) been avoided if, and only if, the concerned MIVs had an effective and appropriate internal control system operational in the first place—*one that did not merely exist on paper but was rather implemented in reality.* This is something that the concerned MIVs will have to self-assess, with regard to their respective organizations and bring about

---

[492] See 'Confessions of a Microfinance Heretic: How Microlending Lost Its Way and Betrayed the Poor' by Hugh Sinclair (http://www.microfinancetransparency.com/). Also refer to the following articles: Why not regulate and supervise microfinance investment vehicles in their country of incorporation? (http://www.moneylife.in/article/why-not-regulate-and-supervise-microfinance-investment-vehicles-in-their-country-of-incorporation/27871.html) by Ramesh S. Arunachalam, August 20, 2012; Triple Jump's Response to Hugh Sinclair's Book: Does It Raise More Questions than Provide Credible Answers? (http://www.moneylife.in/article/triple-jumps-response-to-hugh-sinclairs-book-does-it-raise-more-questions-than-provide-credible-answers/27525.html) by Ramesh S. Arunachalam, August 4, 2012; Why blame the MFIs alone? (http://www.moneylife.in/article/why-blame-the-mfis-alone/26994.html) by Ramesh S. Arunachalam, July 16, 2012; Should not microfinance investment vehicles be judged by the same standards set for retail MFIs? (http://www.moneylife.in/article/should-not-microfinance-investment-vehicles-be-judged-by-the-same-standards-set-for-retail-mfis/27041.html) by Ramesh S. Arunachalam, July 17, 2012; and Does Sinclair's open challenge to the global microfinance industry make his claims true? (http://www.moneylife.in/article/does-sinclairs-open-challenge-to-the-global-microfinance-industry-make-his-claims-true/27106.html) by Ramesh S. Arunachalam, July 20, 2012.

the necessary changes. Regulators/supervisors and other stakeholders including CGAP[493] could also enable these MIVs to assess the quality[494] of their control systems and make the necessary changes.

That said, what then are the key components of such a system?

In my opinion, an effective control system (at any MIV) should have five key elements:

1. An appropriate *control environment*
2. Supported by a proper *risk management system*
3. With *control activities* commensurate with the size, scale, and complexity of investment/operations
4. Aided by a *transparent and accurate accounting, information, and communication systems*
5. Backed by dispassionate *self-assessment/monitoring.*

Among these, the strategic element is an "appropriate control environment." This is in fact an issue that is seldom thought about in practice but one that I believe is very (if not most) crucial to the long-term survival of the MIV.

*Why should each and every MIV have an appropriate control environment?*

This is because the control environment is the foundation on which the MIV's control system is (to be) built. Basically, it reflects the board's[495] (and also senior management's) commitment to strong and effective internal control at the MIV. In other words, it provides the *discipline* and *structure* to the entire (internal) control system. *Without this commitment by the board of directors (and senior management) to strong and effective controls, no (internal) control system (however well designed and structured) can actually work on the ground. And this commitment must clearly be visible throughout the MIV—for all staff to see and emulate. Let us be clear on that!*

*And who has to play a crucial role in establishing this at an MIV?*

At a very basic level, it is an MIV's board of directors (perhaps along with and through senior management) who must assume responsibility for establishing and maintaining an effective internal control system that: (i) meets statutory and regulatory requirements (if any); (ii) protects the MIV, its assets, operations, and investors; and (iii) responds to changes in the MIV's environmental conditions. They need to ensure that the control system operates as it is intended to and is also modified (appropriately) when circumstances so dictate.

And for discharging these duties, the board of directors must fully understand the risks that the MIV could face, set the acceptable limits for these risks, and ensure that senior management takes the steps necessary to identify, monitor, and control these risks. In turn, the senior management must then take the

---

493 *Consultative Group to Assist the Poor* (http://www.cgap.org/p/site/c/).

494 Judging the quality will require not merely the examination of whether or not an appropriate internal control system exists on paper but rather studying if indeed what is said on paper actually works on the ground. That is the key to making inferences about quality.

495 Board = Board of Directors or equivalent as may be as per the legal form of the MIV as per the relevant laws in the country of incorporation.

responsibility to implement the strategies approved by the board, to set appropriate internal control process/procedures, and to monitor the effectiveness of these process/procedures. *There can be no substitute for this.*

This makes it quite clear where the main responsibility for control rests and that is fairly and squarely on the strategic shoulders of the MIV's board of directors (along with the senior management)—not on the *compliance and audit departments*. However, having said that, everyone in an institution shares the responsibility to some extent and that is where the board (through the senior management) must play a catalytic role in shaping a positive control culture throughout the entire MIV.

Thus, a key task for the board (through senior management) is to establish the right culture within the MIV—*a culture in which the importance of internal controls is stressed, and high ethical and integrity standards are promoted, incentivized and adhered to.*

*And this culture cannot be determined simply by what the board or top levels of management (merely) say—it will have to be judged more importantly by what they (actually) do.*

For example, *do the MIVs' policies (remuneration, etc.) reward risk-taking at the expense of accountable and responsible investing?* The pressure (at many MIVs) to disburse more and more loans quickly as well as make rapid equity investments have been known to be associated with remuneration policies that reward (immense) risk taking by MIVs—in turn, this pressure appears to have come from the practical imperative to (immediately) invest (all) the monies available with the MIVs so that there is maximum utilization of the MIV's resources/assets. *Of course, all these are driven by the desire of wanting to have better operational results, attract more capital for deployment and also provide better returns to the primary investors and shareholders of the MIVs.* In a way, this is a cyclical process. Readers may want to recall that many of the large (NBFC) MFIs themselves emulated and replicated the above process at a retail level (kept on disbursing, ignoring the risks at hand) in Andhra Pradesh (during 2005 to 2010), which perhaps resulted in multiple, over- and ghost lending and finally led to the 2010 Andhra Pradesh microfinance crisis. And of course, remuneration policies (including bonuses and stock options) were clearly tied to faster disbursement, all along the financial sector value chain (from MIVs to the retail MFIs).

Likewise, another relevant issue here is the question of *whether the board/senior management at MIVs displays a casual attitude toward breaches of limits? Do they encourage the right attitude toward regulatory compliance? Is there backing and respect at board/senior management levels (at MIVs) for the internal audit and compliance functions and their independence?*

The response of the board/senior management levels at the MIVs to these kinds of issues will clearly determine how other staff (at the MIVs) actually behave in practice, including their attitude to control issues and the overall control environment. This point needs strong emphasis here!

Table 32.1 provides specific examples (not exhaustive) of the differences between policy and implementation (i.e., between what is said and what is actually done) for the benefit of various stakeholders including regulators/supervisors. *One aspect needs clarification here*—I am not arguing that this is happening at every MIV and always so. I am merely providing an illustration of what could happen in terms of differences between policy statements and actual implementation with regard to controls and the implications that this would have in building a positive control culture at an MIV.

Table 32.1 Examples of Differences Between Policy and Implementation

| What POLICY at MIV may say? | What may actually happen during IMPLEMENTATION? |
|---|---|
| **CLAIM:** Strategic goal is to promote inclusive finance through investee | ✓ **DO:** Using the name of financial inclusion, disburse more and more loans as well as make rapid equity investments—without even understanding the absorption capacity of the investees (MFIs), who in turn just lend to low-income clients indiscriminately, causing over-indebtedness and related problems, as it happened in 2010 and before in AP (India)<br>✓ **DO:** Investing without any accountability, merely to push out more and more money collected from primary investors in a short span of time. The idea is to deploy more and more resources as assets in an ongoing manner and get better returns, as it happened in 2010 and before in AP<br>✓ **DO:** Remuneration policies (all levels) at MIV encourage excessive risk taking as it happened in 2010 and before in AP<br>✓ **DO**: Huge bonuses for MIVs' board and/or senior management in short term when the risks are medium and/or long term as it happened in 2010 and before in AP |
| **CLAIM:** Adherence to responsible finance principles, codes of conduct, client protection and other self-regulatory mechanisms | ✓ **DO:** Invest in MFIs (without sufficient monitoring) that engage in over, multiple and/or ghost lending as well as employ coercive collection mechanisms that undermine these well-intended principles, codes, and mechanisms. No better example than what happened in India (AP) in 2010 and before. The case of Sahayata Microfinance also resounds in the memory |
| **CLAIM:** Investment is done after rigorous due diligence and based on objective information so as to protect money of primary investors | ✓ **DO:** Due diligence based on desk research and short field visits which, at best, is part of a checklist compliance process for investing. The example of LAPO is fresh in the memory<br>✓ **DO:** Turn a blind eye to key weaknesses with the investee and ignore credible public domain information pertaining to that: for example, illegal products and actions; inadequate systems; conflict of interests in the MFI board; and so on. The example of LAPO is fresh in the memory<br>✓ **DO:** Send the same information about the investee, contained in the due diligence report done for another investor (at a previous date), to a fresh investor. The net result is one of not presenting the latest and TRUE financial condition (and other parameters) of the investee. The example of LAPO is fresh in the mind.<br>✓ **Do:** Conceal inadequacies and claim to the primary investors that these have been sorted out, when in fact, reality could be different—for example, the MIS could be semiautomated with manual consolidation but the report to a prospective primary investor may say that the MIS is completely automated and integrated. The example of LAPO is fresh in the memory. |
| **CLAIM:** Tell investors that their money is being used for poverty alleviation through enterprise finance | ✓ **DO:** Lend money to MFIs that merely provide consumption loans or consumer financing. What happened in AP in 2010 and before is the best example. |
| **CLAIM:** We have voluntary ceilings on interest rates charged by the investee from low-income people | ✓ **DO:** Ignore credit rating and credible pricing reports that demonstrate "interest rates" much in excess of self-imposed ceiling and/or even rates greater than 100%. The example of LAPO is fresh in the memory. |
| **CLAIM:** Transparent reporting and information based on a proper MIS | ✓ **DO:** Selectively present information or provide factually incorrect information to primary investors and others. The example of LAPO is fresh in the mind. No better example than what happened in India (AP) in 2010 and before. The case of Sahayata Microfinance also resounds strongly in the memory.<br>✓ **DO:** Invest in MFIs—that engage in manipulation of information so as to gain investment—despite knowing that the investee (MFI) is not a transparent one. The example of LAPO is fresh in the memory. No better example than what happened in India (AP) in 2010 and before. The case of Sahayata Microfinance also resounds strongly in the memory. |

The aspect of intended (i.e., existing merely on paper as policy) versus realized (i.e., as seen during implementation) in an "internal control system" is a critical issue. Problems occur when there is a huge gap between the intended "internal control system" and the realized "internal control system." Therefore,

## Chapter 32: Effective Control Systems at MIVs

it is the duty of the board (through guidance to the senior management[496] to ensure that there is a close (if not complete) fit between the *intended* "internal control system" and *realized* "internal control system." The corollary follows that where the fit between "internal control system" and realized "internal control system" is low, the board will have to step in (and get the senior management) to bring about necessary changes. *This would be a critical duty of the board in shaping the control environment.*

Therefore, it would certainly be appropriate to expect the board/management of MIVs—involved in the LAPO case[497] as well as those MIVs who were part of the burgeoning growth of the Indian (AP) microfinance sector[498] during 2008 to 2010—to try and address the key issues given in this chapter and take swift commensurate action to rectify lacunae in their systems.

All these MIVs surely need to introspect with integrity and bring in a positive control environment that can encourage accountable and responsible investing. That alone can usher in an era of responsible microfinance on the ground. And, last but not the least, regulators/supervisors would also need to emphasize the importance of having such a positive and appropriate control environment at MIVs—as part of their overall regulatory framework for MIVs. I hope that the stakeholders developing the regulatory architecture for microfinance accord the requisite importance to issues concerning MIVs, their operations, systems, and regulation/supervision as part of their on-going exercise so as to ensure responsible microfinance on the ground.

---

496 I am not suggesting micromanagement by the board under key circumstances.
497 The MIVs are well known and I do not want to name them here.
498 The MIVs are well known and I do not want to name them here.

# Chapter 33:
# Redeeming the Indian Microfinance Industry: What Needs to Be Done?

As the preceding chapters clearly highlight, the burgeoning growth of the commercial NBFC MFI model in Indian microfinance—during the period April 2008 to March 2010—led to the 2010 Andhra Pradesh microfinance crisis, which was the third in a series of crisis situations (the first being Krishna and the second Kolar) in the past six years. As David Roodman has consistently argued in his blog,[499] the desire to have growth at a burgeoning pace was perhaps one of the major causes of the 2010 AP microfinance crisis. And therefore let us look at some data and understand how this growth actually happened from the Krishna through Kolar to the 2010 AP microfinance crisis. They hold very important lessons—for boards of NBFC MFIs, regulators, supervisors, investors, and others—in terms of how the MFIs grew and what the resultant implications were.

Let us start with data (Table 33.1) for the years 2003–2004, 2004–2005, and 2005–2006—that is, years before and during the Krishna microfinance crisis.

| Table 33.1 Number of Clients and Gross Loan Portfolio (GLP) (in US$) Added by The Five Large AP-Headquartered NBFC MFIs During April 2003–March 2006 | | | |
|---|---|---|---|
| Description | April 2003–March 2004 <br><br> Base year | April 2004–March 2005 <br><br> Year before the Krishna crisis | April 2005–March 2006 <br><br> Year of Krishna crisis |
| Total active clients added in each subsequent year | 195,605 | 713,744 | 1,199,341 |
| Factor by which 'Clients Added' increased in comparison to base year |  | 3.65 | 6.13 |
| Total GLP added in each subsequent year | 19,558,070 | 88,604,617 | 99,384,203 |
| Factor by which 'GLP Added' increased in comparison to base year |  | 4.53 | 5.08 |
| Source: Base data compiled from www.mixmarket.org | | | |

---

499 http://www.cgdev.org/open_book

# Chapter 33: Redeeming the Indian Microfinance Industry: What Needs to Be Done?

As the data in Table 33.1 suggests, growth was extremely significant in terms of clients and gross loan portfolio (GLP) added in the years prior to the Krishna crisis.

1. Specifically, in the year preceding the Krishna crisis (2004–2005), the five large AP-headquartered MFIs added 3.65 times more clients and 4.53 times more GLP, respectively, than in the base year (end March 2004 figures).

2. Further, during the year of the Krishna crisis (2005–2006), the five large AP-headquartered MFIs added 6.13 times more clients and 5.08 times more GLP than in the base year (end March 2004 figures).

3. These were huge numbers by standards that existed then. This rapid growth was perhaps one of the major reasons for the overheating in the Krishna district microfinance market then and, without question, it played a significant part in the resulting (2005-2006) crisis at the local level.

Let us now look at the data in Table 33.2, which is for the years (2006–2007, 2007–2008, 2008–2009, and 2009–2010) after the Krishna crisis. Several trends are discernible from the data.

| Table 33.2 Number of Clients and GLP (in US$) Added by The Five Large AP-Headquartered NBFC MFIs During April 2006–March 2010 | | | | |
|---|---|---|---|---|
| Description | April 2006–March 2007<br><br>Base year (year after Krishna) | April 2007–March 2008<br><br>Year before Kolar | April 2008–March 2009<br><br>Year of Kolar | April 2009–March 2010<br><br>Year after Kolar and before the 2010 AP crisis |
| Total active clients added in each subsequent year | 625,380 | 1,808,223 | 4,165,537 | 5,425,329 |
| Factor by which 'Clients Added' increased in comparison to base year | | 2.89 | 6.66 | 8.68 |
| Total GLP added in each subsequent year | 93,445,254 | 406,465,811 | 590,932,538 | 1,293,133,723 |
| Factor by which 'GLP Added' increased in comparison to base year | | 4.35 | 6.32 | 13.84 |
| *Source*: Base data compiled from www.mixmarket.org | | | | |

As expected, owing to the crisis, the base year (the year after the Krishna crisis, April 2006–March 2007) saw a slowdown and the five large AP-headquartered MFIs (all NBFCs) added just 0.52 times clients and 0.94 times GLP as compared to the previous year (2005–2006, the year of the Krishna crisis). However, thereafter, data suggests that growth was extremely significant in terms of clients and GLP added.

- For example, in the year preceding the Kolar crisis (i.e., 2007–2008) or two years after Krishna, the five large AP-headquartered MFIs added 2.89 times more clients and 4.35 times more GLP, respectively, than in the base year (end March 2007 figures), which had experienced a slowdown as noted earlier.

- Further, in the year of the Kolar crisis (2008–2009), the five large AP-headquartered MFIs added 6.66 times more clients and 6.32 times more GLP than in the base year (end March 2007 figures).

- Last but not the least, in the year after the Kolar crisis (2009–2010)—that is, just before 2010 AP crisis—the five large AP-headquartered MFIs added 8.68 times more clients and 13.84[500] times more gross loan portfolio than in the base year (end March 2007 figures). These are huge numbers by any standards and without doubt they are among the major factors that led to the subprime-like situation in Andhra Pradesh that caused the 2010 microfinance crisis eventually.

So, what are the key learning points that deserve emphasis?

First, clearly, while there was a slowdown after the Krishna crisis, the data show that this slowdown was (at best) temporary. Readers would recall that in 2005–2006 in Andhra Pradesh, when the first major microfinance crisis was experienced in the Krishna district, it was a localized affair and rather limited to Krishna and perhaps Guntur districts, where two of the largest AP-headquartered MFIs[501] were competing fiercely. While there was a lot of rhetoric after the Krishna crisis, in reality, very few lessons were learnt. That is why you see a rather phenomenal growth in terms of clients and GLP added, just two years after the Krishna crisis.

Second, when a similar crisis occurred in Kolar (Karnataka) in 2009, as before, the symptoms of the crisis were perhaps tackled but the inherent causes (the flawed operating model of the NBFC MFIs as Dr C Rangarajan has pointed out) were ignored. In fact, fewer lessons (than after the Krishna crisis) were learnt, and soon the MFIs were back to their old ways of ghost, multiple, and overlending to shared clients in shared JLGs. With senior management and boards of many MFIs looking primarily at (quickly) building a mass of clients (the classic quantity rather than quality aspect), achieving scale rapidly became the most important factor. Client-level controls were forgotten and with the mushrooming of center leaders and others as agents, soon many MFIs started using the decentralized (agency) model to build rapid scale. With their systems and capacities unable to manage this growth, frauds[502] and failures started burgeoning too. The numbers clearly tell the story as the year 2009–2010 (the year

---

500  This should have been higher at 15.60 had the Mix Market retained the original GLP figures that it had put out in 2010/2011 for BASIX and SHARE. For some reason, Mix Market changed its original figures for BASIX and SHARE respectively from US$ 223,229,799 and US$ 490,923,201 to US$ 172,484,946 and US$ 376,593,362 (as on date). I have the original print screen data and other pieces of evidence with regard to the original data put out by Mix Market. There are several other issues with the Mix Market database and I can provide the details if required.
501  Share Microfin Ltd and Spandana Sphoorty Financial Limited.
502  See Chapter 18 on Governance of Risk Management.

## Chapter 33: Redeeming the Indian Microfinance Industry: What Needs to Be Done?

after Kolar) saw an unprecedented growth among the five AP-headquartered MFIs (*many of whom were operating in Karnataka as well*) and the rest is history.

A third additional point needs to be made with regard to 2010 AP microfinance crisis. In the year preceding the 2010 crisis, the growth of MFIs was not only burgeoning in terms of clients added (as compared to the base year) but, more importantly, it was humungous in terms of the GLP added (in reference to the base year). This represents a significant difference between the 2005–2006 Krishna crisis and the 2010 AP microfinance crisis because with regard to the latter, the year preceding the crisis saw MFIs deepen their engagements with clients in terms of larger and perhaps multiple loans. This is evident from the fact that while clients added by five large AP-headquartered MFIs (in 2009–2010) was 8.68 times that of the base year (2006–2007), the GLP added was much higher at 13.84 times the base year. The corresponding figures during Krishna were 6.13 for clients added and 5.08 for GLP added. Therefore, one could argue that while growth that focused on adding more clients (cannibalization of SHGs and market skimming) with (perhaps) lower loan sizes was the undoing of the MFIs in Krishna (2005–2006), growth focused on larger loans, that is, through multiple and ghost loans led to the 2010 AP microfinance crisis.

Fourth, the data from Table 33.3 provides some very interesting trends with regard to why this growth occurred in Indian microfinance across the three years leading up to the 2010 AP microfinance crisis.

Table 33.3 Summary Data for Number of Clients and GLP Added by the Five Large AP-Headquartered NBFC MFIs and Overall Equity Investment into MFIs and DFI/Bank Outstanding in Indian Microfinance

| Description | April 2007–March 2008 Before Kolar crisis | April 2008–March 2009 Year of Kolar crisis | April 2009–March 2010 Year after Kolar and before the 2010 AP crisis | Number of times increase across 2 years |
|---|---|---|---|---|
| Total active clients added in the year by the five large AP-headquartered NBFC MFIs | 1,808,223 | 4,165,537 | 5,425,329 | 3.00 |
| Total gross loan portfolio (in US $) added in the year by the five large AP-headquartered NBFC MFIs | 406,465,811 | 590,932,538 | 1,293,133,723 | 3.18 |
| Total equity investment into Indian microfinance (in US $ million) during period | 118.34 | 141.33 | 345.25 | 2.92 |
| SIDBI loan outstanding (in crores) to MFIs | 950.38 | 2136.89 | 3808.2 | 4.01 |
| Bank loan outstanding (in crores) to MFIs | 2748.84 | 5009.09 | 10147.5 | 3.69 |

*Sources*: www.mixmarket.org, www.nabard.org, www.sidbi.in, www.rbi.org.in and www.microfinance-in-india.blogspot.org

Thus, as seen from the table, one must note that it was during the period of this burgeoning growth (especially April 2009–March 2010) that many of the NBFC MFIs received significant equity investments (from investors/MIVs) and priority sector lending (PSL)/other loan funds from banks/DFIs, post Kolar. The Kolar crisis happened somewhere in January 2009 and if you look at the equity investments and funds from banks/DFIs in the subsequent year, you will clearly understand what I am saying. Without doubt, as is evident from the data, it is clear that despite Kolar, the five AP-headquartered MFIs grew at a fast pace and thereby attracted greater equity investment and also larger amount of DFI/bank funds and used these to grow further. An interesting point to be noted here is that while the five AP NBFC MFIs increased their clients by 3 times across the 24 months, they increased their gross loan portfolio by nearly 3.18[503] times. *This indicates, ceterus paribus, that these five AP NBFC MFIs deepened their portfolio in 2009–2010. This also perhaps provides some surrogate evidence with regard to increasing loan sizes and multiple/ghost lending in 2009–2010.* The following graphs clearly highlight this phenomenon.

**Figure 33.1 Clients (in million) Added in Each Subsequent Year by The Five Large AP-Headquartered NBFC MFIs across Two Crisis Points**

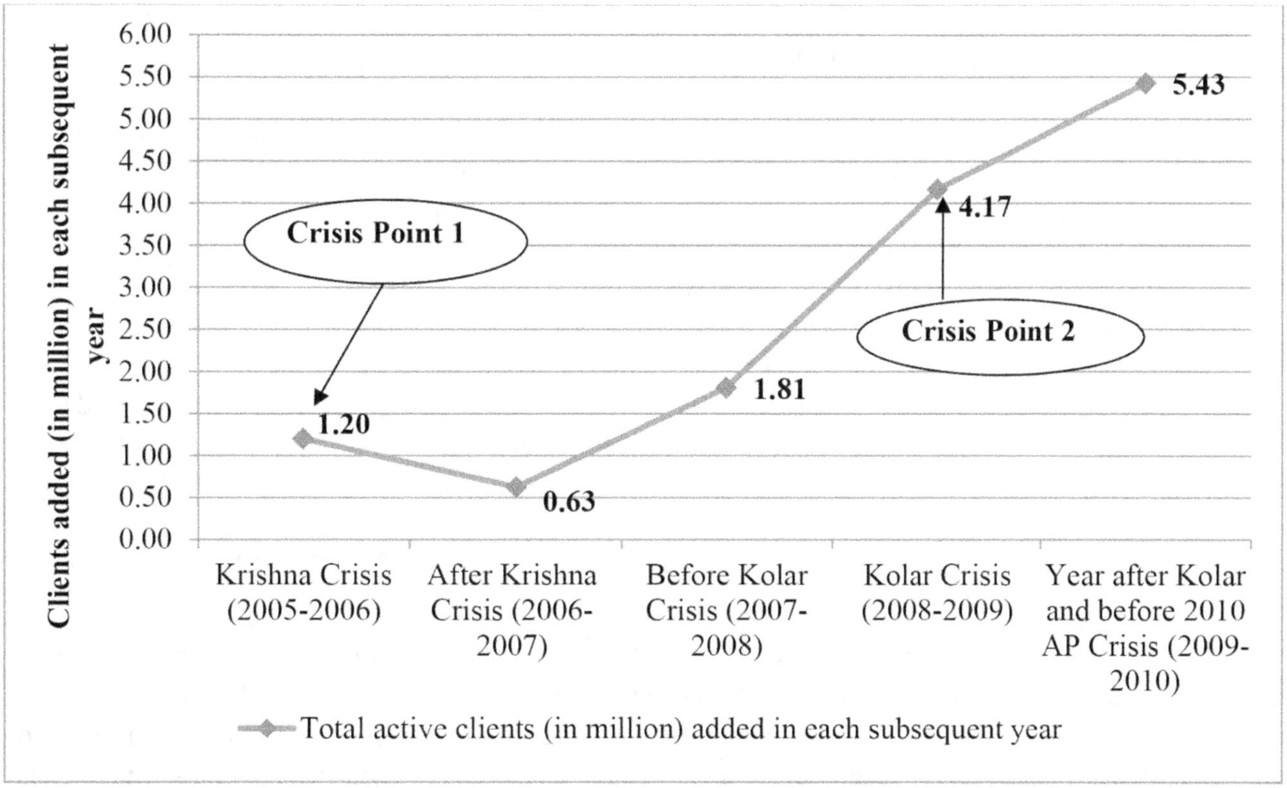

---

[503] This should have been higher at 3.59 had the Mix Market retained the original GLP figures that it had put out in 2010/2011 for BASIX and SHARE. For some reason, Mix Market changed its original figures for BASIX and SHARE respectively from US$ 223,229,799 and US$ 490,923,201 to US$ 172,484,946 and US$ 376,593,362 (as on date). I have the original print screen data and other pieces of evidence with regard to the original data put out by Mix Market. There are several other issues with the Mix Market database and I can provide the details if required.

From the graph, it is clear that despite the two earlier crisis situations in Indian microfinance (Krishna/Kolar), clients added by five large AP-headquartered MFIs significantly increased across the years and rather steeply.

**Figure 33.2 Gross Loan Portfolio (in US$ million) Added in Each Subsequent Year by The Five Large AP-Headquartered NBFC MFIs across Two Crisis Points**

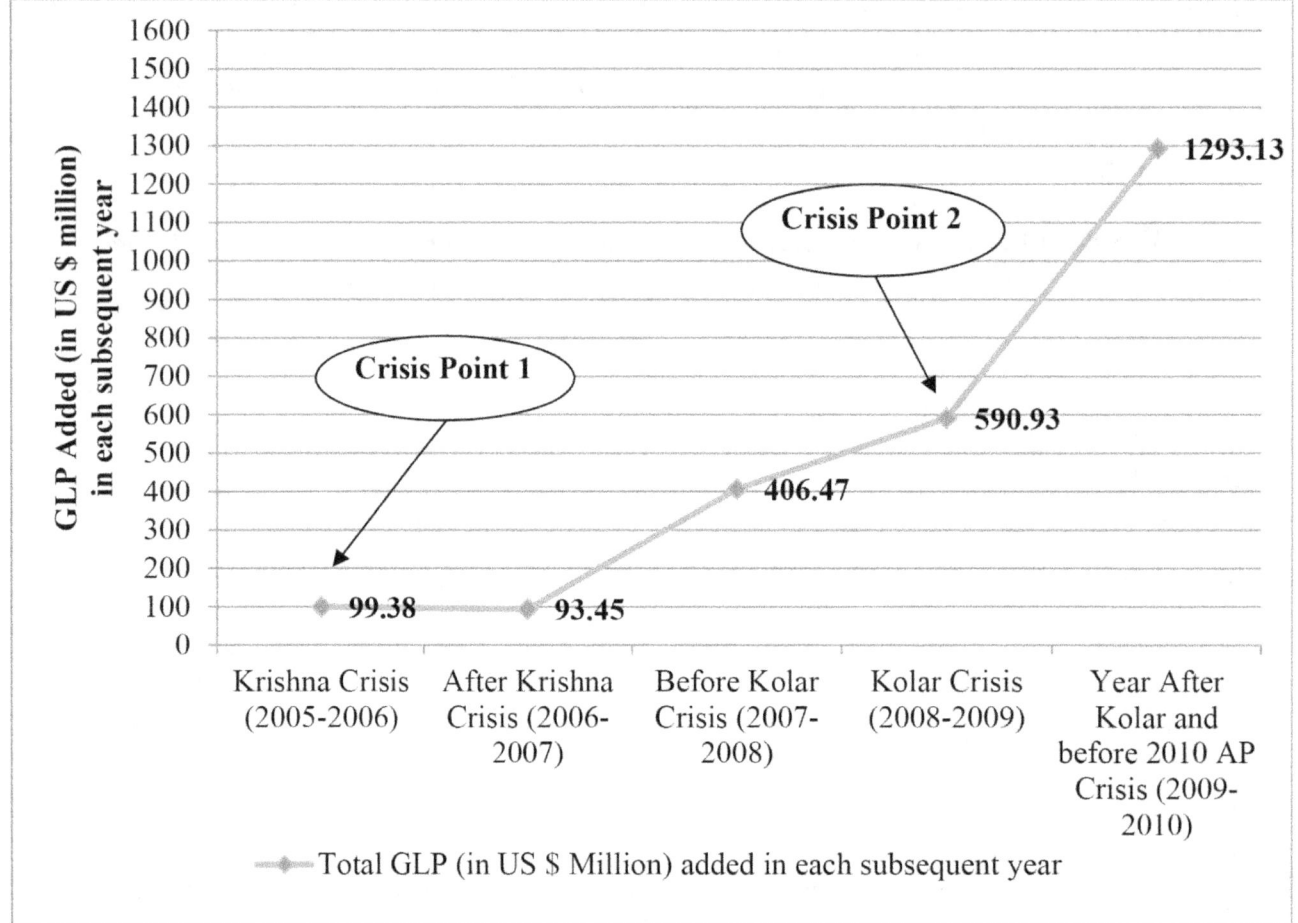

Likewise, the graph also makes it clear that despite the two earlier crisis situations in Indian microfinance (Krishna/Kolar), the GLP added by five large AP-headquartered MFIs steeply increased across the years.

Now, the microfinance industry and other stakeholders (including regulators) were gung-ho about this growth—in the name of financial inclusion—without asking serious questions on how such rapidly burgeoning growth (*emphasis added*) was possible in the first place. Had such questions been asked—especially by the regulators and other stakeholders—at relevant crisis points, then issues such as multiple, over- and ghost lending would have (perhaps) got the attention they deserved and maybe we would not have experienced the 2010 AP microfinance crisis (in its severity).

Never mind. Let us stop crying over spilt milk but let us not forget what has happened in the past in the desire to achieve scale speedily. Going forward, it would be prudent for the various stakeholders[504] (including those developing the regulatory architecture for microfinance) to monitor growth trends closely (quarter on quarter) and constantly keep asking questions such as the following:

✓ How are MFIs growing quarter on quarter? Is the growth unusually large? Is it supply led? Are the growth rates commensurate with the capacity to manage that growth? Are client-level and other internal controls being broken? Is there cause to believe that growth and scale are being rapidly built through multiple, ghost, and overlending? What are the motivations for the concerned institutions (MFIs) to grow this rapidly? To show better operating results? Have greater returns? Pay higher salaries, commissions, and offer sweat equity to staff/management? Get better valuations? Tap capital markets at a premium etc. Enhance financial inclusion?

✓ Are clients having multiple loans and do they appear to be (over)indebted? Are they in a position to repay loans from their known (legitimate) sources of income/cash? Have institutions (for whatever be the reason) provided successive loans (one after another), despite knowing that the concerned clients cannot repay existing (multiple) loans from the known (legitimate) sources of income/cash? Have clients used one loan to repay another loan? Is periodic refinancing required to provide sufficient liquidity to enable the client to service existing debt? Has an additional loan been provided midway through an ongoing loan and, especially, on easier terms? In other words, are clients overleveraged? Have there been a series of delinquent payments and one equalizing payment (often from another loan), and has this pattern been repeated? Have coercive repayment practices been used to ensure better repayment? Has there been a lack of transparency with the product terms and the like, especially, in terms of the effective interest rates as well as other issues?

And if such analysis happens on a regular (quarterly) basis, then, I am sure that the policy as well as regulatory/supervisory failure, so evident from the past crisis situations (including the 2010 AP crisis), will not occur in the future—that alone will serve the cause of financial inclusion and inclusive growth better. And here, it would be good for us to remember the quote of late Shashi Rajagopalan (independent consultant and former RBI director)—one of the most client-sensitive practitioners that microfinance has ever seen—who, commenting on CGAP's paper on SKS Microfinance,[505] noted that:

> "Notwithstanding the sleight of hand by which large numbers of women are shown to be shareholders through MBTs, many NBFC MFIs are closely held companies, and, in my view, statistics quoted by such

---

504 Like the PSCF, MoF, RBI, Microfinance Associations, MIVs, MFIs, and their boards and others such as donors/CGAP.
505 http://www.cgap.org/gm/document-1.9.47613/FN65_Rev.pdf

closely held companies are hard to ascertain. **It appears to be in everyone's interest to pretend that these companies are indeed growing at the rates claimed and that their default rates are indeed the rates claimed.** Anyone buying into these figures, has either never given and collected credit, or, is either incredibly naive, or has a stake in pretending that this is indeed a wonderful gift to the low income group. CGAP is gung-ho about things that it ought to be much more discerning on, if indeed it wants people with low income to truly benefit from regular access to genuine and usable credit."

As someone who has been involved with what is now called the microfinance industry, for a little over two decades, I must say that all is not lost. Indian MFIs and microfinance can salvage the lost ground, but they need to put clients first. For this, they must get back to the basics and do some of the following if indeed they are to rebuild their (lost) credibility and revive the industry.

- ✓ *Build (lasting) client relationships:* In the initial years of microfinance, most MFIs had great social acceptability and local support, because their first and foremost task was getting to know clients rather than mere lending. This has to happen again and MFIs must start to view low-income people not just as mere clients who borrow, but rather respect them as producers of goods and services (micro-entrepreneurs) who contribute to the growth of the country and its economy. MFIs must also be able to empathize with low-income people in terms of the various life-cycle events and situations that they have to confront in their daily struggle for survival. This should result in stronger bonds being built with clients and facilitate the creation of longer lasting mutually beneficial relationships with clients as well as with the larger community.

- ✓ *Recognize the fact that more credit is not always good:* Much of the problems have occurred in India because MFIs got into a race to outwit each other, in terms of building larger loan portfolios and servicing a larger number of clients, to show better results, attract more equity, get greater valuations and create greater wealth for themselves and their shareholders. These objectives resulted in indiscriminate (multiple) lending (and related negative impacts) that created overindebtedness among clients, rather than servicing them in a meaningful manner.

Without question, MFIs must ensure that their strategic vision does not seek to maximize credit (borrowing), but rather attempt to encourage a wide range of need-based financial services (including fair-priced loans) that are appropriate for the particular circumstances of its low-income clients. In fact, their strategic goal must be to minimize destructive (subprime-like) lending, for which they must commit to sound underwriting of loans in line with the borrowers' ability to repay.

- ✓ *Commit to avoiding overindebtedness through various steps:* MFIs should invest in systems and human resources to ensure better loan origination procedures. This apart, they must facilitate mandatory training for low-income clients as well as the field staff to avoid overindebted customers. In fact, both these are not new and many of the MFIs did this in the mid-to-late 1980s and early 1990s. As the CGAP[506] module on delinquency has always stressed, there are no bad borrowers (clients) but only bad loans with institutions being primarily responsible for any delinquency. Therefore, it goes without saying that it is the MFIs that have a major role in reducing delinquency and curbing the development of a poor credit culture. In the long run, MFIs should also look at enhancing their MIS to implement credit scoring and support the establishment of transparent credit bureaus.

✓ *Deliver high-quality and appropriate financial services:* MFIs must also focus on delivering a range of vulnerability-reducing and risk-mitigating financial services (product- and cash-flow-based business cycle loans, post harvest/production loans, savings, insurance, pensions, and the like) as per the needs of clients, rather than thrust more and more standard (Grameen or other type) loans on clients, which are more often used for consumption purposes.

A related issue here is that good service will depend on the ability of all (field) staff to improvise and be flexible in handling sensitive client situations. They will need to learn to balance the benefits of a culture of compliance with a culture of customer service, and at no time should they resort to any unethical means to overcome situations. This essentially pertains to coercive recovery practices that have gained prominence in India during the past few years.

✓ *Set operational, branch, and field staff incentives such that they do not distort the rules under any circumstances:* Incentives to operational managers and branch/field staff have an important role in shaping the MFI in terms of its client orientation. And without any doubt, staff incentives must be in tune with the strategic vision to enable access to a wide range of financial services to low-income people. Therefore, having a narrow incentive scheme that pays attention to either loan disbursement and/or collection will surely set the stage for unethical and fraudulent behavior. In fact, new age financial institutions all over the world ensure that ethical handling of customers and responsiveness to their complaints are an integral part of their incentive and reward systems for staff. MFIs must do the same as well.

*That said, in many places where serious problems such as multiple lending, frauds, high levels of willful default*, the use of agents, and so on, exist on the ground, a common denominator can be usually found, and it is a fact that "staff" turnover has also been very high. One must also remember that all and sundry were hired as staff and especially without sufficient background checks (due diligence) and placed on the job without requisite training. And much of this has happened as the drive to grow

---

[506] Consultative Group to Assist the Poor.

## Chapter 33: Redeeming the Indian Microfinance Industry: What Needs to Be Done?

quickly and reach scale prompted many MFIs (and especially some of the newly established commercially oriented NBFC MFIs) to use all possible methods to achieve this.[507]

In fact, a lot of this has to do with the overall incentive system for staff at MFIs, where the unspoken rule is to either "disburse a lot quickly or perish," as a result of which the decentralized agent model came into vogue. Thus, aspects such as "building scale quickly," the "pressure to reduce interest rates" and the "desire to be a cost leader and maximize profits and value to shareholders," seem to have pushed the Indian microfinance industry into poor human resources practices and that must change for sure.

It must also be noted that working and living conditions of staff in the microfinance industry is dismal. In many places, there are no service rules and, often, it is a very high-pressure, 24×7 schedule. Typically, there are no contracts issued by many institutions and the hiring/firing is done verbally and at the whims and fancy of the superiors. Grievance procedures do not seem to exist in most MFIs, and faced with such a situation, it is hardly surprising that the level of frustration among genuine staff is rather high. In fact, some (good) staff have crossed the line[508] because of such an environment and moved toward (unethical) behavior such as that listed earlier. It is, therefore, imperative that MFIs address the prevalent problems and focus on building professional and ethical human resource systems, with the right incentives, for senior/operational managers and branch/field level staff.

- ✓ *Ensure that senior management and board compensation throughout the microfinance sector value chain is aligned with client interests:* The best example of a poorly aligned compensation system is from the subprime mortgage mess, where actors ranging from frontline personnel to top executives at lending companies, brokerage firms, investment banking companies, and ratings agencies, all responded to a compensation system that encouraged making abusive loans. In fact, *"compensation was one factor among many that contributed to the financial crisis that began in 2007."*[509] I guess that this issue applies to the 2010 AP microfinance crisis situation as well. In future, all stakeholders, including MFIs, should ensure that compensation/incentive systems for senior management and board are driven solely by a common vision in design and delivery of fair and sustainable financial services (including credit) that meets the needs of low-income clients. And without any doubt,

---

507 Some specific comments are in order here: (i) the lack of background checks has meant that staff who have committed frauds in one place (MFI) have got into higher positions in other MFIs and naturally, they also resocialize new staff at the other (new) MFI and attune them toward not-so-good practices. The lack of background checks has also resulted in people with criminal records entering the MFI roster and moving on from one MFI to another, often engaging in increasing frauds at the various levels; and (ii) the lack of training has meant that the staff do not understand the mission of microfinance or that of the MFI and this has again resulted in the excessive drive toward growth, scale and profits—as a result, several MFIs have moved toward using agents for loan disbursement and recovery and also have lent for purposes, that need not be strictly called as microfinance.
508 Nothing however justifies bad behavior by staff.
509 Quoted from BIS paper on Compensation and Corporate Governance, 2010.

such systems should take into account the medium-/long-term risk prevalent in any microfinancing activity.

✓ *Have a mechanism to get client feedback and respond sincerely to customer complaints:* MFIs, at a minimum, should have a designated department (or at least an officer) responsible for handling complaints in a professional and sincere manner. All staff must view customer complaints not just as a valuable source of client feedback but also as useful information for adapting the product and delivery process to better meet client needs. The toll-free complaint number set up by SKS Microfinance and other MFIs deserves mention. And MFIs must attempt to look at such mechanisms to get organized client feedback and channelize the same for delivering responsive financial products in tune with the needs of their clients.

✓ *Ensure transparency on product terms, institutional policies, and operational models and facilitate real-time implementation of stated terms, policies, and models on the ground:* Transparency is extremely critical for MFIs to build trust with clients and all other stakeholders in the current environment. This would include: (i) educating (not just informing) low-income clients on all product terms, as per the contract (including interest to be paid or received); (ii) enabling clients to understand all other policies of the institution (such as penalties for repayment, recovery processes, etc.) and the working model; and (iii) ensuring that these product terms, policies, and models are not distorted during implementation[510] through appropriate controls.

Only this will enable clients to make informed and knowledgeable purchase choices and MFIs must strive to facilitate this. The interest rate issue is critical and clients need to know what they are paying (or receiving) and MFIs must clearly indicate the nominal and effective interest rates as well as total cost to client under normal and delinquent situations. Apart from the transparency aspect, pricing of loans should be fair in that low-income clients do not have to pay for the inefficiency or unnecessarily elaborate policies at MFIs.

To summarize, the role of the board and the senior management in ensuring all these aspects during implementation is critical. In fact, the level of success achieved in translating these intended strategies to realized actions on the ground will almost depend exclusively on the level of commitment and leadership that senior management and board show toward implementing these. And I hope that these leaders recognize that, just like many of us, low-income people want appropriate products and quality service, and that MFIs which focus on meeting client needs in an ethical manner will be the most successful in the long term. Let us make no mistake about that!

---

510 For example, the use of agents and other such mechanisms in the microfinance model during real-time operations must be avoided at all costs and this will have to be done using appropriate human resources policies and staff incentives.

# Chapter 34:
# The 2010 AP Microfinance Crisis: Lessons for International Agencies like CGAP!

The CGAP (Consultative Group to Assist the Poor) could not spot the inherent weaknesses in the commercial microfinance model that it was unabashedly promoting as part of its inclusive finance agenda. This is certainly a reason for self-introspection by its board, senior management, and other stakeholders involved in its governance. Without any doubt, the CGAP, as an institution, should become more accountable to the low-income people, for whom it supposedly exists in the first place—so that they can be really included in a financial sense.

Unfortunately, in India, financial inclusion has translated merely to the delivery of consumption credit (and some small production loans). That consumption credit alone is insufficient to reduce or alleviate poverty is perhaps a no-brainer, for all honest development practitioners. Despite the lack of serious impact studies, for those who have worked at the grassroots and continue to so, it is rather evident that mere access to finance cannot and will not help people come out of poverty. Access to finance is therefore best viewed as a necessary, but not sufficient, condition for poverty alleviation.

While microfinanciers and access to finance enthusiasts can perhaps take comfort in the fact that consumption loans alone cannot make a dent on poverty, there is a caveat in order. They cannot escape the fact that the drive and desire to include low-income people with regard to financial services has resulted in the proliferation of financial services focused on loans and even within loans, primarily consumption lending. The enthusiasm to include low-income people has also led to not-so-good practices including multiple lending, overlending, top-up loans, ghost/*benami* loans, and the like driven by the motivation of some MFIs to generate huge wealth for themselves and their promoters. In fact, one of the major reasons for the 2010 AP microfinance crisis was the mindless drive to include people financially, without asking the question(s) on whether the current bouquet of financial services being offered were indeed appropriate, whether the practices being followed were fair, transparent, legal and ethically sound, and whether the other conditions so necessary for effective use of the financial services existed at the grassroots.

Without question, the onus[511] for this (at least in some *small* part) lies with institutions like the CGAP[512]—which is said to be the foremost agency for promoting financial access to low-income people globally. Without question, the CGAP has played a very important role in the Indian microfinance sector through various efforts over the last decade—ranging from capacity building to credit rating, research[513] on equity, technology, innovation, and the like and dissemination of global best practices to microfinance stakeholders. The CGAP has also been at the forefront providing transparency and other awards[514] as well as grants-in-aid (to the tune of several crores of rupees) to some of the Grameen replicator MFIs[515] that mainly provide consumption loans using a high commercial for-profit strategy. Last but not the least, the CGAP has also (indirectly) facilitated various institutions to invest in many Indian MFIs.

That is not all. At many conferences in India, it is common to see a couple of CGAP staff and they are also often present at discussions (on various occasions) with important microfinance stakeholders in India including DFIs, commercial banks, large MFIs, and even regulators. Further, institutions like CGAP also intervene through projects such as the responsible microfinance project, promoted under the aegis of the World Bank and implemented in India by SIDBI. Thus, in India, CGAP has become synonymous with Grameen MFIs and whenever an MFI gets into some sort of trouble with a state government, the first thing that the MFI does is to argue that it reports to and is recognized by CGAP.[516]

Now, given so much of active interaction with various stakeholders in India and given this leverage, it is indeed an obvious disappointment that CGAP could not spot the inherent weaknesses in the commercial microfinance model that it was unabashedly promoting. Without question, this is surely a reason for self-introspection by its board, senior management, and other stakeholders involved in its governance. And going forward, they would also need to discuss ways in which CGAP, as an institution, becomes more accountable to the low-income people (whom it exists to serve in the first place) and ensures that promoting access to financial services does not in any way infringe on the rights to life, liberty, and pursuit of happiness by such low-income people. Going to scale is critical but scale and growth cannot come at the expense of delivering appropriate financial services through fair, transparent, and legal mechanisms. There can be no compromise whatsoever on that and CGAP must ensure that this basic tenet is internalized in other countries where the microfinance sector is on such a rapid growth path.

Take the case of India—while MFIs grew for different reasons, it was during this period of burgeoning growth (April 2008–March 2010 and thereafter until September 2010) that the hitherto highly

---

511 My intention is not to blame anyone. I am merely highlighting what has happened and would like to see course corrections.

512 The Consultative Group to Assist the Poor, www.cgap.org, is a specialized multidonor body that is housed at the World Bank.

513 CGAP's paper after the first Indian IPO did not seriously discuss the governance problems in the MFI concerned despite many of these issues being found in the public domain (read paper, "Commercialization of Microfinance in India: A Discussion of the Emperor's Apparel," by Prof. Sriram in *EPW*, June 12, 2010, Vol: XLV No: 24).

514 Some of the institutions that received the CGAP transparency award appear to have had serious governance problems.

515 The CEO of one of the Grameen replicator MFIs that CGAP gave a huge grant-in-aid to some years ago was cited by *The Economic Times* in January/February 2011 as having annual compensation much higher than the highest paid CEO of one of India's large private sector banks.

516 If the CGAP is interested, I can share letters that are in circulation.

# Chapter 34: The 2010 AP Microfinance Crisis: Lessons for International Agencies like CGAP!

successful model of JLGs/centers was severely diluted. And the changes did more harm than good to the original concept of joint liability and peer pressure—as several JLGs operated in a mutually reinforcing (cartel-like) manner within a center.

Four issues are relevant here:

- One, the normal and established processes of client acquisition through green field methods—where MFIs laboriously promoted their very own groups and nurtured them and painstakingly created a culture of credit discipline and high repayment based on mutual trust and other aspects—were slowly abandoned by many MFIs because of their urgency to grow fast. Process mapping, which is a good tool by itself, and efficiency goals, which are laudable, were erroneously used to quicken client-acquisition strategies and other related processes. Thus, an undue emphasis was placed on quicker identification of clients, faster processing of loan applications, and so on. And basic issues such as understanding of a client's antecedents and contextual situations, preparation of clients, analysis of client/household loan absorption and debt-servicing capacity and the like—which were the hallmarks of the green field client-acquisition strategy in the traditional Grameen model—were slowly but surely ignored and bypassed.

- Two, given that clients needed to be identified faster and loans disbursed to them quickly, the MFIs concerned had just two options for client acquisition: (i) acquisition—whereby MFIs started taking over the portfolio of smaller MFIs or specific JLGs. Sometimes, SHGs were also taken over (cannibalized) and split into several JLGs (depending on size of SHG); and (ii) mutual sharing—whereby several MFIs decided to share and use their available JLGs/clients on successive days and on the basis of a simple reciprocal arrangement. While both strategies were used, over time, cartels of MFIs started to follow the latter as it was a win-win situation for all of them.

- Three, both of these led to the emergence of power brokers (also called broker agents[517] or ring leaders)—they were basically center leaders (or sometimes, even group leaders, loan officers, and local political honchos) who had access to a captive set of JLGs and clients. These new intermediaries started to match-make with different MFIs on increasingly attractive and exploitative terms. Thus, slowly, these agents became the most powerful pivot in the local microfinance system and various processes were outsourced to them, often without any quality checks. The outsourced processes ranged from client acquisition to KYC documentation, loan disbursement, repayment collection, and

---

517 (a) Implementation safeguards against notorious agents are an imperative for the proposed microfinance bill (http://www.moneylife.in/article/implementation-safeguards-against-notorious-agents-are-an-imperative-for-the-proposed-microfinance-bill/19017.html) by Ramesh S. Arunachalam, August 18, 2011; (b) How and why did microfinance agents become a part of the Indian microfinance business? (http://www.moneylife.in/article/how-and-why-did-microfinance-agents-become-a-part-of-the-indian-microfinance-business/19301.html) by Ramesh S. Arunachalam, August 29, 2011; and (c) Implementation safeguards against notorious agents are an imperative for the proposed microfinance bill (http://www.moneylife.in/article/implementation-safeguards-against-notorious-agents-are-an-imperative-for-the-proposed-microfinance-bill/19017.html) by Ramesh S. Arunachalam, August 18, 2011.

so on. Over time, this outsourcing through agents became an established strategy and the agents became omnipresent and omnipotent in the Indian microfinance industry. They often demanded their pound of flesh and got it, too. It appears that the coercive practices and multiple lending, which have often been cited in the 2010 AP crisis, were due to the presence and use of such agents. It is also clear that, given the burgeoning growth and prevalence of such agent-led decentralized microfinance models, it would be difficult to enforce concepts like social performance[518] on the ground.

- Four, over the period April 2008–March 2010 and thereafter, growth came not from adding fresh clients. Rather, growth came through concurrent loans (from the same MFI) to its clients and multiple lending[519] to shared JLGs/clients, who were serviced by different MFIs on different days. In fact, data reveal that for the six large AP-headquartered NBFC MFIs, while their clients grew by about 1.30 times across two reference periods (April 2008–March 2009 and April 2009–March 2010), the growth in gross loan portfolio across these two periods was about 2.19[520] times, indicating that portfolio deepening had occurred perhaps through larger or successive or multiple loans to the clients.

These concurrent and parallel MFI loans, through shared JLGs and clients, appeared to be God-sent and clients just grabbed them during the phase of burgeoning growth—as by then many of them realized that they could not service their increasing debt. The cases of Zaheera Bhee[521] and others clearly illustrate this. The MFIs too were ecstatic about turbocharging financial inclusion and so were equity investors, banks, regulators/supervisors, policymakers, and other stakeholders including international bodies such as the CGAP. This is a critical point that needs to be noted. The outreach of the Indian microfinance industry even today needs significant correction and revision to reflect this reality of concurrent loans, ghost loans and multiple loans to shared JLGs/clients.

Therefore, it is high time that institutions such as the CGAP[522] recognize and use the following lessons (from the Indian microfinance crisis) with regard to promoting inclusive finance for low-income people in its day-to-day work (globally).

*Lesson 1:* The scope of current inclusive finance practice in India is rather narrow. While the intentions (like the report of the Financial Inclusion Committee and other policy pronouncements) may have been

---

518 http://www.moneylife.in/article/microfinance-will-seal-of-excellence-and-social-performance-management-as-yardsticks-work/20038.html

519 Also ghost lending.

520 This should have been higher at 2.47 had the Mix Market retained the original GLP figures that it had put out in 2010/2011 for BASIX and SHARE. For some reason, Mix Market changed its original figures for BASIX and SHARE respectively from US$ 223,229,799 and US$ 490,923,201 to US$ 172,484,946 and US$ 376,593,362 (as on date). I have the original print screen data and other pieces of evidence with regard to the original data put out by Mix Market. There are several other issues with the Mix Market database and I can provide the details if required.

521 http://microfinance-in-india.blogspot.com/2010/11/can-we-bring-back-ayeshas-ammy.html and Chapter 2.

522 This is also important for stakeholders like the PSCF and others involved in developing the regulatory architecture for microfinance.

# Chapter 34: The 2010 AP Microfinance Crisis: Lessons for International Agencies like CGAP!

to provide low-income clients with access to a wide range of need-based financial services, in reality, the inclusive finance (or financial inclusion) paradigm[523] has mainly led to the proliferation of credit and primarily consumption loans, although there have been some small production/livelihood loans.

*Lesson 2:* Standard (MFI) loans for consumption and/or small production needs, which dominate microfinance (or access to finance) in India today, tend to work well for loan sizes in the range of Rs. 10,000–Rs. 15,000 per client and at most <= Rs. 50,000.

*Lesson 3:* Rs. 50,000 as the loan amount is some sort of *Lakshman Reka*,[524] that the MFIs should not breach, unless they are absolutely sure of the individual/household having the requisite debt servicing ability (could be a livelihood, production unit, and/or labor, etc.) to repay the larger loan. This is the most important lesson from the 2010 AP crisis for MFIs, banks, policymakers, regulators/supervisors, and other stakeholders.

*Lesson 4:* Indiscriminate (and multiple) lending to low-income people under the pretext of furthering financial inclusion—without regard to their (and their families) loan absorption and debt servicing capacity, and especially in the wake of vulnerable livelihoods, can only prove to be a recipe for disaster. As has been demonstrated by the 2010 AP crisis, this will ultimately exclude them altogether from the financial system. As has been argued, when people with weak and vulnerable livelihoods are lent large sums of money (> Rs. 50,000), repayment will either have to come from fresh loans (i.e., greening through concurrent/multiple lending) and/or restructuring of loans. At some point, this cycle will (have to) stop and the bubble will simply burst. These clients will then become financially excluded all over again.

If that is the scenario, then what can institutions such as the CGAP do to help the microfinance industry overcome this precarious situation? First, CGAP can help reengineer the financial inclusion paradigm, to address some of the issues mentioned here. In my opinion, this reengineering should ensure the delivery of quality credit that will reduce risk and vulnerability of low-income clients and give them more choices.[525]

By quality credit, I am arguing for a greater focus on post-harvest and/or post-production financing for agriculture and other sectors that provide (or can provide) significant livelihoods opportunities for low-income people. In other words, among other things, this would call for financing of

---

523 In India, typically, financial inclusion (FI) is presently characterized by (i) preoccupation with opening of savings accounts; (ii) large focus on consumption credit and small production loans; (iii) low outreach with regard to vulnerable groups in agriculture; (iv) lack of suitable and affordable risk management services; and (v) lack of appropriate livelihood financing. The two aspects of lack of suitable and affordable risk management services and lack of appropriate and affordable livelihood financing are noteworthy aspects because they again show the huge gaps between a great vision and intended strategy (the recommendation of the well-intentioned Financial Inclusion Committee) and actual implementation on the ground, which is narrowly focused on consumption and small production credit.

524 A popular metaphor for a line not to be crossed.

525 This can happen through alternative channels that afford lower costs, have greater trust, and high levels of mutual acceptance.

## An Idea Which Went Wrong

agriculture produce/other products[526] marketing—a very critical aspect for small/marginal producers[527] as it has the potential to enhance choices for them in terms of buyers, and so on. Of course, here, the existing relationships would need to be better understood if financial products are to be developed and delivered through appropriate channels.[528] Second, the CGAP must ensure that the focus of financial inclusion is so reengineered such that the delivery of a wide range of financial services (loans, savings, insurance, pensions, etc.) are used strategically to drive higher rewards, better remuneration, and greater power down the value chain as shown in Figure 34.1—otherwise, it will be of limited use.

**Figure 34.1 Tracking Power and Influence within Value Chain Analyses—Example of Agriculture**

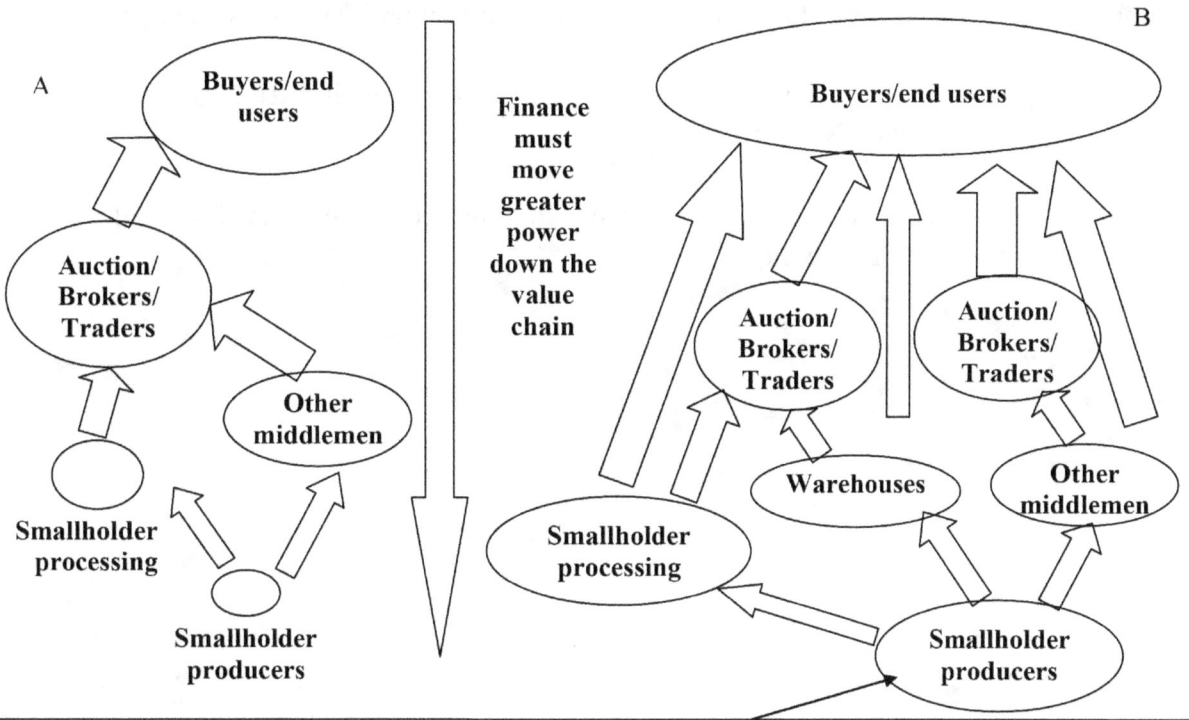

More power and reduced vulnerability for small producers in Scenario B as opposed to Scenario A—as finance gives them staying and bargaining power, reduces their risks, and enables them to get rewards/returns commensurate with the value they create, risk they bear, investment they make, and effort they put in. Note that there are an increased number of players in situation B as opposed to A and there are more choices for the clients as well.

---

526 Like handicrafts, etc.
527 MSMEs as well.
528 And this would need to be validated specifically for a context, a product, and a partner but these are general suggested arrangements.

## Chapter 34: The 2010 AP Microfinance Crisis: Lessons for International Agencies like CGAP!

Hence, the CGAP needs to help initiate a new microfinance paradigm[529] where financial products, mechanisms, and instruments can be used to perform the following:

- Reduce risk/vulnerability[530] in the existing livelihoods of low-income people, arising from various market imperfections—examples include warehouse receipt financing implemented with appropriate safeguards, pro-poor value-chain financing, and so on;

- Help create strong safety and security nets[531] for these low-income clients for a range of aspects as shown in Figure 34.2;

- Enable these low-income clients to pursue diversified/migratory livelihoods where required;

- Facilitate reinclusion of these low-income people (who were once included but subsequently excluded because of fragile livelihoods); and

- Create risk management mechanisms[532] to ensure that they continue to stay financially included, in the context of their fragile livelihoods.

---

[529] *Source*: Adapted from Arunachalam "UNDP Financial Inclusion Strategy in 7 Focus States: Strategic Consideration and Suggestions, UNDP," 2007.
[530] Weather and crop insurance are gaining ground. Contract farming schemes exist but are not producer oriented.
[531] Some innovations exist here for health as well as life coverage but much work is necessary in the nature of product design and also distribution. Micro-pension schemes are also available.
[532] Post harvest loans in fisheries/agriculture and warehouse receipts are examples of such products.

**Figure 34.2 Types of Security for Low-income People: Potential Areas for Servicing by the Inclusive Finance Paradigm**

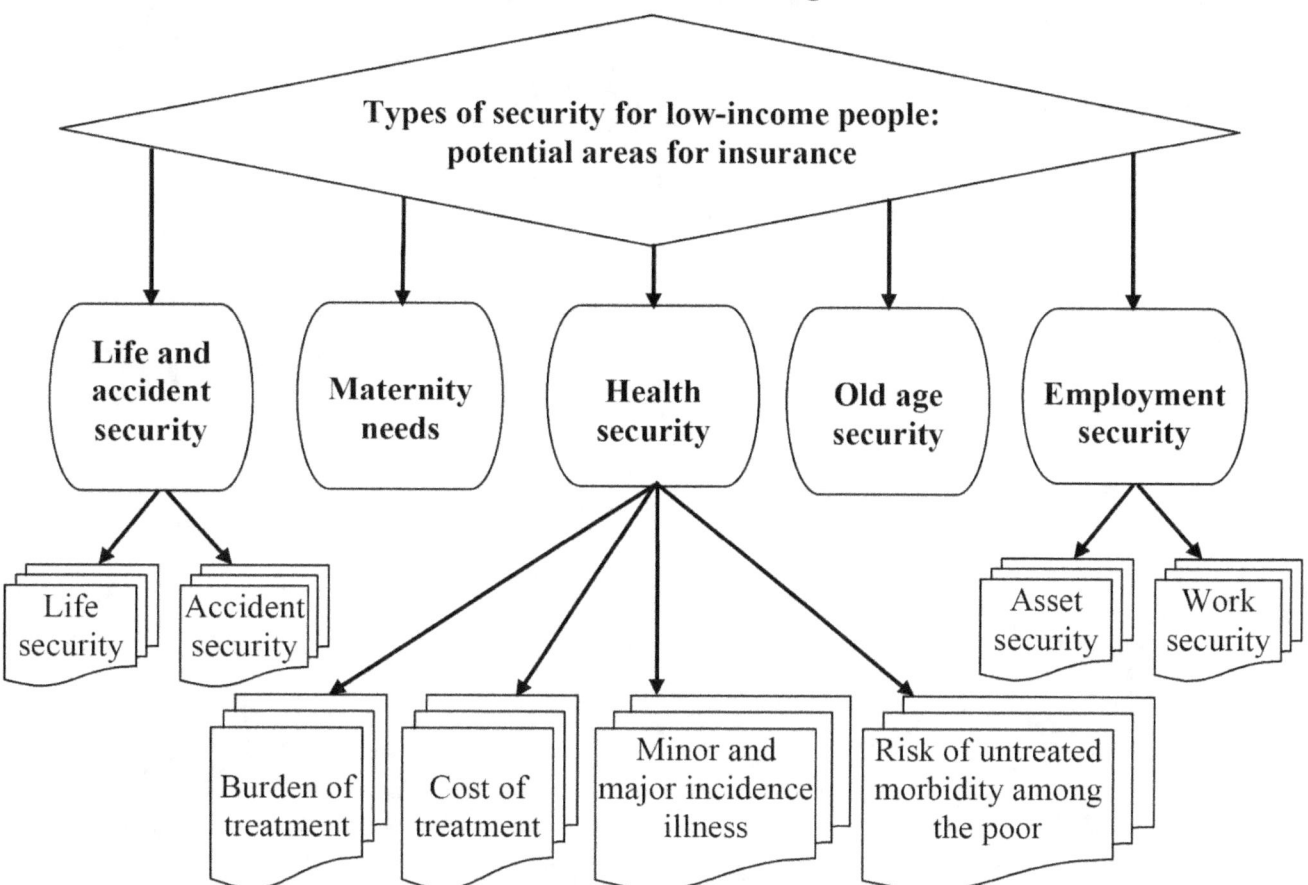

Thus, I would very much like the CGAP to champion the larger cause of reengineering the financial inclusion paradigm to facilitate poverty alleviation on the ground. They have it in their DNA and, in line with their acronym, the CGAP must now become the "Consultative Group to Alleviate Poverty" and assume the lead role in fighting and trying to eradicate poverty globally. I am sure they have the wherewithal and resources to do this and let us hope their governing council, senior management, and other governance structures take this appeal seriously and demonstrate sufficient will to do this in real time, on the ground.

# PART – IV

# Chapter 35:[533]
# Epilogue - Eliminating Conflicts of Interests in Financial Sector Regulation

When I started writing this book, my primary objective was to focus on commercial microfinance as an idea gone wrong in India. The journey through this book should have certainly enabled you, the reader, to understand my perspective on the key antecedents to this and the consequences of the same.

That said, I have all along felt the need to bring a broader financial sector perspective and position the 2010 AP microfinance crisis and subsequent events within the ambit of India's larger financial sector framework. I try to do that in this final chapter using the Reserve Bank of India (RBI) and its legal framework as a fulcrum for my analysis. I am sure that you will find this perspective interesting as it raises important and yet fundamental issues with regard to financial sector regulation and supervision and the conflicts of interests embedded therein.

In fact, I see "conflicts of interest" as one of the major reasons for the lax regulation and supervision of microfinance in India. And, this lax regulation and supervision in turn, permitted the six large AP-headquartered NBFC MFIs in particular (and NBFC MFIs in general) to grow in an irresponsible manner in the years preceding 2010 and thereby led to the actual crisis on the ground. Given that these NBFC MFIs were entities registered with the RBI, it indeed has to shoulder much of the blame for the 2010 AP crisis. In fact, the slack manner in which the NBFC MFIs were supervised is something that Dr Y V Reddy, former RBI governor, has himself admitted. Part of the reason for this laissez-faire supervision by RBI was that the (*old boys*) network of the microfinance sector was able to weave magic in front of the eyes of the RBI and persuade it that *financial inclusion* was the sole objective behind the phenomenal growth of the (NBFC) MFIs. The RBI, on its part, naively accepted the explanations offered by NBFC MFIs and just let them run amok with the unprecedented growth in Andhra Pradesh (in the period 2008–2010 especially). Not to sound like a broken record, but, even a single letter from the RBI to any one of these extremely fast growing NBFC MFIs may have done the trick! But, alas, that was not to be and the rest is history, of course—today, millions of clients have been excluded from the

---

[533] This chapter was written in October 2013, a little after the RBI Governor had announced the new financial inclusion committee under Dr Mor's leadership. In February 2014, the PSCF sent back the MFIDR Bill (2012) to the MoF for revisions.

# Chapter 35: Epilogue - Eliminating Conflicts of Interests in Financial Sector Regulation

financial sector by the very folks whose claim to fame was "financial inclusion" of the poorest and the excluded.

Thus, undoubtedly, the 2010 AP microfinance disaster as well as the previous microfinance crises (in Krishna district in 2006 and Kolar district in 2009), clearly, were symbols of regulatory and supervisory failure in India. The blame for the same has to rest squarely on the shoulders of the board of financial supervision (BFS), RBI, and the Departments of Non-Bank Supervision (DNBS) and Department of Banking Supervision (DBS) at the RBI, both of which come under the BFS.

Clearly, the above-mentioned crises situations also represent dereliction of duty by the RBI (i.e., BFS, DNBS, and DBS) no doubt because they simply watched as the NBFC MFIs regulated by them grew irresponsibly using multiple, ghost and overlending strategies—*which many of the MFIs have themselves admitted to and which have now been well documented*—that pushed poor people to the brink of indebtedness. And indeed personnel of the BFS, DNBS, and DBS just sat in their fancy offices even as these low-income clients were being subjected to complete harassment on the ground. And as the case of Zaheera Bee[534] illustrates, none of the NBFC MFIs followed either the RBI's code of conduct, let alone the self-regulatory codes of their associations (MFIN or Sa-Dhan).

This clearly shows that the three pillars of RBI's regulatory architecture failed miserably: (i) supervision of NBFC MFIs; (ii) protection of poor consumers who were clients of NBFC MFIs; and (iii) use of self-regulatory organizations like MFIN and Sa-Dhan that could do very little to actually protect the end-user poor clients.

And a lot of this happened because industry insiders (from the financial inclusion and microfinance industry) lobbied hard with the RBI to ensure that "financial innovation and financial inclusion" by (NBFC) MFIs did not suffer.[535] And the results are there to see, with several million people excluded from the formal financial system after the 2010 AP crisis—the blame for which should go in part, if not wholly, to the RBI.

Given this discussion, one is tempted to ask, currently, *how accountable has the RBI been and how transparent are its operations?*

Indeed, I was surprised to find that there is no formal mechanism of accountability enshrined in the RBI Act and I quote Dr Subba Rao, former Governor, RBI who argued that:

> *"Neither the RBI Act nor any rules lay down a formal accountability mechanism. In the absence of a specific formulation, the fallback is on the general principle underlying a democracy - which is to render accountability to the parliament through the Finance Minister. The Reserve Bank assists the Finance Minister in answering parliament questions that pertain to its domain. Besides, the Standing Committee on Finance of Parliament summons the Governor for testimony on specific issues including legislations under consideration."*[536]

---

534 See Chapter 2.
535 This was roughly similar to the global financial crisis where steady regulation and supervision were objected to and booted out for the supposed benefit of enhancing financial innovation and financial inclusion.
536 http://www.rbi.org.in/scripts/BS_SpeechesView.aspx?Id=563, point 7

And surely this lack of formal accountability and transparency seems to be showing on the ground as highlighted by a spate of not-so-transparent incidents[537] involving the RBI, which are discussed in detail here:

(a) Take the case of Mr K M Birla,[538] who initially did not resign from the RBI board despite his group company having applied for a banking license. Mr Birla had been appointed to the central bank's board in June 2006. The resignation, which came several weeks after one of the companies in his group—Aditya Birla Nuvo—had applied for a banking licence, is said to have occurred because of the conflict of interest issue. The group and company had all along maintained that there is no conflict of interest. However, the point to note is that *when the Chairman of a Group which applies for a Banking license has been serving as a Director of the RBI for the last several years* and continues to be a director even while the license applications are being processed, there is most certainly a conflict of interest.

In fact, RBI's handling of this conflict of interest matter was highly unprofessional and indecisive (referring it back to the Union Government) until Mr Birla was forced to resign because, according to the media, a member of the Parliamentary Standing Committee on Finance (PSCF) objected. Thus, I was certainly not impressed with the manner in which the RBI handled the resignation of Mr Kumar Mangalam Birla, chairman of the Aditya Birla Group. That Mr Birla was ultimately *forced* to resign from the RBI's central board of directors is a point to be noted and this does not reflect appropriately on the RBI's corporate governance practices.

That someone like Mr Birla, whose group had a strong commercial interest in financial services through subsidiary companies, was allowed to serve on the RBI board (uninterrupted) for many years suggests that he could have perhaps even lobbied for the entry of large business industrial houses into banking. The results are there for everyone to see as when the RBI called for banking licenses in 2013, they strangely permitted the entry of large industrial business groups into banking–a practice hitherto avoided in many countries globally. This, in fact, vitiates the entire bank licensing process in a significant manner as vindicated by the report of the PSCF discussed later.

(b) As written in Livemint[539] and I quote, *"Two months after the deadline for applications for new banks expired, there have been two changes in the list of applicants. One, Value Industries Ltd, a unit of Videocon Industries Ltd, has withdrawn its application for a banking permit, and two, Chandigarh-based real estate and hospitality company KC Land and Finance Ltd has sought a banking licence. The original list of 26 permit seekers, released by RBI on 1 July, did not have this name. Many are finding the*

---

537 During August–October 2013 primarily
538 Mr Birla has also supposedly been named in the CBI first information report (FIR) in the coal scam.
539 http://www.livemint.com/Opinion/l1qAtD6lUqEazr8rszuu6J/Wanted-an-independent-accountable-RBI.html

## Chapter 35: Epilogue - Eliminating Conflicts of Interests in Financial Sector Regulation

*sudden appearance of a new applicant and withdrawal of the Videocon group mysterious."* Whatever be the reasons, I am not sure that this represents the procedural transparency required of institutions like the RBI

(c) When the PSCF was seized of the bank licensing[540] matter, the RBI's tearing hurry in granting banking licenses cannot be rationalized at all. In my humble opinion, irrespective of whatever the RBI says, this action by the RBI (alone) carries huge implications because it shows utter disrespect for parliamentary democracy. In fact, as this manuscript was going through its final edit, the PSCF report on bank licensing had been presented and it opposes many of the aspects in the RBI's currently flawed bank licensing policy, as noted below:

"The Parliamentary Standing Committee on Finance led by BJP leader Yashwant Sinha on Monday submitted a report in Parliament on 'Policy on New Licences in the Banking Sector', where it advocated the RBI to keep industry and banking separate.

"Banking being a highly leveraged business involving public money and public welfare, the Committee are of the considered opinion that it will be more in the fitness of things to keep industry and banking separate. The Committee, therefore desire the Government/Reserve Bank of India to review the licencing guidelines accordingly," the report has recommended.

About two dozens, including corporate houses, are in the fray to obtain bank licenses, which the RBI proposes to grant in the first quarter of 2014. The committee has expressed apprehension that management of private banks may deploy their funds to extend undue favour to own industrial owners, as it was noticed in the pre- nationalised era.

"... The Committee are apprehensive that industrial/ business houses may not be geared to achieve the national objectives of financial inclusion, priority sector lending, etc," the report said. Moreover the committee noted that as on March 2013, out of 15,630 existing private sector bank branches, only 2,699 branches are located in the rural areas i.e. to say only about 17 per cent of the total branches are in the rural areas. "Given such a background, the Committee are apprehensive that industrial/business houses may not be geared to achieve the national objectives of financial inclusion, priority sector lending etc", it added.

The 32-member panel further said that the 'fit and proper' criteria to be used by the RBI to grant licenses "is too ambiguous" and too much scope has been left for subjective discretion of RBI. Having such subjective, ambiguous and open-ended criteria, it said, may leave the doors open for arbitrariness and invite charges of favouritism.

---

540 http://www.moneylife.in/article/does-the-rbi-know-how-much-conflicts-of-interest-it-has-created/34760.html

"The Committee, would therefore, suggest that a more precise, a coherent and objective yardstick/criteria may be formulated to assess the credentials of divergent entities from different sectors in a uniform manner," the report said. To ensure fair-play and justice in the licensing process, it favoured a suitable mechanism to enable aggrieved applicants to seek review of decisions, the panel noted.

Besides, it has recommended raising the minimum capital requirement for raising the minimum capital requirement for the new banks to Rs 1,000 crore from the present Rs 500 crore. On timeline, the Committee recommended the RBI to execute the process of screening and evaluation of applications in a well-defined and transparent manner without leaving any room for speculation or conjecture. The RBI has neither given time limit by which the licences are to be issued nor the number of licenses."[541]

(d) Further, the Banking Selection Advisory Panel[542] had significant conflicts of interests and many weaknesses as a panel. It should also be noted that the panel included several past regulators, who, in my humble opinion, would not have been in a position to dispassionately and objectively analyse past regulatory and supervisory failures at RBI—an aspect so critical for making decisions with regard to providing bank licenses to large industrial corporate groups and NBFC MFIs. Further, it also needs to be emphasized that many panel members[543] have had (and some continue to have) strong associations with institutions that were at the heart of the 2010 AP microfinance crisis. Also, the panel includes regulators whose questionable approach (and actions) during the years preceding the October 2010 AP microfinance crisis had serious consequences in the ground. These certainly resulted in some form of regulatory/supervisory failure which, in turn, exacerbated the 2010 AP microfinance crisis. Therefore, I am not sure that due thought and procedure were applied to deciding on the composition of the Dr Bimal Jalan Banking Selection Advisory Panel. An example should serve to illustrate this better.

Let us consider Dr Nachiket Mor,[544] who was made a member of the above-mentioned (RBI) Banking Services Advisory Panel. Around the same time, Dr Mor also headed the (RBI) Financial Inclusion

---

541 http://www.dailypioneer.com/business/par-panel-suggests-rbi-to-refrain-from-giving-banking-licences-to-corporates.html

542 http://www.moneylife.in/article/reorganising-bank-selection-advisory-panel-is-a-good-governance-imperative-for-the-rbi/34853.html

543 That is why I am insisting on a cooling period when private sector people get into the central bank and further, one should look at the track record and background of these financial sector private players before they are actually posted on the board of a central bank or any of its committees—so that similar conflict of interest situations do not arise. Now, I can provide more details to show that people involved with the 2006 Krishna crisis, the 2009 Kolar crisis and the 2010 AP microfinance crisis and also the irresponsible growth of NBFC MFIs in Andhra Pradesh occupy very important positions at the RBI and especially in various panels. That is why I have written on these topics (somewhat repeatedly) and I hope that we do not face a more serious crisis down the line.

544 Let me at the outset say that I have high regard for Dr Mor (I have said this before) and I say the same now—he is a brilliant professional with lots of energy and experience and I have no personal agenda against him. I like him as a person and, for the record, he and I have enjoyed a great relationship whenever we have met. Professionally, I only question two issues: (i) that someone so closely related to the financial sector occupies very important and multiple positions at the RBI. I fear that things could go wrong as they did in Andhra Pradesh microfinance in 2006 and subsequently in 2010 and also like in the global subprime when insiders did a lot of regulatory damage and (ii) why should someone be so omnipresent and omnipotent at the RBI? Power corrupts even the best individuals and I fear that when someone

# Chapter 35: Epilogue - Eliminating Conflicts of Interests in Financial Sector Regulation

Committee,[545] appointed on September 23, 2013. According to Prof. Sriram[546] (formerly of the Indian Institute of Management, Ahmedabad), Dr Nachiket Mor is said to have played an important role in the irresponsible growth of MFIs and I quote Prof Sriram:

"The microfinance growth and later crisis should be seen as a series of unrelated but connected events and is a typical of other events.

1. Once the NGO MFI achieved a certain amount of scale, it was imperative that they moved to a for-profit format. Unfortunately the Indian law did not allow NGOs to invest in for profits. Please remember, these discussions were happening in the days when MF salaries were modest. So none of the promoters had a personal net worth to invest the minimum capital of Rs.2 crore to set up an NBFC.

2. It was during this time that Mr. Nagarajan a Chartered Accountant based in Delhi came up with the idea of using the surpluses of the NGOs for investment into NBFCs. This was a complicated exercise and needed a pass through SPV which was identified as a series of MBTs. You could see that Mr. Nagarajan was almost the single advisor/chartered accountant for most of the MFIS that moved from NGO to the for-profit format.

3. While technically this was cracked, there was the need to skim 2 crores of cash from the NGO, and park it in an NBFC till the licence was obtained from RBI and the NBFC could start operations. As I told you earlier, none of the promoters seemed to have such ready cash to invest in the capital of the NBFC. However, taking money out of the NGO and granting it to the MBT would mean a bit of shrinking of the operations and in MF activity it is dangerous to signal a winding down, without the risk of large scale default.

4. The NGO-NBFCs needed liquidity. This meant that they had to skim 2crores from the NGO without winding down operations and while being on the tread mill. This is where ICICIs securitisation and SIDBIs Transformation loan came in handy. SIDBI gave a loan of 1 Crore to the NGO. This was the needed liquidity that was transferred to the MBT. The MBT in turn invested it in the NBFC. The NBFC (once it got licence from RBI) then purchased the portfolio of the NGO. The NGO used this proceeds to pay back SIDBI. Thus the portfolio was transferred slowly and seamlessly to the new NBFC.

---

occupies six positions—all related to the RBI, then, things could go wrong. The six positions are (i) a member of the eastern board of RBI; (ii) member of the central board of the RBI; (iii) member of the Financial Inclusion Committee under Dr K C Chakrabarthy; (iv) head of the newly appointed Committee on Financial Inclusion; (v) member of the bank selection advisory panel; and (vi) member of the research advisory panel of CAFRAL (which is said to be housed in the RBI headquarters and completely funded by the RBI). Also, such kind of (over) dependence would never happen in any other central bank. With all due respect, I am not sure that the RBI is acting with accountability, when it puts a single board member on so many non-board committees and panels, which the Board (of which he is part of) will ultimately have to evaluate! That does not seem right!

545 http://www.rbi.org.in/scripts/BS_PressReleaseDisplay.aspx?prid=29606

546 Prof. Sriram's e-mail reply sent to the author, in response to a query raised by the author as a response to an earlier e-mail received from Prof. Sriram. The same can be transparently shared if required.

5. SIDBI's assistance was insufficient to capitalise the NBFC. It was at that time ICICI Bank came in. Their securitisation and partnership model was clearly making the capital of the NGO irrelevant because the portfolio was taken off the balance sheet of the NGO and they were only managing it. Which meant that while portfolios could be sold and converted into cash, the incremental lending could be done off balance sheet as an agent of ICICI Bank. This gave the sense of seamlessness for operations while the NGOs accumulated cash to route it to MBTs and thereafter to the NBFC capital. Here is a link for an article (http://www4.gsb.columbia.edu/filemgr?file_id=646440) by Bindu Anant which argues exactly that. They were lending the balance sheet power of ICICI Bank for entities that were poorly capitalised. While on paper this looked safe, this was excessive leverage because the NGOs were solely operating this portfolio including the origination, paper work, and collection. This was effectively an asset not owned, but under the sole management of the NGO/MFI.

6. At that time, ICICI was under pressure to increase its priority sector lending portfolio because it had at the end of 2002 reverse-merged with ICICI corporation and they had to reach the targets under the combined balance sheet. In addition Dr. Mor who was the ED of ICICI Bank was personally interested in this portfolio and much of it was driven by him. If you look at the press archives and writings during that time, you will clearly see Dr. Mor driving this. There was nobody else (apart from Dr. Mor and his assistants in the Social Investment Group and Rural Banking Group) who were talking about microfinance. No, not even the others in the top management. Also you would see that Dr. Mor, while he had multiple responsibilities in the Bank was disproportionately articulate about microfinance and how they needed to be integrated into the capital markets.

7. I hold that the partnership model which did away with the requirement of capital gave an unnatural (and unrealistic) pace of growth to microfinance institutions at that time. Since a significant portion of the loan portfolio was held outside the balance sheet and was serviced through fee income of being agents of ICICI Bank, the MFIs looked more profitable on a smaller asset base and obviously attracted not only investments but also high valuations. This was a tiger that everybody was riding."

Dr Prabhu Ghate, another respected researcher and author of the first two SoS[547] (MF) reports, similarly noted (in the context of the 2005-2006 Krishna AP microfinance crisis) that:

> "The second enabling cause was the rapid expansion of bank lending to MFIs that took place after 2003 with the introduction of ICICI's partnership model (discussed in Chapter 7A). With the financial constraint on expansion lifted, the MFIs were free to grow as rapidly as they could recruit and lend to new borrowers, or existing borrowers of Velugu or other MFIs."

---

547 State of Sector (Microfinance) Reports brought out by Access Development Services, New Delhi, which also organizes the Annual Microfinance India Summit event in New Delhi (usually in the last quarter of every year).

# Chapter 35: Epilogue - Eliminating Conflicts of Interests in Financial Sector Regulation

*So, I am not sure that it was appropriate to appoint Dr Mor to either the RBI board or the various RBI committees including those mentioned earlier.*

(e) The suddenness with which a new committee on financial inclusion (FI)[548] was appointed by the RBI surprised everyone because a live committee on the same subject had already been functioning at the RBI under Senior Deputy Governor, Dr K C Chakravarthy, since 2012.

*That is not all.* The composition of this new FI committee left a lot to be desired as many members of this committee had significant conflicts of interests. Apart from being closely related to each other in a professional sense, a couple of the members of the FI committee represented institutions that had directly applied for the banking license. Also, there were many members of the committee who represented (and/or served on the boards of) institutions that had significant relationships with various banking license applicants[549]. Further, many of the institutions—*that the new financial inclusion committee members represent (directly or indirectly)*—also had very significant commercial interests in the area of financial inclusion. And what is really shocking is that this insider (industry) committee with the above-mentioned characteristics was to draft the overall vision and recommend the regulatory architecture for the broad area of financial inclusion. This was surely a recipe for big time disaster as past global crises have clearly demonstrated.

And the icing on the cake was the fact that this committee ran parallel to the Banking Selection Advisory Panel (in terms of its time frame) and the chair of the FI committee was also a member of the Banking Selection Advisory Panel. As noted before, recall that two banking applicants were themselves part of the financial inclusion committee and also the fact that several members of this committee represented institutions (directly or indirectly) that had provided (or were providing) debt, equity, and other support (in a commercial manner) to the banking applicants and other microfinance industry players—in other words, they all had significant professional interest in these banking applicants as well as other microfinance institutions, some of whom were also involved in the 2010 AP microfinance crisis. As a highly reputed professor of finance at IIM Bangalore so aptly put it, the new RBI financial inclusion committee appointed on September 23, 2013, *had no conflicts but only interests.*

(f) Further, when the PSCF was looking at the broad subject matter of financial inclusion through the prism of the Microfinance Institution Development and Regulation (MFIDR) Bill, the RBI's action of appointing a new financial inclusion committee smacked of total disregard for the Indian Parliament. I simply did not understand the need for preempting Parliament!

---

548 http://www.moneylife.in/article/rbis-new-financial-inclusion-committee-rife-with-conflicts-of-interests/34638.html
549 One such institution has indeed received a banking license!

Thus, given these factors, I strongly felt that the time has come to make the RBI, India's central bank, more accountable, to the people of India. With its wide-ranging powers and greater impact on all aspects of the economy, the accountability of the RBI assumes even greater importance and should not be ignored. Indeed, as Mr Surjit Bhalla and others have long argued, *"The time has come for accountability at the RBI. This institution makes decisions that affect the fortunes (lately misfortunes) of many Indians, rich and poor."*[550] And this accountability will have to come in several transparent ways and these are discussed extensively here:

*Institutional accountability of the RBI,* as a central bank, can come in two major ways: (i) short-term measures such making the board of RBI accountable and the aspects associated with this; and (ii) long-term measures such as making the RBI directly accountable to Parliament and the mechanisms that go with it. While it is easy to propose long-term measures and distract from the real issue at hand, in my opinion, certain short-term steps can and should be immediately taken by Dr Rajan (the RBI governor, who has sweeping powers) and the Ministry of Finance to make the RBI more administratively accountable and this is first highlighted.

Simple things, as given here, can be done to facilitate RBI's accountability in the short term. Just as charity begins at home, accountability must start with the RBI board, which is in fact the first and most important layer in a multilayered accountability process. Long-term measures such as the RBI governor reporting to Parliament and other such aspects *(discussed later in this chapter)* can happen eventually, as also the formal adoption of the (proposed) Indian financial code. However, as Dr Rajan has so convincingly argued many times, there are low hanging fruits to be plucked and they need to be harvested right away (in the short-term) with regard to the issue of making RBI more accountable.

But before we discuss the substantive issues, let us go back to the RBI Act, 1934,[551] whose preamble notes that the primary function of RBI is as follows:

> *"... to regulate the issue of Bank Notes and keeping of reserves with a view to securing monetary stability in India and generally to operate the currency and credit system of the country to its advantage."*[552]

Therefore, as India's central bank *that has been created by society at large (and not just governments or politicians),* the RBI has one key objective—*the need to preserve the value of the bank notes which it has been mandated to issue for use by all of us.* I emphasize maintenance in value because any erosion of this value would mean that we, the people, would lose the overall value of our wealth. To me, that would amount to a betrayal of the trust which, we, the people, have placed in RBI as the central bank. And in my opinion, this trust cannot be built either by government ownership of the RBI or the laws that have helped establish it, but rather by the efficiency, professionalism, integrity, and adherence to

---

550  http://www.indianexpress.com/news/holding-rbi-accountable/888648/
551  http://www.rbi.org.in/scripts/OccasionalPublications.aspx?head=Reserve%20Bank%20of%20India%20Act
552  Source: RBI Act of 1934, 2 of 1934, page 12 of pdf file from RBI site -http://rbidocs.rbi.org.in/rdocs/Publications/PDFs/RBIA1934170510.pdf

# Chapter 35: Epilogue - Eliminating Conflicts of Interests in Financial Sector Regulation

good governance by those who run the RBI. And of those who run the RBI, the most important, in my opinion, is the board of the RBI, which is sacrosanct and must be so maintained. Thus, the first line of accountability would have to be the board of RBI and it must be made accountable to the people of India. That said, what then are the changes required to ensure this?

Specifically, this, in effect, would translate into the following:

a. *Using the board as the key evaluator of RBI's performance:* Treating the board as the key evaluator of RBI's performance[553] as also that of the governor (both as a leader and manager). The nonexecutive (independent) members must be capable of performing this task appropriately and independently. At a later stage, the RBI could even consider the establishment and use of an independent "lead nonexecutive director" position and facilitate regular independent meetings of the nonexecutive directors (alone) so that the above is achieved in an objective manner.

b. *Ensuring a transparent board appointment process:* Competency-based processes must be used for selection of people (who have the capacity, ethics, skills, and orientation) to serve on the RBI board. Filling up vacancies on the RBI board should thus be through proper procedure, involving a search and selection committee with at least two to four names being proposed for each board vacancy. The Finance Ministry can easily do this and thereby set the highest standards of corporate governance to the RBI as an institution. If appointment of board members is compromised, then, corporate governance and accountability of the RBI as an institution (and, more importantly, as India's central bank) would suffer, as seems to be the case because of certain events.[554]

*Thus, the need of the hour is a transparent board appointment policy for the RBI* and this policy must also ensure that directors have adequate skills and experience (apart from the availability of time to do their job effectively). The policy must also ensure that the overall composition of the RBI's board of directors is suitably diverse—including more women, youth, and individuals with the requisite skills (and appropriate backgrounds) on the RBI board is perhaps a way to improve the boards' overall functioning and effectiveness. The policy must also ensure that conflict of interest issues are taken into account with regard to board appointments so that the independence of the nonexecutive directors is not compromised, under any circumstances (whatsoever).

c. *Establishing critical non-negotiables for Board composition:* People who have an ongoing direct commercial interest in the provision of financial services (through banking companies, NBFCs, equity investments in such institutions and other related institutions) should *not* be appointed to the board. This single step should go a long way in enhancing the accountability of the RBI as an institution and must be implemented forthwith. Likewise, relatives and/or very close friends of the RBI staff

---

553 Other than monetary policy, which would have to be dealt with separately!
554 http://www.moneylife.in/article/should-the-rbi-be-made-more-accountable-mdashpart1/34926.html

*(including the governor, deputy governors, executive directors and other board members)* should *not* be appointed to the RBI board. Similarly, it may be wiser to keep politicians out of the RBI board. Let me make one thing clear here. This is not an exhaustive list of non-negotiables. *Rather, it must be viewed as a starter's set that provides examples of the kind of relationships that are better avoided to enable effective functioning of the RBI board and more importantly, facilitate public confidence with regard to the same.*

Otherwise, serious conflicts of interests and related situations, like what happened in the case of Mr Rajat Gupta, could happen here, much to the detriment of the reputation of the RBI. This is not to be construed that people with a background in economics, finance, business administration, and related areas should not be appointed to RBI board. They can be, provided, they meet the minimum non-negotiable criteria, such as those mentioned. In fact, the Financial Sector Legislative Reforms Commission has made (similar) good suggestions in this regard.[555]

Let me give you a couple of examples to explain this further. Take the case of Mr K M Birla. By virtue of having served on the RBI board for several years, he could have lobbied[556] (with the RBI) to facilitate the entry of large industrial business groups into banking–a practice that is still avoided in many countries. Note that the current round of banking licenses to be given by the RBI includes large industrial business groups as applicants for banking licenses.

Likewise, it is completely inappropriate for people like Dr Mor to serve on the RBI board given that he was and still appears to be connected with the IFMR Trust[557] (at least there are some websites and

---

555 I have adapted Clause 2 (c) to include any financial service provider.
"9. (1) Members of the Reserve Bank Board must be fit and proper persons, having expertise in dealing with matters relating to banking, payments and monetary
(2) A person cannot be appointed as a member on the Reserve Bank Board if such a person
(a) is an employee of the Central Government, except in case of the nominee members;
(b) is a member of Parliament or a state legislature;
(c) is a director, employee or officer of any banking or financial service provider;
(d) is a director, employee or officer of any system provider;
(e) is a member of an advisory council of the Reserve Bank; or
(f) is a member of the Monetary Policy Committee, other than –
(i) the Reserve Bank Chairperson; or
(ii) the executive member designated by the Reserve Bank Board to serve on the Monetary Policy Committee."
556 Under the circumstances, it is a very reasonable assumption.
557 Quoted from the State of the Sector Report, 2012, Sage Publications, Page 116—"ICTPH and Sughavazhvu are working with IFMR Rural Finance, the Kshetriya Gramin Financial Services (KGFS) network of small branch-based village banks and insurance partners, to design and market a product that will couple fixed-price, pre-paid primary care and insurance mechanisms to pool risk for secondary and tertiary care." According to this source, *"The IKP Centre for Technologies in Public Health (ICTPH) and partner Sughavazhvu Health Care are demonstrating an innovative managed healthcare model designed to provide high-quality, cohesive and low-cost health services to rural populations. SughaVazhvu Health Care Pvt. Ltd. is a wholly owned subsidiary of IKP Trust."* (Page 116).
Independently, The websites of ICTPH (http://www.ikptrust.org.in/ikp-centre-for-technologies-in-public-health.html), Sughavazhvu Health Care Pvt. Ltd (http://www.sughavazhvu.co.in/about-us.html) and IKP Trust (http://www.ikptrust.org.in/index.html) show Dr

# Chapter 35: Epilogue - Eliminating Conflicts of Interests in Financial Sector Regulation

documents that say he is still connected[558]), which has strong interests in the financial sector through its involvement with financial inclusion and also its investments in NBFC MFIs.

Look at it this way. The RBI is the regulator and supervisor of the financial sector in India and the board is involved in many critical deliberations related to the financial sector. What assurance can the RBI board provide that these important discussions and decisions will not be shared by nonexecutive directors with their parent (or related) organizations that have some form of commercial interest in the financial sector? In fact, providing RBI board membership to anyone connected with institutions that have a strong commercial interest in the financial sector will, for the above-mentioned reason, give undue advantage to these institutions as they will gain access to what economists often call *"superior information."* Dr Rajan should be able to understand this better than anyone else!

And this is not to say that people who have in the past served in organizations with a commercial interest in the financial sector cannot become board members of the RBI. Maintaining a cooling period of between 3–5 years before they are appointed to the RBI board seems an advisable strategy.

Again, let me remind the readers that the case of Mr Rajat Gupta looms large and should not be forgotten. Therefore, it would be prudent and appropriate if those with strong and ongoing commercial interests in the financial sector are not made board members of the RBI.

d. *Circumscribing the term of an RBI board member:* Restricting board terms for people (on the RBI board) to a maximum of 8 years (2 terms of four years each) and ensuring regular induction of new members is critical. When board members get older than the furniture in the boardroom, experience suggests that they could be compromised in different ways and, therefore, 'unrestricted board terms' as practice, is better avoided. This needs to be implemented immediately at the RBI.

e. *Facilitating evaluation of board member performance:* Having a compulsory formal evaluation of the functioning of the RBI's board of directors by an external independent evaluator is necessary. And the results of this evaluation should be made available to the public—officially publishing the evaluation (on their website) is an aspect that could also be considered by RBI. It goes without saying that independent evaluators—individuals and/or institutions—must not have had a material relationship (as defined in common parlance) with the RBI.

---

Nachiket Mor as a director. In addition, the websites of ICAAP (http://www.ikptrust.org.in/ikp-centre-for-advancement-in-agricultural-practice.html) shows Dr Nachiket Mor as a director and also says that: *"IKP Centre for Advancement in Agricultural Practices (ICAAP) (http://advanceagripractice.in) is jointly owned by IKP Trust (51%) and IFMR Trust (49%) (www.ifmr.co.in) and is a Company under Section 25 of the Companies Act (1956)."* One other point–Ms Sucharita Mukherjee is a director serving on the boards of IFMR Trust and ICTPH. Lastly, IFMR Rural Channels is a part of the IFMR Trust group.

558 This is where a disclosure code for board members at RBI would have helped clarify the facts

f.  *Ensuring RBI board members do not get involved in non-board activities:* Ensuring that board members do not head or serve on other RBI committees (outside of the RBI board) concurrently is a very important issue. The RBI board's primary task, as noted earlier, is very clear—to monitor RBI's performance and that of its executives including the governor and act as the first stage of defence in the multilayered accountability mechanism. That being the case, they cannot and should not serve on any committees other than board subcommittees. For example, during the 2010 AP microfinance crisis, the committee headed by Mr Yezdi Malegam is a perfect example of a committee appointed appropriately as it was entirely a board subcommittee. I have no issues with that.

    However, take the case of the new Financial Inclusion Committee headed by Dr Mor, who is also a central board member nominated from the eastern board. That is not appropriate because Dr Mor, being a part of the central board, will have a natural duty to evaluate the work of the RBI, which would also include these very advisory committees. This is indeed a serious conflict of interest and that is why board members should perform only roles meant for them. Likewise, Dr Mor's participation in the RBI (external) banking selection advisory panel is again highly inappropriate for the same reasons.

g.  *Reducing key person dependence:* Look at the key person dependence at RBI on Dr Mor, especially in 2013. This is clearly bad practice of corporate governance and it reduces the accountability of RBI as an institution. As noted earlier, Dr Mor had been made the chair of the newly constituted financial inclusion committee (September 23, 2013), was part of the banking selection advisory panel (October 4, 2013) and may also have been a member of other board subcommittees.

    As at October 2013, Dr Mor was a member of the eastern board of RBI, member of the central board of the RBI, member of the financial inclusion committee under Dr K C Chakrabarthy, head of the newly appointed committee on financial inclusion, member of the bank selection advisory panel, member of the research advisory panel of CAFRAL (which is said to be housed in the RBI headquarters and completely funded by the RBI) and may have been part of several other committees.[559] See the following news item:

    > **"Nachiket Mor likely to be appointed RBI deputy governor: report**
    > *Contify Banking – Mon 4 Nov, 2013 7:42 PM IST*
    > Nachiket Mor, once tipped to head India's largest private sector lender ICICI Bank, is likely to be appointed as a Deputy Governor of the Reserve Bank of India in 2014, the Business Standard reported. Mor, 49, is currently a director of the central board of the RBI. He was appointed to this post in May earlier this year. Following his appointment to the RBI, Mor has been given major responsibilities. RBI Governor

---

559 It has also been mentioned that he was part of the search committee for selecting the director of the National Institute of Bank Management (NIBM), Pune. If true, the key person dependence gets even higher.

# Chapter 35: Epilogue - Eliminating Conflicts of Interests in Financial Sector Regulation

Raghuram Rajan, just within days of taking over the reins of the central bank on September 4, named Mor as the head of a 13-member committee to formulate a plan for financial inclusion in the country. Mor is also part of the four-member high-level advisory committee to vet new banking licenses. Former RBI Governor Bimal Jalan is heading this committee. Of the current four RBI Deputy Governors, the tenures of the two -- Anand Sinha and K C Chakrabarty end in January and June 2014, respectively. Therefore, the appointment of the IIM Ahmedabad graduate as a Deputy Governor is likely to come as early as 2014. **Mor and Rajan were batchmates in IIM Ahmedabad.**"[560]

This would never happen in any other central bank. With all due respect, I am not sure that the RBI is acting with accountability, when it puts a single board member on so many non-board committees and panels, *which the Board (of which he is part of) will ultimately have to evaluate!* And given Dr Mor's links (as noted earlier)[561] with the IFMR trust, which works with NBFCs MFIs and is involved with financial inclusion, I am indeed sure that what is happening is *not* at all appropriate from an accountability perspective.

h. *Emphasizing procedural accountability:* If you look at causes for the global subprime crisis (and the same is true of the AP 2010 microfinance crisis) and I quote from The Financial Crisis Inquiry Report (FCIC) report which notes that:

> **"Dramatic failures of corporate governance and risk management at many systemically important financial institutions were a key cause of this crisis.** *There was a view that instincts for self-preservation inside major financial firms would shield them from fatal risk-taking without the need for a steady regulatory hand, which, the firms argued, would stifle innovation. Too many of these institutions acted recklessly, taking on too much risk, with too little capital, and with too much dependence on short-term funding. In many respects, this reflected a fundamental change in these institutions... which focused their activities increasingly on risky trading activities that produced hefty profits. They took on enormous*

---

[560] http://in.finance.yahoo.com/news/nachiket-mor-likely-appointed-rbi-141203022.html. Also see http://www.business-standard.com/article/finance/rbi-may-have-more-role-for-nachiket-113110300206_1.html. Both these articles suggest that he could even become a Deputy Governor at RBI.

[561] Quoted from State of the Sector Report, 2012, Sage Publications, page 116 –"ICTPH and Sughavazhvu are working with IFMR Rural Finance, the Kshetriya Gramin Financial Services (KGFS) network of small branch-based village banks and insurance partners, to design and market a product that will couple fixed-price, pre-paid primary care and insurance mechanisms to pool risk for secondary and tertiary care." According to this source, *"The IKP Centre for Technologies in Public Health (ICTPH) and partner Sughavazhvu Health Care are demonstrating an innovative managed healthcare model designed to provide high-quality, cohesive and low-cost health services to rural populations. Sughavazhvu Health Care Pvt. Ltd. is a wholly owned subsidiary of IKP Trust."* (Page 116)
Independently, The websites of ICTPH (http://www.ikptrust.org.in/ikp-centre-for-technologies-in-public-health.html), Sughavazhvu Health Care Pvt. Ltd (http://www.sughavazhvu.co.in/about-us.html) and IKP Trust (http://www.ikptrust.org.in/index.html) show Dr Nachiket Mor as a director. In addition, the websites of ICAAP (http://www.ikptrust.org.in/ikp-centre-for-advancement-in-agricultural-practice.html) shows Dr Nachiket Mor as a director and also says that: *"IKP Centre for Advancement in Agricultural Practices (ICAAP) (http://advanceagripractice.in) is jointly owned by IKP Trust (51%) and IFMR Trust (49%) (www.ifmr.co.in) and is a Company under Section 25 of the Companies Act (1956)."* One another point–Ms Sucharita Mukherjee is a director serving on the boards of IFMR Trust and ICTPH. Lastly, IFMR Rural Channels is a part of the IFMR Trust group.

*exposures in acquiring and supporting subprime lenders and creating, packaging, repackaging, and selling trillions of dollars in mortgage-related securities, including synthetic financial products. Like Icarus, they never feared flying ever closer to the sun."*[562]

And the results are there to see for all of us from both the global subprime and the 2010 AP microfinance crisis.

Likewise, the proposed financial inclusion committee under Dr Mor was to recommend the overall regulatory architecture for the financial inclusion sector. As noted earlier, the Dr Mor committee *comprised (at least in majority) of industry insiders with significant conflicts of interests (such as linkages to those who had applied for a banking license and those connected to banking license applicants) and those having direct/indirect linkages with institutions with a commercial interest in financial inclusion.* That this committee was to recommend the regulatory framework for financial inclusion is surely akin to what happened in the global subprime as noted earlier. And by appointing such an industry insider committee, the RBI had shown that it did not have the *procedural accountability* required of a central bank. The same is the case with the banking selection advisory panel, which is again an inappropriately constituted body! In fact, the manner and urgency with which both these committees had been set up, especially when both topics were (then) the subjects of discussion at the Parliamentary Standing Committee on Finance[563] (PSCF), certainly showed that the RBI had not followed the norms of *procedural accountability* expected of central banks.

i. *Adopting an official formal code of conduct publicly:* Lastly, an official code of conduct needs to be *formally* and publicly adopted by the RBI board with regard to various aspects, including activities and roles that board members can engage in (as board members of the RBI) and disclosures to be made them with regard to conflicts of interest and several other issues. As Dr Subba Rao, the former Governor has said, an informal code is perhaps in place at the RBI; however, let me state unequivocally that no informal code can be a substitute for a formal official code[564] adopted publicly. And indeed disclosures on various aspects including conflicts of interest must form a critical part of this code.

Overall, what needs to be emphasized here is that the RBI has fair practice and other codes for various stakeholders including NBFCs. Given this, is it not fair that the RBI has an official code adopted formally for its board and staff? And once adopted formally, it should be available publicly and board

---

[562] Source: The Financial Crisis Inquiry Report-Final Report of the National Commission on the Causes of the Financial and Economic Crisis in the United States, The Financial Crisis Inquiry Commission, Pursuant to Public Law 111-21, January 2011, Official Govt Edition.
[563] http://www.moneylife.in/article/should-the-rbi-be-made-more-accountable-mdashpart1/34926.html
[564] I have not come across a comprehensive formally adopted official code of conduct for RBI board members and staff, to the best of my knowledge. In fact, if such a code did exist, then, disclosures on various conflicts of interests should have also happened but I am not aware any such disclosures.

## Chapter 35: Epilogue - Eliminating Conflicts of Interests in Financial Sector Regulation

members would have to make appropriate disclosures as per the code. This is a very simple task to set the ball rolling for greater institutional accountability and Dr Rajan must push hard to get this done quickly so that *'the RBI indeed becomes the change that it wants to ultimately see on the ground in India's financial sector'*.

Thus, accountability and ethics are very crucial to the survival of the financial sector and there is no doubt that there has been a systemic breakdown in the accountability and ethics globally across the financial sector in the past few years, leading to various forms of economic crisis, the effects of which we are still experiencing! As all of you would agree, the integrity and credibility of financial markets and peoples' trust in these markets are of paramount importance to the economic health of countries and India is no exception to this basic dictum. And therefore, without any doubt, the stability, soundness, safety and sustained prosperity of India's financial system and larger economy rely fundamentally on the notions of fairness, transparency, and accountability. In other words, the RBI must ensure this happens consistently at all levels in the financial sector, where by the concerned stakeholders (be it regulators, supervisors, banks, NBFCs, MFIs, and others) produce services of high quality and conduct themselves fairly and with a high degree of transparency and accountability. As India's central bank, the RBI must start to facilitate this process of metamorphosis, which is required **now**, more than ever before! *In other words, unless the RBI becomes the change that it wants to see on the ground in the financial sector, I am afraid that there will be very little action on the ground in terms of accountability!*

That said, what else needs to be done to help move the RBI to a more accountable entity, especially from a long-term perspective? I *discuss this briefly hereafter!*

First, there is the issue of legal accountability. As in many other countries (the US and elsewhere), this would require the governor of the RBI to depose on a quarterly or semi-annual basis before a select committee of Parliament such as the Parliamentary Standing Committee on Finance (PSCF). Ideally, this deposition should follow the policy pronouncements made by the RBI. Being an unelected individual with such huge powers, the RBI governor must clearly be subject to parliamentary accountability, apart from the existing mechanisms. This would also mean to suggest that the RBI governor should, therefore, be appointed by a Parliamentary Committee and also be capable of being removed by them, if the situation so demands!

And, as noted in the media, Dr Duvvuri Subbarao, former governor of RBI, has argued for the same and I quote him:

> "The Reserve Bank must tender accountability in order to claim and enjoy autonomy from the government... We must be conscious to the fact that we are unelected officials. And our mandate is that the government has appointed us. In order to claim, demand autonomy from the government, and to enjoy that autonomy, we must remember that we must tender accountability... Reserve Bank must take its accountability seriously if it wants to be knowledge institution.... The governor should go before a select committee of the Parliament... Just like it

*happens in US, UK, where the governor goes and gives evidence before the committee. In India too, the governor must go and tender accountability to members of Parliament select committee. That will be a good practice,"*[565]

Second, while parliamentary accountability is crucial, it cannot however be a substitute for the basic accountability of the RBI to the non-executive members of the RBI board—especially, from an operational perspective. Here, I would like to humbly state that these board members must become serious and active players in the immediate accountability of the RBI and the governor—that is why they are in the RBI board in the first place. Let us face it! The RBI is a great example of a central bank that has, by and large, individual-centric decision making. Whether it is monetary policy or any other function, the governor unquestionably reigns supreme. An added factor makes the respected governor omnipresent and omnipotent at the RBI—the high level of discretion currently available to him[566] (which I am not questioning here).

Given these, my *overall point is simple:* subject the presently available huge discretionary decision-making powers with the RBI governor to normal checks and balances (of good governance) so as to facilitate greater accountability in decision making! Put differently, make the governor answerable to the nonexecutive members of the board of the RBI. *In fact, at this basic level, the nonexecutive members of the RBI board must make the governor and RBI accountable for the use of the countries' (scarce) resources, performance of regulatory and supervisory functions and the consequences of their actions.* Thus, as at the Bank of New Zealand, what is needed is a framework of accountable autonomy where the governor (along with his team) are the primary decision-makers at the central bank and the board exclusively engages in a monitoring role, evaluating the performance of the central bank and the governor.

Third, facilitate the transition from being an individual-centric decision maker (that most RBI governors have tended to be) to one who uses the collection potential and wisdom of RBI's deputy governors, executive directors, and others. This model of central banking is certainly not without merits and must be tried before it is dismissed. More importantly, this would certainly call for the creation of an empowered monetary policy committee along with voting rights—an advisory committee would not be enough here as it fixes no responsibility at all. Of course, this would also require that clear mandates and objectives exist (for the RBI) along with inflation and other targets. To reiterate, *there is considerable evidence globally from the experience of central banks to show that group-based collective decision making has led to better results and actions on the ground for the economy as compared to highly individualistic decision making that most of our RBI governors have tended to engage in!*[567]

Fourth, the RBI must not only be audited by independent external auditors but, more importantly, it should also be subject to audit by the CAG (the Comptroller and Auditor General). Look at the example of Bundesbank (Germany), which is a much-cited example of a central bank in Europe. It is said to be

---

565 http://www.hindustantimes.com/business-news/businessbankinginsurance/rbi-must-tender-accountability-to-enjoy-autonomy-subbarao/article1-1086671.aspx

566 There has been no lady governor to the best of my knowledge.

567 Those of you who are interested in getting more information on this may contact me at r_arunachalam@hotmail.com and I would be most happy to share whatever evidence I have on hand from global experiences.

## Chapter 35: Epilogue - Eliminating Conflicts of Interests in Financial Sector Regulation

subject to both independent external audits as well as oversight by the supreme audit authority (federal court of auditors). I fail to understand the logic that the RBI is different and therefore needs no CAG oversight. In fact, parliamentary (and legal) accountability will be enhanced significantly, if and only if the RBI is subject to a CAG audit!

Last but not the least, there is so much lobbying that happens by firms and individuals in the financial services industry, and especially with the regulator. The RBI must be more transparent about such lobbying. Without any doubt, the right to voice our concerns and interests, and thereby attempt to influence public policy, is fundamental to any democracy like India. Many stakeholders including individuals, businesses, *industry associations*, advocacy organizations and other stakeholders have this fundamental right. However, lobbying is indeed facing a crisis of legitimacy (e.g., the controversial Radia[568] tapes have revealed a lot). It is also very big business, especially for those representing these companies and (sometimes, even) foreign countries. Even the normally passionate civil society lobbying has started to acquire significant commercial dimensions, often galvanizing support for an extraordinary range of objectives. Without any doubt, the sheer numbers of lobbyists and the huge resources at their command perhaps even threaten to overwhelm and/or co-opt public (minded) officials and the RBI is no exception to this trend—*in fact, there was said to be significant lobbying by industry associations and others before, during, and after the 2010 AP microfinance crisis.*

Another issue is relevant here. Scale notwithstanding, lobbying, as a strategy, is also debatable for several reasons. Many a time, sadly, the spirit of law is not observed. Further, sometimes undue influence falls into too few hands, or into the hands of those with very narrow commercial interests—*I have pointed out instances* (in this chapter) *where a single person held six high-profile positions related to the RBI*. And of course, likewise, conflicts of interests in the recent financial inclusion and banking selection advisory committees appointed by the RBI have also been discussed threadbare in this chapter.

All of these, in short, show that there is an accountability deficit, especially concerning lobbying with the financial sector regulator, the RBI. Concrete action is therefore needed to make such lobbying more transparent and accountable and here again the buck stops with the RBI in the financial sector and it must show a clear actionable way forward—so that it is not only becomes accountable but is also perceived to be accountable, by the people of India as well as other nations.

---

568 http://en.wikipedia.org/wiki/Radia_tapes_controversy and http://www.outlookindia.com/article.aspx?268618

# PART – V

# Appendix 1 Growth of Number of Active Borrowers and GLP From 2000 to 2005

| Table 1.1 Number of Active Borrowers From 2000-2005 | | | | | | |
|---|---|---|---|---|---|---|
| Name of Institution | 2000 | 2001 | 2002 | 2003 | 2004 | 2005 |
| SHARE | 30,629 | 48,868 | 85,644 | 132,084 | 197,722 | 368,996 |
| SPANDANA | 1,695 | 4,358 | 13,206 | 34,095 | 110,011 | 385,996 |
| SKS | 191 | 1,068 | 5,080 | 11,127 | 24,799 | 73,635 |
| BASIX | 12,626 | 13,889 | 26,630 | 40,379 | NA | 89,953 |
| AML | 0 | 0 | 0 | 0 | 0 | 127,696 |

Source: Compiled from www.mixmarket.org

| Table 1.2 Growth of Number of Active Borrowers From 2000-2005 | | | | | | | |
|---|---|---|---|---|---|---|---|
| Name of Institution | Clients Added up to 2001 Since 2000 | Clients Added up to 2005 Since 2001 | Total Clients Added up to 2005 After 2000 | Total Clients Added up to 2005 After 2000 (in million) | Client Growth 2001-2000/ Total Clients Added After 2000 (A) (in %) | Client Growth 2005-2001/Total Clients Added After 2000 (B) (in %) | Sum of Columns A+B (in %) |
| SHARE | 18,239 | 320,128 | 338,367 | 0.338 | 5.39 | 94.61 | 100.00 |
| SPANDANA | 2,663 | 381,638 | 384,301 | 0.384 | 0.69 | 99.31 | 100.00 |
| SKS | 877 | 72,567 | 73,444 | 0.073 | 1.19 | 98.81 | 100.00 |
| BASIX | 1,263 | 76,064 | 77,327 | 0.077 | 1.63 | 98.37 | 100.00 |
| AML | 0 | 127,696 | 127,696 | 0.128 | 0.00 | 100.00 | 100.00 |

Source: Compiled from www.mixmarket.org

| Table 1.3 Gross Loan Portfolio (in US $) From 2000-2005 | | | | | | |
|---|---|---|---|---|---|---|
| Name of Institution | 2000 | 2001 | 2002 | 2003 | 2004 | 2005 |
| SHARE | 2,398,837 | 3,515,924 | 5,780,393 | 10,366,842 | 18,902,664 | 40,199,809 |
| SPANDANA | 104,512 | 288,302 | 954,979 | 3,209,636 | 10,170,677 | 54,596,594 |
| SKS | 15,115 | 64,472 | 278,514 | 1,073,950 | 2,702,832 | 7,604,875 |
| BASIX | 2,551,195 | 3,280,883 | 4,547,453 | 6,441,700 | 8,874,025 | 13,003,910 |
| AML | 0 | 0 | 0 | 0 | 0 | 13,849,627 |

Source: Compiled from www.mixmarket.org

| Table 1.4 Growth of Gross Loan Portfolio (in US $) from 2000-2005 | | | | | | | |
|---|---|---|---|---|---|---|---|
| Name of Institution | GLP Added up to 2001 Since 2000 | GLP Added up to 2005 Since 2001 | Total GLP Added up to 2005 After 2000 | Total GLP Added up to 2004 After 2000 (in million) | GLP Growth 2001-2000/ Total GLP Added After 2000 (A) (in %) | GLP Growth 2005-2001/ Total GLP Added After 2000 (B) (in %) | Sum of Columns A+B (in %) |
| SHARE | 1,117,087 | 36,683,885 | 37,800,972 | 37.801 | 2.96 | 97.04 | 100.00 |
| SPANDANA | 183,790 | 54,308,292 | 54,492,082 | 54.492 | 0.34 | 99.66 | 100.00 |
| SKS | 49,357 | 7,540,403 | 7,589,760 | 7.590 | 0.65 | 99.35 | 100.00 |
| BASIX | 729,688 | 9,723,027 | 10,452,715 | 10.453 | 6.98 | 93.02 | 100.00 |
| AML | 0 | 13,849,627 | 13,849,627 | 13.85 | 0.00 | 100.00 | 100.00 |

Source: Compiled from www.mixmarket.org

# Appendix 2 The Financial Marketplace for Low-income People in India

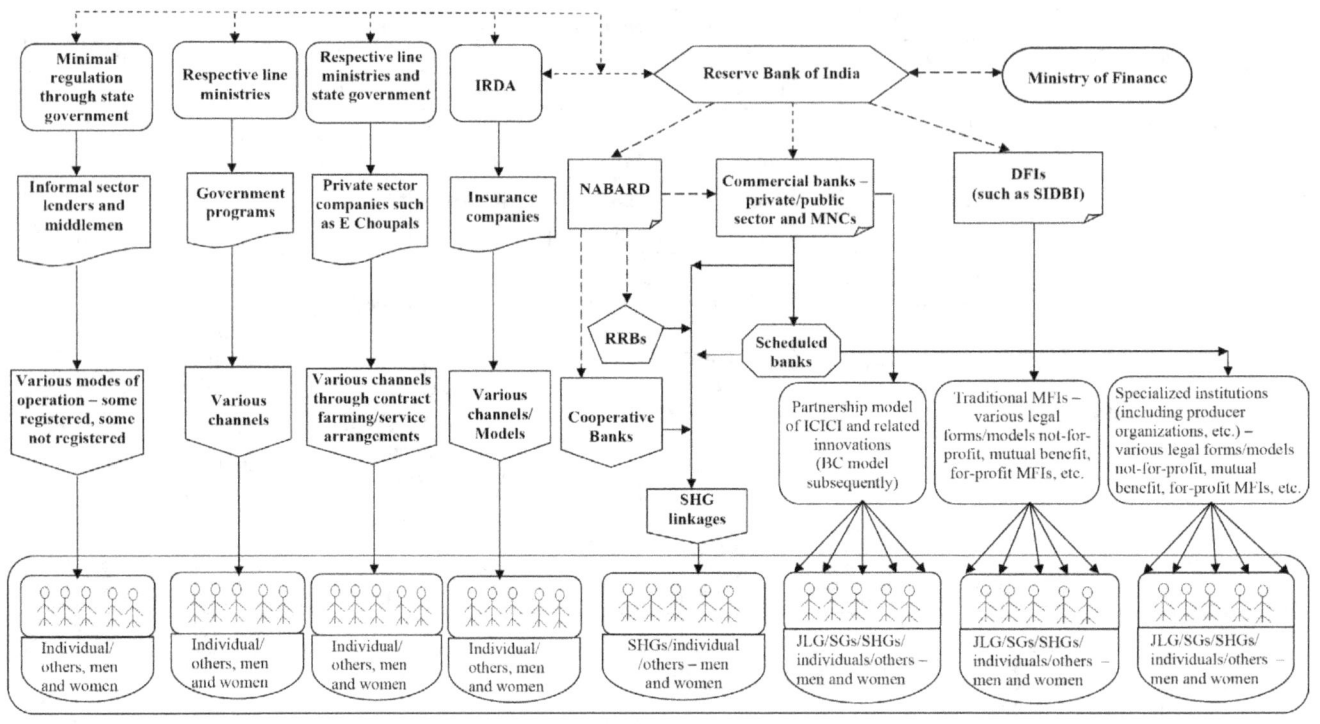

# Appendix 3 Growth of Equity Investments, GLP, and Number of Active Borrowers for the Two Reference Periods

| Group A MFIs (Equity Investor Favorites or Equity Leaders) | Period: April 2006–March 2008 | Period: April 2008–March 2010 | Remarks |
|---|---|---|---|
| Number of MFIs | 5 | 6 | One extra MFI in April 2008–2010, which started operations in 2008 |
| Equity infusion (in million dollars) | 144.53 | 486.58 | A sum of $646.97 million came in after April 2007 (and until July 2010); of this, $528.63 million came in during April 2008–July 2010 |
| Total portfolio addition for all MFIs in 24 months (in million dollars) | 504.08 | 2014.49 | This represents an increase of 4.00 times across the two periods |
| Total portfolio addition for all MFIs per month (in million dollars) | 21.00 | 83.94 | Note that the equivalent amount added every month during the 24-month period of April 2008–March 2010 is almost equal to one-fourth of what SKS put up through its relatively huge IPO. In other words, at the pace of growth during the period, the IPO money could have been exhausted in just four months by the six MFIs. This reflects the burgeoning rate at which these MFIs grew |
| Total portfolio addition per MFI per month (in million dollars) | 4.20 | 13.99 | One extra MFI in April 2008–2010, which started operations in 2008 |
| Total new clients added for all MFIs for 24 months | 2.45 million | 10.46 million | This represents an increase of 4.27 times across the two periods |
| Total new clients added for all MFIs per month | 102,073 | 435,971 | One extra MFI in April 2008–March 2010, which started operations in 2008 |
| Total new clients added per MFI per month | 20,414 | 72,661 | One extra MFI in April 2008–2010, which started operations in 2008 |
| Total new clients added per MFI per day | 671 | 2389 | The value for a day is derived by dividing the (monthly) number by 30.42 |
| Total new JLGs per MFI per day | 134 | 478 | A JLG typically has five members |
| Total new centers per MFI per day | 20 | 69 | A center usually consists of seven JLGs, but could vary by model and adaptation strategies used by MFI |

# Appendix 4 Loans Disbursed by Banks and SIDBI and Loans Outstanding to Banks and SIBDI

### Table 4.1 Loans Disbursed by Top 5 Banks to MFIs During 2009–2010

| Serial No | Name of bank | Loans disbursed by banks to MFIs during 2009–2010 | |
|---|---|---|---|
| | | No. of MFIs | Amount (in Rs. Lakhs) |
| 1 | HDFC Bank | 47 | 146,346.5 |
| 2 | Corporation Bank | 28 | 78,335.85 |
| 3 | Axis Bank | 52 | 64,564.52 |
| 4 | Punjab National Bank | 9 | 63,750 |
| 5 | Syndicate Bank | 12 | 51,011 |

*Source:* Compiled from Status of Micro Finance in India – 2009-10, by NABARD

### Table 4.2 Loans Outstanding of Top 5 Banks (for Loans Given to MFIs) as on September 30, 2010

| Serial No | Name of bank | Outstanding bank loans against MFIs as on September 30, 2010 | |
|---|---|---|---|
| | | MFIs | Amount (in Rs. Lakhs) |
| 1 | HDFC Bank | 73 | 132,400.4 |
| 2 | Axis Bank | 84 | 120,776.7 |
| 3 | Punjab National Bank | 13 | 106,934 |
| 4 | State Bank of India | 205 | 87,619 |
| 5 | IDBI Bank | 41 | 60,360.4 |

*Source:* Compiled from Status of Micro Finance in India – 2009-10, by NABARD

### Table 4.3 SIDBI Loans Disbursed and Outstanding to MFIs-2007-2010, (in Rs. Lakhs)

| Year | 2007-2008 | 2008-2009 | 2009-2010 |
|---|---|---|---|
| Loan disbursed | 69580 | 168675 | 266575 |
| Loan outstanding | 95038 | 213689 | 380820 |
| Percentage (%) of SIDBI's loan outstanding to total SIDBI+ commercial banks | 25.69% | 29.90% | 27.29% |

### Table 4.4 DFI/Bank Loans Disbursed to MFIs (2007–2010), Top 5 Institutions (in Rs. Lakhs)

| Ranking | 2007–2008 | | 2008–2009 | | 2009–2010 | |
|---|---|---|---|---|---|---|
| | Bank | Amount | Bank | Amount | Bank | Amount |
| 1 | HDFC Bank | 73,059 | SIDBI | 168,675 | SIDBI | 266,575 |
| 2 | SIDBI | 69,580 | ICICI Bank | 82,517 | HDFC Bank | 146,347 |
| 3 | Axis Bank | 55,450 | HDFC Bank | 78,671 | Corporation Bank | 78,336 |
| 4 | State Bank of India | 13,270 | Axis Bank | 62,624 | Axis Bank | 64,565 |
| 5 | ICICI Bank | 10,954 | Indian Overseas Bank | 24,445 | Punjab National Bank | 63,750 |

*Source:* Compiled from Status of Micro Finance in India – 2009-10, by NABARD

### Table 4.5 DFI/Bank Loans Outstanding (for Loans Given to MFIs, 2007–2010), Top 5 Institutions (in Rs. Lakhs)

| Ranking | 2007–2008 | | 2008–2009 | | 2009–2010 | |
|---|---|---|---|---|---|---|
| | Bank | Amount | Bank | Amount | Bank | Amount |
| 1 | SIDBI | 95,038 | SIDBI | 213,689 | SIDBI | 380,820 |
| 2 | HDFC Bank | 75,418 | HDFC Bank | 94,417 | HDFC Bank | 132,400 |
| 3 | Axis Bank | 52,190 | ICICI Bank | 80,220 | Axis Bank | 120,777 |
| 4 | ICICI Bank | 41,071 | Axis Bank | 75,822 | Punjab National Bank | 106,934 |
| 5 | State Bank of India | 27,507 | ING Vyasa Bank | 47,406 | State Bank of India | 87,619 |

*Source:* Compiled from Status of Micro Finance in India – 2009-10, by NABARD

# Appendix 5 AP versus Other State MFIs, Clients and GLP Added

Table 5.1 Andhra Pradesh versus Other State MFIs Clients Added, April 2006–March 2008 and April 2008–March 2010 and Client Growth, 2008 minus 2006 and 2010 minus 2008, as a Percentage of Total Clients Added After 2006

| State of MFI | State of origin and headquarters | Legal status | Clients added April 2006–March 2008 | Clients added April 2008–March 2010 | Total clients added from April 2006 to March 2010 | Total clients added after 2006, up to 2010 (in millions) | Client growth 2008–2006/total clients added after 2006 (A) (in %) | Client growth 2010–2008/total clients added after 2006 (B) (in %) | Sum of columns (A+B) (in %) |
|---|---|---|---|---|---|---|---|---|---|
| AP-headquartered MFIs' total | Andhra Pradesh | 6 | 2,441,853 | 9,757,489 | 12,199,342 | 12.20 | 20.02 | 79.98 | 100.00 |
| Other state MFIs' total | New Delhi, West Bengal, Karnataka, and Tamil Nadu | 8 | 1,435,194 | 4,519,865 | 5,955,059 | 5.96 | 24.10 | 75.90 | 100.00 |
| NBFC total | For-profit NBFC | 13 | 3,536,865 | 13,626,752 | 17,163,617 | 17.16 | 20.61 | 79.39 | 100.00 |
| Non-NBFC total | Trust | 1 | 340,182 | 650,602 | 990,784 | 0.99 | 34.33 | 65.67 | 100.00 |

*Source*: Compiled from www.mixmarket.org.

Table 5.2 Andhra Pradesh versus Other State MFIs, GLP (in US $) Added April 2006–March 2008 and April 2008–March 2010 and GLP Growth 2008 minus 2006 and 2010 minus 2008, as a Percentage of Total GLP Added After 2006

| State of MFI | State of origin and headquarters | Legal status | GLP added April 2006–March 2008 | GLP added April 2008–March 2010 | Total GLP added April 2006–March 2010 | Total GLP added up to 2010 after 2006 | GLP growth 2008–2006/total GLP added after 2006 (A) (in %) | GLP growth 2010–2008/total GLP added after 2006 (B) (in %) | Sum of columns (A+B) (in %) |
|---|---|---|---|---|---|---|---|---|---|
| AP-headquartered MFIs' total | Andhra Pradesh | 6 | 501,085,380 | 1,911,680,234 | 2,412,765,614 | 2412.77 | 20.77 | 79.23 | 100.00 |
| Other state MFIs' total | New Delhi, West Bengal, Karnataka, and Tamil Nadu | 8 | 195,983,350 | 701,154,992 | 897,138,342 | 897.14 | 21.85 | 78.15 | 100.00 |
| NBFC total | For-profit NBFC | 13 | 636,270,137 | 2,561,260,554 | 3,197,530,691 | 3197.53 | 19.90 | 80.10 | 100.00 |
| Non-NBFC total | Trust | 1 | 60,798,593 | 51,574,672 | 112,373,265 | 112.37 | 54.10 | 45.90 | 100.00 |

*Source*: Compiled from www.mixmarket.org.

**Appendix 6 Growth of AP-headquartered MFIs During April 2006-March 2010 and Various Critical Parameters**

| Critical parameters | End March 2006 | End March 2007 | End March 2008 | End March 2009 | End March 2010 | Total Clients and GLP Added 2010-2006 | Total Clients and GLP Added 2008-2006 | Total Clients and GLP Added 2010-2008 |
|---|---|---|---|---|---|---|---|---|
| Total number of active borrowers (six large AP-headquartered MFIs) | 2,245,617 | 2,870,997 | 4,687,470 | 8,925,799 | 14,444,959 | 12,199,342 | 2,441,853 | 9,757,489 |
| Total number of active borrowers (all AP-headquartered MFIs) | 2,492,783 | 3,263,164 | 5,068,152 | 9,558,192 | 15,259,366 | 12,766,583 | 2,575,369 | 10,191,214 |
| Percentage of active borrowers of six large AP-headquartered MFIs/total AP-headquartered MFI active borrowers | 90.08 | 87.98 | 92.49 | 93.38 | 94.66 | 95.56 | 94.82 | 95.74 |
| Total GLP of the six large AP-headquartered MFIs (in dollars) | 228,639,018 | 322,084,272 | 729,724,398 | 1,327,790,043 | 2,641,404,632 | 2,412,765,614 | 501,085,380 | 1,911,680,234 |
| Total GLP (all AP-headquartered MFIs; in dollars) | 257,082,764 | 375,997,898 | 797,577,454 | 1,424,282,206 | 2,796,641,660 | 2,539,558,896 | 540,494,690 | 1,999,064,206 |
| Percentage of GLP of the six large AP-headquartered MFIs/total AP-headquartered MFIs' GLP | 88.94 | 85.66 | 91.49 | 93.23 | 94.45 | 95.01 | 92.71 | 95.63 |

*Source*: Compiled from www.mixmarket.org

# Appendix 7 E-mails to RBI Board and SEBI Chairman

1. **E-mails to RBI Board**
From: shashi_r@sify.com
To: r_arunachalam@hotmail.com
Subject: Fw: From Ramesh
Date: Sun, 25 Jul 2010 20:33:22 +0530
1 attachment
MF_IPO_CorpGov_23rdJuly2010_448PM.pdf (866.1 KB)

FYI - Shashi

----- Original Message -----
**From:** Shashi Rajagopalan
**To:** Governor, Reserve Bank Of India; Thorat, Usha; Gokarn, Dr. Subir; ymalegam@sbbandco.com; a.vaidyanathan053@gmail.com; Gopinath, S; Chakrabarty, Dr. K C; subbarao@gmail.com
**Sent:** Sunday, July 25, 2010 8:27 PM
**Subject:** Fw: From Ramesh

The attached yet-to-be-edited draft adds to the earlier paper from Sriram and I have Ramesh's permission to share it with you, and he hopes to send you the finalised version as soon as it is ready. What the RBI needs to do or not (in the light of such information) is best left to those of you who are in the hot seat/s. However, we should consider the logic of including closely held (notwithstanding the garb of the MBTs) for-profit MFI loans under priority sector lending, given that ascertaining end use/end borrower is nigh impossible.

Tomorrow we start our exploratory visit to rural thrift and credit cooperatives to fine tune the RBI study design and I am really looking forward to learning from the focussed approach. Warm regards to all,

Shashi

----- Original Message -----
**From:** Ramesh S. Arunachalam
**To:** shashi_r@sify.com; Ramesh S. Arunachalam; black berry
**Sent:** Friday, July 23, 2010 8:51 PM
**Subject:** FW: From Ramesh

# Appendix 7 Emails to RBI Board and SEBI Chairman

Dear Shashi

Greetings and here is the paper I promised to send you.

Pls treat this as informal and pls do give me your feedback

Thanks

Warm Regards

Ramesh

---

From: r_arunachalam@hotmail.com
To: ajaytankha@gmail.com; brijmohang@hotmail.com; viji.das@ananyafinance.com; navin.anand@un.org.in; shepherddevorg@gmail.com; shrin54@yahoo.co.in; vivek.siffs@gmail.com; m-mishra@dfid.gov.uk; m-sengupta@dfid.gov.uk; mssriram@gmail.com; neelaiah_asp@sify.com; nverma@worldbank.org; sanjaysinha@edarural.com; seeta.prabhu@undp.org; prasad@caspian.in; mona@caspian.in; dasviji@icenet.co.in; dasviji@youtele.com; arora_psd@yahoo.co.uk; fernandez@myrada.org; aliasghar60@gmail.com; baladeb@gmail.com; girija41@yahoo.com; dattasankar@thelivelihoodschool.org; smitapremchander@gmail.com; tara01@gmail.com; tara@gidr.ac.in; jayshreevyas@gmail.com; vijaymahajan@basixindia.com; vipin@accessdev.org; suryamani@accessdev.org; bindu.ananth@ifmrtrust.co.in; cjoseph@axisbank.com; achla@sa-dhan.org; titus@sa-dhan.org; prema.gera@undp.org; vasudevanpn@equitas.in; m-nath@dfid.gov.uk; prakash.lb@gmail.com; a.kanitkar@fordfound.org; ninanayar@hotmail.com; dhan@md3.vsnl.net.in; creddy@apmas.org; yesuthasen@gmail.com; board@sa-dhan.org; srinivas.bonam@indusind.com; bonam_2000@yahoo.com; ratnesh@undp.org; nachiket@nachiketmor.net
CC: r_arunachalam@hotmail.com; arunachalam@airtel.blackberry.com; r_arunachalam1@rediffmail.com
Subject: From Ramesh
Date: Fri, 23 Jul 2010 17:43:06 +0530

Dear All

Greetings! Many thanks for the wonderful responses that you have all provided, either by mail or telephone

I sincerely thank you all for the kind feedback.

On my part, I have tried my best to look at every word and remove any (possible) subjectivity from the 1st version of the paper.

When I started this paper, it was to look in the issues raised by Prof Sriram and now, I think I am done with this research and it is up to all of you – the leaders and pioneers in the sector – to carry on the agenda of Corporate Governance forward.

I would very much value your feedback on the paper. Please do write back to me or call me (+919840082065), which ever is easier. Thanks

The IPO is indeed a hall mark event for Indian micro-finance and I would like to congratulate the Indian micro-finance sector, the SKS company and its promoters (including the founder, the MBTs and key employees) on this event.

At the same time, the global financial crisis has left behind some serious lessons in corporate governance and compensation that, we, in micro-finance should not and cannot ignore. As the BIS paper on the above argues, **"Compensation…is one factor among many that contributed to the financial crisis that began in 2007. Action to address unsound compensation systems must therefore be embedded in the broader financial reform program, built around a substantially stronger and more resilient global capital and liquidity framework. Action …must be speedy, determined and coherent. Urgency is particularly important to prevent a return to the compensation practices that contributed to the crisis."**

Prof Sriram's article in the EPW was indeed a seminal, thought provoking piece on the aspect of Compensation and Corporate Governance in the commercializing Indian Micro-finance sector. I have tried to contribute, in my own little way, to Prof Sriram's work, by closely looking at the various issues raised in his paper. And attached is a revised version of the paper for further comments and feedback. Thanks in advance for the same

I had one final request and that is regarding the use of this paper and I would be grateful if you respect my sentiments on this and thanks again in advance – At the outset, let me clarify that this paper has been written primarily for learning and discussion purposes and therefore, I strongly discourage the use of this paper for any other purposes. I would also be very grateful if you do not circulate the paper to others outside of this group, as it can be used for other purposes

Thanks again and have a wonderful week-end and I will be in touch with you all in mid-august again!

Thanks

Warmest Regards

Ramesh

---

From: r_arunachalam@hotmail.com
To: ajaytankha@gmail.com; brijmohang@hotmail.com; navin.anand@un.org.in; shepherd-devorg@gmail.com; shrin54@yahoo.co.in; vivek.siffs@gmail.com; m-mishra@dfid.gov.uk; m-sengupta@dfid.gov.uk; moumita.sensarma@in.abnamro.com; mssriram@gmail.com; nachiket.mor@icicibank.com; neelaiah_asp@sify.com; sanjaysinha@edarural.com; seeta.prabhu@undp.org; srinivas.bonam@in.abnamro.com; prasad@caspian.org; mona@caspian.org; dasviji@icenet.co.in; dasviji@youtele.com; arora_psd@yahoo.co.uk; fernandez@myrada.org; aliasghar60@gmail.com; baladeb@gmail.com; girija41@yahoo.com; dattasankar@theliveli-hoodschool.org; smitapremchander@gmail.com; tara01@gmail.com; tara@gidr.ac.in; vijaymahajan@basixindia.com; vipin@accessdev.org; suryamani@accessdev.org; bindu.ananth@ifmrtrust.co.in; cjoseph@axisbank.com; achla@sa-dhan.org; titus@sa-dhan.org; prema.gera@undp.org; vasudevanpn@equitas.in; m-nath@dfid.gov.uk; prakash.lb@gmail.com; a.kanitkar@fordfound.org; dhan@md3.vsnl.net.in; nverma@worldbank.org
CC: r_arunachalam@hotmail.com; arunachalam@airtel.blackberry.com
Subject: Most Confidential
Date: Wed, 21 Jul 2010 10:30:53 +0530

Dear All

Greetings!

Good Morning! I have been depressed ever since, I got to know of the happenings at SKS as I always thought that SKS was among the most well run and transparent organizations. I had even intended to subscribe during the IPO

Prof Sriram's paper uprooted my foundations and left me searching - it indeed was a real eye opener. As I have told him often, this was simply brilliant work. Yet, I could never digest and accept the issues he had raised and found it hard to believe

So, ON MY OWN, I set out to (myself) look at all issues raised by Prof Sriram in my slow manner over the last 2 months – the attached paper is the outcome of my work.

It specifically looks at almost every issue raised by Prof Sriram's in his paper and uses these as a fulcrum to analyse the Corporate Governance situation. Basically, I have listed the issue identified by Prof Sriram, and then tried to get at the facts and analyse them and then, raise some key questions and also outline implications (for all stakeholders including the retail investor).

Please note that I have done this for my own satisfaction and it is not intended for publication and/or any other use (at this time).

However, after I completed the same, I felt it important that I share this with all of you as I have known several of you for almost 12 to 14 years and have learnt a lot from you all. I also felt that it would be important to place on record my observations on Prof Sriram's paper and the happenings in SKS, before the IPO opens next week.

Kindly go through attached paper and as leaders and pioneers in micro-finance, I expect you all to guide the sector appropriately. I would be grateful if you could accord the highest priority to this and thanks again!

**Kindly do not circulate this paper outside of this group and I have not (so far) sent it to anyone outside of this closed group!**

Thanks and I do look forward to hearing from you all!

Thanks

Warm Regards

Ramesh

## 2. E Mail to SEBI Chairman

From: **Ramesh S. Arunachalam** (r_arunachalam@hotmail.com)
To: surajmohanm@sebi.gov.in; black berry (arunachalam@airtel.blackberry.com); Ramesh S. Arunachalam (r_arunachalam@hotmail.com)
Sent: 26 July 2010 13:12PM

# Appendix 7 Emails to RBI Board and SEBI Chairman

Dear Sir

Thanks

Contents noted

Will get back to you, if required. I am still saying that I would have passed on information very useful to SEBI, if I had been given a meeting with Chairman Sir or Whole time member. I respect the fact that they do not want to meet me and I am sure they are busy but I am comfortable meeting them and handing over things.

Thanks

Best

Ramesh

# Appendix 8 E-mail to Buy ESPS Shares for Consultant

**From:** YYYYYYYYYYY
**Sent:** 06 August 2009 16:12
**To:** XXXXXXXXX
**Subject:** Your resignation - ZZZZZZZZ

Sir – We need to close this issue as well. If you say I would touch base with MM Sir. Thanks, TTTTTT

**From:** XXXXXXXXX
**Sent:** Tuesday, July 28, 2009 11:09 AM
**To:** YYYYYYYYYYY
**Subject:** Your resignation - ZZZZZZZZ

Pl discuss

**From:** YYYYYYYYYY
**Sent:** Tuesday, July 28, 2009 11:02 AM
**To:** XXXXXXXXX
**Subject:** Please opine

DRAFT email to MM Sir

Dear MM Sir –

Hope you are doing well.

Would need your guidance with respect to purchasing of ESPS Shares by ZZZZZZZZ as July 31, 2009 is his last working day.

Taking instructions from your under mentioned email, we approached NNNNNNN (F&A) and he needs your confirmation.

Thanks,

## Appendix 8 E-mail to Buy ESPS Shares for Consultant

YYYYYYYYYY
**From:** MM
**Sent:** Saturday, July 04, 2009 3:24 AM
**To:** DDDDDDDD
**Cc:** SSSSSSSSS; XXXXXXXXXX
**Subject:** Your resignation - ZZZZZZZZZZ

ZZZZZZZ,

Please draw the fund for purchase of ZZZZZ shares from my personal account. And please do not insist on a non compete. I will explain when we speak next.

MM

# Appendix 9 E-mail to Bankers

From: r_arunachalam@hotmail.com
To: vrrao@syndicatebank.co.in; selvam_ib74@yahoo.com; selvaur@indian-bank.com; slkumbhare@yahoo.co.in; sme@pnb.co.in; cmprisec@centralbank.co.in; pramodmarar@hsbc.co.in; umesh.jain@idbi.co.in; dikholesuresh@yahoo.com; prasanta.sahu@axisbank.com; dgm.mc@sbi.co.in; shrikant.srivastava@rbs.com; karuna.sharma@yesbank.in; viji.das@ananyafinance.com; vasumathi.parthasarathy@sc.com; hari.rajagopal@rabobank.com; waikar@unionbankofindia.com; waikarpb@yahoo.co.in; sldikhole@unionbankofindia.com; kundan.tiwari@hdfcbank.com; m.venkiteswaran@axisbank.com; manohara@hdfcbank.com; vaibhav.agarwal@icicibank.com; gouri.sankar@sc.com; ajay.b@ingvysyabank.com; venkatesh.challawar@hdfcbank.com; balajisiyer@hsbc.co.in; narendranathm@dcbl.com; hariharan.k@yesbank.in; nk.maini@sidbi.in; gaurav.saboo@citi.com; headoffice.afd@bankofindia.co.in; anandilal@denabank.co.in; hopslb@pnb.co.in; arindom.datta@rabobank.com; lnvrao@unionbankofindia.com; kosaraju@unionbankofindia.com; bs.sivakumar@kotak.com; nandita.prabhu@sc.com; nkmaini@sidbi.in; rewari@sidbi.in; r_arunachalam@hotmail.com; arunachalam@airtel.blackberry.com
Subject: RE: Most Urgent, Official Mail, Most Confidential
Date: Fri, 15 Oct 2010 13:25:10 +0530

3 attachments
1_CGAP_article_Response_Ramesh_1812_4thOctober2010.pdf (69.5 KB), 6_MF_IPO_CorpGov_23rdJuly2010_
514PM.pdf (866.0 KB), 7_Main_Paper_Annex1_4.pdf (1360.3 KB)

Dear All

I foget to attach the papers and thanks and apologies!

Warm Regards

Ramesh

------------------------------------------------- --------------------------------------------------

# Appendix 9 E-mail to Bankers

From: r_arunachalam@hotmail.com
To: vrrao@syndicatebank.co.in; selvam_ib74@yahoo.com; selvaur@indian-bank.com; slkumbhare@yahoo.co.in; sme@pnb.co.in; cmprisec@centralbank.co.in; pramodmarar@hsbc.co.in; umesh.jain@idbi.co.in; dikholesuresh@yahoo.com; prasanta.sahu@axisbank.com; dgm.mc@sbi.co.in; shrikant.srivastava@rbs.com; karuna.sharma@yesbank.in; viji.das@ananyafinance.com; vasumathi.parthasarathy@sc.com; hari.rajagopal@rabobank.com; waikar@unionbankofindia.com; waikarpb@yahoo.co.in; sldikhole@unionbankofindia.com; kundan.tiwari@hdfcbank.com; m.venkiteswaran@axisbank.com; manohara@hdfcbank.com; vaibhav.agarwal@icicibank.com; gouri.sankar@sc.com; ajay.b@ingvysyabank.com; venkatesh.challawar@hdfcbank.com; balajisiyer@hsbc.co.in; narendranathm@dcbl.com; hariharan.k@yesbank.in; nk.maini@sidbi.in; gaurav.saboo@citi.com; headoffice.afd@bankofindia.co.in; anandilal@denabank.co.in; hopslb@pnb.co.in; arindom.datta@rabobank.com; lnvrao@unionbankofindia.com; kosaraju@unionbankofindia.com; bs.sivakumar@kotak.com; nandita.prabhu@sc.com; nkmaini@sidbi.in; rewari@sidbi.in
CC: r_arunachalam@hotmail.com
Subject: Most Urgent, Official Mail, Most Confidential
Date: Fri, 15 Oct 2010 13:01:04 +0530

**Dear All**

Greetings and apologies for a long posting! And please treat this mail as very confidential!

I am very sad that SIDBI (and the lenders forum), the primary body responsible for the MFI model is unable to give me time to listen to confidential aspects with regards to MFIS, ESPECIALLY WHEN THERE IS SO MUCH CONTROVERSY ABOUT MFIS and the MF sector is burning! I am grateful for all of you who have written to me individually but there has been no formal response from the lenders forum or SIDBI, the convener of the lenders forum and hence, I have to write this mail. Kindly do not misunderstand. Thanks!

As a professional who has spent 23 years working in 550 districts of India and also many countries, I wanted to share some very critical information about the MF sector, in confidence. Please recall that I have already sent you a paper on Corporate Governance and I attach the same with a few others.

As suicides mount and not-so-legal practices appear to abound, I thought you all including SIDBI should be appraised of the complete situation first and IMMEDIATELY as SIDBI and the banks have been responsible for nurturing and growing this sector. If SIDBI and the banks do not act now, much of the good work could be lost for ever. That is the sense of urgency....here

There seem to be very serious corporate governance violations in several MFIs and I wanted to talk about this in person to you all (as I have already been threatened for the papers that I have written, where I question seemingly illegal practices in MF and MFIs). These institutions appear to pose a huge risk to the financial sector and are already intermediating large amounts of money, and SIDBI/Banks have significant stake in them. Codes of conduct do not seem to work on the ground and what MFIs say on paper and do are actually very different. Rating or loan portfolio audits of MFIs do not seem to have unearthed the kind of problems that have been unearthed recently - SKS which has consistently received great ratings does appear to have serious corporate governance issues and there is prima facie evidence available. Like wise, research has tended to be somewhat superficial and often supporting MFIs, when their practices are really questionnable - please see critique of CGAP paper on SKS attached, where there are several omissions. SKS is in fact the tip of the iceberg and there is much more happening in the MF industry in India. That is why I felt it important to share critical issues from the field so that the newly formed (forming) lenders forum can play a real effective role and get the facts and figures, from the field right. It would have helped the forum function more effectively

It is in larger national interest that I wanted to present to SIDBI and the banks in the lenders forum but somehow that has not been possible. I wanted to set the record straight and send this mail officially to you all, so that I am not failing in my duty as a citizen of this country. As the crisis deepens, a lot is at stake and for SIDBI/banks as well...and please remember that a lot of the money that you have all lent are public deposits and SIDBI/banks will be answerable when serious **systemic** issues surface. Please do not say that no body volunteered to tell you. I have and this mail is proof of my repeated requests, which have not been accepted by SIDBI/Banks.

To tackle this crisis and clean up Indian microfinance, the MF community in India (lenders and banks included) must FIRST come out of their mode of denying that nothing is wrong...unless, we accept problems, we cannot effect changes and let us not repeat the same mistake that happened with sub-prime where most people pretended that all was well, until the crisis brought us crashing to the ground. I hope the same does not happen here in India with regard to microfinance. And this is where SIDBI/Banks can play a positive role but seem reluctant to do so. And we are losing precious time...

I am recording the same here again and am still very keen to meet you both - SIDBI as well as with other lenders...I hope you understand and will appreciate the urgency and do the needful. Again, forgive me for writing to you again and my profuse apologies if I have caused any inconveniences.

# Appendix 9 E-mail to Bankers

Thanks and pls ack receipt of this mail.

Warm Regards

Ramesh

**PS: BRIEF SUMMARY OF SITUATION IN MICROFINANCE**

I want to say that the situation in MF in Andhra Pradesh (AP) and other parts of India are worsening day by day and suicides are occurring fairly regularly. While suicides may not be because of MFI loans, a huge MFI loan repayment could act as trigger and lead to the concerned person committing suicide. This becomes even more likely, when other coping and crsis handling mechanisms have been exhausted. There are several points that I want to make in this regard:

Aggressive (Predatory) lending appears to be practiced by many MFIs and delinquencies/defaults also seem to be increasing...and in many cases, the lack of integrated MIS (across products and geographies) means that the real extent of the delinquency problem may not be known. As I reported earlier, in several sampled portfolios, I have witnessed ghost clients and non-MF clients (being targeted) and also seen the phenomenon of broker agents who are the major cause of multiple lending - the real National extent of this problem must be accessed through a national study done by neutral non-sectoral people (to avoid conflicts of interest), using a rigorous approach and appropriate sample.

Growth is burgeoning in microfinance and to a great extent, growth is temporarily shrouding many problems. However, appropriate MFI systems and commensurate MFI capacity to manage burgeoning growth do not exist, especially at the field level. Cash handling and management are still nascent and as a result, frauds appear to be on the increase (significantly!) The decentralised model has also meant that KYC documentation is very poor, MIS is inaccurate (with altered business rules sometimes), internal controls are weak and frauds are galore!

Amidst all of this, people with 2/3/4/5 loans (in ranges of Rs 15000 - 35000 each) seem unable to make (weekly) payments and in some cases, when confronted by field workers/toughs and/or criminal elements (hired by broker agents), they are perhaps turning to commit suicide. A few such cases that I am currently looking at seems to suggest that the tactics and processes used by MFIs to recover money perhaps cannot be called, under any circumstances, as acceptable practice (some of the instances include kidnapping, harassment, etc). This aspect is further compounded by the fact the rapid growth has meant that there is no proper training/orientation for staff - who then behave as they like

The HR function in MFIs is also very weak and staff are over worked and fatigued (6 AM to 11PM in many cases and their working/living conditions are pathetic). Hence, they are more prone to cut corners and also engage in frauds. Their frustration is also perhaps causing them to behave high-handedly with clients - who are also harassed by toughs and criminals hired by broker agents, a growing phenomenon. Staff unions have come up in many districts/some states and there are few cases where unions have wanted to stop repayment to the parent MFI. There are cases where sets of branches and/or an area or regional office are threatening to break away and/or have broken away from the MFI, causing huge losses. All of you must remember that a lot of this is loan money from banks, which, as Dr Y V Reddy, former Governor RBI said, are indeed public deposits. This is why it is even more urgent to take stock of the situation

Further, it is becoming increasingly clear that the effective interest rates charged by many MFIs are not what they claim these to be. I have observed EIRs in the range of 36 - 54% in several cases and the decentralised model adopted by many MFIs is permitting staff excesses in this regard

All said and done, the Indian MF bubble is getting bigger and closer to bursting, day by day...

Most importantly, the negative publicity for MFIs has meant that in many places, people are now trying to violently protest against MFI excesses, which is not a good thing (I do not justify violence of any manner and for any cause). In short, microfinance and MFIs are slowly losing acceptability among the people... What is very sad is the fact that MFIs are slowly losing their creditability, both in the eyes of the people and state - who now see MFIs as formalised money-lenders and mere vehicles for making money of the poor.

The fact of the matter is that many MFIs have not helped their causes with poor Corporate Governance, Conflicts of interest at various levels, Inadequate checks and balances over executive decision making and behaviour, Lack of transparent reporting to the outside world, Lack of truly independent directors, Insufficient transparency about ownership/control, related-party transactions and the (group's) overall financial position etc

I really hope that the Indian MF industry is able to wade through this crisis (unscathed)? The regulators and lenders have a very serious responsibility in ensuring this as otherwise, between Rs 20000 - Rs 25000 crores could be at stake...

# Appendix 10 Tampering with Legal Records

**From:** xxxxxxxxx [mailto: xxxxxxxxx]
**Sent:** 05 September 2009 19:09
**To:** xxxxxx; yyyyy; zzzzzzz
**Cc:** xxxxxx; yyyyyyy
**Subject:** ESPS - activity

Dear All

**Subject:** ESPS – Old Finance agreement (page which contains the schedule) to be replaced with revised one.

**Steps taken till date:**

First meeting was conducted on **August 31, 2009**; decision made to replace the page from the finance agreement and get the signatures from concerned employees, after reviewing documents.

xxxxxxx (legal representative) and xxxxxxxxxx (HR representative) will be working on this. As agreed upon the print outs will be taken in the legal dept premise as the legal team holds the custody of the hard copies of existing documents.

Revised Financial agreement received on **September 01, 2009** which was forwarded by xxxxx (F & A) on August 31, 2009.
· The present documents have been assigned serial number and alignment noted by xxxxxxx.
· Old continuation sheets (black and white logo) procured from Admin by xxxxxxxxxx.

No activity on September 02, 2009 as xxxxxxx is ill.

**September 03 and 04, 2009** was a holiday.
**September 05**, xxxxxxx to send the soft copy of the list and xxxxxxxxxx to list the RO/BO against the names to be dispatched.

**Problems:**

It is very difficult to match the paper quality and the print color of the existing documents.

**Further POA:**

We will print the letters on September 07, 2009 (xxxxxxx & xxxxxxxxxx to start at 10.30 am) and send out the couriers on September 09, 2009.

Regards

Xxxxxxxxxx

# Appendix 11 Laundry List of Issues Corporate (Mis) governance that was Internally Shared at a Large NBFC MFI in 2009

1. FC Minutes- Not made nor signed, only extracts prepared. At Board Meetings these extracts were placed, without any signatures. Minutes have to be statutorily placed, which has NOT happened. This is Non Compliance. Till now the FC Minutes have NOT been given to Sectl, despite repeated reminders.

2. ALM Minutes- Last Year in July'08 First Meeting held. Minutes not yet signed by the then Chairman. The Chairman was xxxx xxx xxx. This year Minutes not yet prepared and approved.

3. Sectl Audit- There are many Non Compliances. There are cases where Minutes have been altered/changed, clearly attracting Sections 463 and 464 of the IPC relating to Forgery and making False Documents. Action to be taken after due Investigation.

4. AGM Minutes- Last Year AGM Not prepared. Earlier ones and post last AGM, Minutes of either AGM or EGM Not prepared, clearly Contravention of Companies Act'1956. All Directors can be held responsible.

5. EGM 2007- The Notice and the Minutes show ESOP to XY and ZW. Necessary Forms have been filed with ROC. BUT actually they have been issued ESPS and Equity Shares. Hence, the ESPS and the Shares issued to these Employees are null and void ab initio. Consequences are disastrous from the Company side and so from all the Directors side. How this will be rectified, God only knows.

6. Ind. Drs- The way the AOA are worded, even if any of the Independent Directors hold one share of the Company, they will not remain Independent Director of the Company. It is amazing that none from the Company has ever looked at this lacunae!

7. 187C of the Companies Act'1956- Due to the Financing Agreement and the Back to Back Agreements with the EWT Trust, ESPS Shareholders cannot attend nor vote at any General Meetings of the Company. Don't know if this was considered earlier by the Company as the

General Meetings of the Company wrongly talk of Five Members present in person BUT no names have been given nor attendance signatures taken.

8. Share Certs Reconciliation- NO Board approvals obtained for Printing of share Certificates at any point of time. Left, right and Centre Share Certificates have been printed without any checks and balances. Clear cut Violations attracting penal provisions!

9. Section 77(2A) of the Companies Act'1956 relating to ESPS and Trust- The current practice will play foul of the provisions of the Companies Act'1956, which the Company has been advised to STOP such practice.

10. Sitting Fees- Sitting Fees is payable as per AOA of the Company to all Directors. Cheques on many occasions issued, not taken, returned etc. The Accounts of the Company have been prepared on this basis. Unless, the Board takes on record, wavier of Sitting fees by all/any, The sitting Fees are to be paid. This is again violation of the Provisions of Companies Act'1956- Surprisingly no one has ever seen this not even the Auditors!

11. Counterfeited Notes- There is RBI Policy to be strictly followed. This is not the case here.

12. Issue of ESOPs to a Consultant- ESOPs cannot be issued to anyone other than Permanent Employees and Directors. 50,000 ESOPs have been issued to xxxx, who is a consultant.

# Appendix 12: Who is an Independent Director and Who Should be Treated as an Independent Director?

*Given the importance of independent directors, the determination of who is an independent director and who should be treated as an independent director becomes very important.* Two key questions arise here: (a) How to make this determination of a director's independence; and (b) What objective criteria can be effectively used in microfinance in India and especially for unlisted companies (NBFCs MFIs) involved in financial intermediation. I offer some suggestions here and these can be used by the concerned stakeholders as part of their current efforts in developing the regulatory framework (including corporate governance guidelines) for the crisis-ridden Indian microfinance industry.

Firstly, for an MFI director to be considered independent, it must be conclusively and affirmatively determined that the director has no material[569] relationship (whether financial, business, personal or otherwise) with the MFI, or any of its sister concerns or subsidiaries or affiliates or group entities, either directly or as a partner, shareholder or officer or employee of an institution, which in turn has a relationship with them. This is very critical. Further, in making the determination of independence, a director's relationships can be deemed immaterial as long as the following standards are met:

a) *Director's relationships:* The director is not, and has not been within the previous three years, an employee of the MFI or any of its subsidiaries or affiliates or sister concerns or any other group institution.

b) *Relationships of the director's immediate family:*[570] No member of the director's immediate family is/has been, within the previous three years, an executive officer of the MFI or any of its subsidiaries, or affiliates, or sister concerns, or any other group institution.

c) *Compensation of director/family members:* Neither the director nor any member of his or her immediate family has received, during any 12-month period, within the previous three years, significant[571]

---

[569] "Materiality" is to be considered from the standpoint of the director and that of each person or organization with which the director is affiliated, including organizations of which the director is a partner, shareholder, or officer. The determination that, as to each director individually, there is no material relationship (whether financial, business, personal, or otherwise) will have to be made after due consideration of the information provided by the director and any other information that may be known to the board. The purpose is ultimately to determine whether a director has any relationship with the MFI that may interfere with the exercise of the director's independence with regard to the MFI and its management.

[570] "Immediate family" means a director's spouse, parents, stepparents, children, stepchildren, siblings, mothers- and fathers-in-law, sons- and daughters-in-law, brothers- and sisters-in-law, and any person (other than a tenant or employee) who comprise the director's household, but not the physical space necessarily.

[571] This has to be debated and decided accordingly, as per consensus. The concerned stakeholders would have to take the initiative in this regard.

direct compensation from the MFI, or any of its sister concerns, or subsidiaries, or affiliates, or group institutions (including without limitation, any consulting, advisory or other compensatory fees) except (1) fees which the MFI pays to its directors for their services as members of the board, and members or chairs of board committees, and (2) fixed amounts of deferred compensation for prior service, which is not contingent in any way on continued service; provided that compensation paid to an immediate family member for service as an employee other than an executive officer will not be considered in determining the director's independence, so long as the compensation is comparable to the compensation paid to other similarly situated employees.

d) *Director's/family members' relationship with MFI auditors:* The director is not a partner or an employee with a firm that is the internal or external auditor for the MFI, or any of its sister concerns or subsidiaries or affiliates or group institutions; nor is any member of the director's immediate family a partner with such a firm or an employee who participates in the firm's audit and/or tax compliance practice (as well as similar tasks); nor has the director or any member of the director's immediate family, within the previous three year's been a partner or employee with such a firm that has, within that time, personally worked on the audit of an MFI or any of its sister concerns or subsidiaries or affiliates or group institutions.

e) Compensation committee *aspects for director/family members:* Neither the director, nor any member of his or her immediate family is employed, or has been employed, within the previous three years, as an executive officer of any company whose compensation committee, at the same time, included an individual who currently serves as an executive officer of an MFI or any of its sister concerns or subsidiaries or affiliates or group institutions.

f) *Director/family members' relationships with MFI service providers:* The director is not an employee, nor is any member of his/her immediate family an executive officer of another company where payments by the MFI to that company or from that company to the MFI, including their respective subsidiaries and affiliates or sister concerns, for property or services, have exceeded more than 2% of the other company's consolidated gross revenues in any of the other company's past three fiscal years.

However, notwithstanding anything to the contrary in standards #a through #e, no MFI shall treat as categorically immaterial, but instead will discuss case by case and will disclose (i) any relationship between a director and the MFI or any of its sister concerns or subsidiaries or affiliates (or group institutions) that is required to be disclosed under the relevant section of the Indian Companies Act, 1956 (and other SEBI/RBI directives from time to time) and (ii) any contributions made by the MFI or any of its sister concerns or subsidiaries or affiliates to any tax-exempt organization of which a director serves as an executive officer if, within the preceding three years, such contributions in any single fiscal year exceeded 2% of the tax-exempt organization's consolidated gross revenues.

# Appendix 13 Open Letter to Right Honorable Andrew Mitchell

Respected Sir,

Good afternoon! I am delighted that The UK Department for International Development (DFID) is launching SAMRIDHI (a programme promoting microfinance and impact investment in India) in partnership with SIDBI in your esteemed presence (Sir) at 6pm today, the 16th December (Friday) at the British Council Division, Kasturba Gandhi Marg, New Delhi. Much as I wanted to attend the same, I am unable to do so and hence, this open letter Sir for your kind consideration and necessary action.

Sir, I wanted to draw your attention to some key lessons and findings from the Code of Conduct (CoC) assessments of eight Indian MFIs sponsored as part of the SIDBI World Bank "Scalling up Sustainable and Responsible Microfinance Project" (http://www.sidbi.com/micro/WorldBankInitiative.htm). The findings are very relevant to the SAMRIDHI programme to be launched as noted above.

Sir, in an earlier article (Have sophisticated thermometers ever reduced the temperature?), I pointed to some real peculiar findings from the above Code of Conduct Assessment (COCA) reports where by the fastest growing NBFC-MFIs received the higher (better) scores. This was counter intuitive because it is now widely accepted that burgeoning growth of MFIs caused the 2010 microfinance crisis in Andhra Pradesh—a state which DFID can take great pride in having nurtured significantly through its seminal poverty alleviation and rural livelihoods projects.

Sir, this peculiar fining made me go deeper into the COCA assessments—and not to my surprise, I found that there were too many free points that were awarded as part of the COC assessments (The award of free points in microfinance code of conduct assessments). I must also record that I came across several instances of subjectivity and inconsistencies in the aforementioned COCA reports (Subjectivity and inconsistencies in microfinance code of conduct assessments). I would be grateful if you can read these carefully as they have tremendous implications for DFID's work globally in relation to microfinance, financial inclusion and inclusive growth! Thank you sir!

And through this open letter, I also wanted to share some key findings from the aforementioned COCA reports. This again should prove extremely useful to DFID not only in its fight against global poverty but also for the SAMRIDHI programme that is being launched today!

Sir, all along I have been saying that two crucial aspects in microfinance (client origination/targeting and loan appraisal) have been neglected in favour of unprecedented growth *(caused by a desire to fully commercialise microfinance and rapidly enhance access/outreach of such services)* and this has resulted in the present crisis. The above eight COCA assessments present additional evidence in support of my above assertion and I briefly summarise the key issues hereafter for your kind understanding:

a) On client origination and targeting, it has been found that unauthorised agents were very much present in the operational areas of (some) MFIs. Further, the COCA reports themselves suggest that Ujjivan, Equitas and Basix have used unauthorised agents to source and target new clients. Further, according to the COCA report, Cashpor is said to have experienced this in the past (at least until 2008). While no cases were found at Arohan, the COCA report concludes that Arohan needs to apply internal check systems at all times so as to prevent the risk of informal agents (existing in their operational areas) from infiltrating into their system. And the assessments found no evidence (with regard to use of agents) at SKDRDP, Bandhan and ASA. Not surprisingly, Ujjivan, Basix and Equitas are among the fastest growers (between Apr 2009 and Sept 2010) in this group of eight MFIs for whom COC assessments have been attempted by the SIDBI World Bank responsible microfinance project.

This apart, the COCA report on of one MFI (http://www.sidbi.in/Micro/COCA%20Equitas.pdf) shows how the use of unauthorised agents evolved and this affords very valuable lessons for DFID:

"From November 2010, the organisation has done away with sales targets as well as the direct monetary incentives for enrolment of clients for its Sales Officers to reduce the likelihood of the Sales Officers misrepresenting indebtedness of clients.... In the past, Equitas has faced problems pertaining to involvement of unauthorised agents in the client origination process, particularly in some of the branches of Chennai, primarily on account of high sales targets of the SOs and weaker controls."... "In M2i's opinion, despite all sincere efforts, some of these agents may still be in existence (though their influence may now be low)". (Pages 6 and 7)

And a reading of the above COCA report clearly shows that only a crisis could incentivise the MFI to change it is policies. The findings given in the report are best interpreted as follows:

# Appendix 13 Open Letter to Right Honorable Andrew Mitchell

- The MFI had 'high sales targets'. (http://www.sidbi.in/Micro/COCA%20Equitas.pdf, page 7)
- The MFI had 'direct monetary incentives for enrolment of clients for its sales officers'. (page 6)
- There was a 'likelihood of sales officers misrepresenting indebtedness of clients'. (page 6)
- The MFI 'faced problems pertaining to involvement of unauthorised agents in the client origination process, particularly in some of the branches of Chennai primarily on account of high sales targets of the sales officers and weaker controls'. (page no 7)
- The MFI had an 'incentive for collections at the branches and there was a monetary penalty in case collections are not 100%'. (page no 14)
- And interestingly, what needs to be noted from the COCA assessment is that, the MFI still received a score of 7.6 out of 9 on client origination and targeting and it also had the highest overall score (88%) in the pool of COCA assessments (*please look at Annex 1 page 18 and Section 1: Scores and facts in the above report, page 2*).
- I leave it to you as the reader to judge whether this COCA rating is indeed appropriate?

Therefore, it becomes clear that the above not-so-appropriate practices were changed only due to the 2010 crisis and herein lies the most important lesson from Indian microfinance that DFID should not ignore:

- The desire for very rapid (burgeoning) growth driven by the need to scale up outreach and enhance financial access through full blown commercialization has resulted in many MFIs allowing these (not-so-good) practices (use of agents to source and target clients, etc) to creep into their organizations.
- The desire for rapid growth and complete commercialization thus appears to have led many MFIs to cut corners and provide lower quality services to its clients.
- The significance of the above finding from the COCA reports that agents were used to turbo charge growth in Indian microfinance further corroborates the following direct evidence (through three e-mails) already available from the field (please see previous Moneylife article on agents -MFIN-NCAER study: Here's the proof that microfinance agents are thriving in Tamil Nadu)
- Now, a very important question here is who pushed these MFIs to grow this way? Was it the promoters or senior management, equity investors, bankers, policy makers, technical support organisations or others? I have already tried to provide some answers to this in previous articles (Lessons from the commercial micro-finance model in India; Dissecting the mechanics of growth in Indian microfinance; and The special category of NBFC MFIs: Lessons for the Department of Non-Bank Supervision, RBI)

b) Likewise, on loan appraisal, the Ujjivan COCA report says:

"At present, information pertaining to income, expenses as well as indebtedness of the clients used for credit analysis is what is self reported by the clients. Given the profile of its clientele, it may not be possible for the organization to obtain documentary evidence of the income, expenses and indebtedness." (http://www.sidbi.com/micro/COCAUjjivan.pdf, page 11)

Sir, this is the omnipresent reality in microfinance as MFIs typically work with poor clients in the informal sector. Some MFIs use tools (like housing index, asset means test, PPI tool) to estimate the income levels of the clients. But it is impossible to get the exact information from a poor household operating in the informal sector.

The only way to get a better insight on the loan absorption and repayment capacity of the clients is to invest in a long-term relationship with them. However, this requires considerable time and may not deliver the best financial results for the MFI in the short term (but from a longer term perspective, the clients will be better off and that is what ultimately matters). And, most importantly, this calls for a strict "no" to use of unauthorised agents in client origination and targeting so that a good direct relationship can be built with clients. And according to the COCA report, the only MFI that seems to have invested in such a relationship is SKDRDP:

As the COCA report says "The SHGs are required to conduct weekly meetings and undertake compulsory savings for a minimum period of three months before they become eligible to undergo the process of grading. Only SHGs receiving satisfactory performance grades are eligible for applying for loans." (http://www.sidbi.com/micro/COCA%20SKDRDP.pdf, page 7)

Yet Sir, it is ironical the SKDRDP has received the lowest COCA score! C'est la vie!

Sir, in summary, in many MFIs that had an emphasis on rapid growth, loans were disbursed (indiscriminately) at the fastest rate possible. And greening, informal collateral and abusive collateral substitutes (Tackling informal collateral and collateral substitutes in Indian microfinance) were used to collect back the loans – *primarily because the agents behaved like local level thugs.* Not enough time was taken by the MFIs to really get to know the clients and to be able to assess their (true) capacity to service the debt. The case of BASIX, which is generally known as one of India's better MFIs, amply demonstrates this. The fast growth trajectory prevalent in the Indian microfinance industry *(much of BASIX's peer MFIs in Andhra Pradesh grew at much faster rates than BASIX, prior to 2009)* perhaps pushed well intentioned organisations like BASIX *(which had sound lending systems originally and I can vouch for how good it was in its early years as an NBFC)* to sacrifice their proper lending methodology – that is why as the M2i report on Basix argues,

"However, it was observed that the practice of recording the existing loans of clients in not uniformly practiced across all the units. We found during client interviews that some of the clients had borrowed from other MFIs but this had not been recorded in their loan forms. In one of the units—Kamareddy in Andhra Pradesh—a random inspection of 15 loan appraisal forms revealed that none of them had a mention of any other lender. It is improbable that none of the clients would have borrowed from any other MFI in the region given the prevalence of MFIs. Also, interviews with the LSPs revealed that nearly 70% of his clients had borrowings from other MFIs." (http://www.sidbi.com/micro/COCA%20Samruddhi.pdf, Page 12)

And this is confirmed by none other than the then CEO of BASIX, who candidly said to *The Economic Times,*

"That (following sound lending practices) is where we failed," says Sajeev Viswanathan, CEO of Basix. MFIs lent liberally to individuals who didn't have a corresponding ability to repay. The mismatch had to hurt sometime, and that's what is happening now….Mr Viswanathan says MFI lending in Andhra rose from Rs5,000-Rs6,000 crore in 2009 to Rs9,000 crore this year." (From Microfinance: What's wrong with it, by M Rajshekhar, *Economic Times*, November 2010)

Sir, all of the above is fine but what then are the positives from the SIDBI-World Bank sponsored COCA reports? After having analysed eight assessments, the most positive aspect that emerges is the fact that the presence and use of unauthorised agents in Indian microfinance has now been (officially) acknowledged and admitted. I say officially because of the COCA reports are sponsored by the SIDBI-World Bank project and that puts these findings in a different plane altogether. And M2i, SIDBI and the World Bank certainly need to be complemented for their courage to bring the (widespread?) use of agents in Indian microfinance officially out into the open. Kudos to all of them!

A major disappointment however is the fact that those MFIs engaged in such (undesirable) practices have been rewarded with highest scores for Code of Conduct Compliance. As a result, not much value can be attached to the scores resulting from the assessments. And without question, as J Nunnally, the Psychometric Guru would argue, the COCA tool will need significant revamping for it to become a reliable and valid psychometric measure, capable of portraying ground level reality in an accurate and unbiased manner. And given that Sa-Dhan and MFIN have just released a joint code of conduct in Indian microfinance, it is only natural that they take on this task of creating an appropriate tool—one that rewards actual implementation rather than glorious intentions on paper.

Sir, coming back to the SAMRIDHI, a programme promoting microfinance and impact investment, I have tried my best to present you with relevant facts and details (in the public domain) with regard to the practice of microfinance in India. I would be very grateful if you can use your good offices to ensure that the available lessons and learning are factored into the implementation of the DFID SIDBI SAMRIDHI programme (being launched today) as well as the DFID Poorest States Inclusive Growth (PSIG) project that is to be implemented in the near future! And please be rest assured sir that your kind intervention will not only enable millions of low income people in India to have a better quality life but also be an integral part of the inclusive growth story in India!

# Appendix 14 Glossary

| | |
|---|---|
| AP | Andhra Pradesh |
| AGM | Annual General Meeting |
| AIM | Asian Institute of Management |
| AKMI | Association of Karnataka Microfinance Institutions |
| AML | Asmitha Microfin Limited |
| APMAS | Andhra Pradesh Mahila Abhivruddhi Society |
| ASAP | As Soon As Possible |
| BASIX | Bhartiya Samruddhi Finance Limited |
| BFS | Board of Financial Supervision |
| BIS | Bank for International Settlements |
| BoP | Bottom of Pyramid |
| BSE | Bombay Stock Exchange |
| CAFRAL | Centre for Advanced Financial Research and Learning |
| CAG | Comptroller and Auditor General |
| CAGR | Compound Annual Growth Rate |
| CB | Credit Bureau |
| CDFG | Community Development Finance Group |
| CDO | Collateralized Debt Obligation |
| CEO | Chief Executive Officer |
| CFO | Chief Financial Officer |
| CGAP | Consultative Group to Assist the Poor |
| CMF | Centre for Micro Finance |
| CoC | Code of Conduct |
| COO | Chief Operating Officer |
| CRISIL | Credit Rating Information Services of India Limited |
| DB | Deutsche Bank |
| DBS | Department of Banking Supervision |
| DFIs | Development Finance Institutions |
| DFN | Development Finance Network |
| DNBS | Department of Non-Bank Supervision |
| DRHP | Draft Red Herring Prospectus |
| EIR | Effective Interest Rate |
| EPW | Economic and Political Weekly |
| ES | Emergency and Setbacks |
| ESOP | Employee Stock Option Plan |

| | | |
|---|---|---|
| ESPS | | Employee Share Purchase Scheme |
| ET | | Economic Times |
| FCIC | | Financial Crisis Inquiry Commission |
| FCRA | | Foreign Regulation (Contribution) Act |
| FEMA | | Foreign Exchange Management Act |
| FI | | Financial Inclusion |
| FICCI | | Federation of Indian Chambers of Commerce and Industry |
| FY | | Financial Year |
| GLP | | Gross Loan Portfolio |
| HDFC | | Housing Development Finance Corporation |
| HR | | Human Resource |
| HSBC | | Hong Kong and Shanghai Banking Corporation |
| HT | | Hindustan Times |
| IA | | Internal Audit |
| ICICI | | Industrial Credit and Investment Corporation of India |
| ICTPH | | IKP Centre for Technologies in Public Health |
| IDs | | Independent Directors |
| IFC | | International Finance Corporation |
| IFMR | | Institute for Financial Management and Research |
| IIMA | | Indian Institute of Management, Ahmedabad |
| IMF | | International Monetary Fund |
| IPC | | Indian Penal Code |
| IRDA | | Insurance Regulatory and Development Authority |
| IT | | Information Technology |
| JLG | | Joint Liability Group |
| KBSLAB | | Krishna Bhima Samruddhi Local Area Bank Limited |
| KYC | | Know Your Customer |
| LAB | | Local Area Bank |
| LAC | | Loan Absorption Capacity |
| LAPO | | Lift Above Poverty Organization |
| LCE | | Life Cycle Events |
| LIBOR | | London Interbank Offered Rate |
| MACS | | Mutually Aided Cooperative Societies |
| MBT | | Mutual Benefit Trust |
| MCR | | Malegam Committee Report |
| MD | | Managing Director |
| MF | | Microfinance Focus |
| MFI | | Microfinance Institution |

# Appendix 14 Glossary

| | |
|---|---|
| MFIDRB | Microfinance Institution Development and Regulation Bill |
| MFIN | Microfinance Institutions Network |
| MFP | Microfinance Practice |
| MFPF | Microfinance Portfolio |
| MIS | Management Information System |
| MIVs | Microfinance Investment Vehicles |
| MoF | Ministry of Finance |
| MOU | Memorandum Of Understanding |
| MSME | Micro Small and Medium Enterprises |
| NA | Not Applicable |
| NABARD | National Bank for Agriculture and Rural Development |
| NABFINS | NABARD Financial Services Limited |
| NBFC | Non-Banking Financial Company |
| NCAER | National Council for Applied Economic Research |
| NCDs | Nonconvertible Debentures |
| NGOs | Non-governmental Organizations |
| OBC | Other Backward Class |
| OD | Overdue |
| P/BV | Price to Book Value |
| PAR | Portfolio At Risk |
| PAT | Profit After Tax |
| PDS | Public Distribution System |
| PE | Private Equity |
| PSCF | Parliamentary Standing Committee on Finance |
| PSL | Priority Sector Lending |
| PSLF | Priority Sector Lending Funds |
| QIP | Qualified Institutional Placement |
| RBI | Reserve Bank of India |
| RBS | Royal Bank of Scotland |
| RE | Regular Events |
| ROC | Registrar of Companies |
| RoE | Return on Equity |
| RPCD | Rural Planning and Credit Department |
| RRBs | Regional Rural Banks |
| RTI | Right to Information |
| SEBI | Securities and Exchange Board of India |
| SEC | Securities and Exchange Commission |
| SERP | Society for Elimination of Rural Poverty |

| | |
|---|---|
| SFMC | SIDBI Foundation for Micro Credit |
| SHGs | Self-Help Groups |
| SIDBI | Small Industries Development Bank of India |
| SKSML | SKS Microfinance Limited |
| SoS | State of the Sector |
| SROs | Self-Regulatory Organizations |
| TA | Total Assets |
| TFC | Transaction Financial Cost |
| ToT | Training of Trainers |
| UN | United Nations |

www.ingramcontent.com/pod-product-compliance
Lightning Source LLC
Chambersburg PA
CBHW081717170526
45167CB00009B/3605